AF896505

Resilient and Friendly Living Environments

Editors-in-Chief

Yibin Ao, College of Environment and Civil Engineering, Chengdu University of Technology, Chengdu, Sichuan, China

Haimei Li, Humanities and Law School, Chengdu University of Technology Chengdu, Sichuan, China

Homa Bahmani, College of Environment and Civil Engineering, Chengdu University of Technology, Chengdu, Sichuan, China

Editorial Board Members

Jason Cao, Humphrey School of Public Affairs, University of Minnesota, Minneapolis, MN, USA

Jian Zuo, School of Architecture and Built Environment, University of Adelaide, Adelaide, SA, Australia

Chuan Chen, Business School, Sichuan University, Chengdu, Sichuan, China

The paramount goal of this series is to be a groundbreaking resource for professionals, practitioners, and enthusiasts dedicated to shaping resilient, friendly, and inclusive environments. This series aims to empower its readers with cutting-edge insights and practical tools to design spaces that seamlessly blend sustainability, adaptability, and cultural sensitivity. By delving into such topics, the series strives to provide a holistic perspective on creating environments that prioritize the well-being and interconnectedness of diverse communities. Moreover, the series also seeks to guide the development of frameworks that evolve with the ever-changing needs of societies, ensuring that the built environment remains responsive and relevant over time. Ultimately, this book series aspires to be a catalyst for positive transformation, encouraging a paradigm shift in the way we conceptualize, design, and interact with the spaces we inhabit. This series covers a broad spectrum of topics related to building environments that stand resilient and friendly, with a special emphasis on inclusivity for individuals of all ages. The series encompasses but is not limited to:

- Sustainable and Adaptive Design: Guidance on creating environments that are environmentally sustainable and capable of adapting to changing circumstances.
- Cultural Considerations in Design: Insight into designing spaces that respect and reflect the cultural diversity of communities which promote a sense of belonging among individuals.
- Supportive Infrastructure: Detailed examinations of infrastructure elements that contribute to the overall well-being, safety, and accessibility of diverse communities. It can also include wellness initiatives that address physical, mental, and emotional well-being.
- Designing for All Ages: Foster an inclusive environment that values diversity. This includes promoting equal opportunities, and ensuring that everyone feels welcome and respected. In-depth discussions on creating infrastructure and spaces that caters to the unique needs of both children and older adults is also of great importance.
- Community Engagement: Practical approaches to involving the community in the design process and ensuring that the built environment aligns with their needs and preferences.
- Safety Measures and Disaster Risk Reduction: Prioritize safety and security to ensure a comfortable and secure environment. This includes physical safety measures as well as fostering a culture of respect and mutual support.
- Technological Integration: Explorations of how technology can be seamlessly integrated to enhance connectivity, flexibility, and inclusivity within the built environment.
- Collaborative Spaces: Design work and learning environments that facilitate collaboration. This can involve open-plan workspaces, collaborative tools, and flexible seating arrangements that encourage interaction and teamwork.
- Adaptive Policies and laws: Establish policies and laws that are adaptable to changing circumstances. This flexibility allows for the accommodation of diverse needs and ensures that policies remain relevant and effective over time.

This book series is a valuable resource for architects, designers, urban planners, educators, and anyone interested in the intersection of design, community, and well-being. The series aims to inspire and guide readers in creating environments that not only withstand challenges but also flourish as vibrant and inclusive spaces for everyone.

Haimei Li • Ping Liang

The Legal System for the Protection of Children's Rights in China

Springer

Haimei Li
Humanities and Law School
Chengdu University of Technology
Chengdu, Sichuan, China

Ping Liang
Humanities and Law School
Chengdu University of Technology
Chengdu, Sichuan, China

ISSN 3005-1681 ISSN 3005-169X (electronic)
Resilient and Friendly Living Environments
ISBN 978-981-95-9924-0 ISBN 978-981-95-9925-7 (eBook)
https://doi.org/10.1007/978-981-95-9925-7

© The Editor(s) (if applicable) and The Author(s), under exclusive license to Springer Nature Singapore Pte Ltd. 2026

This work is subject to copyright. All rights are solely and exclusively licensed by the Publisher, whether the whole or part of the material is concerned, specifically the rights of translation, reprinting, reuse of illustrations, recitation, broadcasting, reproduction on microfilms or in any other physical way, and transmission or information storage and retrieval, electronic adaptation, computer software, or by similar or dissimilar methodology now known or hereafter developed.
The use of general descriptive names, registered names, trademarks, service marks, etc. in this publication does not imply, even in the absence of a specific statement, that such names are exempt from the relevant protective laws and regulations and therefore free for general use.
The publisher, the authors and the editors are safe to assume that the advice and information in this book are believed to be true and accurate at the date of publication. Neither the publisher nor the authors or the editors give a warranty, expressed or implied, with respect to the material contained herein or for any errors or omissions that may have been made. The publisher remains neutral with regard to jurisdictional claims in published maps and institutional affiliations.

This Springer imprint is published by the registered company Springer Nature Singapore Pte Ltd.
The registered company address is: 152 Beach Road, #21-01/04 Gateway East, Singapore 189721, Singapore

If disposing of this product, please recycle the paper.

Preface

In the context of rapid social development and accelerated urbanization, the protection of children's rights has become an increasingly important topic. Since China's ratification of the United Nations Convention on the Rights of the Child in 1991, the construction of a legal framework for safeguarding children's rights has been continuously advancing. China has consistently attached great importance to the protection of children's rights, gradually establishing a comprehensive legal system grounded in the Constitution and supported by legal statutes such as the Civil Code of the People's Republic of China, the Criminal Law of the People's Republic of China, and the Law of the People's Republic of China on the Protection of Minors.

Throughout my practical and research endeavors, I have maintained a close focus on issues related to the protection of children's rights, witnessing firsthand the continuous improvement of China's legal framework in this domain. However, challenges and issues persist in the implementation process, including regional disparities in the protection of children's rights and the need for further refinement of legal enforcement mechanisms. These observations have motivated me to conduct in-depth research on the legal system for safeguarding children's rights and to advocate for its enhanced effectiveness.

This book represents a synthesis and refinement of my research findings. It begins with an introduction to the provisions and evolutionary trajectory of the Constitution of the People's Republic of China concerning children's rights, elucidating the significance and developmental context of the legal framework for children's rights protection. Subsequent chapters elaborate on the stipulations and safeguarding mechanisms pertaining to children's rights in laws such as the Civil Code of the People's Republic of China and the Criminal Law of the People's Republic of China. Through meticulous analysis of specific legal provisions, this work aims to clarify the structure and content of China's legal system for children's rights protection, highlighting the pivotal roles of various laws in different dimensions of safeguarding children's rights.

The research methodology employed in this study involves legal text analysis, encompassing a comprehensive review of relevant laws and regulations in China.

This approach demonstrates the practical application of the legal framework for children's rights protection, as well as the existing circumstances within this system.

I would like to express my sincere gratitude to my co-author, Liang Ping, whose scholarly rigor and invaluable professional contributions were instrumental to the success of this research. I am also deeply thankful to my colleagues Juan Wei, Liyuan Deng, Ya Wang, Yao Zhao, Hongying Li, Shuangqing Tao, and Qiuyu Hu for their assistance and support during the writing process. Their insightful suggestions played a crucial role in enhancing the quality of this book. Furthermore, I hope this work will provide some reference and inspiration for all those concerned with the protection of children's rights, thereby contributing to the continuous improvement and development of China's legal system in this field.

This book represents only a preliminary exploration of the legal framework for children's rights protection. As society continues to progress and the landscape of children's rights protection evolves, numerous issues warrant further in-depth research and discussion. I remain committed to this field and will strive to make greater contributions to the advancement of children's rights protection.

Chengdu, China
23 September 2025

Haimei Li

Competing Interests The authors have no competing interests to declare that are relevant to the content of this manuscript.

Contents

Chapter 1
Constitutional Guarantees for Children in the People's Republic of China

1.1 Introduction

If the young people are strong, the country will be strong. The struggle and legacy of children determine the strength and stability of a nation's future, while the degree of protection afforded to children's rights determines the nation's future development and destiny. Chinese President Xi Jinping has profoundly emphasized: "Cultivating children is a strategic task with long-term significance." and "the Party and the government must always care about children of all ethnic groups, striving to create better conditions for their study and growth." Chinese President Xi Jinping also demanded that "the whole society should understand, respect, care for, and serve children, and provide them with a good social environment." These important discourses of the new era all indicate the value of respecting the status of minors and the firm national stance on protecting minors, with Xi Jinping at the core of the CPC Central Committee and the whole Party (Sun, 2021).

As a signatory state of the Convention on the Rights of the Child, China has been actively taking various measures to implement the provisions of the Convention. As a State Party to the United Nations Convention on the Rights of the Child (CRC), China has been actively taking various measures to implement the Convention. Adhering to the core principle of the best interests of the child, China has formed a legal protection system for children with Chinese characteristics: rooted in the Constitution, centered on specialized child protection laws and constitutional chapters, and supplemented by other relevant provisions, thereby aligning domestic child protection concepts with international standards in a precise manner.

From a historical perspective, children and their rights are social products and creatures of the era, primarily achieved through legal norms, particularly constitutional regulations.

The Constitution of the People's Republic of China is the highest legal authority and the fundamental law of China. the Constitution of the People's Republic of

© The Author(s), under exclusive license to Springer Nature Singapore Pte Ltd. 2026

H. Li, P. Liang, *The Legal System for the Protection of Children's Rights in China*, Resilient and Friendly Living Environments,
https://doi.org/10.1007/978-981-95-9925-7_1

China is the fundamental law of the state, possessing the highest legal authority. It stipulates the state's basic system, the fundamental rights and duties of citizens, the organization and powers of state organs, and essential symbols such as the national flag, emblem, anthem, and capital. Covering all aspects of citizens' lives and national governance, it serves as the general charter of state governance. This chapter introduces how the Constitution, as the core foundation of the socialist legal system for child protection, fulfills the spirit of the CRC by providing constitutional guarantees for children's rights, guiding specialized child protection laws, and laying down fundamental concepts of child protection in line with China's national conditions.

1.2 The Evolution of Children's Rights and Interests in the Constitution of the People's Republic of China (1954-Present)

1.2.1 The Basic Development of China's Constitution

The Constitution of the People's Republic of China (1982) is the fundamental law of China, with supreme legal authority, serving as the basis for all other legislation, none of which may contravene it. The first PRC Constitution was promulgated in 1954 and was subsequently comprehensively revised in 1975, 1978, and 1982. In addition, it has been amended five times (1988, 1993, 1999, 2004, 2018) to meet the needs of political, economic, social, and cultural development, thereby providing a solid constitutional foundation for governance, safeguarding people's rights, and maintaining national unity and social stability.

On September 21, 1949, *the First Plenary Session of the Chinese People's Political Consultative Conference* (CPPCC) adopted the Common Program of the Chinese People's Political Consultative Conference, which had the nature of a provisional constitution. It elected the Central People's Government Committee and declared the establishment of the People's Republic of China. This serves as both the program of the united front of the Chinese people's democracy and acted as a provisional constitution.

On September 29, 1949, the First Plenary Session of the Chinese People's Political Consultative Conference (CPPCC) formally adopted the Common Program of the Chinese People's Political Consultative Conference (hereinafter referred to as the Common Program), which possessed the character of a provisional constitution. At the same session, the Central People's Government Committee was elected, and the founding of the People's Republic of China (PRC) was proclaimed.

Apart from its preamble, the Common Program consists of seven chapters—General Principles, Organs of State Power, Military System, Economic Policies, Policies on Culture and Education, Ethnic Policies, and Foreign Policies—comprising a total of sixty articles. It functioned not only as the program of the Chinese people's democratic united front but also as a provisional constitution. On October 1, 1949, the People's Republic of China was officially founded.

On September 20, 1954, the First Session of the First National People's Congress (NPC) formally adopted and promulgated the *Constitution of the People's Republic of China (1954)*, also known as the "Fifty-Four Constitution." As the first constitution of New China and the first socialist constitution, it established the fundamental political system of the People's Republic, for the first time stipulating that "all power in the People's Republic of China belongs to the people." It advanced and improved the development of the people's democratic regime and inaugurated a new era of socialist democracy and the rule of law (Wang & Bi, 2022).

In August 1973, the Central Committee of the Communist Party of China decided to convene the National People's Congress to revise the constitution. On January 17, 1975, the First Session of the Fourth NPC formally adopted the *Constitution of the People's Republic of China (1975)*, also referred to as the "Seventy-Five Constitution." In order to meet the needs of a new historical period and to undertake the task of building a strong socialist state, the First Session of the Fifth NPC, on March 5, 1978, carried out a comprehensive revision of the "Seventy-Five Constitution" and adopted the *Constitution of the People's Republic of China (1978)*, also known as the "Seventy-Eight Constitution."

Subsequently, on December 4, 1982, the Fifth Session of the Fifth NPC formally adopted and promulgated the *Constitution of the People's Republic of China (1982)*, commonly referred to as the "Eighty-Two Constitution," which remains the constitution currently in force. The "Eighty-Two Constitution" inherited and further developed the basic principles of the "Fifty-Four Constitution," summarized China's socialist development experience, and drew upon international experience. It is the fundamental law with Chinese characteristics, suited to the requirements of China's socialist modernization. The constitution is composed of a "Preamble" and four chapters—General Principles, Fundamental Rights and Duties of Citizens, Structure of the State, and the National Flag, National Anthem, National Emblem, and the Capital—comprising a total of 138 articles.

Since the promulgation and implementation of the 1982 Constitution ("Eighty-Two Constitution"), it has been amended five times—in 1988, 1993, 1999, 2004, and 2018—through constitutional amendments, in response to the practices and developmental needs of China's reform, opening-up, and socialist modernization.

1.2.2 The Confirmation of Constitutional Qualifications for Chinese Children

Since modern times, the development of children's rights in the constitution has undergone a process from nonexistence to existence, and from implicit to explicit recognition. Children have evolved from having an "invisible" status without constitutional identity to being prominently qualified for protection by explicit provisions in the Constitution. Children were not recognized as independent rights holders and their rights were only implicitly covered under family or general citizen provisions—to explicit and systematic constitutional protections (Wang, 2019).

Looking back at this process, earlier constitutions often failed to explicitly define children as independent subjects of rights. Instead, children were largely regarded as appendages of the family or society, with their rights scattered across provisions on marriage and family or embedded within general statements of citizens' rights, thereby remaining in a vague state of "implicit protection." With the advancement of social civilization and the rise of rights-consciousness, the particular value of children as distinct rights-bearing subjects gradually came to be recognized and accepted. Constitutional texts began to move beyond traditional paradigms: from initial principled declarations, to the addition of specific rights provisions, and eventually to the establishment of systematic norms of protection. In this progressive trajectory, children gradually acquired the status of constitutional subjects explicitly protected under the law.

In the contemporary era, this trend has become even more pronounced. Constitutional texts have explicitly incorporated children's rights within their scope of protection, not only affirming children's independent constitutional status, but also specifying, through dedicated legal provisions or clauses, core entitlements such as the rights to survival, development, and protection. Children's rights have thus become an indispensable component of the constitutional rights system, embodying the extension and deepening of contemporary rule of law's humanistic concern from adults to minors.

When it comes to how children possess constitutional qualifications similar to adults, we can discuss that from both formal and substantive perspectives. Normatively, children are defined as all persons under the age of 18; substantively, they are recognized as individuals with incomplete physical and mental maturity, lacking full legal capacity. The constitutional recognition of children balances their equal legal personality with the necessity for special protection due to their developmental vulnerabilities. Thus, children's constitutional subject status is both general and special: they are equal citizens yet in need of additional safeguards.

In normative terms, a child is generally defined as any person under the age of eighteen; in substantive terms, however, a child refers to an individual whose physical and mental development is immature due to age, and who therefore does not possess full legal capacity. Within the legal context, the substantive concept of the child is characterized by duality and particularity, encompassing four dimensions.

In normative terms, a child is generally defined as any person under the age of eighteen; in substantive terms, however, a child refers to an individual whose physical and mental development is immature due to age, and who therefore does not possess full legal capacity. Within the legal context, the substantive concept of the child is characterized by duality and particularity, encompassing four dimensions.

First, it constitutes the logical starting point for the protection of children's rights—namely, the principle of equal constitutional subjecthood. Children, like adults, possess equal personality and legal capacity; regardless of age differences, the fundamental rights they enjoy as citizens do not essentially differ from those of adults at the constitutional level and are equally safeguarded by the fundamental law of the state.

Second, it provides the essential basis for children's special protection, namely the "incompleteness" of their legal capacity. While children's capacity for rights is consistent with that of adults, their capacity for conduct and responsibility is comparatively limited. They cannot independently perform all civil legal acts, nor can they fully assume legal consequences in the way adults can.

Third, it reflects the non-equivalence between children's capacity for rights and their other capacities, highlighting the necessity of "protection" and "assistance" in the realization of children's rights. Children's capacity for rights may exist in separation from their capacity for conduct and responsibility: they may hold certain rights without the ability to exercise them independently or to bear the corresponding legal responsibilities. For example, while children are legally entitled to the right to education, the exercise of this right depends on the assistance of legal guardians, such as parents.

Fourth, the limitations of children's capacities can be attributed to specific causes. Their origin lies in the immaturity of physical and mental development due to age, which fundamentally differs from restrictions on legal capacity arising from special circumstances such as mental disorders or intellectual disabilities. The former is temporary and universal, reflecting the natural course of individual growth, whereas the latter entails persistent impairments affecting particular groups. Consequently, the legal responses and modes of protection differ between the two.

Thus, children's universal acquisition of constitutional subject status is both general and special: they are citizens in the general sense but also a distinct category of subjects. The fact that children have not yet reached the statutory age of majority does not preclude them from substantively attaining constitutional subjecthood. On the contrary, it is precisely because of their distinctive physical and mental characteristics that children require the highest level of protection afforded by the constitution as the fundamental law.

In addition, in contemporary constitutions, children's general subject qualification for rights is mainly obtained in two ways: firstly, by acquiring nationality to become citizens of a country; secondly, contemporary constitutions universally establish the principle of equal protection, prohibiting discrimination based on age, thus even children who have not reached the age of majority can obtain constitutional qualifications like adult citizens. From this, we can ascertain how Chinese children enjoy constitutional qualifications. According to Article 33, Paragraph 1 of *the Constitution of the People's Republic of China* (1982), "All persons holding the nationality of the People's Republic of China are citizens of the People's Republic of China," indicating that the Chinese Constitution protects children's rights of name and nationality, clarifying the external source of rights for Chinese children to enjoy constitutional qualifications, namely, first acquiring Chinese nationality, which is a prerequisite for obtaining constitutional qualifications for Chinese children. Besides, in formal terms, according to relevant laws such as *the Law of the People's Republic of China on the Protection of Minors*, under Chinese law, "minors" are defined as "citizens under the age of eighteen," which is entirely consistent with the definition of children under *the United Nations Convention on the Rights of the Child*. From the aforementioned substantive perspective, children have equal rights and obligations as adults, enjoying the constitutional qualifications they deserve, and should not be deprived of constitutional qualifications or discriminated against based on age. However, on another level, due to the young age and insufficiently mature physical and mental development characteristics of children, *the Constitution of the People's Republic of China* sets many special protection provisions for children, which will be elaborated in the following sections.

1.2.3 The Development of Child Protection in the Chinese Constitution

With the inclusion of social welfare rights centered around the right to protection and benefit in the Weimar Constitution, children were recognized for their equal rights and autonomy in post-World War II constitutions, marking a new stage in the development of children's rights. In contemporary times, the constitutionalization of *the Convention on the Rights of the Child* has become a new trend in the development of children's rights. The Constitution is a sacred scripture filled with people's rights, and human rights protection is the core value of modern constitutions. The protection of children through the constitution is truly achieved through the protection of their various rights.

The Constitution of the People's Republic of China actively responds to the implementation of the protection of children's various rights as stipulated in *the United Nations Convention on the Rights of the Child.* Meanwhile, the appearance of children and the protection of children have been continuously reshaped and improved in different periods of constitutional texts in China.

The Constitution of the People's Republic of China (1954), China's first socialist constitution, contains two provisions related to children. Article 94 of the "54 Constitution" stipulates: "Chinese citizens have the right to education. The state establishes and gradually expands various schools and other cultural and educational institutions to ensure that citizens enjoy this right." It also states, "The state pays special attention to the physical and intellectual development of the youth." Article 96 provides: "Marriage, family, mothers, and children are under the protection of the state." This constitution primarily delineates two fundamental rights for children: the right to education and the right to protection. It largely establishes the normative foundation for children's rights in the subsequent three constitutions.

The Constitution of the People's Republic of China (1975) and the Constitution of the People's Republic of China (1978) also do not neglect constitutional protection for children in China. Article 27 of the Constitution of the People's Republic of China (1975) stipulates: "Citizens have the right to work and the right to education. Workers have the right to rest and the right to material assistance when they are old, sick, or disabled." It also states, "Marriage, family, mothers, and children are under the protection of the state." Article 51 of the Constitution of the People's Republic of China (1978) provides: "Citizens have the right to education. The state gradually increases various types of schools and other cultural and educational facilities to popularize education, ensuring that citizens enjoy this right." It also states, "The state pays special attention to the healthy growth of young people." Article 53 of the Constitution of the People's Republic of China (1978) provides: "Marriage, family, mothers, and children are under the protection of the state." Particularly the Constitution of the People's Republic of China (1978), essentially restores the provisions of the 1954 Constitution regarding children's rights. It can be observed that the protection of children's rights through constitutional means has always been a fundamental principle of modern Chinese constitutions.

The Constitution of the People's Republic of China (1982) stipulates the rights of children in both general and specific provisions. Firstly, Article 33 of the 1982 Constitution provides as a general provision: "All citizens of the People's Republic of China are equal before the law." "The state respects and safeguards human rights." This provision constitutes the fundamental core of citizens' basic rights under the Chinese Constitution, and naturally, children, as citizens, are entitled to the general basic rights prescribed by the Constitution. Additionally, Article 46 explicitly states: "The state shall nurture the comprehensive development of the youth, minors, and children in morality, intellect, physique, etc." Simultaneously, the Constitution also explicitly states the protection of children by the state and prohibits child abuse.

Secondly, the specific provisions in the Constitution of the People's Republic of China (1982) outline the specific rights of children. Article 46 provides children's rights to education and development: "Chinese citizens have the right and duty to receive education." "The state shall nurture the comprehensive development of the youth, minors, and children in morality, intellect, physique, etc." Article 49 specifies the protection of children by the state and the right to parental care: "Marriage, family, mothers, and children are under the protection of the state." "Parents have the obligation to support and educate their minor children." This article also prohibits child abuse: "It is prohibited to abuse the elderly, women, and children." Compared to the "54 Constitution," the "82 Constitution" inherits the provisions concerning children's rights to education and protection while also adding the rights of children to parental care and provisions against child abuse, further expanding the scope and depth of constitutional protection for children's rights.

These provisions constitute the fundamental basis for China's legislative work on child protection, providing a solid constitutional guarantee for the construction of a legal system safeguarding children's rights. They vividly demonstrate the continuous strengthening of the Constitution of the People's Republic of China in protecting children, the steady expansion of the scope of rights, and the increasing diversification of protective mechanisms. At present, China has essentially established a child rights protection legal system with Chinese socialist characteristics: the Constitution as the foundation; specialized legislation—the Law of the People's Republic of China on the Protection of Minors and the Law of the People's Republic of China on the Prevention of Juvenile Delinquency—as the core; and other laws, such as the Civil Code of the People's Republic of China and the Criminal Law of the People's Republic of China, serving as valuable supplements. Within this entire legal framework for child protection, the Constitution of the People's Republic of China, as the fundamental law, performs a leading and overarching role.

1.3 The Protection of Children's Rights and Interests Is Directly Reflected in the Constitution of the People's Republic of China

The discovery of humanity is fundamentally the discovery of human rights. However, the discovery of human rights is not a sudden, widespread process; rather, it is a gradual and slow evolution. In this process, the emergence and development of children's rights from nonexistence to existence, from implicit to explicit, have also occurred. Constitutional texts embody the fundamental values of a nation, and constitutional language represents the finest expression of a people. The Constitution is intimately related to the future of a country and the destiny of its people. From a historical perspective, children's and children's rights are products of history and social construction, safeguarded through a series of laws and regulations.

Article 4 of *the Convention on the Rights of the Child* requires contracting states to take all appropriate legislative, administrative, and other measures to implement the rights recognized in the Convention. Constitutionalizing the rights of the Convention can be viewed broadly as part of these "legislative measures," urging contracting states to "incorporate into their constitutions provisions that reflect key principles of the Convention on the Rights of the Child." The Constitution of the People's Republic of China actively incorporates the protection of children into its constitutional text, thus laying a solid foundation for China's legal system for the protection of children.

1.3.1 Protection of the Basic Human Rights of the Child

As the first comprehensive treaty elaborating on children's rights and freedoms, *the Convention on the Rights of the Child* establishes the principles of the best interests of the child, non-discrimination, respect for the views of the child, and the right to survival and development to guide legislative, judicial, and administrative protection activities for children in all countries.

As rights holders, children have dual identities: as human beings and as minors. Therefore, compared to adult rights, children's rights possess commonalities and differences. As rights of a special subject, children's rights have their unique characteristics. Firstly, the source of children's rights has an empowering nature;

secondly, the exercise of rights is highly dependent; the scope of rights has certain differences; moreover, the efficacy of rights has priority.

Among them, according to the specificity of rights, children's rights can be divided into basic rights and special rights. Basic rights are internationally recognized, namely, the constitutional basic rights enjoyed by children as citizens, similar to adults, such as the right to life, dignity, freedom, and other basic human rights. Special rights refer to the rights enjoyed exclusively by children as children, also known as children's privileges, including rights to education, protection, freedom from harm, and so on, in various aspects of life, learning, and development.

The safeguarding of human rights is the core value and basic value of the Constitution, and the fundamental purpose and value of the Constitution lie in safeguarding the rights of citizens. The Constitution of the People's Republic of China achieves this by ensuring the basic human rights of children as a foundation, thereby extending to protect other specific rights of children, including the right to education, the right to protection, the right to be free from harm, and others. The following will focus on how the Constitution of the People's Republic of China explicitly safeguards the basic rights of children through Article 33 of the constitutional text.

Article 33
All persons holding the nationality of the People's Republic of China are citizens of the People's Republic of China.

All citizens of the People's Republic of China are equal before the law.

The state shall respect and protect human rights.

Every citizen shall enjoy the rights prescribed by the Constitution and the law and must fulfill the obligations prescribed by the Constitution and the law.

Article 33, Clause 1 of the Constitution of the People's Republic of China delineates the appearance of constitutional qualifications for Chinese children, namely, obtaining Chinese nationality: "All persons holding the nationality of the People's Republic of China are citizens of the People's Republic of China." Naturally, all children holding the nationality of the People's Republic of China are citizens of the People's Republic of China. This clause indicates that the Chinese Constitution guarantees children's rights to their names and nationality, which is consistent with Article 7 of the Convention on the Rights of the Child, which stipulates that "every child shall be registered immediately after birth and shall have the right from birth to a name, the right to acquire a nationality..."

At the same time, Clause 1 of Article 33 also includes the conditions for acquiring constitutional qualifications for Chinese children. In contemporary constitutions, the general legal status of children's rights is mainly obtained in two ways: firstly, children obtain nationality to become citizens of a country (Clause 1 of Article 33 of the Chinese Constitution falls into this category). Secondly, contemporary constitutions universally establish the principle of equal protection, prohibiting discrimination based on age, so that even children under the age of 18 can obtain constitutional qualifications like adult citizens. This second scenario is reflected in

Clause 2 of Article 33 of *the Constitution of the People's Republic of China (Naftali,* 2019*)*.

Clause 2 of Article 33 of the Constitution of the People's Republic of China indicates that the Chinese Constitution grants every citizen (including every child) the right to equal protection, which is consistent with Article 2 of the Convention on the Rights of the Child: "States Parties shall respect and ensure the rights outlined in the present Convention to each child within their jurisdiction without discrimination of any kind, irrespective of the child's or his or her parent's or legal guardian's race, color, sex, language, religion, political or other opinion, national, ethnic or social origin, property, disability, birth or other status." This reflects the principle of non-discrimination and embodies the concept of equality before the law. For any child in China, from birth to adulthood, the Constitution of the People's Republic of China will always protect their basic human rights, including the right to life, the right to a name, personal freedom, and dignity, ensuring that they are free from all discrimination and unequal treatment based on gender, ethnicity, religion, disability, or any other status.

Article 33, Clause 3 of the Constitution of the People's Republic of China, "The state respects and guarantees human rights," embodies the protection of basic human rights for all Chinese citizens, including Chinese children, under the Chinese Constitution. This is also the spiritual core of the Constitution as a human rights protection document, specifically protecting children's rights to life, health, personal freedom, and dignity, among other personal and personality rights. Meanwhile, Clause 4 of Article 33 reflects the principle of consistency between rights and obligations, meaning that while children enjoy the rights guaranteed by the Constitution, they also have the responsibility to fulfill the obligations stipulated by the Constitution.

Overall, Clause 1 of Article 33 of the Constitution of the People's Republic of China provides comprehensive protection for children's rights, precisely reflecting the full recognition of children's legal status by the Constitution. Children obtaining full constitutional qualifications marks the starting point for a series of comprehensive protections. Clause 2 of Article 33, by establishing the principle of constitutional equality and prohibiting discrimination based on age, effectively includes children within its protective scope. As general subjects of constitutional rights, children are entitled to the same dignity and respect as adults, including equal constitutional rights, such as equal rights to education, participation, development, and protection, which will be further elaborated in the following sections.

1.3.2 Other Specific Provisions of Children's Rights

The Convention on the Rights of the Child (UNCRC) points out that children's most basic rights can be summarized as fourfold: the right to survival, the right to protection, the right to development, and the right to participation. The right to survival entails the right of all children to survive and to have access to feasible, the highest standard of medical care. The right to protection involves safeguarding children from discrimination, as well as from physical and economic exploitation and abuse. It includes protection from armed conflict, abandonment, and neglect, and ensuring appropriate care or rehabilitation services whenever needed. The right to development encompasses access to all formal and informal education and providing children with a conducive moral and social environment to meet their physical, psychological, and spiritual developmental needs. The right to participation refers to children's right to participate in family culture and life, including the right to express opinions on matters affecting them (Duan, 2019).

Article 94 of the Constitution of the People's Republic of China (1954) stipulates: "Citizens of the People's Republic of China have the right to receive education, and the state particularly cares for the physical and intellectual development of the youth. Marriage, family, mothers, and children are protected by the state." This provision embodies the spirit of safeguarding children's "right to participation" as stated in the UNCRC, establishing special protection for children's rights and laying the foundation for the current constitution's protection of children's rights. The Constitution of the People's Republic of China (1982), building upon the Constitution of the People's Republic of China (1954), further develops provisions for the protection of children's rights.

1.3.2.1 Participation Rights (Article 35)

Article 35
Citizens of the People's Republic of China shall enjoy freedom of speech, the press, assembly, association, procession and demonstration.

Article 15 of the United Nations Convention on the Rights of the Child stipulates freedom of association and peaceful assembly. In line with this, Article 35 of the Constitution of the People's Republic of China (1982) guarantees all citizens, including children, the freedom of speech, of the press, of assembly, of association, of procession, and demonstration. This provision embodies the basic principle of respecting children's views and opinions as enshrined in the UNCRC, and it is also a positive affirmation of children's participation rights (Zhang & Chen, 2021).

1.3.2.2 Freedom of Religious Belief (Article 36)

Article 36
Citizens of the People's Republic of China shall enjoy freedom of religious belief.

No state organ, social organization, or individual shall coerce citizens to believe in or not to believe in any religion, nor shall they discriminate against citizens who believe in or do not believe in any religion.

The state shall protect normal religious activities. No one shall use religion to engage in activities that disrupt public order, impair the health of citizens, or interfere with the state's education system.

Religious groups and religious affairs shall not be subject to control by foreign forces.

Article 14 of the United Nations Convention on the Rights of the Child respects and protects children's freedom of religious belief. Similarly, respecting and protecting children's freedom of religious belief is also a basic principle in the Constitution of the People's Republic of China, protected by laws and regulations at all levels. Freedom of religious belief is a part of personal freedom and constitutes a basic human right. In China, no child will be discriminated against or treated unfairly due to their religious beliefs or lack thereof.

The curriculum in Chinese schools, including legal education, ethnic unity education, and moral education, features content related to the state's policy of religious freedom. At the same time, China adheres to the principle of separating religion from education, and no organization or individual may use religion to interfere with school education and public education, nor may they use religious activities to obstruct the implementation of compulsory education.

1.3.2.3 The Right to Education and the Right to Development (Article 46)

The comprehensive development of individuals is primarily achieved through various forms of education, and education plays a crucial role in the formation and development of children's independent personalities. The right to education belongs to the category of developmental rights among children's basic rights, hence modern constitutions universally emphasize the protection of citizens' right to education and children's right to compulsory education.

The right to education for children is also an important right enshrined in the United Nations Convention on the Rights of the Child. The right to education for children encompasses a rich array of rights, mainly including the rights to equality, non-discrimination, protection from abuse, access to information, and participation in decision-making. These rights are stipulated in Articles 28 and 29 of the Convention on the Rights of the Child, aiming to safeguard children's right to education for the full development of their personality, intellect, and physical and mental abilities, while nurturing respect and responsibility towards human rights, others, and the natural environment. Article 46 of the Constitution of the People's Republic of China actively implements the protection of the right to education and the right to comprehensive development for Chinese children.

Article 46

Citizens of the People's Republic of China shall have the right and the obligation to receive education.

The state shall foster the all-round moral, intellectual, and physical development of young adults, youths, and children.

Schools are the primary sites for children's growth, and children's healthy development is inseparable from school education. The Constitution of the People's Republic of China (1982) makes explicit provisions for children's right to education at school. On this basis, the Education Law of the People's Republic of China, the Higher Education Law of the People's Republic of China, and the Compulsory Education Law of the People's Republic of China all stipulate children's equal right to education.

According to the *Outline for the Development of Chinese Children (2021–2030)*, the coverage of compulsory education in China has continued to expand. By the end of 2020, the gross enrollment rate in preschool education had reached 85.2 percent, the retention rate in nine-year compulsory education stood at 95.2 percent, and the gross enrollment rate at the senior secondary level was 91.2 percent. These figures indicate that China has gradually realized equal opportunities for children to exercise their right to education. At the same time, substantive equality in children's right to education in China is primarily reflected in the widespread availability of "high-quality" and "high-standard" compulsory education. This signifies a gradual shift from the guarantee of "equality of educational opportunities" toward "equality of educational quality," while applying the principle of equality in safeguarding children's right to education.

The evolution of China's current legal framework also demonstrates this progression. Provisions concerning children's right to education have developed from ensuring the basic right of school-age children to enroll—namely, "compulsory education for all"—which addressed the quantitative aspect of equal access, to guaranteeing that school-age children receive education of high or comparable quality—namely, "compulsory education of equivalent quality for all."

Additionally, disabled children also have the right to equal access to education. Article 25 of the Law of the People's Republic of China on the Protection of Persons with Disabilities stipulates: "Ordinary primary schools and junior secondary schools must admit disabled children and adolescents who can adapt to their learning and life... Ordinary preschool education institutions should admit disabled preschoolers who can adapt to their life." This embodies the right to equal access to education and is in line with the non-discrimination principle in the Convention on the Rights of the Child.

1.3.2.4 The Right to Protection—The Right Protects Children from Harm (Article 49)

Children are the future and hope of the nation. However, due to their physical and psychological developmental stage, their rights are more vulnerable to infringement compared to adults, and the forms of violation they encounter are more concealed. Therefore, it requires us to pay more attention to the protection of children's rights.

The right to protection of children is the right for children to obtain care from families, schools, communities, other organizations, and the entire society in accordance with the law, to be free from harm, persecution, and harmful influences. From the Constitution of the People's Republic of China to basic laws, specialized laws, and judicial interpretations, a zero-tolerance attitude is adopted toward violence against children. The act of abusing children violates their personal rights, and from the perspective of national kinship, children are not only the hope of the family but also the future of the country. Illegal criminal acts that harm the physical and mental health of children must be severely punished by law.

This includes the issue of child abuse in domestic violence. "Child abuse is a legal issue, don't hesitate on this issue. Violence against children, regardless of the purpose, must be prohibited. Because all harm to children is often done in the name of love." As stipulated in the Convention on the Rights of the Child, countries should protect children from physical and mental abuse, harm, humiliation, neglect, abuse, or exploitation.

Article 49
Marriage, families, mothers, and children shall be protected by the state.

Both husband and wife shall have the obligation to practice family planning.

Parents shall have the obligation to raise and educate their minor children; adult children shall have the obligation to support and assist their parents.

Infringement of the freedom of marriage is prohibited; mistreatment of senior citizens, women, and children is prohibited.

Article 49 of the Constitution of the People's Republic of China (1982) provides comprehensive and general protection for children as a group. As the mother law and the fundamental law, the constitution has the highest efficacy. Its basic principles serve as a normative basis for the special protection of children's rights, making children the general subject of constitutional rights. Other basic rights provisions such as personal rights, freedom of communication, and the right to communication secrecy are also applicable.

At the same time, Article 49 of the Constitution of the People's Republic of China (1982) presents implicit legislative requirements for the protection of minors. To ensure its practical application, China has successively promulgated the Law of the People's Republic of China on the Prevention of Juvenile Delinquency and the Law of the People's Republic of China on the Protection of Minors, which are laws applicable to the entire group of minors.

The 20th National Congress of the Communist Party of China emphasized, "Protect the legitimate rights and interests of children. The state, family, and society play crucial roles in maximizing the survival and development of children. This is determined by the characteristics of children themselves and the roles they play in society. As mentioned earlier, the right to education stipulated in Article 46 of the Constitution of the People's Republic of China (1982) is based on schools as construction sites. Therefore, as the most intimate environment for children's growth, families are the first place for children to receive education after birth. The constitution protects children's right to a happy family and enables them to grow up healthily under the care and education of their parents. As the fundamental law, this provision echoes the principle of equality enshrined in Article 33. Specifically addressing vulnerable groups such as orphans and children with disabilities, it establishes special protections and achieves a unity of formal and substantive equality through "reasonable differential treatment," thereby embodying the Constitution's precise concern for special groups.

To implement the spirit of the Constitution, China has successively enacted the Law of the People's Republic of China on the Protection of Minors, the Law of the People's Republic of China on the Prevention of Juvenile Delinquency, and the Civil Code of the People's Republic of China, which specify children's rights to maintenance as well as the rights and limitations of family guardianship. In 2021, the Law of the People's Republic of China on the Promotion of Family Education was adopted, further linking Article 49, paragraphs 1 and 3 of the Constitution. By emphasizing the construction of "family, family education, and family values," this law seeks to prevent domestic violence, promote the all-round development of children in morality, intellect, physical fitness, aesthetics, and labor, and thereby establish an institutional chain of "constitutional principles — specialized legislation — implementing laws."

The deeper significance of Article 49 of the Constitution of the People's Republic of China lies in its clarification that the protection of children is not solely the responsibility of either the family or the state, but rather a systematic endeavor requiring the coordinated governance of society, schools, families, and government. This not only provides the highest legal foundation for the source of children's rights but also demonstrates China's determination to construct a comprehensive and multi-level legal system for the protection of children (Zheng, 2020).

1.4 Summary

The Constitution of the People's Republic of China is the fundamental law of China, serving as the general outline for governing the country and ensuring national security, with the highest legal status, authority, and effectiveness.

The importance China places on the protection of children's rights is evident through the explicit provisions of *the Constitution of the People's Republic of China*. Safeguarding children's rights requires the guidance and protection provided by both the Constitution and specific laws. The Constitution serves as the fundamental mother law, and comprehensive protection for children is more clearly seen in China's basic laws such as *the Criminal Law of the People's Republic of China*, *the Civil Code of the People's Republic of China*, or specialized laws for child protection like the Law of *the People's Republic of China on the Protection of Minors* and the Law of *the People's Republic of China on the Prevention of Juvenile Delinquency*.

The Constitution of the People's Republic of China plays a guiding role in leading other laws to protect children. The emphasis in the Constitution on equality for all, respect for children's rights and freedoms, ensuring children's education, and protecting children from harm, embodies similar principles as those highlighted in *the United Nations Convention on the Rights of the Child*, such as nondiscrimination, freedom of thought, belief and religion, and protection from abuse. Chinese law strives to implement and respond to international policies, seeking alignment with international standards.

In summary, *the Constitution of the People's Republic of China* and *the Convention on the Rights of the Child* demonstrate a high level of consistency in protecting children's mental well-being, providing solid and the highest legal protection for safeguarding children's mental health. Of course, the vitality of the constitution lies in its implementation, and its authority is also derived from implementation. The actual realization of children's constitutional rights protection still requires specific implementation through other legislation, administrative measures, and actions.

References

Duan, L., Jia, W., & Xiaojing, X. (2019). Children in ancient law: Normative description and value analysis. *Journal of Tangshan College, 32*, 6.

Naftali, O. (2019). Rights of children and youth in China: Protection, provision and participation. In *Handbook on human rights in China* (pp. 273–299).

Sun, Q. (2021). The construction path of China's juvenile justice system. *Political Science and Law, 6*.

Wang, J. (2019). Changes and development of youth rights protection in 70 years of new China. *China Youth Social Science, 38*, 126–134.

Wang, Y., & Bi, Z. (2022). A centennial review of the rule of law construction process of the Communist Party of China. *Theoretical Observation, 2*, 14–16.

Zhang, Y., & Chen, X. (2021). Realistic dilemmas and solution paths of minors in realizing the right to participate in family affairs. *Journal of Liaoning Public Security and Judicial Administration Cadre College, 5*, 96–100.

Zheng, S. (2020). Analysis and reconstruction of the legal protection system of left-behind children - from the perspective of the constitution. *Journal of Hebei Youth Management Cadre College, 32*, 70–76.

Chapter 2
The Civil Code of the People's Republic of China: Foundations for the Civil Rights and Protection of the Child

2.1 Introduction

The Civil Code of the People's Republic of China is the country's first law named as a civil code. Since its inception and drafting, it has carried the noble aspirations and strong expectations of building a country ruled by law, and has been incorporated into the top-level design of the national governance system and modernization of governance capabilities. In the construction of the legal system for safeguarding children's rights and interests, *the Civil Code of the People's Republic of China* plays an indispensable role in protecting children's civil rights and interests.

As the "declaration of the rights of the people in the new era," the Civil Code of the People's Republic of China runs through the development ideology centered on the people, focusing on meeting the needs of the people for a better life, embodying the full guarantee of the people's rights. *The Civil Code of the People's Republic of China* consists of 7 parts and 1260 articles, including the general principles, property rights, contract rights, personality rights, marriage and family rights, inheritance rights, tort liability, and supplementary provisions, covering various aspects of social life, also known as the "encyclopedia of social life." In the compilation process, multiple provisions protecting the rights and interests of minors were specifically established, playing a comprehensive and three-dimensional role in protecting the rights and interests of minors, adding a significant touch to the construction of the legal system for protecting the rights of minors.

This chapter, combining with relevant articles, takes the perspective of children's rights, from the general provisions of children's civil capacity, civil act capacity, statute of limitations in litigation, to the specific protection of children's personal rights and property rights, and further to the exercise of the right to request and remedies when children's personal or property rights are impaired or infringed upon. It interprets how the Civil Code of the People's Republic of China serves as a new era declaration of rights protection in our country, how it multi-dimensionally

© The Author(s), under exclusive license to Springer Nature Singapore Pte Ltd. 2026
H. Li, P. Liang, *The Legal System for the Protection of Children's Rights in China*, Resilient and Friendly Living Environments,
https://doi.org/10.1007/978-981-95-9925-7_2

and comprehensively protects the healthy growth of minors in legislation, how it responds to and implements the principles of maximizing children's interests such as respecting children's opinions, safeguarding children's rights and freedoms, and protecting children from all forms of violence in the United Nations Convention on the Rights of the Child.

2.2 The Civil Law Protection of Children's Rights and Interests

As the "encyclopedia of social life", *the Civil Code of the People's Republic of China* provides guidance and protection for people in all aspects of daily life, from cradle to grave, from day to night, from basic necessities to marriage and funeral rites. In terms of time span, this protection spans a person's entire life, covering various aspects of rights. From the fundamental nature of civil law, its protection of children mainly focuses on two aspects: personal and property. The general principles of *the Civil Code of the People's Republic of China* establish the basic rights of children throughout their growth period, such as civil capacity and capacity for civil acts. The specific provisions ensure comprehensive protection for children in terms of personal and property rights. Moreover, when children's rights are infringed upon, corresponding legal remedies are provided to achieve multidimensional protection for children. The following will introduce the specific content of the protection of children's rights in *the Civil Code of the People's Republic of China*, ranging from general provisions to specific regulations, covering various systems such as guardianship, inheritance, adoption, and family (Guo, 2021).

2.2.1 *General Provisions*

The general provisions of child rights protection in *the Civil Code of the People's Republic of China* are reflected in its general principles. At the beginning of the code, it defines children as natural persons under the age of eighteen. This definition aligns with the concept of *the Convention on the Rights of the Child*, considering individuals under the age of 18 as children requiring more attention. It also extends the starting point of protection to before birth, during the prenatal period. Based on this, the general principles of *the Civil Code of the People's Republic of China* also make important provisions regarding children's civil capacity and capacity for civil acts, providing comprehensive and reasonable protection for children throughout their growth period, from prenatal to reaching the age of 18.

2.2.1.1 Protection of Children Before Birth (Prenatal Period)

The Civil Code of the People's Republic of China provides comprehensive protection for the life of the fetus during the prenatal period and grants reasonable property rights to the fetus. It stipulates that the fetus has its own right to inherit property; if the guardian of the fetus accepts property gifted by others on behalf of the fetus, then that property belongs to the fetus itself. Parents, as legal representatives before the fetus born, have the right to assert corresponding rights in court. However, all of this is contingent upon the successful birth of the fetus; otherwise, these provisions are deemed not to have occurred. Detailed provisions can be found in Article 16 of *the Civil Code of the People's Republic of China*:

> **Article 16**
> ***If there are interests of the fetus to be protected, such as inheritance of estates or acceptance of gifts, the fetus is deemed to have the capacity for civil rights. However, if the fetus is stillborn, its capacity for civil rights does not exist from the outset.***

While property rights are protected, *the Civil Code of the People's Republic of China* also provides corresponding guarantees for the personal rights of the fetus. Firstly, activities related to human genes, human embryos, and medical and scientific research must be conducted lawfully and reasonably, without using fetuses for research that violates ethics or laws. Secondly, husbands are obliged to care for their wives during pregnancy and for the child until they reach one year of age, and they are prohibited from initiating divorce during this period. Articles 1009 and 1082 of *the Civil Code of the People's Republic of China* provide provisions regarding this matter.

> **Article 1009**
> ***Medical and scientific activities related to human genes, human embryos, and similar matters shall comply with laws, administrative regulations, and relevant state provisions. They shall not endanger human health, violate ethical principles, or harm public interests.***

> **Article 1082**
> ***During pregnancy, within one year after childbirth, or within six months after termination of pregnancy, the husband shall not initiate divorce proceedings. However, this provision does not apply if the wife initiates divorce or if the People's Court deems it necessary to accept the husband's divorce request.***

2.2.1.2 Protection of Children Aged Under 18

As stated in the Convention on the Rights of the Child, children inherently possess the rights to survival, development, protection, and participation from the moment of their birth. Chinese law recognizes that children, as natural persons, possess absolute capacity for civil rights. Article 13 of *the Civil Code of the People's Republic of China* clarifies this:

Article 13
Natural persons have the capacity for civil rights from the time of birth until death, enjoy civil rights in accordance with the law, and bear civil obligations.

Although children do not have the same rights and obligations as adults in terms of capacity for civil acts, they still possess certain civil rights and obligations. Respecting and protecting the rights of children is a social responsibility, and each of us should contribute to safeguarding their rights, and creating a safe, healthy, and harmonious environment for their growth and development (Gong, 2021).

Regarding capacity for civil acts, *the Civil Code of the People's Republic of China* classifies civil subjects into those with full capacity for civil acts, those with limited capacity for civil acts, and those without capacity for civil acts, based on whether the civil acts correspond to their age, intelligence, and mental health status. Age is the primary criterion for distinguishing these three categories of subjects, corresponding to three different stages of childhood in China: under 8 years old, 8–18 years old, and 16–18 years old. Tailoring targeted protection for children's civil rights and interests according to their different stages of development is more conducive to their growth and development (Xiong, 2015).

Children under the age of 8 are considered to have no capacity for civil acts and thus cannot perform valid civil legal acts. However, their guardians have the right to represent them in civil activities. Legislators consider children of this age to be too young and in the initial stages of growth and development. Although they have some intelligence, they cannot engage in civil activities rationally. This provision can be found in Articles 20, 21, and 144 of *the Civil Code of the People's Republic of China.*

Article 20
Individuals under the age of eight are deemed to lack the capacity for civil acts and shall have their civil legal acts carried out by their statutory representatives.

Article 21
The statutory representatives of individuals lacking capacity for civil acts or individuals with limited capacity for civil acts are their guardians.

Article 144
Civil legal acts performed by individuals lacking capacity for civil acts are invalid.

Children aged 8–18 are considered individuals with limited capacity for civil acts. They can independently engage in civil legal acts that purely benefit themselves or those that are appropriate for their age, intelligence, and mental health status. If they undertake other civil legal acts, as long as their guardians agree or ratify, they also have legal effect. For these children, they have reached a certain level of intelligence, and possess the ability to recognize and judge matters to a certain extent. Therefore, the law recognizes their limited capacity for civil acts, granting them the right to make choices in accordance with their cognitive level and the freedom to carry out certain civil legal acts. However, considering that children aged 8–18 are still relatively young and their intellectual development is not yet complete, they cannot independently understand and judge their actions and their consequences. Thus, they only possess partial legal capacity, not full legal capacity. Whether the civil legal acts performed by children are appropriate for their age, intelligence, and mental health status, the court may determine from the degree of relevance to their lives, whether they can understand their actions and foresee the corresponding consequences based on their intellectual and mental health conditions, as well as the subject matter, quantity, price, or remuneration, etc. This provision can be understood from Articles 19 and 145 of *the Civil Code of the People's Republic of China*:

Article 19
Individuals aged over eight but under 18 are deemed individuals with limited capacity for civil acts. Their civil legal acts shall be conducted by their statutory representatives or shall be valid if carried out independently and purely for their own benefit or are appropriate for their age and intelligence, with the consent or ratification of their statutory representatives.

Article 145
Civil legal acts performed by individuals with limited capacity for civil acts, which are purely beneficial or appropriate for their age, intelligence, and mental health status, are valid. Other civil legal acts they undertake shall be valid with the consent or ratification of their statutory representatives.

For children aged 16–18, who have acquired independent living capabilities and rely primarily on their own labor income, they may be deemed individuals with full capacity for civil acts. Like adults, they can independently engage in civil legal acts and enjoy the rights and obligations of civil activities on an equal basis with adults. With the development of society and the economy, the living standards of residents are improving, and many children demonstrate cognitive and functional abilities beyond their peers. For example, some individuals may be capable of employment at the age of 16. Considering the reality in China, many children aged 16–18 are living independently without relying on their parents (Guo, 2008). Therefore, the law designates them as individuals with full legal capacity for acts, aligning with the prevailing social conditions. This provision, which integrates with the actual societal context, can be found in Article 18 of *the Civil Code of the People's Republic of China*:

Article 18
Adults are individuals with full capacity for civil acts and can independently engage in civil legal acts. Individuals aged over sixteen who primarily rely on their labor income for livelihood are deemed individuals with full capacity for civil acts.

Furthermore, the Civil Code of the People's Republic of China specifies a statute of limitations of three years for lawsuits seeking protection of civil rights in court. However, for two types of civil cases involving harm to children—cases where guardians harm children and cases where children suffer from sexual abuse—the starting point for calculating the statute of limitations is specifically regulated to ensure genuine protection of children's rights.

As mentioned earlier, before children attain full capacity for civil acts, their guardians act on behalf of them to carry out civil legal acts. When children's rights are violated, their statutory representatives have the right to initiate lawsuits in court to help protect their interests. However, there are many irresponsible guardians who not only fail to provide assistance to children but also perpetrate harm against them. Particularly in cases of child sexual abuse, due to guardians being unaware, concealing information, or because the child's immature mental state prevents them from timely reporting to the guardians, the law explicitly stipulates the postponement of the commencement of the statute of limitations for the right to litigate, allowing children to have sufficient time to seek legal remedies. This is specifically outlined in Articles 180, 190, and 191 of *the Civil Code of the People's Republic of China*:

Article 188
The statute of limitations for lawsuits seeking protection of civil rights in court is three years. If the law provides otherwise, it shall be followed accordingly.

Article 190
The statute of limitations for the right to litigate of individuals lacking capacity for civil acts or individuals with limited capacity for civil acts against their statutory representatives shall be calculated from the date of termination of such representation.

Article 191
The statute of limitations for the compensation claims of minors who have suffered sexual abuse shall be calculated from the date when the victim reaches the age of eighteen.

For children who lack or partially possess capacity for civil acts, the Civil Code of the People's Republic of China has established a comprehensive guardianship system (further discussed later), ensuring the protection of children's rights. In summary, by granting civil capacity to fetuses, and distinguishing children's capacity for civil acts based on different stages of growth, the law not only aligns with the developmental characteristics of children but also better achieves the fundamental purpose of protecting children's rights. The Civil Code of the People's Republic of China considers children's interests from multiple perspectives, providing comprehensive protection throughout their entire growth period.

2.2.2 *Protection of Children's Personal Rights*

Building upon the general protective provisions for children at different stages of development, *the Civil Code of the People's Republic of China* (PRC) ensures the protection of children's personal and property rights through specific institutional arrangements. Regarding the protection of personal rights, this primarily manifests in various systems such as guardianship, family, and adoption (Zhang & Kollnig, 2024).

2.2.2.1 Guardianship

Guardianship refers to the legal system of supervising and protecting the personal, property, and other legitimate civil rights of individuals who lack or partially possess the capacity for civil acts. The person fulfilling the guardianship duties is referred to as the guardian, while the individual under supervision and protection is the ward. China's guardianship system encompasses guardianship for children and for adults with limited or no capacity for civil acts. Here, we primarily focus on and elucidate guardianship for children.

Regarding the guardianship system, pursuant to the provisions of the Civil Code of the People's Republic of China, guardianship is primarily categorized into statutory guardianship, testamentary guardianship, designated guardianship, and consensual guardianship.

The specific provisions mentioned above can be found in Articles 26–30 and 32 of *the Civil Code of the People's Republic of China.*

Article 26
Parents have the obligation to nurture, educate, and protect their minor children. Adult children have the obligation to support, assist, and protect their parents.

Article 27
Parents are the guardians of their minor children. If the parents of a minor child have died or are incapable of guardianship, the following individuals with guardianship capacity shall assume guardianship in the following order: (1) grandparents; (2) elder siblings; (3) other individuals or organizations willing to act as guardians, subject to the consent of the residents' committee, village committee, or civil affairs department at the minor's place of residence.

Article 29
If the parents of the ward serve as guardians, they may designate a guardian through a will.

Article 28
Adults lacking or partially possessing capacity for civil acts shall have guardians appointed by individuals with guardianship capacity in the following order: (1) spouse; (2) parents, children; (3) other close relatives; (4) other individuals or organizations willing to act as guardians, subject to the consent of the residents' committee, village committee, or civil affairs department at the place of residence of the ward.

Article 30
Individuals with legal guardianship qualifications may agree to designate a guardian. The designation of a guardian through agreement shall respect the true intentions of the ward.

Article 32
If there is no individual with legal guardianship qualifications, the guardianship shall be assumed by the civil affairs department, or by the residents' committee or village committee at the place of residence of the ward, provided they meet the conditions for performing guardianship duties.

In cases of guardianship disputes, the Civil Code of the People's Republic of China provides corresponding dispute resolution mechanisms and a system of temporary guardianship. When a guardianship dispute arises, there are two ways to designate a guardian: first, through appointment by the residents' committee, village committee, or civil affairs department; second, by directly applying to the court for appointment. The former is not a prerequisite for the latter. Once the court designates a guardian, the appointed guardian cannot refuse. However, if the guardian appointed by the residents' committee, village committee, or civil affairs department disagrees, they may apply to the court. Specific provisions can be found in Article 31 of *the Civil Code of the People's Republic of China*:

Article 31
In cases where there is a dispute over the appointment of a guardian, the guardian shall be designated by the residents' committee, village committee, or civil affairs department at the place of residence of the ward. If any party disagrees with the designation, they may apply to the People's Court for the appointment of a guardian. Relevant parties may also directly apply to the People's Court for the appointment of a guardian.

The residents' committee, village committee, civil affairs department, or People's Court shall respect the true intentions of the ward and appoint a guardian from among individuals with legal guardianship qualifications based on the principle most favorable to the ward.

Before designating a guardian in accordance with the provisions of the first paragraph of this article, if the personal rights, property rights, and other

lawful rights and interests of the ward are in a state of no protection, the residents' committee, village committee, relevant organizations stipulated by law, or civil affairs department at the place of residence of the ward shall serve as temporary guardians.

Once appointed, the guardian may not be changed arbitrarily. Any unauthorized change does not exempt the appointed guardian from responsibility.

The central content of guardianship is guardianship duties, which mainly include the right to personal guardianship, property guardianship, and the power of agency in civil acts and civil litigation. If the guardian fails to fulfill their guardianship duties or infringes upon the lawful rights and interests of the ward, they shall bear legal responsibility. The provisions regarding guardianship duties are mainly presented in Articles 34–35 of *the Civil Code of the People's Republic of China.*

Article 34

The duties of a guardian include representing the ward in carrying out civil legal acts and protecting the ward's personal rights, property rights, and other lawful interests. The rights arising from the guardian's lawful performance of guardianship duties are protected by law. If a guardian fails to fulfill their guardianship duties or infringes upon the lawful rights and interests of the ward, they shall bear legal responsibility. In the event of emergencies such as sudden incidents where the guardian is temporarily unable to perform their duties and the ward's life is left unattended, the residents' committee, village committee, or civil affairs department at the ward's place of residence shall arrange necessary temporary care measures for the ward.

Article 35

The guardian shall perform his guardianship duties in accordance with the principle of being most beneficial to the ward. The guardian shall not dispose of the property of the ward except to safeguard the interests of the ward. The guardian of a minor shall, when performing the duties of guardianship, when making a decision related to the interests of his ward, respect the true will of his ward in light of the age and intellectual status of his ward. In performing the duties of guardianship, the guardian of adults shall respect the true wishes of the ward to the greatest extent, and guarantee and assist the ward in performing civil legal acts commensurate with his intellectual and mental health status. The guardian shall not interfere with the affairs that the ward is able to handle independently.

About the guardian's revocation and restoration, as well as the termination of the guardianship, the article 36–39 of *the Civil Code of the People's Republic of China* stipulates and lists the statutory circumstances. It is necessary to note that there is no limit to the subject order of the application for the revocation of the guardian qualification, once the statutory circumstances for the revocation of the guardian qualification arise, the relevant individuals and organizations stipulated in this article can apply to the people's court for the revocation of the guardian qualification. When the civil affairs department applies to the people's court for the revocation of the guardian qualification, it is not on the premise that other relevant individuals and organizations do not apply, as long as there are objective reasons for the revocation of the guardian qualification, the civil affairs department can apply to the people's court for the revocation of the guardian qualification. The people's court appoints a new guardian according to law, which is usually applicable to the situation where there is no guardian to perform the guardianship duty due to the revocation of the guardian qualification.

The subject of the revocation of the guardian qualification shall still bear the obligations of paying maintenance, support and maintenance, and the system of restoring the guardian qualification for the first guardian of parents and children. Three typical situations are listed for the termination of the guardianship relationship, and the guarantee stipulation is made. In some cases of termination of guardianship, such as the death of the guardian, loss of guardianship ability or cancellation of guardianship qualification, the guardian still needs to be guardian, shall be based on the specific circumstances, in accordance with the provisions of the law to determine the guardian.

For the cancellation and restoration of the guardian and the termination of the guardianship, the provisions of *the Civil Code of the People's Republic of China* are mainly concentrated in Articles 36–39.

Article 36

Where a guardian has performed any of the following acts, the people's court shall, upon request of a relevant individual or organization, disqualify the guardian, adopt necessary temporary measures, and appoint a new guardian in the best interest of the ward in accordance with law: (1) engaging in any acts which severely harm the physical or mental health of the ward; (2) failing to perform the duties of the guardian, or being unable to perform such duties but refusing to delegate all or part of the duties to others, thus placing the ward in a desperate situation; or (3) engaging in other acts which severely infringe upon the lawful rights and interests of the ward. The relevant individual and organization referred to in this Article include any other person legally qualified to be a guardian, the residents' committee, the villagers' committee, a school, a medical institution, the women's federation, the disabled persons' federation, a child protection organization, a legally established organization for senior people, the civil affairs department, and the like. Where the aforementioned individual and organization other than the civil affairs department, as stated in the preceding paragraph, fail to request the people's court to disqualify the guardian in a timely manner, the civil affairs department shall initiate such a request to the people's court.

Article 37
A parent, child, or spouse legally obligated to pay for his ward's support shall 7continue to perform such obligations after being disqualified as a guardian by the people's court.

Article 38
Where a ward's parent or child, who has been disqualified as a guardian by the people's court for reasons other than having committed an intentional crime against the ward, and who has truly repented and mended his ways, applies to the people's court for being reinstated, the people's court may, upon considering the actual situation and upon the satisfaction of the prerequisite that the true will of the ward is respected, reinstate the guardian, and the guardianship between the ward and the guardian subsequently appointed by the people's court after the disqualification of the original guardian shall thus be terminated simultaneously.

Article 39
A guardianship is terminated under any of the following circumstances:
(1) the ward has obtained or regained full capacity for performing civil juristic acts; (2) the guardian has become incompetent to be a guardian; (3) the ward or the guardian deceases; or (4) Any other circumstance in which the people's court determines to terminate the guardianship. Where a ward is still in need of a guardian after the termination of the guardianship, a new guardian shall be appointed in accordance with law.

The guardianship system of the child in China has formed a set of system with Chinese characteristics, which plays a role in protecting the legitimate rights and interests of the child from multiple dimensions and aspects. As the smallest unit of society and the first front of child protection, the Civil Code of the People's Republic of China expounds the legal aspects of guardianship of the child in China from a more comprehensive and systematic perspective, and establishes a guardianship system based on family guardianship and state guardianship (Xia, 2018).

2.2.2.2 Civil Law Norms on Family Relations

Family is the basic social unit of the child's life. The special protection of the child's family rights and interests is the consistent principle of marriage and family legal system in China. The maximization of the child's interests has been the consensus of the international community. The Civil Code of the People's Republic of China's Marriage and Family Code especially emphasizes the protection of the child's interests, including prohibiting abuse, protecting the child's education and other systems, among which Article 1041 is another emphasis on the protection of minors' legitimate rights and interests in China's Civil Code.

Article 1041
Marriage and family are protected by the State. A marriage system based on freedom of marriage, monogamy, and equality between men and women is implemented. The lawful rights and interests of women, minors, the elderly, and persons with disabilities are protected.

In *the Civil Code of the People's Republic of China*, the Marriage and Family Code stipulates prohibited acts between families to emphasize the prohibition and avoidance of harm to the child. Specifically, the prohibited acts within the family include: abuse between family members, which refers to the use of beatings, cold starvation, illness without treatment and other methods to destroy and torture family members, so that they suffer physical and mental pain; Abandonment among family members is the failure of a person who has a duty to support, bring up or maintain a person who is old, young, ill or otherwise unable to live independently. In violation of the prohibitions, if one party maltreats or abandons a family member, resulting in divorce, the party without fault may claim compensation for divorce damages. If the circumstances of maltreatment or abandonment of family members are egregious, they shall constitute the crime of maltreatment or abandonment and shall be sanctioned by the Criminal Law. The prohibition of interfamily in *the Civil Code of the People's Republic of China* is mainly reflected in Article 1042.

Article 1042
Arranged marriages, mercenary marriages, and other acts interfering with the freedom of marriage are prohibited. The exaction of money or other property by way of marriage is prohibited. Bigamy is prohibited. No one who has a spouse may cohabit with another person. Domestic violence is prohibited. Maltreatment or desertion of family members is prohibited.

The protection of minors at the family level is mainly reflected in the legal provisions of parental support obligations. Both husband and wife shall enjoy equal rights to bring up, educate and protect the child under the age of 18, and shall jointly undertake corresponding obligations. Husband and wife have equal status in marriage and family relations, equally perform the rights prescribed by law, and jointly undertake many obligations in the upbringing, education a protection of minor children. The legal provisions of *the Civil Code of the People's Republic of China* on parental rearing obligations are mainly presented in Articles 1058 and 1067.

Article 1058
Both spouses have equal rights and joint duties to raise, educate, and protect their minor children.

Article 1067
Where parents fail to fulfill their duty to raise their children, a minor child or an adult child who is incapable of supporting himself has the right to claim child support payments against his parents. Where an adult child fails to fulfill

the duty to support his parents, his parents who lack the capacity to work or are in financial hardship have the right to claim support payments against the adult child.

The education and protection of the child is a common concern in today's society. Family legislation should be based on the child. The Civil Code of the People's Republic of China clearly stipulates the education and protection of the child by parents, better safeguarding the legitimate rights and interests of the child, and maximizing the interests of the child. In order to urge parents to fulfill their duties and obligations in educating and protecting the child, and to fully guarantee the healthy development of the child, the Civil Code of the People's Republic of China confirms that parents shall bear civil liability for the tortious acts of the child. As legal guardians of the child, parents have the right to educate and discipline the child through appropriate means within the scope of the law. The education of the child by parents is an important function of the family. At the level of education, parents should take correct measures to care for, guide and cultivate the child so that they can receive compulsory education according to law and ensure their healthy physical and mental development. At the level of protection, parents, as guardians of the child, should avoid the child from being infringed on their right to education from the outside world. For details, see *the Civil Code of the People's Republic of China.*

Article 1068
Parents have the right and duty to educate and protect their minor children. Where a minor causes damage to others, his parents shall bear civil liability in accordance with the law.

The Civil Code of the People's Republic of China also provides legal provisions on the rights and obligations of parents who remarry, the biological father or mother of an illegitimate child, and the step-parents. This reflects the concept of equality under the rule of law, and is also the principle of non-discrimination emphasized by *the United Nations on the Rights of the Child.* Family members other than parents will also bear corresponding obligations under certain conditions. Grandparents, maternal grandparents, elder siblings who are financially capable shall have corresponding obligations to bring up the child whose parents have died or whose parents are unable to bring them up. It reflects the protection and care of the whole family for minors. The specific provisions of *the Civil Code of the People's Republic of China* are mainly concentrated in articles 1070–1075.

Article 1070
Parents have the right to inherit their children's estates, and vice versa.

Article 1071
Children born out of wedlock have equal rights as children born in wedlock, and no organization or individual may harm or discriminate against them. A natural parent who does not have physical custody of his out-of-wedlock child

shall pay child support for such child who is a minor or who is an adult but incapable of supporting himself.

Article 1072
Stepparents shall not maltreat or discriminate against a stepchild, and vice-versa. Provisions of this Code governing the parents-children relationship shall apply to the rights and duties between a stepmother or a stepfather and a stepchild who has been raised and educated by such stepfather or stepmother.

Article 1073
Where a parent challenges maternity or paternity with just cause, the parent may file a lawsuit with the people's court for affirmation or denial of such maternity or paternity. Where an adult child challenges maternity or paternity with just cause, he may file a lawsuit with the people's court for affirmation of such maternity or paternity.

Article 1074
Paternal or maternal grandparents, if financially capable, have the duty to raise their minor grandchildren whose parents are deceased or are incapable of such raising. Paternal or maternal grandchildren, if financially capable, have the duty to support their grandparents whose children are deceased or are incapable of providing such support.

Article 1075
Elder brothers or sisters, if financially capable, have the duty to raise their minor siblings whose parents are deceased or are incapable of such raising. Younger brothers or sisters who have been brought up by their elder siblings and who are financially capable have the duty to support such elder siblings who lack both the capacity to work and the means to support themselves.

It can be seen that the legal provisions of the Marriage and Family section of *the Civil Code of the People's Republic of China* reflect the special protection of the rights and interests of the child' families. It protects the body, property and other legitimate rights and interests of the child from infringement from the aspects of principle requirements, prohibitive provisions, parental rearing obligations, education and protection obligations, and even the protection of the child in special families.

2.2.2.3 Civil Law Norms on Adoption

Adoption refers to the natural person adopting another person's child as his own child, which is a legal act of creating a fictitious blood parent-child relationship under the legal framework. This is the identity legal relationship based on the legal effect of the act of adoption. The fictitious parent-child relationship of blood relatives has the same rights and obligations as natural blood relatives (Xiang & Yang, n.d.).

Firstly, the Civil code of our country stipulates the basic principles that are most beneficial to the adoptee; The Basic principle of protecting the legitimate rights and interests of adoptees and adopters and the basic principle of prohibiting the sale of minors. These principles are designed to fundamentally eliminate any harm to the physical and mental growth of the child. Polymers refer to Article 1044 of *the Civil Code of the People's Republic of China*.

Article 1044
Adoption shall be in compliance with the principle of acting in the best interest of the adoptee, and the lawful rights and interests of both the adoptee and the adopter shall be protected. Trafficking minors in the name of adoption is prohibited.

Secondly, the law strictly defines the qualifications for adoption, so as to ensure that adopters can provide stable growth environment and good educational conditions for adopted child. Provide adequate living expenses and education, have a good home education atmosphere, and be able to ensure good care and attention for the adoptee. The provisions of *the Civil Code of the People's Republic of China* on the eligibility for adoption are mainly presented in Articles 1093–1104.

Article 1093
The following minors may be adopted: (1) an orphan bereaved of parents; (2) a minor whose natural parents cannot be traced; or (3) a minor whose natural parents are incapable of raising him due to unusual difficulties.

Article 1094
The following individuals and organizations may place a minor for adoption:(1) the guardian of an orphan;(2) a children's welfare institution; (3) a minor's natural parents who are incapable of raising him due to unusual difficulties.

Article 1095
Where neither of the parents of a minor has full capacity for performing civil juristic acts, and where they may seriously harm the minor, the guardian of the minor may place such minor for adoption.

Article 1096
Where a guardian intends to place an orphan under his guardianship for adoption, he shall obtain the consent of the person who has the duty to raise the orphan. Where the person with the duty to raise the orphan does not consent to the adoption and the guardian is unwilling to continue exercising guardianship, a successive guardian shall be appointed in accordance with the provisions of Book One of this Code.

Article 1097
Where the natural parents intend to place their child for adoption, they shall act in concert. Where one of the natural parents is unknown or cannot be traced, the other parent may place the child for adoption by himself.

Article 1098
A prospective adopter shall meet all the following conditions:(1) having no child or only one child;(2) being capable of raising, educating, and protecting the adoptee;(3) not suffering from any disease that is deemed medically unfit to be an adopter;(4) having no criminal record unfavorable to the healthy growth of the adoptee; and reaching the age of thirty.

Article 1099
Adoption of a child from one's collateral relatives by blood of the same generation and up to the third degree of kinship may be exempted from the restrictions provided in Subparagraph (3) of Article 1093, Subparagraph (3) of Article 1094, and Article 1102 of this Code. Adoption of a child by an overseas Chinese from his collateral relatives by blood of the same generation and up to the third degree of kinship may also be exempted from the restrictions prescribed in Subparagraph (1) of Article 1098 of this Code.

Article 1100
A childless adopter may adopt two children, and an adopter with one child may adopt only one more child. Adoption of an orphan, a minor with disabilities, or a minor in a children's welfare institution whose natural parents cannot be traced may be exempted from the restrictions provided in the preceding paragraph and Subparagraph (1) of Article 1098 of this Code.

Article 1101
Where a person with a spouse intends to adopt a child, the person and his spouse shall jointly adopt the child.

Article 1102
Where a person without a spouse intends to adopt a child of a different gender, the prospective adopter shall be at least forty years older than the adoptee.

Article 1103
A stepparent may, with the consent of the natural parents of the stepchild, adopt the stepchild, and such adoption may be exempted from the restrictions provided in Subparagraph (3) of Article 1093, Subparagraph (3) of Article 1094, Article 1098, and Subparagraph (1) of Article 1100 of this Code.

Article 1104
Both adoption and placing for adoption shall be based on mutual consent. Where a minor adoptee is aged eight or above, his consent shall be obtained.

Third, the Civil Code also makes clear provisions on the procedure of adoption. First of all, certain procedures shall be carried out between the intended adopter and the adoptee, including written application, consultation and agreement. The purpose of these programs is to ensure that both sides of the true wishes and adequate communication, and clear the rights and obligations of both sides. Secondly, prospective adopters need to go through the court's review and approval. The court will examine the qualifications, conditions, and wishes of the prospective adopter and hear the views of the parties concerned. The adoption is legally effective only after the approval of the court, which is also to protect the rights and interests of the adopted child. Finally, once the adoption is established, the court will register the adoptive relationship on a factual basis. The purpose of registration is to ensure the legitimacy of the adoptive relationship, and traceability, provide the basis for the exercise of relevant rights and interests. For details, please refer to Article 1105–1110 of *the Civil Code of the People's Republic of China.*

Article 1105
Adoption shall be registered with the civil affairs department of the people's government at or above the county level. The adoptive relationship is established upon registration. In the case of adopting a minor whose parents cannot be traced, the civil affairs department for adoption registration shall make public notice prior to the registration. The parties to an adoptive relationship may enter into an adoption agreement on a voluntary basis. Upon request of both parties or one of the parties to an adoptive relationship, an adoption shall be notarized.

Article 1106
Upon establishment of an adoptive relationship, the public security department shall facilitate household registration for the adoptee in accordance with the relevant regulations of the State.

Article 1107
An orphan or a child whose natural parents are incapable of raising him may be raised by the relatives or friends of his natural parents. The provisions of this Chapter shall not apply to the relationship between two persons one of whom is raised by the other.

Article 1108
Where one spouse is deceased and the surviving spouse intends to place their minor child for adoption, the parents of the deceased spouse shall have priority in raising the child.

Article 1109
Foreign nationals may adopt children in the People's Republic of China in accordance with law. The adoption of a child by a foreign national in the People's Republic of China shall be subject to the review and approval of the competent authorities of the foreign national's country of residence in

accordance with the law of that country. The foreign adopter shall submit documents issued by the competent authorities of his country of residence certifying such personal information as his age, marital status, occupation, financial situation, physical condition, and whether he has a criminal record. The foreign adopter shall conclude a written agreement with the person who places the child for adoption and register the adoption in person with the civil affairs department of the people's government at the level of provinces, autonomous regions, or municipalities directly under the State Council. The certifying documents provided in the preceding paragraph shall be authenticated by the diplomatic authorities of the country in which the foreign national resides or by an agency authorized by the said diplomatic authorities, and then authenticated by the embassy or consulate of the People's Republic of China in the said country unless otherwise provided by the State.

Article 1110
Where an adopter or a party placing a child for adoption requires that the adoption be kept confidential, the other persons shall respect their will and shall not disclose it.

Finally, in the Marriage and Family part of the Civil Code of the People's Republic of China, the last part of the adoption chapter is the specific provisions on the effect of adoption. The establishment of the adoption relationship is of great significance to the protection of the legitimate rights and interests of the child. According to the provisions of the Civil Code, adoptees have the same legal status as their own children. This means that the adoptee has the same rights and obligations as the biological child, including inheritance rights, custody rights, maintenance rights, etc. Furthermore, once an adoption has been established, it cannot be arbitrarily altered or revoked. Only under special circumstances, such as serious abuse by the intended adopter or great harm to the interests of the adoptee, can the court terminate the adoption by law. This regulation aims to protect the stability and legitimate rights and interests of adoptees from abuse and harm. See Articles 1111–1118 of *the Civil Code of the People's Republic of China.*

Article 1111
Upon establishment of an adoptive relationship, the provisions of this Code governing the parent-child relationship shall apply to the rights and duties between the adoptive parents and the adopted children. The provisions of this Code governing the relationship between children and the close relatives of their parents shall apply to the rights and duties between the adopted children and the close relatives of their adoptive parents. Upon establishment of an adoptive relationship, the rights and duties arising between the adoptee and his natural parents as well as the latter's other close relatives shall be terminated.

Article 1112
An adopted child may take the surname of his adoptive father or mother, or may retain his original surname upon consent of all the parties to the adoption.

Article 1113
An adoption shall be void when it constitutes a void civil juristic act as provided in Book One of this Code or violates the provisions provided in this Book. A void adoption has no legal effect ab initio.

Article 1114
No adopter may dissolve an adoptive relationship before the adoptee has reached the majority age unless there is an agreement between the adopter and the party who places the child for adoption to dissolve such relationship. Where an adoptee is aged eight or above, his own consent thereto shall be obtained. Where an adopter fails to perform the duty to raise the adoptee or commits maltreatment, desertion, or other acts infringing upon the lawful rights and interests of the minor adoptee, the person who has placed the child for adoption has the right to request that the adoptive relationship be dissolved. Where an adopter and a party who has placed a child for adoption fail to reach an agreement for the dissolution of the adoptive relationship, either party may file a lawsuit with the People's Court.

Article 1115
Where the relationship between adoptive parents and adult adoptive children deteriorates and they are unable to live together, the adoptive relationship may be terminated by agreement. If no agreement can be reached, a lawsuit may be brought before a people's court.

Article 1116
Where the parties agree to terminate the adoptive relationship, they shall register the dissolution of the adoptive relationship with the civil affairs department.

Article 1117
After the dissolution of the adoptive relationship, the rights and obligations between the adopted child and the adoptive parents and other close relatives shall be eliminated, and the rights and obligations between the adopted child and the birth parents and other close relatives shall be restored by itself.

Article 1118
After the dissolution of the adoptive relationship, adult foster children brought up by their adoptive parents shall pay living expenses to the adoptive parents who lack the ability to work and lack sources of livelihood. If the adoptive relationship is terminated because the adoptive child maltreats or abandons the adoptive parents when they come of age, the adoptive parents may ask the adoptive child to compensate for the alimony paid during the adoption period. If the birth parents request the dissolution of the adoptive relationship, the adoptive parents may ask the birth parents to properly compensate the alimony paid during the adoption period; However, the adoptive relationship shall not be terminated due to the abuse or abandonment of the adopted child by the adoptive parents.

It can be seen that *the Civil Code of the People's Republic of China* protects the legitimate rights and interests of minors as adoptees by providing specific provisions on the eligibility, procedure, and effectiveness of adoption. As far as possible, unaccompanied children are provided with a good family environment and educational conditions so that they can enjoy the same rights and status as their own children.

2.2.3 Civil Law Protection of Children's Property Rights

The Civil Code of the People's Republic of China also has detailed provisions on the protection of the child's property rights and interests, so as to comprehensively protect the healthy growth of minors.

First of all, the child's property rights are protected by guardians. The guardian's duties in protecting the child include protecting the personal rights, property rights, and other lawful rights and interests of the ward. The guardian shall not dispose of the ward's property except to safeguard the ward's interests. The rights of a guardian arising from the performance of his duty of guardianship according to law shall be protected by law. If a guardian fails to perform his guardianship duties or infringes upon the lawful rights and interests of his ward, he shall bear corresponding legal liabilities. If the guardian is temporarily unable to perform his duties of guardianship due to a sudden accident or other emergencies, and the person under his guardianship is left uncared for in his life, the resident's committee or villagers committee in the place where the person under his guardianship lives or the civil affairs department shall arrange necessary temporary measures for the guardian to take care of his life. When a guardian of a minor performs his guardianship duties and makes a decision related to the interests of the ward, he shall respect the true intention of the ward in light of the age and intellectual status of the ward. See Article 34–35 of *the Civil Code of the People's Republic of China*.

Article 34
The duties of a guardian are to represent the ward to perform civil juristic acts and to protect the personal, proprietary, and other lawful rights and interests of the ward. A guardian's rights arising from the performance of his duties as required by law are protected by law.

Article 35
The guardian shall perform his duties in the best interest of the ward. A guardian shall not dispose of the ward's property unless it is for protecting the interests of the ward.

Secondly, *the Civil Code of the People's Republic of China* provides for the protection of the child's property rights: First, the child has the right to receive gifts. The donor donates his property to the minor without compensation, and the minor who is the donee expresses acceptance of the gift and then becomes the owner of the donated property. Secondly, the inheritance rights of the child are specially protected by law. Thirdly, there are also special provisions for the protection of remuneration received by the child. See Articles 18, 19, 1124, and 1142 of *the Civil Code of the People's Republic of China.*

Article 18
An adult has full capacity for performing civil juristic acts and may independently perform civil juristic acts.
A minor aged 16 or above whose main source of support is the income from his own labor is deemed as a person with full capacity for performing civil juristic acts.

Article 19
A minor aged 8 or above has limited capacity for performing civil juristic acts and may perform a civil juristic act through or upon consent or ratification of his legal representative, provided that such a minor may independently perform a civil juristic act that is purely beneficial to him or that is appropriate to his age and intelligence.

Article 1124
A successor who, after the opening of succession, disclaims an inheritance shall manifest his decision in writing before the estate is disposed of. In the absence of such a manifestation, he is deemed to have accepted the inheritance. A donee-by-will shall, within 60 days after he learns of the testamentary gift, manifest his decision to accept or disclaim it. In the absence of such a manifestation within the specified period, he is deemed to have disclaimed the gift.

Article 1142
A testator may revoke or alter a will he has made. Where a testator who, after making a will, acts inconsistently with the content of his will, the pertinent part of the will is deemed to be revoked. Where several wills have been made and their contents are inconsistent, the will made last in time shall prevail.

It can be seen that although the child does not have full capacity for civil rights and civil conduct, under the protection of *the Civil Code of the People's Republic of China*, their personal property can be obtained through inheritance, donation, legal labor, and other means. The lack of full capacity for civil conduct and rights cannot prevent them from becoming "property holders".

2.2.4 Mechanisms for Protecting Children's Rights in Tort

As qualified as qualified civil subjects, children enjoy full personal rights and property rights. Children are endowed with their due rights and interests, and when their rights and interests are infringed, their legal representatives are required to help protect their civil rights. The infringement of children is the infringement of personal rights and property rights, and *the Civil Code of the People's Republic of China* provides comprehensive provisions for corresponding relief.

2.2.4.1 Legal Remedies for Children's Personal Rights

The protection of children's personal rights is a concrete embodiment of the concepts related to the United Nations Convention on the Rights of the Child and the Constitution of the People's Republic of China in the Civil Code of the People's Republic of China. In the protection of children's rights, personal rights are the basis, and children's personal rights are the most likely to be violated. When children's personal rights and interests are violated, families, society, and the state need to provide relief. Families and educational institutions are obviously the fields of children's main activities, and the infringement of children's personal rights also mainly occurs in the above fields. For this reason, the Civil Code of the People's Republic of China fully provides for the guardianship of guardians and relief after the infringement of educational institutions (Lao, 2022).

If the guardian is not fully or negligent in performing the duty of guardianship of the child, which infringes on the physical and mental health of the supervised children and is not conducive to the growth of the child, *the Civil Code of the People's Republic of China* stipulates the right to apply to the people's court for the revocation of the guardian qualification, as specified in articles 36,190 and 191:

> **Article 36**
> ***If the guardian is under any of the following circumstances, the people's court shall, upon the application of relevant individuals or organizations, arrange necessary temporary guardianship measures, and appoint the guardian according to the principle of being most conducive to the ward: (1) acts that seriously damage the physical and mental health of the ward; (2) delay in performing the guardianship duties, or refuse to entrust the guardianship duties to others, causing the ward in distress; (3) other acts that seriously infringe upon the lawful rights and interests of the ward. The relevant individuals and organizations stipulated in this Article include: other persons with guardianship qualifications according to law, residents 'committees, villagers' committees, schools, medical institutions, women's federations, disabled persons' federations, minor protection organizations, organizations for the elderly established according to law, civil affairs departments, etc. Where an individual or organization other than the Civil Affairs Department prescribed in the preceding paragraph fails to timely apply to the People's Court for the revocation of guardianship, the Civil Affairs Department shall apply to the People's Court.***

> **Article 190**
> ***The limitation of action for a person without civil capacity or with limited civil capacity for a right of claim against his legal agency shall be counted from the date of termination of the legal agency.***

Article 191
The limitation of action for the right to claim damages for sexual assault by a minor shall be calculated from the date when the victim reaches the age of 18.

The primary party responsible for the protection of children's rights and interests is the guardian. However, when the guardian infringes on the child's physical and mental health, the main relief channel is to revoke the guardian's guardianship qualification, and a new guardian should be determined according to law, based on the principle of what is most beneficial to the child. That is, the dynamic system theory is adopted to formulate the guardian consideration factors, Specifically, the close degree of life and emotional connection with the ward in all qualified guardians, As in the regular years of living with a supervised child, Grandparents, or maternal grandparents who have established good close relationships with their children; The guardianship in accordance with the law; Whether there are illegal and criminal situations that are not conducive to the performance of their guardianship duties, Such as adultery children; The guardianship capacity, will and conduct of persons qualified for guardianship according to law If the property status is better than other qualified guardians, The best guardian will be determined in the case of stronger guardianship will or good conduct.

The subject applying for the cancellation of the guardianship qualification covers the qualified individuals and organizations to the state. When the individuals and organizations fail to fulfill their duties, the Civil Affairs Department on behalf of the government shall apply to the People's Court for the cancellation of the guardianship qualification of the above guardians, so as to protect the rights and interests of children from the perspective of state rights.

At the same time, if the guardian infringes on the child during the existence of the guardianship relationship, in view of the child's ability to resist and the dilemma of protecting their own rights and interests, in order to extend the starting point of the child to maximize the calculation of the limitation of action until the termination of the guardianship relationship. If the guardian has sexually abused a child, the limitation of action shall be calculated according to the psychological maturity, cognitive ability and identification ability of the child when the child reaches a certain degree.

In addition to guardians, kindergartens, schools or other educational institutions are the second most important places for children to grow up besides families. These institutions aim to cultivate children's cognitive and recognition abilities, improve children's cognition, work, living together, and survival ability, and reserve corresponding abilities for children to enter the society after growing up. This means that almost all children will be gathered in the above places, resulting in the hidden danger to children's personal safety, which can be seen in Article 1199–1201 of *the Civil Code of the People's Republic of China:*

Article 1199
If a person with no capacity for civil conduct suffers personal injury during his study or living in a kindergarten, school, or other institution of education, the kindergarten, school, or other institution of education shall bear tort liability; however, those who can prove that he has performed his duties of education and administration shall not bear tort liability.

Article 1200
Where a person with limited capacity for civil conduct suffers personal injury during his study or life in a school or other institution of education, and the school or other educational institution fails to fulfill his duties of education and management, he shall bear tort liability.

Article 1201
If a person with limited capacity without civil conduct or during studying or living in a kindergarten, school, or other institution of education, the third party shall bear the tort liability; if a kindergarten, school, or other educational institution fails to fulfill its administrative duties, it shall bear the corresponding supplementary liability. A kindergarten, a school, or any other institution of education may, after assuming the supplementary responsibility, seek compensation from a third party.

Thus, although the education institution is not a guardian of children, but in the process of the growth of children. Schools are central to where children spend most of their developmental time, but children in the education institutions of learning and life during the infringement is common. It is because of education institutions plays an important role in the process of children growth, so when children in education institutions, according to the children's self-protection ability and schools should supervise the education institutions of children without civil capacity, limited capacity for civil conduct children share the corresponding liability share. The school shall undertake the special obligation of causing damage to the students due to its violation of its education and management duties. The obligations of the school should be determined based on the knowledge and cognitive development of children of different ages, and the responsibility of the school is determined for whether the school is at fault, the causal relationship between the fault and the result of the accident.

At the same time, *the civil code of the People's Republic of China* based on children's intelligence, understanding development, will have no civil capacity for the age of eight children in the education institutions during learning and life by personal infringement, direct presumption education institutions at fault, by the education institutions to their no fault burden of proof. In addition, when the infringed child is infringed by the third party, he can directly choose the third party to bear all the tort liability. If the educational institution fails to fulfill its management duty, the infringed child can also claim that the educational institution should bear the corresponding liability within the scope of the fault of the educational institution.

2.2.4.2 Legal Remedies for the Property Rights of Children

When children's property rights are infringed upon, China will provide relief according to law. *The Constitution of China* stipulates citizens 'lawful private property shall not be infringed upon, and the state protects citizens' private property rights and inheritance rights in accordance with the law. The main property protection of children is reflected in articles 1155, 1142, 1130, 1159 and 1067 of *the Civil Code of the People's Republic of China*:

> **Article 1155**
> ***When the inheritance is divided, the share of the fetal inheritance shall be retained. When the fetus is delivered and is dead, the retained shares shall be handled according to legal inheritance.***
>
> **Article 1142**
> ***The will shall keep the necessary share of the estate for the heir who lacks the ability to work and has no source of income.***
>
> **Article 1130**
> ***Heirs who have special difficulties in living and lack the ability to work shall be taken care of when distributing the estate.***
>
> **Article 1159**
> ***In dividing the estate, the taxes and debts payable by the decedent shall be paid off; however, the necessary estate shall be reserved for the heir who lacks the ability to work and has no source of income.***
>
> **Article 1067**
> ***If the parents fail to perform the obligation of bringing up, the minor child or the adult child who cannot live independently shall have the right to ask their parents to pay the maintenance fee.***

If the above provisions, the testamentary inheritance should leave the corresponding share of the child's property. If the testator does not retain the share of the fetus and does not retain the appropriate share of the estate for the heir who lacks labor ability and has no source of income, the estate shall leave the necessary estate for the heir, and the rest can be dealt with reference to the principle of distribution determined by the will.

If the child's share of due property is infringed, the limitation of action may be calculated from the date when the legal agent knows or should know that the rights are damaged and the obligor. Guardian shall be in accordance with the principle of the most beneficial to children management, children the corresponding property. But if the guardian does not abuse the child's property in accordance with their guardianship duties, but instead attributes the child's property to their own use, the children obtain full civil capacity or in the original legal relationship terminate and determine the new legal agent, the corresponding civil subject know or should know rights damage when calculated, by the new legal agent or children after full civil capacity can be in accordance with the people's court in accordance with the lawsuit, to protect the children's legal property rights.

During the growth of children, the parents have the obligation to bring up their children. If one or two parties do not bring up the children, they may request the people's court to pay the children's living expenses, education expenses, medical expenses and other maintenance fees. At the same time, the cost is not fixed. If the original amount of the child is insufficient to maintain the actual living standard; if the child needs to increase beyond the original amount, the people's court shall support it.

In short, *the Civil Code of the People's Republic of China* provides the substantive relief provisions for the infringement of children's personal rights and property rights according to the principle of most conducive to the protection of minors. It covers the cases of individuals and organizations infringing upon the rights and interests of children, and stipulates the subject of appropriate relief and responsibility. It is the practice of the spirit of *the United Nations Convention on the Rights of the Child* to maximize the survival and development of children, but also the specific provisions and implementation of the protection of children's rights and interests in the Constitution of China.

2.3 Summary

Montesquieu once said, "In the motherly eyes of the civil law, every man is the whole country." Minors and adults also have the same capacity for civil rights and have the capacity for civil conduct. Minor is a special legal identity granted to a natural person by law. This special status does not give a natural person a privilege, but to a legal status under special protection.

This chapter closely follows the context of rights, By exhausting all the laws related to the protection of minors in *the Civil Code of the People's Republic of China*, Interpretation of *the Civil Code of the People's Republic of China* for the special physical and mental characteristics of minors, Around the children's personal rights and property rights, How to set up special protection from the general provisions, specific protection and relief methods when rights are infringed, The protection of children's personal rights is mainly carried out from three aspects: guardianship, family and adoption; The protection of children's property rights mainly starts from inheritance, acceptance of gifts and remuneration; Therefore, the relief method is also different from the different attributes of the right to suffer damage.

The civil code of the People's Republic of China of the whole compilation process, is to follow the United Nations on the convention on the rights of the children "children's interests maximization principle" under the premise of considering the provisions of child protection, establish the most beneficial in the adoptee principle, such as emergency for unattended children established neighborhood committees, village committee custody and so on is the embodiment of this principle. The principle of "the most beneficial to minors" frequently used in *the Civil Code of the People's Republic of China* is the local expression of "the principle of maximizing children's interests" in China, which contains the concept of child protection, such as the priority of the interests of minors and the greatest interests of minors.

The Civil Code of the People's Republic of China on the protection of the rights and interests of minors is all-dimensional and multi-dimensional, reflecting the modern concept of the protection of minors in the era of globalization. The provisions of *the Civil Code of the People's Republic of China* have the property of basic norms. which not only construct the basic legal concept for the laws on the protection of other minors, but also directly determine the rationality and effectiveness of the application of the law on the protection of other minors. On the other hand, this is also the Chinese wisdom of China's child legal protection system in response to China's voice and contribution from *the United Nations Convention on the Rights of Children* from the perspective of children's civil rights standard. With the progress of The Times, the renewal of the rule of law concept, *the civil code of the People's Republic of China* will build a more perfect children security system of socialism with Chinese characteristics play a more and more important role, will continue in the set up the protection of children's civil social atmosphere, create good, harmonious and healthy growth environment for children (Dai, 2022).

References

Dai, L. (2022). Study on the problem of approval of prosecution in the cases of underage minors. *Prevention of Juvenile Delinquency Research, 2*, 42–50.

Gong, H. (2021). Realistic problems and solutions in minors 'community corrections-analysis of relevant data based on the survey of minors' crimes in T City. *China Prison Journal, 3*, 17–22.

Guo, K. (2021). On the civil code and the principle of most favorable to minors. *China Youth Social Science, 1*, 118–125.

Guo, Z. (2008). The "contract theory" of labor relations and its practice. *Social Science Research, 4*.

Lao, K. (2022). Improvement of relief mechanism for student injury accidents in primary and secondary schools. *Journal of Chinese Academy of Social Sciences University, 2*, 41–53.

Xia, Y. (2018). A discriminative analysis of the legislative style of minor guardianship in the Civil Code. *Jurist, 4*, 1–15+191.

Xiang, S., & Yang, X. (n.d.). The main differences and important provisions between the civil code and the repealed contract law and other nine laws — case analysis of the adoption chapter.

Xiong, M. (2015). *Research on the system of behavioral capacity of natural person*. Wuhan University.

Zhang, L., & Kollnig, K. (2024). Theory and practice: the protection of children's personal information in China. *International Data Privacy Law, 1*, 37–52.

Chapter 3
Criminal Law in the People's Republic of China: Principles and Practices in the Protection of the Child

3.1 Introduction

The Criminal law, as a substantive legal norm, regulates crimes and their legal consequences. It details whether a person's conduct constitutes a crime and the corresponding penalties and criminal liability when it does. The interests it protects and the objects it regulates include national security, public safety, economic order, and the personal and property rights of individual citizens; criminal law does not only punish crime, but also strikes a balance between punishing crime and safeguarding human rights. Criminal law, as the legal norm with the most severe means of sanction, includes deprivation of important rights and interests such as life, freedom, property and qualification, etc. Based on the principle of modesty and clarity of criminal law, as the "last line of defense" for the protection of the society, the criminal law can be brought into play only when the other sectoral laws are unable to adequately protect a certain social interest. It is only when other sectoral laws are unable to adequately protect certain social interests that criminal law can be brought into play as a sanction to maintain social order and safeguard human rights.

The United Nations Convention on the Rights of the Child clearly defines the principle of respect for the rights and dignity of the child and requires States parties to guarantee the child's right to survival and development, the most important of which is the child's right to protection, i.e. to ensure that the child is protected from harm. Therefore, in the construction of the legal system for the protection of children's rights and interests, the criminal law, as the "last resort", has made more detailed provisions for the protection of children's rights and interests. The protection of children's rights and interests in the specific provisions of the law is mainly reflected in two aspects: when a child, as a perpetrator, violates the criminal law, a series of substantive and procedural provisions are stipulated to ensure that the child's substantive and procedural rights are fully safeguarded. When a child's personal and property rights are violated by another person, the Criminal Law

© The Author(s), under exclusive license to Springer Nature Singapore Pte Ltd. 2026

H. Li, P. Liang, *The Legal System for the Protection of Children's Rights in China*, Resilient and Friendly Living Environments,
https://doi.org/10.1007/978-981-95-9925-7_3

provides for corresponding crimes that carry heavier penalties for the perpetrator of the crime, thus safeguarding the rights and interests of the child (Shang & Katz, 2014)

Based on the relevant provisions of the Criminal Law of the People's Republic of China on the protection of children's rights and interests, this chapter will be divided into two parts to elaborate on the embodiment of *the United Nations Convention on the Rights of the Child* in China's criminal law and the protection of children's rights and interests: the conviction and sentencing of children based on the principles of humanitarianism and modesty in criminal law when children are the subjects of crime; and the conviction and sentencing of the perpetrators of criminal acts when children are the victims of aggression. Chinese criminal law adopts a four-component model for criminalization and sentencing, which means that the establishment of a crime under the criminal law requires both the subjective and objective elements of the crime, which include the object of the crime, the objective aspect of the crime, the subject of the crime and the subjective aspect of the crime.

3.2 Criminal Law Regulations on Children as Subjects of Criminal Liability

Article 37 of *the United Nations Convention on the Rights of the Child* specifies that States parties shall not impose the death penalty or life imprisonment without the possibility of release on persons under 18 years of age who have infringed penal law. Article 40, paragraph 2, of *the Convention on the Rights of the Child* establishes the principle of legality in determining whether an act of a child constitutes a crime, and "a child shall not be charged with or recognized as having infringed the penal law by reason of acts or omissions not prohibited by the law of the State or by international law". While States parties are obliged to "provide for the promotion or establishment of legislation applicable to children alleged to have, accused of, or recognized as having infringed the penal law, which establishes a minimum age below which a child shall be considered incapable of infringing the penal law".

In keeping with its commitment to the Convention, and in order to better implement the principle of maximizing the interests of the child, *the Criminal Law of the People's Republic of China*, in accordance with the characteristics of children's physical and mental development, divides the age of responsibility of a child into 4 stages when a child's infringement of the rights and interests of others may constitute a crime, so as to determine whether or not the child has the capacity to be held criminally liable. It also sets out the corresponding limitations on the criminal law offences that may be committed by children at each stage of the process, and details the sentencing elements of the eventual penalties for children involved in the criminal justice system.

3.2.1 System for Determining the Age of Criminal Responsibility

China clearly defines a child who is under the age of 18, which is consistent with the provisions of *the United Nations Convention on the Rights of the Child*, and if a child is to be held criminally responsible, he or she should reach the appropriate age of criminal liability. The age of criminal responsibility is the age set by law that must be reached when the perpetrator should be held criminally liable for the socially dangerous acts prohibited by the criminal law that he or she has committed. The United Nations Convention on the Rights of the Child also clearly stipulates that "States Parties shall set a reasonable minimum age of criminal responsibility", and if the child involved in the criminal offense is below the minimum age of criminal responsibility, it is directly recognized that he or she does not have the age of criminal responsibility. However, if the age of the child meets the minimum age of criminal responsibility, the child is deemed to have the capacity to recognize and control the criminal act he or she has committed and is then capable of assuming criminal responsibility. Therefore, according to the principle of simultaneous existence of behavior and responsibility, the child should bear the corresponding criminal responsibility for the criminal behavior he or she has committed. As a member of the Convention on the Rights of the Child, China has scientifically and reasonably categorized children's capacity for criminal responsibility into four stages according to their age, namely, under the age of 12, under the age of 12 but not under the age of 14, under the age of 14 but not under the age of 16, and under the age of 18, in accordance with the state of general development of the child's mind and his or her capacity for cognition and recognition. If a child under the age of 12 violates the relevant provisions of the Criminal Law, it is directly recognized that such a child does not have the capacity to violate the Criminal Law; a child who has reached the age of 16 is directly regarded as having the capacity to be criminally liable, and shall independently bear the consequences of criminal liability for all criminal acts committed by him or her (Jiang, 2022). For details, see Article 17 of *the Criminal Law of the People's Republic of China*:

> **Article 17**
> ***A person who has reached the age of 16 shall be criminally responsible for committing a crime. A person who has attained the age of fourteen but not yet sixteen and commits the crimes of intentional homicide, intentional injury resulting in serious bodily injury or death, rape, robbery, drug trafficking, arson, explosion or the release of dangerous substances shall be held criminally liable. A person who has reached the age of twelve or less than fourteen, who commits the crimes of intentional homicide or intentional injury resulting in death or serious injury resulting in serious disability by particularly cruel means, under aggravating circumstances, and is approved by the Supreme People's Procuratorate for recourse to prosecution, shall be held criminally liable. A person under the age of eighteen who is held criminally responsible***

in accordance with the preceding three paragraphs shall be given a lighter or mitigated punishment. If a person is not criminally punishable because he or she is under the age of 16, his or her parents or other guardians shall be instructed to discipline him or her; where necessary, specialized correctional education shall be provided in accordance with the law.

The general standard of measurement for the minimum age of criminal responsibility set by the member States of *the Convention on the Rights of the Child* is the cognitive ability and control capacity at the time of the commission of the crime; if the perpetrator has the cognitive ability and control capacity at the time of the commission of the crime, he or she should be deemed to have the capacity of criminal responsibility, and having the capacity of criminal responsibility is a general principle and an international consensus in determining the minimum age of criminal responsibility. At the same time, *the United Nations Standard Minimum Rules for the Administration of Juvenile Justice* stipulates that the minimum age of criminal responsibility varies considerably from one Member State to another due to historical, cultural and other factors. The most important consideration is whether the child meets the mental and psychological requirements for criminal responsibility, in which the child's ability to recognize and understand is the main factor in determining whether he or she is capable of assuming criminal responsibility for a violation of the law. If the age of criminal responsibility is set too low or there is no age limit, the very act of establishing the concept of responsibility ceases to have any meaning.

In line with the principle of prioritizing the "protection of children's rights", and according to the improvement of China's material level, children's education has been more comprehensively covered by children's pre-school and primary education, and at the same time, parents' ability to educate their children and their level of education have also improved to some extent, as well as children's cognitive ability and their level of cognition have also risen to some extent. The age of criminal responsibility for children is therefore set at 12 years, which is reasonable. The general cognitive ability and physical and mental development level of children under the age of 12 are not sufficient to enable them to independently carry out criminal activities on their own, and even if the corresponding conditions are met, the following two aspects of the problem will arise if they are ultimately judged to be criminally liable: On the one hand, such children may not be able to understand the significance of punishment, and the imposition of punishment on them does not serve as a disciplinary measure; on the other hand, allowing them to assume criminal responsibility will cause them to be separated from parental supervision, resulting in a lack of coexistence with their parents to a large extent, which makes it impossible for them to receive due education in the best stage of cognitive development, and thus makes them disconnected from the society and unable to get along with other people in a good way after serving their sentences. This leads to more serious problems for the child, and may even lead to a vicious circle in which the child is unable to acquire a sense of belonging and commits crimes repeatedly, thus making China's adoption of the four stages of the age of responsibility a further safeguard for the rights and interests of the child. After the minimum age of criminal responsibility is met, there are further restrictions on the crimes that can be committed by children of different ages according to their level of knowledge, i.e. their cognitive ability and control. Thus, for children who have reached the age of 12 but not yet 14 years old, most of them are in the middle school learning stage, have been educated for six years in elementary school, and are receiving middle school education in middle school, and they are already enough to recognize the harm of intentional homicide, intentional injury causing serious injury to another person, etc., and if they have caused the above results by particularly cruel means, it is enough to show that the children's subjective malignancy is great. At this time, the child is capable of recognizing the social harm of his or her own actions and should therefore bear the corresponding criminal responsibility. Children who have reached the age of 14 but not yet 16 are in the middle and high school stages of education and have higher cognitive ability and control than children in the previous stage. Most children who have reached the age of 16 have completed China's nine years of compulsory education, at which point there is little difference in their cognitive ability and control compared to adults, so there are no longer any restrictions on the crimes that they may ultimately be convicted. However, in view of their physical and mental developmental characteristics, mitigating or extenuating circumstances are more often taken into account in the determination of their sentences. In addition, China has adopted legislation that clearly stipulates the minimum age of criminal responsibility, the age range at which a person should be held criminally responsible, and a two-tiered mechanism for the judicial organs to determine the de facto age of a child at the time of the commission of a crime, in accordance with specific rules and the actual situation, so as to safeguard the rights of the child to the fullest extent possible.

3.2.2 *Special Legal Regime for the Conviction and Sentencing of Children*

The United Nations Convention on the Rights of the Child requires States parties to implement the principle of maximizing the interests of the child and safeguarding the child's right to survival and development to the maximum extent possible when convicting and sentencing children. China's Criminal Law therefore contains restrictive provisions on the conviction and sentencing of children of the four aforementioned age groups for the various crimes they commit. The Criminal Law of the People's Republic of China, as the basic law, provides for the corresponding conviction and sentencing of children as perpetrators. On this basis, the Supreme People's Court of the People's Republic of China has refined the corresponding provisions in judicial practice, thereby fully safeguarding the rights and interests of children.

3.2.2.1 Specific Provisions of the Penal Code

The criminalization of children is detailed in Article 17 of *the Criminal Law of the People's Republic of China*, supra, which states that children under the age of 12 years are not subject to criminal penalties for any offense, as the law directly establishes that those below the minimum age of criminal responsibility of 12 years do not have the capacity for criminal responsibility. If a child who has reached the age of 12 but not yet reached the age of 14, if his or her behavior is physically consistent with intentional homicide or intentional injury resulting in death or causing serious injury by particularly cruel means resulting in serious disability under aggravating circumstances, and procedurally the Supreme People's Procuratorate approves the pursuit of the prosecution, the people's court shall ultimately ascertain the facts of the child's crime in accordance with the provisions of the law and make a judgment centrally as to whether or not the child's behavior constitutes a crime and the final penalty if it does. Thus, at this stage, the final conviction of a child requires the circumstances of the crime to be extremely serious and the approval of the Supreme People's Procuratorate for the prosecution of such a child, in order to better safeguard the rights and interests of the child and his or her future development. In addition to the above, even if a child who has reached the age of 12 but is not yet 14 acts in a manner consistent with other crimes, a child who has reached the age of 12 but is not yet 14 may not be convicted or punished for any reason or on any charge, which is a concrete manifestation of the principle of the law of crimes and punishment in safeguarding the rights and interests of children. If a child has reached the age of 14 but not yet 16, he or she shall be held criminally liable only if he or she commits the crimes of intentional homicide, intentional injury resulting in serious bodily injury or death, rape, robbery, trafficking in narcotics, arson, explosion, or the throwing of dangerous substances. The first two of these are extremely serious consequences for the right to life and the right to the body of others, which cannot be remedied, and their crimes are extremely serious; while the crime of rape seriously infringes on the right to sexual autonomy of others, the crime of robbery adopts violent means to force others to take their property, which is more harmful to the right to a person of others, and the crime of trafficking in narcotics is detrimental to the social and public order and the interests of the State, while the crimes of setting fires, explosions, and throwing dangerous substances are dangerous to the unspecified public, which are dangerous to the public. The crime of drug trafficking causes damage to public order and national interests, while arson, explosions, and the release of dangerous substances pose a danger to unspecified members of the public. The above acts were committed by children with great subjective malice, and children of this age are capable of recognizing the harmful consequences for others or for the public interest of society and of controlling their own actions; in short, children between the ages of 14 and 16 are already capable of recognizing the harmful effects of the above acts on other people and society, and thus the imposition of criminal penalties is in accordance with the principle of the appropriateness of punishment to the crime. In short, children between the ages of 14 and 16 are capable of recognizing the dangers of such acts to others and to society, and the imposition of criminal penalties on them is consistent with the principle of appropriateness of punishment. A child who has reached the age of 16 and has violated any provision of the Criminal Law shall be subject to the appropriate criminal punishment.

On the basis of the principle of modesty, Criminal Law provides for the sentencing of children, that is to say when sentencing a criminal, the sentence shall be imposed in accordance with the facts of the crime, the nature of the crime, the circumstances and the degree of harm to society, in accordance with the relevant provisions. Thus, after the People's Court has characterized a child's criminal conduct, it is required to quantify the penalty that he or she will ultimately receive in accordance with the circumstances of the crime and the degree of subjective malice, as embodied in Article 49 of *the Criminal Law of the People's Republic of China:*

> **Article 49**
> ***The death penalty shall not be applied to persons who were under eighteen years of age at the time of the commission of the crime and to women who are pregnant at the time of the trial.***

The crime referred to in the above-mentioned article 49 refers to the commission of a criminal act by a child, based on the principle that the age of responsibility and the capacity to be responsible coexist at the time of the perpetrator's act, and thus not the age of 18 at the time of the application of the penalty, and that the death penalty shall not be applied to a child who was under 18 at the time of the commission of the crime, but who has attained 18 years of age at the time of the trial. This is a concrete expression of the purpose of Article 1 of the Convention on the Rights of the Child in Chinese criminal law, which specifies that "A child means every human being below the age of 18 years unless under the law applicable to the child, majority is attained earlier". The age of majority for a child is 18 years, and adulthood signifies the ability to assume responsibility for one's own actions. therefore, the non-application of the criminal law of deprivation of life to crimes committed by children under 18 years of age is consistent with the principle of maximum protection for children in China, and at the same time gives the children who have violated the criminal law mentioned above the opportunity to rehabilitate themselves.

3.2.2.2 Further Additions to Judicial Interpretations

Judicial interpretations are the refinement and supplementation of criminal law provisions by the highest judicial organ of the People's Republic of China in accordance with the law, without violating *the Constitution of the People's Republic of China* or the basic provisions of *the Criminal Law of the People's Republic of China*, and are constitutional, serious, authoritative and legally effective. In order to safeguard the rights and interests of children on all fronts, China has issued judicial interpretations that safeguard the rights and interests of children as follows.

The Interpretation of the Supreme People's Court on Several Issues Concerning the Specific Application of the Law in the Trial of Criminal Cases Involving Minors (2006) stipulates that, even if a child who has reached the age of 16 and is not yet 18 commits an act of theft, if he or she meets the relevant constitutive elements, but is able to truthfully confess all the facts of the theft after the crime has been committed, and is active in returning the stolen goods and meets one of the specific circumstances, the child's actions are not recognized as a violation of the criminal law. And in which further quantified the children after the crime of sentencing. The detailed provisions on the criminalization of theft are reflected in Article 9 of the Judicial Interpretation:

Article 9

The person who has reached the age of sixteen or less than eighteen years of age has not committed theft more than three times, although the amount of theft has reached the standard of "larger amount", but after the crime is discovered, the person can truthfully confess all the facts of the theft and actively return the stolen goods, and has one of the following circumstances, it can be recognized as "the circumstances of the crime are significantly less serious and less harmful", and is not considered a crime: the crime is not considered a crime. Less harmful", is not considered a crime:

(1) is deaf and dumb or blind;
(2) Playing a secondary or auxiliary role in the joint theft, or coerced;
(3) Other minor circumstances.

Sixteen years of age less than eighteen years of age, attempted theft or suspension, may not be considered a crime.

Sixteen years of age but not yet eighteen years of age, theft of their own family or close relatives, or theft of other relatives, but other relatives request not to be prosecuted, may not be treated as a crime.

The term "not considered a crime" in the above provision means that a child who is not ultimately found to have committed the above acts does not constitute a crime and is not subject to a penalty. According to the foregoing, the age of full criminal responsibility is 16 but not yet 18 years, and therefore only this category of children can be addressed with regard to theft. Attempted theft means that the child fails to realize his or her criminal purpose in the course of the theft, not because of his or her own subjective will, while suspension of theft means that the child is willing to stop the act of theft, both of which do not cause any actual damage to other people's property, and thus are not considered to be criminally punishable. The family, as the basic unit of society, is able to tolerate each other and share property; if a child steals from the family or from close relatives within three generations or steals from other relatives but the other relatives understand and do not pursue the case, it is ultimately determined that the child's actions have not violated the criminal law. If an adult acts in accordance with the above provisions, he or she shall be held criminally liable.

In addition, the principle of simultaneous existence of conduct and responsibility is a derivative of the principle of responsibilization, which is one of the principles of criminal law. The principle of simultaneous existence of conduct and responsibility means that the perpetrator of an intentional crime has the corresponding capacity for criminal responsibility at the time of committing the act that violates the criminal law, and the important basis for measuring the existence of the capacity for criminal responsibility is whether or not the perpetrator has reached the corresponding age of criminal responsibility. In the case of crimes committed by children, it is manifested in the fact that a child can be convicted and punished only if he or she had the appropriate age of criminal responsibility at the time of the commission of the crime. After conviction, the child is punished only if he or she meets the age requirement at the time of the commission of the crime, i.e., when determining the final penalty for the child, the child will be given a lighter or less severe penalty only for crimes committed before he or she reaches the age of 18. This is specified in Article 12 of the Judicial Interpretation:

Article 12
If a perpetrator commits an act that endangers society both before and after he reaches the legal age of criminal responsibility, he shall only be held criminally liable in accordance with the law for the acts that endanger society that he commits after he reaches the legal age of criminal responsibility.

If the perpetrator commits different kinds of criminal acts both before and after he reaches the age of 18, he shall be given a lighter or more lenient punishment in accordance with the law for crimes committed before he reaches the age of 18. If the perpetrator commits the same kind of criminal act before or after he reaches the age of 18, he shall be given a lighter or mitigated punishment in accordance with the law for crimes committed before he reaches the age of 18 when determining the sentence.

Other sentencing provisions for children under the age of 18 in conflict with the law are set out in articles 13-15 of the Judicial Decree:

Article 13
Life imprisonment may be applied to minors who commit crimes only if the crimes are extremely serious. Life imprisonment is generally not imposed for crimes committed by persons who have reached the age of 14 but not yet 16.

Article 14
Except for the provisions of the Criminal Law which stipulate that additional deprivation of political rights "shall" be imposed, additional deprivation of political rights shall not normally be imposed on juvenile offenders.

If additional deprivation of political rights is imposed on a juvenile offender, the sentence shall be lenient in accordance with the law.

The provisions of the preceding paragraph shall apply to the imposition of additional deprivation of political rights on offenders who were minors at the time of the commission of the alleged crime but who have reached the age of majority at the time of trial.

Article 15
Where a minor offender commits an offense for which confiscation of property or a fine is "concurrently" provided for in the criminal law, the corresponding property penalty shall be imposed in accordance with the law; where a minor offender commits an offense for which confiscation of property or a fine is "concurrently" provided for in the criminal law, the property penalty shall not be imposed as a general rule. Property penalties shall be imposed.

The above provisions indicate the principle of leniency or mitigation when a child commits a crime, and restrict the imposition of life imprisonment on children to those who commit extremely serious crimes with great subjective malice and extreme cruelty, such as those who slash the victim dozens of times, resulting in the death of another person or disability, and so on, may be subjected to life imprisonment. Which has reached the age of 14 but not yet 16 years of age is generally not applicable to life imprisonment. In such cases, it is "possible" to apply life imprisonment, thus giving the adjudicator the authority to weigh the situation in the light of the actual circumstances, rather than applying life imprisonment absolutely. In addition, with regard to the additional penalty of deprivation of political rights, political rights should be the rights that citizens enjoy as a matter of course. When sentencing children for violations of the criminal law, in view of the child's physical and mental development and his or her best interests, additional penalties of deprivation of political rights are generally not imposed on children. If the provisions of the criminal law stipulate that a child "may also" be subject to confiscation of property or a fine, property penalties are generally not imposed for crimes committed against children in order to safeguard the child's right to survival and development. Even if the additional penalty of a fine is ultimately applied to the child, the maximum amount of the fine is limited, taking into account the child's capacity to bear it, and his or her guardian or other persons are allowed to pay it voluntarily on his or her behalf.

In summary, China, as a member of the United Nations Convention on the Rights of the Child, recognizes to the greatest extent possible the inherent right to life of every child and ensures to the greatest extent possible the survival and development of the child when the child, as the subject of a crime, may have violated the criminal law, which is reflected in the criminal law of China by the criminalization of the child, which establishes the corresponding age of criminal responsibility in accordance with the child's state of psychological and physiological development and the division of the child's age into age groups. The criminalization of children is reflected in China's Criminal Law, which establishes the corresponding age of criminal responsibility according to the age of the child's psychological and physical development. The law also restricts the amount of punishment for a child according to the subjective state of mind and objective behavior of the child at the time of the commission of the criminal act, as well as the circumstances of the crime and the physical and mental condition of the child, in order to safeguard the growth of children. In judicial practice, the People's Courts and People's Procuratorates, in order to better safeguard the rights and interests of children, have made a series of detailed provisions, which are implemented in practice, in an effort to safeguard the rights and interests of children.

3.3 Protection of Children's Rights as Victims

The United Nations Convention on the Rights of the Child sets out the duty of States parties to take a range of measures to ensure the child's personal and property rights. It specifies that the child has the right to the protection of the law and that States parties shall ensure that the child is protected against unlawful acts, and therefore shall provide for special or aggravated penalties for offences and sentences in the event that the child is harmed. In this regard, China's criminal law imposes heavier or more severe penalties on the basic penalty for acts committed by others that violate children's personal and property rights, mainly in the areas of personal and property rights (Children's Division, 2023).

3.3.1 Criminal Law Protections for Children's Personal Rights

The protection of children's personal rights, namely, the right to life and physical health, sexual autonomy, marriage and family, and the right to physical integrity and human dignity, is also regulated by China's Criminal Law (Nagornaya, 2018).

Firstly, China's criminal law safeguards children's right to life and physical health in all respects, in accordance with the law. Due to children's incomplete physical and mental development and their insufficient social awareness, they are less capable of discerning their own health and the magnitude of the harm done to them by the actions of others (Babanina et al., 2021). Therefore, even if the perpetrator obtains the child's commitment before violating the child's right to life and health, i.e., satisfies the condition of "the victim's commitment," the perpetrator is not exempted from criminal liability for this reason. In this regard, China's criminal law provides for specific penalties for violations of children's right to life and health, as reflected in Article 234 of *the Criminal Law of the People's Republic of China*:

> **Article 234**
> ***Anyone who removes the organs of a person without his or her consent, or removes the organs of a person under the age of eighteen, or forces or deceives another person to donate his or her organs, shall be convicted and punished in accordance with the provisions of the crimes of intentional homicide or intentional injury.***

It is easy to see that the above provisions fully guarantee the child's right to life and physical health. Although children have independent personality, but their physiological and psychological characteristics are not yet fully developed, unable to fully recognize the harm of certain acts on their own, and the criminal perpetrator of the act of removing the organs of a child under 18 years of age, if he adopts the means of deceiving the child that the removal of the organs will not cause any harm to his body, causing the child to fall into a false understanding, so as to cooperate with the perpetrator of the crime; or by means of coercion to force the child, so as to remove the organs of the child, the perpetrator's behavior must be consistent with the crime of intentional homicide or intentional injury, and ultimately to be convicted. or by forcing the child to do so, thereby removing the child's organs, the perpetrator's conduct must be consistent with the crime of intentional homicide or intentional injury, which will ultimately result in a conviction and punishment, and if his or her conduct has resulted in extremely serious consequences for the child, the punishment shall be aggravated. The perpetrator often uses the defense of obtaining the "victim's consent", which is not justified on the basis of the characteristics of the child's physical and mental development and the principle of maximizing the interests of the child, which is a manifestation of the principle of "paternalism" in criminal law. This is the embodiment of the principle of "paternalism" in criminal law. In the case of organ harvesting, even an adult cannot fully recognize the harmful consequences that may result from the harvesting of organs. As minors who are not fully developed physically and mentally, children are even less able to recognize the act of organ harvesting, and cannot be expected to fully recognize the harmful consequences of organ harvesting and waive the right to recourse to the results of such damage to their own bodies. Furthermore, in the case of criminal acts, the waiver of harmful consequences permitted by the criminal law is limited to those containing less than minor injuries. Thus, the act of a child removing his or her own organs due to coercion or deception or the act of removing organs with the child's consent cannot be an exculpatory reason for the offender to be exempted from the penalty, i.e., such an act cannot be a victim's promise that the act of the criminal offender should be recognized as the crime of intentional injury or intentional homicide, and that if there is a coercive or deceptive act that leads to a serious and grave result, the penalty should be heavier in terms of the basic penalty (Zhu, 2024).

Secondly, China's criminal law safeguards the sexual rights of children and their physical and mental health in accordance with the law (Chen & Lyu, 2021). Children are still in a state of physical and psychological development, and their ability to recognize and identify sexual rights is not yet sufficient to enable them to exercise their sexual autonomy. Some perpetrators take advantage of this to violate children's sexual autonomy, harming their physical and mental health or enticing them to commit crimes. *The United Nations Convention on the Rights of the Child* requires States parties to "undertake to protect the child from all forms of sexual exploitation and sexual abuse and. To this end, State parties shall take all appropriate measures, including bilateral and multilateral measures, to prevent the inducement or coercion of a child to engage in any unlawful sexual practice, the use of the child in prostitution or other unlawful sexual practices or the use of the child in obscene performances and as subjects of obscene materials". Thus, in order to safeguard the above-mentioned rights of the child, China's corresponding criminalization and sentencing are set out in detail in articles 236, 237, 301, 358, and 359 of *the Criminal Law of the People's Republic of China*:

Article 236
Anyone who rapes a woman by violence, coercion, or other means shall be sentenced to three to ten years' imprisonment.

Anyone who rapes a young girl under the age of 14 shall be punished severely for rape.

If a person rapes a woman or a young girl under the age of fourteen, he shall be sentenced to fixed-term imprisonment of not less than ten years, life imprisonment, or the death penalty if any of the following circumstances apply:

(1) Raping a woman or raping a young girl under aggravating circumstances;
(2) Raping a woman or raping a young girl by more than one person;
(3) Raping a woman or raping a young girl in public in a public place in public;
(4) Gang rape by two or more persons;
(5) Rape of a young girl under ten years of age or causing injury to a young girl;
(6) Causing serious injury or death to the victim or causing other serious consequences.

The above article protects the sexual rights of young girls. When the victim is a young girl under 14 years of age, even if the act is consented to by the young girl, it is still rape in nature and shall be punished severely within the corresponding sentencing range when the final penalty is imposed. In the event of aggravating circumstances or causing serious mental damage to a young girl or raping a young girl by more than two persons, committing rape in a public place, i.e., a place with the possibility of many people passing by, gang-raping a young girl by more than two persons, and causing serious injury to the young girl or death or other serious consequences, the Criminal Law stipulates that the penalty shall be imprisonment for a term of not less than 10 years, life imprisonment or the death penalty. The death of the young girl, including suicide, is an aggravating circumstance on top of the basic penalty.

Article 237
Anyone who molests a child shall be sentenced to imprisonment for a term of not more than five years; if any of the following circumstances apply, he or she shall be sentenced to imprisonment for a term of not less than five years:

(1) Whoever molests a child for more than one person or repeatedly;
(2) Whoever gathers a crowd to molest a child, or molests a child in public in a public place under aggravating circumstances;
(3) Causing injury to a child or other serious consequences;

Furthermore, if any of the following circumstances exist—molestation of multiple children or repeated molestation of a child, group molestation or molestation in public places, or causing physical harm to a child—heavier penalties shall be imposed.

Article 236
A person who has special duties such as guardianship, adoption, caretaking, education, medical care, etc., over a female minor who has reached the age of 14 but has not yet reached the age of 16 and who has sexual intercourse with such a female minor shall be sentenced to fixed-term imprisonment of not more than three years; if the circumstances are aggravated, he or she shall be sentenced to fixed-term imprisonment of not less than three years but not more than 10 years.

Anyone who commits the acts in the preceding paragraph and at the same time constitutes an offense under article 236 of this Law shall be convicted and punished in accordance with the provisions on heavier penalties.

A perpetrator who meets the above conditions is guilty of sexual assault by a person in a position of care, regardless of whether he or she has obtained the consent of the girl of that age or whether he or she has resorted to violence. If the crime of rape is committed at the same time, the penalty for the crime shall be the one that is more severe, and the crime of rape shall be recognized as the final crime.

Article 301
Anyone who induces a minor to participate in a gathering for debauchery shall be subject to a heavier penalty in accordance with the provisions of the preceding paragraph.

Article 358
Anyone who organizes or forces another person into prostitution shall be sentenced to fixed-term imprisonment of not less than five years and not more than ten years and shall be fined; if the circumstances are serious, he or she shall be sentenced to fixed-term imprisonment of not less than ten years or life imprisonment and shall be fined or have his or her property confiscated. Anyone who organizes or forces a minor into prostitution shall be given a heavier penalty in accordance with the preceding paragraph.

Article 359
A person who induces a young girl under the age of fourteen to engage in prostitution shall be sentenced to not less than five years' fixed-term imprisonment and shall be fined.

If another offender induces a minor to participate in the criminal activity of mobbing or organizing or forcing a child offender to engage in prostitution or induces a young girl under 14 years of age to engage in prostitution, he or she shall be subject to a heavier penalty on the basis of the corresponding offense. As minors are not yet mentally mature at this stage, other offenders who involve minors in criminal activities in the manner described above shall be subject to heavier or more severe penalties.

Furthermore, China safeguards the physical health of children in marriage and the family in accordance with the law. In this regard, the Criminal Law contains detailed provisions on violations of children's physical and mental health by family members, as set out in articles 260 and 261 of *the Criminal Law of the People's Republic of China*:

Article 260

Anyone who abuses a family member under aggravating circumstances shall be sentenced to fixed-term imprisonment of not more than two years, criminal detention, or control.

A person who commits the crime in the preceding paragraph and causes serious injury or death to the victim shall be sentenced to fixed-term imprisonment of not less than two years and not more than seven years.

The first paragraph of this article shall be dealt with only if there is a complaint, unless the victim is incapable of making a complaint or is unable to do so due to coercion or intimidation.

The United Nations Convention on the Rights of the Child stipulates the right of the child to protection, and if a family member with whom the child lives regularly and consistently tortures the child physically or mentally, the child may institute criminal proceedings in his or her own name in accordance with the law. If the child is unable or afraid to institute criminal proceedings for other reasons or if the child is seriously injured or dies as a result of long-term or short-term abuse by a family member living together, the public prosecutor's office shall institute public proceedings in accordance with the law. The result of serious injury or death includes serious injury or death caused by an abused child who is unable to bear it and takes action to injure himself/herself or commits suicide, and if, in the course of prolonged abuse, some of the behaviors are consistent with intentional injury or intentional homicide, the crime of abuse and the crimes of intentional injury and intentional homicide shall be punished together as one crime. In the crime of long-term abuse, the mental and physical damage caused to the child by family members living together is so great that if it is in line with the acts of abuse, intentional injury, or intentional homicide, it will be convicted and punished in accordance with the corresponding crimes; if it is not in line with the corresponding crimes, the perpetrators will be punished according to the other chapters of this book, such as the Anti-Domestic Violence Law, the Law of Punishment for Administration of Public Security and other provisions, so as to safeguard the child's physical, mental and spiritual health and fulfill the commitment to *the United Nations Convention on the*

Rights of the Child. Mental health of children and fulfill the promise of *the United Nations Convention on the Rights of the Child.*

Article 261
Anyone who refuses to support the elderly, young, sick, or otherwise incapable of an independent living person who is under an obligation to do so, under aggravating circumstances, shall be sentenced to fixed-term imprisonment of not more than five years, criminal detention, or control.

The United Nations Convention on the Rights of the Child requires state parties to guarantee the maintenance of children. Thus, if a person who is obliged to maintain a child fails to do so, thereby placing the child in a state of danger, he or she commits the crime of abandonment. The crime of abandonment is recognized when a person who is obliged to support a child, such as a parent or an orphanage, refuses to do so, thereby endangering the child's survival and development. If the child's life is in imminent danger as a result of the failure of the person who is obliged to maintain the child, such as abandoning the child in an unoccupied place, the act is considered to be intentional homicide.

Finally, China safeguards the personal freedom of children in accordance with the law. The United Nations Convention on the Rights of the Child requires that "States Parties shall take all appropriate national, bilateral and multilateral measures to prevent the abduction of, the sale of or traffic in children for any purpose or in any form." In this regard, the criminal law penalizes violations of children's personal freedom mainly in articles 240, 241, 261, 262, 416, 244, 260, 347, and 353 of *the Criminal Code*:

Article 240
Anyone who abducts women or children shall be sentenced to fixed-term imprisonment of not less than five years and not more than ten years and shall be fined; if any of the following circumstances applies, he or she shall be sentenced to fixed-term imprisonment of not less than ten years or life imprisonment and shall be fined or have his or her property confiscated; and if the circumstances are particularly serious, he or she shall be sentenced to the death penalty and to have his or her property confiscated:

(1) A leading member of a group that abducts and traffics women and children; (2) abducting and trafficking three or more women and children; (3) raping a woman who has been abducted and trafficked; and (4) enticing, forcing a woman who has been abducted and trafficked to engage in prostitution, or selling a woman who has been abducted and trafficked to another person for the purpose of forcing her to engage in prostitution;(5) Kidnapping women or children for the purpose of selling them, using violence, coercion or anesthesia; (6) Stealing infants or young children for the purpose of selling them; (7) Causing serious injury, death or other serious consequences to the trafficked women or children or their relatives; (8) Selling women or children outside the country. Trafficking in women and children means one of the acts of abducting,

kidnapping, buying, selling, transporting, or transiting women and children for the purpose of selling.

Trafficking refers to the act of abducting, kidnapping, buying, selling, transporting, and relaying children for the purpose of selling them, which infringes on their personal rights and human dignity, and the sale of children as commodities infringes on their right to personality, and thus constitutes an attempt to constitute the crime, which does not require that the perpetrator actually sell the child, as long as he or she performs the aforementioned acts with the purpose of selling them, that is, to constitute a crime. If the circumstances provided for in the law are caused during this period, the penalty is aggravated to a maximum of the death penalty.

Article 241

Anyone who buys an abducted or trafficked woman or child shall be sentenced to fixed-term imprisonment of not more than three years, criminal detention, or control.

Anyone who buys a trafficked woman and forcibly has sexual relations with her shall be convicted and punished in accordance with the provisions of Article 236 of this Law.

Anyone who buys an abducted or trafficked woman or child and unlawfully deprives or restricts her of her personal freedom or commits a criminal act such as injuring or insulting her shall be convicted and punished in accordance with the relevant provisions of this Law.

Anyone who buys an abducted woman or child and commits the criminal acts stipulated in paragraphs 2 and 3 shall be punished in accordance with the provisions of this Law, which stipulate that several crimes shall be punished together.

Anyone who buys an abducted woman or child and sells her again shall be convicted and punished in accordance with the provisions of Article 240 of this Law.

If a person who buys an abducted woman or child does not abuse the child and does not prevent her from being rescued, he or she may be given a lighter penalty; and if, in accordance with the wishes of the woman, he or she does not prevent her from returning to her original place of residence, he or she may be given a lighter or mitigated penalty.

In addition to the above, if the offender knows that he/she is buying a trafficked child, but still negotiates the price with the trafficker and eventually receives the trafficked child, he/she commits the crime of buying a trafficked child. If other acts, such as rape or indecent assault, are committed on this basis, the crime of buying a trafficked child shall be punished together with the other crimes, but if the trafficked child is eventually sold, the crime of child trafficking shall be punished.

Article 262

Anyone who abducts a minor under 14 years of age from his family or guardian shall be sentenced to not more than five years' fixed-term imprisonment or detention.

If the perpetrator abducts a child under 14 years of age without the intention of selling or extorting property, and the child is separated from his or her family or guardian, he or she is convicted and punished for the crime of child abduction. The crime is committed even with the consent of the child. If the child is abducted and other crimes are committed against the child, the offender shall be punished for both crimes; if the child is abducted and then sold, the crime of child abduction and sale shall be punished, because the abduction of the child is a means to an end and the sale of the child is the end, which is an end in itself, and the crime of the end shall be punished by conviction.

Article 416

If an employee of a State organ who is responsible for rescuing a woman or child who has been abducted, trafficked, or kidnapped receives a request for rescue from the abducted, trafficked, or kidnapped woman or child and her or his or her family members or receives a report from another person and fails to rescue the abducted, trafficked or kidnapped woman or child, thereby causing serious consequences, he or she shall be sentenced to fixed-term imprisonment of not more than five years or to penal servitude.

If an employee of a State organ who has the duty to rescue a woman or child uses his or her official position to impede rescue, he or she shall be sentenced to fixed-term imprisonment of not less than two years and not more than seven years; if the circumstances are less serious, he or she shall be sentenced to fixed-term imprisonment of not more than two years or to criminal detention.

If a member of a State organ charged with the duty of rescuing abducted or trafficked children fails to carry out his or her duty of rescue in accordance with the law, and serious consequences result, he or she shall be convicted and punished for the crime of failing to rescue an abducted or trafficked child. At the same time, if they use the convenience of their position to hinder the rescue, they shall be convicted and punished for the crime of hindering the rescue of trafficked or abducted children. This requires that the staff of State organs should carry out appropriate rescue activities immediately after receiving information that a child has been abducted or trafficked or kidnapped, and requires the staff of State organs to fulfill their duty to act and to bear criminal liability if they fail to fulfill their duty to act or if they use their official position to impede the rescue activities.

Article 244

If, in violation of the regulations governing labor management, a person employs a minor under the age of 16 to perform excessively strenuous physical labor, or engages in work at high altitude or in an underground workplace, or performs labor in a hazardous environment, such as an explosive, flammable, radioactive, or poisonous environment, and if the circumstances are serious,

the person directly responsible shall be sentenced to not more than three years' fixed-term imprisonment or detention, and shall also be punished with a fine; and if the circumstances are particularly serious, the person shall be sentenced to not less than three years and not more than seven years imprisonment shall be sentenced to fixed-term imprisonment of not more than three years or criminal detention, and shall be fined.

If any of the acts in the preceding paragraph cause an accident and constitute another crime, he or she shall be punished in accordance with the provisions on the combination of several crimes.

If an employer violates this provision by hiring a child under the age of 16 to engage in the activities described above, the employer will be convicted and punished for the crime of unlawful employment of child labor, which is a reflection of the fact that, as stated in the United Nations Convention on the Rights of the Child, "States Parties shall take legislative, administrative, social and educational measures to ensure the healthy development of the child. Therefore, the minimum age for employment should be stipulated", which is embodied in China's criminal law, the minimum age for employing workers is 16 years old, if the employer violates this provision and employs them to engage in hazardous labor, then they shall bear the corresponding criminal responsibility; if they employ them to engage in other labor, if they are in line with Law of the People's Republic of China on Public Security Administration Penalties or other legal punishment, they shall be given the corresponding punishment, so as to safeguard the rights and interests of children.

Article 260

If a person who is responsible for the guardianship or care of a minor, an elderly person, a sick person, or a disabled person abuses the person under his guardianship or care under aggravating circumstances, he shall be sentenced to fixed-term imprisonment of not more than three years or to criminal detention.

If a unit commits the crime in the preceding paragraph, the unit shall be sentenced to a fine, and the persons in charge and others directly responsible shall be punished in accordance with the provisions of the preceding paragraph.

If a person or organization responsible for the custody or care of a child commits an act of abuse, such as physical or mental torture, the person or organization responsible for the custody or care of the child is convicted and punished for the crime of abuse of a person under his or her custody or care, and the organization is usually a kindergarten or an orphanage, for example. In addition, if a person who is responsible for the guardianship or care of a child forces the child to use doping substances in sports or induces or deceives the child to use doping substances for a long period of time, or organizes the illegal use of doping substances by the child in a way that causes other serious damage to the child's physical and mental health, he or she will be convicted and punished for this crime.

Article 262

Anyone who, by means of violence or coercion, organizes persons with disabilities or minors under the age of 14 to beg shall be sentenced to fixed-term imprisonment of not more than three years or criminal detention and a fine; if the circumstances are serious, he or she shall be sentenced to fixed-term imprisonment of not less than three years but not more than seven years and a fine.

Anyone who organizes minors to engage in theft, fraud, robbery, extortion, or other activities in violation of public security management shall be sentenced to fixed-term imprisonment of not more than three years or criminal detention and fined; if the circumstances are serious, he or she shall be sentenced to fixed-term imprisonment of not less than three years but not more than seven years and fined.

If the perpetrator threatens or otherwise coerces a child under 14 years of age to engage in begging activities, he or she shall be punished for the crime of organizing children to beg, an act that clearly violates the child's personal freedom and human dignity. At the same time if the perpetrator uses children's mental immaturity to organize children to implement theft, fraud or snatching, extortion, and extortion of other people's property, with the organization of minors to carry out the crime of violating the public security management activities, convicted and punished, if their behavior constitutes a theft, fraud, snatching, extortion and other crimes of indirectly positive offenders, i.e., the formation of the children's dominance, then the theft of the crime of criminalization and so on to convicted and punished.

Article 347

Anyone who uses or abets a minor to smuggle, sell, transport, or manufacture drugs, or who sells drugs to a minor, shall be given a heavier penalty.

Article 353

Anyone who induces, abets, deceives or forces a minor to take or inject drugs shall be subject to a heavier penalty.

If the offender uses a child or abets a child to commit the drug crimes mentioned above or sells drugs to a minor, he or she shall be given a heavier punishment while being convicted of the crime of smuggling, trafficking, transporting, or manufacturing drugs. If the child is induced, abetted or deceived, or forced to take or inject drugs, he or she shall be given a heavier punishment on top of the original offense.

3.3.2 Legal Protections of Children's Property Rights Under Criminal Law

With regard to safeguarding children's property rights, children's property rights are protected in accordance with the law. In judicial practice, property crimes such as robbery and extortion require that the "larger amount standard" be met, whereas if the perpetrator robs or extorts property from an elderly person, a child, a pregnant woman, a person with a baby, a person with a disability, or a person who has lost the ability to work, the perpetrator is only required to pay 50 percent of the "larger amount standard" to be deemed to have reached the larger amount, and the perpetrator is then convicted and punished. The perpetrator may be deemed to have committed a greater amount of the crime if he or she meets 50 percent of the "greater amount criterion", and the perpetrator may then be convicted and punished. By lowering the criminalization criteria for those who infringe on the property rights of children and persons with infants, the material resources needed by children in their growth are more comprehensively safeguarded, and children's healthy growth is cared for. In addition, if the perpetrator of uses of minor violence against children to rob children of a small amount of property if the behavior meets the characteristics of the crime of provoking trouble, the crime of provoking trouble can be convicted and punished. When the perpetrator commits the crime of telecommunication network fraud, the perpetrator of the crime shall be punished severely on the basis of the standard sentence in accordance with the law, if the perpetrator adopts telecommunication network fraud against persons with disabilities, the elderly, schoolchildren or persons who have lost the ability to work.

In summary, if another person violates a child's right to life, the Criminal Law of the People's Republic of China provides for the protection of the child's right to life, etc., and stipulates in it the corresponding heavier or more severe penalties. The Criminal Law of the People's Republic of China also provides for a lower standard of criminalization than the general standard of criminalization in the case of violations of the property rights of children, and there are also aggravating circumstances in the penalties involved. As a result, China's criminal law comprehensively safeguards children's personal and property rights; at the same time, in view of the physical and psychological characteristics of children, the standard of criminalization for perpetrators of crimes against children is lower than that of ordinary perpetrators, while the penalties are higher than those for ordinary perpetrators.

3.4 Summary

When children prosper, the country prospers; when children are strong, the country is strong. Children are the cornerstone of a country's sustainable development and strength. Since becoming a member of *the United Nations Convention on the Rights of the Child*, China has always practiced the principle of maximizing the rights and interests of children and has stipulated the protection of children's rights and interests in its laws and regulations, building a perfect system for protecting children's rights and interests and safeguarding the rights and interests of children in all aspects of their growing process. The prerequisite for the healthy growth of children is that their rights and interests are protected by law, and the prerequisite for their survival and development is their right to life and to continued existence. Thus, China's criminal law provides that when children infringe on the rights and interests of others, the characteristics of their physical and mental development are taken into account, and the convictions and sentences are limited accordingly, with the principles of "no criminalization, fewer penalties, and more prudent penalties" as the basis for safeguarding the rights and interests of children (Zhou, 2021). When a child's rights and interests are violated by others, most of the crimes are punishable by heavier or more severe penalties. This maximizes the implementation of the relevant provisions of the Chinese Constitution and the United Nations Convention on the Rights of the Child, thereby safeguarding human rights while better protecting legal interests, and insisting on the equal importance of the two in order to protect children as they grow up (Chao, 2022).

Research in China's academic and practical circles on children infringing others' rights and interests and others infringing on children's rights and interests is becoming increasingly in-depth. It is believed that with the continuous improvement of research methods, legislative techniques, and theoretical knowledge, the future legislation and practice of safeguarding children's rights and interests under criminal law will become increasingly perfected, thereby forming a more comprehensive and perfect normative system for the protection of children's rights and interests. This will advance the construction of a child-friendly nation and create a nurturing environment for children's growth (Wang & Zhang, 2015).

References

Babanina, V., Ivashchenko, V., Grudzur, O., & Oleksandr, Y. (2021). Criminal protection of children's life and health: International experience. *Cuestiones Politicas, 71.*

Chao, Y. (2022). The development of right protection for juveniles of China. From childhood to the right to a dignified old age human rights and institutions, 243.

Chen, J., & Lyu, J. (2021). Interpretative perspectives and regulatory boundaries of the crime of sexual assault by persons with special care duties. *Journal of Central South University (Social Science), 5*, 53–64.

Children's Division. (2023). *Top ten progresses in child welfare and child protection in 2022 and trends in 2023*. Public Interest Times.

Jiang, M. (2022). Study on the minimum age of criminal responsibility for members of the United Nations. *Legal Science (Journal of Northwest University of Politics and Law), 2*, 89–100.

Nagornaya, I. I. (2018). Ensuring rights and legitimate interests of minors by means of criminal law. *Law: Journal of the Higher School of Economics, 84.*

Shang, X., & Katz, I. (2014). Missing elements in the protection of children: Three cases from China. *Journal of Social Service Research, 4*, 545–559.

Wang, H., & Zhang, X. (2015). On the criminal law protection of minors from the victim's perspective. *Inner Mongolia Social Sciences (Chinese Edition), 4*, 94–98.

Zhou, G. (2021). Progress in criminal legislation and judicial prospects: An overall review of the "Criminal Law Amendment 11". *Law Science, 1*, 18–35.

Zhu, J. (2024). Revisiting the implementation of China's juvenile justice philosophy from the "Criminal Law Amendment 11". *Journal of Southeast University (Philosophy and Social Science), S1*, 95–101.

Chapter 4
The Law on the Protection of the Child in China: Comprehensive Safeguards and the Six Protection Regimes

4.1 Introduction

The most sacred faith of mankind is in the child, and the most important obligation of mankind is to ensure that the rights of the child are respected and their well-being is protected, so that they can be free from fear and poverty, growing up in peace (Annan, 2000).The child is a special group with immature physical and mental development and special physiological and psychological characteristics. They are in great need of special care and love from the state, society, schools, and families. As natural beings, children need material support and spiritual care from family and society; as social beings, they are inevitably influenced by social culture, customs, traditions, habits, lifestyles, and various forms of consciousness. It is therefore incumbent upon the State, society, schools, and families to amplify the positive impact on children and to avoid or reduce the negative impact (Liu, 2022).

Chinese Government has always attached great importance to the protection of children's rights and interests and has never given up its efforts, especially in the formulation, promulgation, and implementation of laws and regulations on child protection (Hämäläinen et al., 2023). In the early days of the United Nations Convention on the Rights of the Child, 17 provinces, autonomous regions, and municipalities in China, including Shanghai, Fujian, Hunan, Beijing, Liaoning, Guizhou, and Henan, successively formulated child protection regulations. Guided by *the Constitution of the People's Republic of China*, China adopted the Law of *the People's Republic of China on the Protection of Minors* (the child) (2021) for the first time in September 1991, which specifically protects the legitimate rights and interests of citizens under the age of 18, and has gradually established a legal system for the protection of children's rights with the Law as the core. As stated in article 2 of *the United Nations Convention on the Rights of the Child*: "States Parties shall take all appropriate measures to ensure that the child is protected against all forms of discrimination or punishment on the basis of the status, activities, expressed

© The Author(s), under exclusive license to Springer Nature Singapore Pte Ltd. 2026

H. Li, P. Liang, *The Legal System for the Protection of Children's Rights in China*, Resilient and Friendly Living Environments,
https://doi.org/10.1007/978-981-95-9925-7_4

opinions, or beliefs of the child's parents, legal guardians, or family members." *The Law of the People's Republic of China on the Protection of Minors* (the child) (2021), as a comprehensive law in the field of child protection, aims to protect the basic rights of children's healthy growth, including the rights to survival, development, protection, and participation, so as to ensure that the legitimate rights and interests of children are effectively protected. As the progress of The Times has put forward new and higher requirements for child protection, China has kept pace with The Times and revised *the Law of the People's Republic of China on the Protection of Minors* (the child) (2021) three times in 2006, 2012 and 2020, to meet the maximum demand for the protection of children's rights and interests (Ma & Bo, 2023).

On June 1, 2021, the newly revised Law of the People's Republic of China on the Protection of Minors (the Child) (2021) was officially implemented, which is divided into general provisions, family protection, school protection, social protection, network protection, government protection, judicial protection, legal liability, and supplementary provisions, totaling nine sections and 132 articles. The new law proposes "six protection systems" for the child, including family, school, society, network, government, and judiciary, which have made a top-level legal design for the construction of the legal system for the protection of children's rights in China and have played an important role in safeguarding and protecting children's legitimate rights, protecting children's physical and mental health, and promoting children's all-round development (You & Li, 2021). This chapter will interpret the specific content of the Law of the People's Republic of China on the Protection of Minors (the child) (2021) (2021) based on the legal provisions, introduce readers to the general principles and relevant provisions of China's child protection work, and elaborate on the "six protection systems" for the child established by the law, namely family protection, school protection, social protection, network protection, government protection, and judicial protection (Yao & Chen, 2021a, 2021b).

4.2 The Concrete Presentation of the Protection of the Child in the Law of the People's Republic of China on the Protection of Minors (the child) (2021)

Since its implementation on January 1, 1992, *the Law of the People's Republic of China on the Protection of Minors* (the child) (2021) (2021) has been promulgated for more than 30 years, the protection object has been adjusted from the original "under 25 years old" to "under 18 years old". The legislative intention has changed from the original aim of "protecting teenagers from corrupt ideas and preventing teenagers from breaking the law and committing crimes" to the current "comprehensive protection of children". *The Law of the People's Republic of China on the Protection of Minors* (the child) (2021) takes the four rights of children as its legislative philosophy, namely, survival, development, protection, and development, and makes clear provisions in the General provisions on the basic principles of child protection, the rights enjoyed by children, and the subjects responsible for child protection (Articles 1–14). On this basis, this Law establishes the "six protection systems" for the child of "family, school, society, network, government, justice" (Articles 15–16), and defines the relevant legal responsibilities (117–129). At the same time, Article 131, this Law proposes that China shall not only protect children of Chinese nationality but also protect foreigners and stateless persons under the age of 18 in China. The following is an explanation of the contents of the Law of the People's Republic of China on the Protection of Minors (the child) (2021) (2021) so that readers can understand the core foundation of China's legal system for the protection of children's rights (Yao & Chen, 2021a, 2021b).

4.2.1 General Provisions of the Law of the People's Republic of China on the Protection of Minors (the child) (2021)

The Law of the People's Republic of China on the Protection of Minors (the child) (2021) further improves the establishment of China's legal system for the protection of children's rights, including the general principles for protecting children, strengthening the protection of children's rights. The law clarifies the responsibilities of different subjects of children in different living, learning, and recreational environments, in particular, it strengthens the State's responsibility to protect and establishes a mandatory reporting system for close contact of children when the rights of children are violated, which echoes many provisions of the United Nations Convention on the Rights of the Child. For example, non-discrimination against children (Article 2 of the Convention), the principle of the best interests of the child (Article 3 of the Convention), the protection of children's rights to life, survival and development (Article 6 of the Convention), and respect for children's views (Article 12 of the Convention), which provide new guidance for the development of the protection of children's rights in China.

The Law of the People's Republic of China on the Protection of Minors explicitly stipulates at the outset that its subjects of protection are individuals under the age of eighteen. It further delineates its legislative purpose: to safeguard the physical and mental health of minors, to protect their lawful rights and interests, to promote their all-round development in morality, intellect, physical fitness, aesthetics, and labor, to foster socialist builders and successors endowed with ideals, morality, culture, and discipline, and to nurture a new generation capable of assuming the historic mission of national rejuvenation. Relevant provisions refer to Articles 1 and 2 of this Law:

Article 1
This Law is enacted in accordance with the Constitution for the purpose of protecting the physical and mental health of minors, safeguarding their lawful rights and interests, promoting their all-round development morally, intellectually, physically, art and working, and training them in builders of and

successors to the socialist cause with lofty ideals, sound morality, good education and a good sense of discipline, and training them to take on the responsibility of national rejuvenation new era.

Article 2
Minors as used in this Law refer to citizens under the age of eighteen.

Building upon this legislative purpose, Articles 3 and 4 of the General Provisions of the Law of the People's Republic of China on the Protection of Minors establish two fundamental principles of child protection, namely the principle of safeguarding the basic rights of children and the principle of the best interests of the child, thereby providing clear guidance for the handling of all matters concerning child protection. Articles 5 through 14 further specify the respective responsibilities of the state, society, schools, and families in ensuring the protection of minors.

4.2.1.1 Principle of Protection of the Fundamental Rights of the Child

Article 3
The state protects minors' rights to survival, development, protection, and participation. Minors shall enjoy equal rights in accordance with the law, and shall not be discriminated against by their nationality, race, gender, household registration, occupation, religious belief, educational level, family status, physical and mental health status, etc.

The first principle is the "Principle of Protection of the Fundamental Rights of the Child Children enjoy the right to survival, development, protection, and participation, and the state shall give special and priority protection to children in light of their physical and mental development characteristics, so as to ensure that their legitimate rights and interests are not infringed upon. Among them, the "right to survival" includes the right to life security and the right to livelihood security. That is, all children have the right to live and enjoy basic living conditions, as well as the right to receive the highest attainable standard of health care. *The Law of the People's Republic of China on the Protection of Minors* (the child) (2021) emphasizes that family members, schools, and the government have the obligation to protect children's right to survival, and those who infringe on children's personal rights constitute a crime, refuse to raise the child, drown and abandon babies will be held legally responsible. The "right to development" refers to the right of the child to the full development of his or her physical and mental abilities and all forms of education, both formal and non-formal, as well as to an environment and living conditions conducive to his or her physical, mental, spiritual, moral and social development. *The Law of the People's Republic of China on the Protection of Minors* (the Child) (2021) emphasizes the need to ensure the full development of children in the physical, intellectual, spiritual, moral, personal, and social aspects. The "right to protection" means that the child shall be protected from discrimination, exploitation, torture, ill-treatment, abandonment, or neglect of care, and children shall have the right to appropriate care or rehabilitation services when they need them. *The Law of the People's Republic of China on the Protection of Minors* (the child) (2021) explicitly forbids discrimination based on children's religious beliefs, educational level, family status, physical and mental health status, as well as discrimination based on the status of children's parents or other guardians. The "right to participation" refers to the right of children to participate in family, cultural, and social life, including giving their opinions and recommendations on the matters facing them. Both *the United Nations Convention on the Rights of the Child* and *the Law of the People's Republic of China on the Protection of Minors* (the Child) (2021) emphasize that the child is a whole human being and maintains that the child is an independent individual, a member of the family and society, with rights appropriate to his age and stage of development. These fundamental rights are designed to ensure the health, safety, education, and dignity of children, giving them the opportunity to develop into individuals able to participate in society and contribute.

4.2.1.2 Principle in the Best Interests of the child

Article 4

The Principle in the Best Interests of minors shall be adhered to in the protection of minors. The handling of matters involving minors shall meet the following requirements: (1) give minors special and priority protections, (2) respect minors' personal dignity, (3) protect minors' privacy and personal information, (4) adapt to the laws and characteristics of minors' physical and mental health development, (5) hear minors' opinions, (6) combine protection and education.

The second is "Principle in the Best Interests of the child". As early as the 1950s, the United Nations General Assembly adopted the Declaration on the Rights of the Child, which published the ten principles on the rights of children, proposing for the first time that "the best interests of the child should be the first consideration". Article 3 of the Convention on the Rights of the Child also states that: "In all actions concerning children, whether undertaken by public or private social welfare institutions, courts of law, administrative authorities or legislative bodies, the best interests of the child shall be a primary consideration." It states that public and private social welfare institutions, courts, administrations, and legislative bodies should abide by this principle. According to *the Law of the People's Republic of China on the Protection of Minors* (the child) (2021), it is necessary to adhere to the "Principle in the Best Interests of the child". When dealing with matters involving children, one must take into account the development interests and fundamental interests of children in a comprehensive and long-term way, give children special and priority protection, respect their personal dignity, and protect their privacy and personal information. Listen to the opinions of children and ensure the maximum realization of children's interests. The "Principle in the Best Interests of the Child" is reflected in all aspects of this Law, and is also the guiding principle for building the legal system for the protection of children's rights in China. For example, according to the guiding principle, the Civil Code of the People's Republic of China stipulates that courts should respect the true wishes of minor children over the age of 8 when hearing divorce cases involving the raising of minor children.

The establishment of the above general principles provides specific guidance for clarifying the responsibilities of the family, school, government, and society, specifically as outlined in Articles 3 and 4 of the Law of the People's Republic of China on the Protection of Minors (the child) (2021):

4.2.1.3 The Legislative Purpose and General Principles

The General Provisions of *the Law of the People's Republic of China on the Protection of Minors (2021)* clarify the responsibilities of various types of subjects in different living, learning, leisure, and entertainment environments. The state, society, schools, families, and other organizations shall provide protection and education for the growth of children. For details, see Articles 5 and 6 of this Law:

Article 5
The state, society, schools, and families shall conduct education among minors in ideals, morality, science, culture, rule of law, national security, health, and Labor, strengthen education in patriotism, collectivism, and socialism with Chinese characteristics, and cultivate public virtues of loving the motherland, the people, Labor, science and socialism. Resist the erosion of capitalism, feudalism, and other decadent ideas, and guide minors to establish and practice socialist core values.

Article 6
The protection of minors shall be the joint responsibility of state organs, armed forces, political parties, people's organizations, enterprises and institutions, social organizations, urban and rural grass-roots mass self-governing organizations, guardians of minors, and other adults. The state, society, schools, and families shall educate and help minors to safeguard their legitimate rights and interests and enhance their awareness and ability to protect themselves.

The healthy growth of children requires the joint protection of multiple entities, among which the state is the most powerful backing for the protection of children's rights and interests. Therefore, *the Law of the People's Republic of China on the Protection of Minors (2021)*, while clarifying the responsibility to protect different subjects, emphasizes in particular the responsibility of the state to protect. First, it clarifies the state's responsibility to ensure the realization of children's basic rights, that is, the government should act as the last shield for the protection of children's rights, and protect children's rights to survival, development, protection, participation, and other rights. Second, it clarifies the duties of the state in the guardianship.

This Law establishes that the guardianship of the state is higher than the rights of the parents. When the parents are unable, unfavorable, or refuse to perform the guardianship, the state has the power and responsibility to intervene or even take over the guardianship of the parents. However, it should be noted that the state's parental rights should not be abused. The state should take measures to guide, support, help, and supervise the parents or other guardians of children to perform their guardianship duties, and should not easily interfere with the parental rights, only if forced to deprive the guardians, especially the guardianship of the parents. However, it should be noted that the parental authority of the State cannot be abused, and the State shall take measures to guide, support, assist, and supervise the parents or other guardians of children in the performance of their guardianship duties, and shall not arbitrarily interfere with parental authority at will, and may only deprive guardians, especially parents, of their guardianship rights when they are forced to do so. Third, the State is required to include child protection in national economic and social development plans and government budgets. Fourth, it is clarified that the government is to take the lead in establishing mechanisms for child protection work, and people's governments at the county level or above shall establish coordination mechanisms for efforts on the protection of minors, to plan, coordinate, supervise, and guide the work of relevant departments, and at the same time have the civil affairs departments of people's governments at the county level or above undertake specific work. Fifth, it emphasizes the national construction of disciplines and majors related to the protection of children and encourages and supports scientific research in child protection. Sixth, the State shall establish a system of statistical surveys on children, conduct statistics, surveys, and analyses on children's health, education, and other conditions, and release relevant information on child protection. In addition, while the state provides security, social organizations including the Communist Youth League and the Women's Federation should assist and cooperate in order to safeguard the legitimate rights and interests of minors. The state will commend and reward the organizations and individuals who have made outstanding achievements in the protection of children. For relevant legislative provisions, please refer to Articles 7–10 and 12–14 of the Law of the People's Republic of China on the Protection of Minors *(2021)*:

> **Article 7**
> ***The parents or other guardians of minors shall bear guardianship duties over minors in accordance with law. The State is to employ measures to guide, support, assist, and supervise minors' parents or other guardians in the performance of guardianship duties.***
>
> **Article 8**
> ***People's governments at the county level or above shall include efforts on the protection of minors in the citizens' economic and social development plans, and the relevant expenses shall be included in the budgets of the governments at that level.***

Article 9
People's governments at the county level or above shall establish coordination mechanisms for efforts on the protection of minors, to plan, coordinate, supervise, and guide relevant departments to do a good job of efforts on the protection of minors within the scope of their respective duties. The specific work of the coordination mechanism is to be undertaken by the civil affairs department of the people's government at the county level or above, and the people's government at the provincial level may also determine that other relevant departments are to undertake it on the basis of actual local conditions.

Article 10
The Communist Youth League, women's federations, trade unions, disabled persons' federations, working committees for the care of the next generation, youth federations, student federations, young pioneers, and other people's organizations, and relevant social organizations shall assist all levels of people's government and their relevant departments, people's procuratorates, and people's courts in efforts to protect minors, and preserve the lawful rights and interests of minors.

Article 12
The State encourages and supports scientific research on the protection of minors, establishing relevant disciplines, setting up relevant majors, and strengthening the cultivation of talents.

Article 13
The State is to establish and complete a system for statistical surveys of minors, carrying out statistics, investigations, and analyses of minors' health, education, and other such conditions, and publishing information related to the protection of minors.

4.2.1.4 The Mandatory Reporting System

While stipulating that different entities bear the responsibility for the protection of children's rights, *the Law of the People's Republic of China on the Protection of Minors (2021)* pays special attention to the prevention and priority protection of child harm and establishes a mandatory reporting system for cases of violations against children from the legal level. This law requires that state organs, residents' committees, villagers' committees, units with close contact with children, and their staffs, who discover in the course of their work that children's physical and mental health has been violated, are suspected to have been violated, or are facing other dangerous situations, shall immediately report to the relevant departments such as public security, civil affairs, and education (Chen & Zhang, 2023).

The mandatory reporting system is widely used worldwide for the protection of children as a vulnerable group, and its core content is the response model when reports of suspected child abuse and neglect are received. The Anti-Domestic Violence Law of the People's Republic of China, which came into effect in March 2016, has enshrined mandatory reporting of domestic violence against children and set out the post-reporting response process. *The Law of the People's Republic of China on the Protection of Minors (2021)* reaffirms the mandatory reporting system for cases of violations against children, and the Supreme People's Procuratorate of China and other competent authorities of other countries have also refined the relevant provisions accordingly, clarifying that the mandatory reporting system must be activated immediately in any of the following circumstances.

The child has suffered or is suspected to have suffered abnormal damage to his or her reproductive organs or private parts.

(2) Female children under the age of 14 have suffered or are suspected of being sexually assaulted, pregnant, or miscarried.

(3) Pregnancy or miscarriage caused by a female child over the age of 14 who has suffered or is suspected of having suffered sexual assault.

(4) The child has multiple physical injuries, severe malnutrition, unconsciousness, or is or is suspected of being subjected to domestic violence, bullying, abuse, beating, or being anesthetized.

(5) Serious student bullying

(6) The child is disabled or dies due to suicide, self-injury, work-related injury, poisoning, being anesthetized, beaten, or other abnormal reasons.

(7) The child has been abandoned or left unattended for a long time.

(8) It is discovered that children are being organized to beg.

As a new system in China's judicial protection system for children, the "Mandatory Reporting System for Cases of Violations against Children" plays an important role in preventing and discovering cases of violations against children, providing timely assistance to child victims, and effectively protecting the legitimate rights and interests of children. For specific legislative provisions, please refer to Article 11 of *the Law of the People's Republic of China on the Protection of Minors (the child) (2021).*

Article 11

Any organization or individual discovers circumstances that are detrimental to the physical and psychological health of minors or infringe upon the lawful rights and interests of minors, and has the right to dissuade or stop them, or to submit a report or accusation to the relevant departments such as for public security, civil affairs, and education.

Where state organs, residents' committees, villagers' committees, units with close contact with minors, and their staffs, discover in the course of their work that minors' physical or psychological health has been violated, is suspected to have been violated, or that they are facing other dangerous situations, they shall immediately report to the relevant departments such as for public security, civil affairs, and education.

When relevant departments receive reports, accusations, or reports involving minors, they shall promptly accept and dispose of them in accordance with law, and inform the relevant units and personnel of the outcome of the disposition in an appropriate manner.

To sum up, as the most important content of the legal system for the protection of children's rights, the General Provisions (Articles 1–14) of *the Law of the People's Republic of China on the Protection of Minors (the child) (2021)* start from general provisions, clearly put forward the legislative purpose of protecting children's rights and interests, the general principles for protecting children, the state to implement the relevant institutional provisions for child protection, and put forward that the protection of children's rights is the common responsibility of the whole society.

4.2.2 "Six Protection Systems" for Children's Rights

In order to ensure the effective promotion of the protection of children's rights and interests, *the Law of the People's Republic of China on the Protection of Minors (the child) (2021)* gives children basic rights at the legal level, establishes general principles for the protection of children, and proposes the "six major protections" for children at the specific implementation level, namely family protection, school protection, social protection, online protection, government protection, and judicial protection. From the perspective of different subjects and specific functions and responsibilities, a protective net has been woven for the protection of children's rights.

4.2.2.1 Family Protection Under the Six Protection Systems (Articles 15–24 of the Act)

Article 18 of the United Nations Convention on the Rights of the Child clearly states that parents have the primary responsibility for the development of their children and that States should provide them with appropriate assistance and the development of nurseries. The family is the primary place for children to live and grow, and it is in the family that they accept social norms, form values, establish life goals, develop behavioral habits and life skills, and develop a sense of responsibility. Children have not yet matured physically and psychologically, their world view, outlook on life, and values have not yet been fully formed, they do not have a clear understanding of the rights and obligations stipulated by the law, as well as public order and good customs, and their awareness and ability to protect themselves are still poor, so the law needs to pay more attention to family protection (Xu et al., 2023).

Family protection refers to the protection of children by parents or other guardians, including care and ideological education in life. Family protection is an important link of child protection work, the quality of family protection, directly affects the growth of the child. *The Law of the People's Republic of China on the Protection of Minor (2021)* proposes at the beginning of "Family Protection" that parents or other guardians shall learn about family education, accept guidance on family education, and create a good, harmonious and civilized family environment. Among them, it focuses on the refinement of the guardianship responsibilities of children's parents or other guardians, clarifies the safety and security obligations of parents, establishes several systems including temporary guardianship and long-term guardianship, and regulates entrusted care, especially for the lack of guardianship of left-behind children and other groups in rural areas.

Firstly, *the Law of the People's Republic of China on the Protection of Minors* (2021) emphasizes the importance of family education. Family education refers to the cultivation, guidance, and influence of parents or other guardians on children's moral character, physical fitness, life skills, cultural accomplishments, behavioral habits, and so forth, in order to promote their comprehensive and healthy growth. For details, see Article 15 of this Law:

Article 15

Children's parents or other guardians shall learn about family education, accept guidance on family education, and create a good, harmonious, and civilized family environment. Other adult family members living together shall assist the child's parents or other guardians in raising, educating, and protecting the child.

Secondly, *the Law of the People's Republic of China on the Protection of Minors (2021)* emphasizes the guardianship duties of parents and other guardians. The guardian here refers to the person who supervises and protects the child's person, property, and all other lawful rights and interests. In general, parents or other guardians should perform the following guardianship duties:

1. Perform guardianship duties and support obligations for children in accordance with the law. Specifically, it includes: (1) protecting the personal health and safety of children under guardianship. (2) To protect their right to name and honor, and to cultivate and educate them morally, intellectually, physically, and so on; Violations of children's property by others may be eliminated in a timely manner, and children's property may be disposed of on the premise that it is beneficial to the interests of the child. (3) Acting for the civil liability of children for damage caused to the state, the collective, and others. (4) Raise and care for children materially, and provide children with living expenses, medical expenses, and education expenses. While performing guardianship and care obligations for children, parents, and other guardians must not abuse or abandon children, must not discriminate against female children or children with disabilities, and must not drown or abandon infants. Otherwise, they shall bear legal responsibility in accordance with the law.

2. Respect children's right to receive education, and must ensure that school-age children receive compulsory education in accordance with regulations and that children who receive compulsory education in school must not be allowed to drop out of school. Regardless of the reason, children who are out of school or drop out of school are derelict on the part of their parents, and to a certain extent, they infringe upon the legitimate rights and interests of children.
3. Respect children's right to receive education, and must ensure that school-age children receive compulsory education in accordance with regulations and that children who receive compulsory education in school must not be allowed to drop out of school. Regardless of the reason, children who are out of school or drop out of school are derelict on the part of their parents, and to a certain extent, they infringe upon the legitimate rights and interests of children.
4. Children shall not be married or betrothed. The Civil Code of the People's Republic of China stipulates that the age of marriage for Chinese citizens is not earlier than 22 years old for men and 20 years old for women. In terms of age, it is illegal for parents to allow children to marry. Parents may not allow or compel a child to marry, nor may they enter into a marriage contract for the child. This is also an aspect of the family protection that parents give to their children.
5. Children shall not be married or betrothed. The Civil Code of the People's Republic of China stipulates that the age of marriage for Chinese citizens is not earlier than 22 years old for men and 20 years old for women. In terms of age, it is illegal for parents to allow children to marry. Parents may not allow or compel a child to marry, nor may they enter into a marriage contract for the child.

In addition to the above-mentioned aspects, parents or other guardians should also carry out other aspects of family protection that are appropriate, appropriate, timely, and effective according to the child's physical and mental characteristics and different circumstances. For details, please refer to Articles 16–18 and 20 of t*he Law of the People's Republic of China on the Protection of Minor (2021):*

Article 16

The parents or other guardians of minors shall perform the following guardianship duties: (1) provide minors with safeguards for their lives, health, safety, etc., (2) pay attention to minors' physical and psychological conditions and emotional needs, (3) educate and guide minors to abide by discipline and law, (4) Carry out safety education for minors to improve their awareness and ability to protect themselves; (5) Respect minors' right to education, and ensure that minors of appropriate age receive and complete compulsory education in accordance with the law; (6) Guarantee minors' rest, Time for recreation and physical exercise, guide minors to engage in activities that are beneficial to their physical and mental health; (7) Properly manage and protect minors' assets; (8) Represent minors in carrying out civil juristic acts in accordance with law; (9) Prevent and stop minors' negative conduct and illegal and criminal conduct, and conduct reasonable discipline; (10) Other guardianship duties that shall be performed.

Article 17

The parents or other guardians of minors shall perform the following guardianship duties: (1) provide minors with safeguards for their lives, health, safety, etc., (2) pay attention to minors' physical and psychological conditions and emotional needs, (3) educate and guide minors to abide by discipline and law, (4) Carry out safety education for minors to improve their awareness and ability to protect themselves; (5) Respect minors' right to education, and ensure that minors of appropriate age receive and complete compulsory education in accordance with the law; (6) Guarantee minors' rest, Time for recreation and physical exercise, guide minors to engage in activities that are beneficial to their physical and mental health; (7) Properly manage and protect minors' assets; (8) Represent minors in carrying out civil juristic acts in accordance with law; (9) Prevent and stop minors' negative conduct and illegal and criminal conduct, and conduct reasonable discipline; (10) Other guardianship duties that shall be performed.

Article 18

Parents or other guardians of minors shall provide a safe family living environment for minors and promptly eliminate safety hazards that may cause injuries such as electric shock and scalding falls; Take measures such as educating minors to obey traffic rules by equipping them with child safety seats to prevent them from being injured by traffic accidents; Improve the awareness of outdoor safety protection, to avoid minors drowning animal injury and other accidents.

Article 20

Parents or other guardians of minors who discover that the physical and mental health of minors has been infringed, suspected to have been infringed, or other legitimate rights and interests have been infringed, shall promptly understand the situation and take protective measures; If the situation is serious, it shall immediately report to the civil affairs education department of public security.

In addition, *the Law of the People's Republic of China on the Protection of Minor (2021)* re-emphasizes the "principle of the best interests of the child" in the "family section", and parents should listen to the opinions of the child before making decisions related to the rights and interests of the child, based on the child's age and intellectual development. When parents divorce, they shall properly handle matters such as the upbringing, education, visitation, and property of minor children, hear the opinions of children who have the ability to express their wishes and must not compete for custody rights by snatching or hiding minor children. Articles 19 and 24 of this Law provide for this:

Article 19
The parents or other guardians of minors shall, on the basis of the minors' age and intellectual development, listen to the opinions of minors and give full consideration to their true wishes before making decisions related to the rights and interests of minors.

Article 24
When a minor's parents divorce, they shall properly handle matters such as the minor child's upbringing, education, visitation, and property, and hear the opinions of the minor who has the ability to express his or her wishes. Custody must not be fought for by means such as snatching or hiding minor children.

After a minor's parents divorce, the party who does not directly raise the minor child shall follow the time and method determined by the agreement, the people's court's judgment, or mediation, and visit the minor child without impacting the minor's studies and life, and the party directly raising the minor shall cooperate, except where the people's court has suspended visitation rights in accordance with law.

Finally, in order to effectively protect the legitimate rights and interests of children, *the Law of the People's Republic of China on the Protection of Minors (2021)* also sets up a temporary entrusted care system and a long-term entrusted care system.

Temporary entrusted care means that parents cannot leave children unsupervised, especially children under the age of eight and children who require special care for psychological or physical reasons. If there is a legitimate reason why guardianship duties cannot be performed in a timely manner, parents shall entrust persons with the capacity to take care of the child temporarily, but must not entrust the child to the temporary care of four categories of persons: persons with no capacity for civil conduct, persons with limited capacity for civil conduct, persons with serious infectious diseases, and other persons who are not suitable.

Long-term entrusted care refers to situations where parents or other guardians who are unable to fully perform guardianship duties within a certain period of time due to reasons such as going out to work, and shall entrust a person with full capacity for civil conduct to take care of them on their behalf. In determining the client, it shall comprehensively consider the connection between the moral character, family status, physical and mental health status, and the emotional life of the child, and listen to the opinions of children who have the ability to express their will, and shall not be regarded as the client under any of the following circumstances: (1) have committed sexual assault, abuse, abandonment, trafficking, violence and injury and other illegal and criminal acts; (2) drugs, alcohol, gambling, and other bad habits; (3) has refused to perform or long-term neglect to perform the duties of guardianship and care; (4) Other circumstances in which it is not appropriate to act as a principal.

At the same time, parents need to pay attention to the following obligations: first, inform the entrusted person about the care, second, parents should strengthen communication with schools and kindergartens, third, they should strengthen family care with minor children, and fourth, if left-behind children's psychological and behavioral abnormalities are discovered, they should take timely interventions. For details, please refer to Articles 21–23 of *the Law of the People's Republic of China on the Protection of Minors (2021)*:

Article 21
The parents or other guardians of minors must not leave minors under the age of 8 or who need special care due to physical or psychological reasons unsupervised, or place them in temporary care by persons who lack civil capacity, have limited civil capacity, suffer from serious infectious diseases, or are otherwise unsuitable.

Minors' parents or other guardians must not allow minors under the age of 16 to live alone from their guardianship.

Article 22
Where the parents or other guardians of minors are unable to fully perform their guardianship duties within a certain period of time due to reasons such as going out to work, they shall entrust a person with full capacity for civil conduct who has the capacity to take care of them to do so on their behalf.

When determining the person to be represented, the parents or other guardians of minors shall comprehensively consider circumstances such as their moral character, family status, physical and psychological health, and emotional ties to the minor's life, and hear the opinions of the minor who has the ability to express their wishes.

In any of the following circumstances, they must not be the person being retained: (1) they have committed illegal or criminal acts such as sexual assault, abuse, abandonment, trafficking, or violent harm; (2) they have bad habits such as drug abuse, alcoholism, or gambling; (3) they have refused to perform or have neglected to perform their guardianship or care duties for a long time; (4) they are otherwise unfit to serve as the entrusted person.

Article 23
Minors' parents or other guardians shall promptly inform the minors' schools, kindergartens, and residents' committees and villagers' committees of their actual place of residence in writing of the circumstances of the entrusted care, and strengthen communication with the minors' schools and kindergartens.

After minors' parents or other guardians receive notice from the entrusted person, residents' committees, villagers' committees, schools, kindergartens, and so forth about minors' psychological or behavioral abnormalities, they shall promptly employ intervention measures.

4.2.2.2 School Protection Under the Six Protection Systems (Articles 25–41 of the Act)

Article 28 of the United Nations Convention on the Rights of the Child clearly states that all children in the world have the right to education and that schools should guarantee equal access to education on the basis of respect for children's human dignity. In the "six protection systems" for the child established by *the Law of the People's Republic of China on the Protection of Minor (2021)*, "School Protection" responds to the Convention on the Rights of the Child by legally stipulating that schools should ensure the realization of the rights of minor students from the perspectives of "impart knowledge and educate" and "safety guarantee".

School protection refers to the special protection implemented by relevant schools for minor students and kindergarten children in accordance with the law. The schools referred to here include ordinary primary and secondary schools, various vocational and technical schools, special education schools for the blind, deaf, dumb, and mentally handicapped, infant and child care service institutions, early education service institutions, and various literary and artistic, sports, martial arts, and special craft schools that enroll children (Wang, 1994).

In terms of "impart knowledge and educate", this law clarifies the proper and prohibited behaviors of schools in the performance of their educational and childcare duties, and in terms of "safety guarantee", this law stipulates the mechanism for ensuring campus safety and the measures to deal with emergencies including school bullying, as well as mandatory reporting requirements for schools and teachers and other staff.

In 2021, the Ministry of Education of the People's Republic of China promulgated the Provisions on the Protection of Minors in Schools, which is guided by the Law of the People's Republic of China on the Protection of Minors (2021), and in accordance with the Constitution of the People's Republic of China and other laws, systematically integrates relevant systems, and clarifies school protection responsibilities, management requirements, working mechanisms, and supervision measures.

The task of "impart knowledge and educate" is not only to impart knowledge to students, but also to create a good educational atmosphere in teaching, so that students can acquire natural behavior and habits, and ultimately shape a sound personality spirit. *The Law of the People's Republic of China on the Protection of Minors (2021)* summarizes the responsibilities of schools in "teaching and educating people" as follows: (1) fully implement the national education policy and promote the all-round development of minor students, (2) respect the personal dignity of minor students and not discriminate against students, (3) protect the right to education of minor students and not arbitrarily expel students, (4) not increase the learning burden of minor students, and pay attention to multi-faceted training. Specifically, it can be understood from the following four aspects.

Firstly, *the Law of the People's Republic of China on the Protection of Minors (2021)* clarifies that all types of educational institutions should do a good job of protecting children, from infancy to adulthood. Schools shall fully implement the state's education policy, establish a system for the protection of minor students, not only cultivate students' cognitive ability, ability to cooperate, innovate, and cultivate practical ability, but also cultivate them to develop good habits of behavior and law-abiding, and comprehensively promote children's development; Extracurricular training establishments and so forth shall do a good job of protection efforts on the basis of the characteristics and laws of children's growth at different ages. For details, please refer to Articles 25, 26, and 41 of this Law.

Article 25
Schools shall fully implement the national education policy, persist in cultivating morality, implement quality education, improve the quality of education, pay attention to cultivating minor students' cognitive ability, cooperation ability, innovation ability, and practical ability, and promote the all-round development of minor students. Schools shall establish a system for the protection of minor students, complete norms of student conduct, and cultivate positive habits of minor students' compliance with discipline and law.

Article 26
Kindergartens should do a good job in childcare and education, follow the laws of children's physical and mental development, implement enlightenment education, and promote the harmonious development of children's physique, intelligence, morality, etc.

Article 41
Infant and child care service establishments, early education service establishments, off-campus training establishments, off-campus childcare establishments, and so forth, shall refer to the relevant provisions of this chapter and do a good job of efforts to protect minors on the basis of the characteristics and laws of minors at different ages.

Secondly, in line with the concept of respecting children's human rights, *the Law of the People's Republic of China on the Protection of Minors (2021)* emphasizes that schools should respect and protect the personal dignity of students and must not insult students.

On the one hand, schools shall treat every student equally, and shall not discriminate against or treat students differently on the basis of their or their parents' ethnicity, race, gender, household registration, occupation, religious belief, education level, family status, physical and mental health, and so forth. It is necessary to respect students' reputations, protect and cultivate students' sense of honor and responsibility, and commend and reward students for being open, fair, and just; no words, deeds, or methods that demean or insult students, their parents, or specific groups to which they belong must be used in education and management. On the other hand, schools should care for minor students, and conduct social life guidance and mental health counseling based on the characteristics of their physical and mental development. Care shall be provided to students with family difficulties or physical or mental disabilities; Schools shall cooperate with relevant government departments to establish information archives for left-behind minor students and minor students in difficulty, and carry out care and support efforts.

It is important to point out that in order to fully protect the human dignity of children, the Chinese government has issued a number of legal documents with more detailed provisions under the guidance of *the Law of the People's Republic of China on the Protection of Minor (2021)*. For example, in order to create a lively educational ecology, protect students' vitality, and promote students' all-round development, schools must not set up management measures that infringe on students' personal freedom, and must not set unnecessary restrictions on students' freedom of speech and deeds such as normal communication, games, and out-of-class activities during recess and other non-teaching hours. In order to protect students' privacy and self-esteem, reduce comparisons, avoid discrimination, and alleviate test-taking pressure, schools and teachers are prohibited from disclosing students' test scores and rankings, but schools are required to take measures to facilitate parent's access to students' grades and other academic information. For another example, schools should respect students' rights to participate and express themselves, guide and support students' participation in the formulation of school charters, school rules and discipline, and class conventions, and should listen to students' opinions in an appropriate manner when handling matters related to students' rights and interests.

For the foregoing, please refer to Articles 27, 29, and 30 of the Law of the People's Republic of China on the Protection of Minors (2021).

Article 27
Teachers and staff of schools and kindergartens shall respect the personal dignity of minors, and must not carry out corporal punishment, covert corporal punishment, or other acts that insult the personal dignity of minors.

Article 29
Schools shall care for and care for minor students, and shall not discriminate against students on the basis of family, physical, psychological, or academic ability. Care shall be provided to students with family difficulties or physical or mental disabilities; Schools shall cooperate with relevant government departments to establish information archives for left-behind minor students and minor students in difficulty, and carry out care and support efforts.

Article 30
Schools shall, on the basis of the characteristics of minor students' physical and mental development, conduct social life guidance, mental health counseling, adolescent education, and life education.

Thirdly, *the Law of the People's Republic of China on the Protection of Minors (2021)* clearly states that schools should respect and protect students' right to education. At present, China implements a nine-year compulsory education system, and the state guarantees free education for school-age children, who can learn various knowledge and skills through compulsory education schools. Compulsory education schools must not expel or covertly expel students, and must not deprive students of their right to accept and complete compulsory education in school by means such as long-term suspension of classes or persuasion to leave school. For details, see Article 28 of this Law.

Article 28
Schools shall protect the right of minor students to receive education, and shall not expel or covertly expel minor students in violation of state regulations.

Schools shall register minor students who have dropped out of school and persuade them to return to school if they have not completed compulsory education.

Finally, *the Law of the People's Republic of China on the Protection of Minors (2021)* requires schools to pay attention to the multi-faceted cultivation of students, and not to increase their learning burden. On the one hand, schools should not only ensure that students learn theoretical knowledge, but also cultivate students' practical ability and do a good job in mental health counseling. Schools shall regularly organize children to participate in labor to help them master the necessary labor knowledge and skills; they should carry out publicity and education activities such as diligence and thrift, opposition to waste, cherishing food, and civilized diet, so as to help children develop civilized, healthy, and environmentally friendly living habits. On the other hand, schools shall scientifically and reasonably arrange students' work and rest time at school in accordance with regulations, ensuring that students have the opportunity and time to rest, participate in recreational activities, and physical exercise, and must not uniformly require students to come to school to participate in curriculum and teaching activities before the prescribed class time. Compulsory education schools must not occupy legally-prescribed national holidays, rest days, or winter and summer vacations to organize students to make up classes collectively; Kindergartens and extracurricular training institutions must not conduct primary school curriculum education for preschool children. For details, see Articles 31–33 of this Law.

Article 31
Schools shall organize minor students to participate in daily life labor, production labor, and service labor appropriate to their age, and help minor students master the necessary labor knowledge and skills, and develop good labor habits.

Article 32

Schools and kindergartens shall carry out publicity and education activities such as diligence and thrift, opposition to waste, cherishing food, and civilized diets, to help minors establish an awareness that waste is shameful and that thrift is proud, and develop civilized, healthy, green, and environmentally friendly living habits.

Article 33

Schools shall cooperate with the parents or other guardians of minor students to reasonably arrange their study time and ensure their time for rest, recreation, and physical exercise. Schools must not occupy legally-prescribed national holidays, rest days, and winter and summer vacations to organize group make-up classes for minor students in the compulsory education stage, increasing their learning burden. Kindergartens and extracurricular training establishments must not conduct primary school curriculum education for preschool minors.

In terms of "safety guarantee", when students enter the campus to study and live, they are temporarily separated from the protection of the family, and the degree of supervision of parents and other guardians over the children at this time is greatly reduced, so the school should implement the safety management responsibilities to protect the personal safety of students during the school period. The Law of *the People's Republic of China on the Protection of Minors (2021)* stipulates the mechanism for ensuring campus safety and the handling of emergencies and establishes measures for the prevention, control, and handling of student bullying and campus sexual assault, as well as mandatory reporting requirements for schools and teachers, which are mainly reflected in three aspects.

First, the law provides principled provisions regarding student safety. The Law of the People's Republic of China on the Protection of Minors stipulates the following requirements: (1) schools must provide adequate health care facilities, maintain campus hygiene, and implement disease prevention measures; (2) schools are prohibited from organizing or requiring students to participate in disaster relief, hazardous work, commercial activities, or any other activities deemed inappropriate for minors; (3) schools must establish and improve systems for school bus safety management. Institutions offering school bus services are required to designate safety management personnel, conduct regular safety inspections of school buses, provide safety education to drivers, and deliver corresponding safety education to students; (4) schools may not adopt the destruction of property as a means of education or discipline. Where schools temporarily confiscate illegal or unauthorized items brought onto campus by students, such items must be managed collectively and handled in accordance with relevant regulations; (5) schools are prohibited from collecting fees in violation of regulations, and may not compel or impose conditions requiring students or their parents to donate money or materials, purchase goods or services, or otherwise provide financial or material support; (6) in formulating emergency response measures, schools must prepare contingency plans for natural disasters, accidents, public health incidents, and other emergencies or accidental injuries in light of actual circumstances, equip necessary facilities, and conduct regular drills; and (7) where a student suffers personal injury on campus or during extracurricular activities organized by the school, the school is obligated to provide immediate first aid, manage the situation appropriately, promptly inform the student's parents or guardians, and report the matter to the relevant authorities.

Where a child is injured in the school or during an off-campus activity organized by the school, the school shall immediately provide first aid, properly handle it, promptly notify the child's parents or other guardians, and report it to the relevant departments.

For details, see Articles 34–38 of this Law:

Article 34
Schools and kindergartens shall provide necessary health care conditions, and assist the health departments in completing health care efforts for minors in schools and kindergartens.

Article 35
Schools and kindergartens shall establish safety management systems, conduct safety education for minors, improve security facilities, and allocate security personnel, to ensure the safety of minors' persons and property while in school and kindergarten. Schools and kindergartens must not carry out educational and teaching activities in school buildings or other facilities or venues that endanger minors' physical safety or physical and psychological health. Schools and kindergartens arranging for minors to participate in group activities such as cultural entertainment and social practice shall protect minors' physical and psychological health and prevent the occurrence of personal injury accidents.

Article 36
Schools and kindergartens that use school buses shall establish and complete school bus safety management systems, equip safety management personnel, conduct regular safety inspections of school buses, conduct safety education for school bus drivers, and explain school bus safety riding knowledge to minors, and cultivate emergency response skills for minors in school bus safety accidents.

Article 37
Schools and kindergartens shall, as needed, formulate plans for responding to emergencies and accidental injuries such as natural disasters, accidents, and public health incidents, equip them with appropriate facilities, and conduct necessary drills on a regular basis.

Article 38

Schools and kindergartens must not arrange for minors to participate in commercial activities, and must not market to minors and their parents or other guardians, or require them to purchase designated goods and services. Schools and kindergartens must not cooperate with off-campus training establishments to provide paid course tutoring for minors. Where minors have personal injury accidents on campus or in kindergartens, or during off-campus or off-campus activities organized by the school or kindergarten, the school or kindergarten shall immediately provide first aid, properly handle it, promptly notify the minors' parents or other guardians, and report to the relevant departments.

Second, there are special provisions for dealing with school bullying and sexual assault. Article 19 of the United Nations Convention on the Rights of the Child states: "States shall protect children from physical and mental abuse, injury or abuse, neglect, abuse or exploitation, including sexual abuse." In response to the spirit of the Convention, *the Law of the People's Republic of China on the Protection of Minors (2021)* clearly states that schools should establish a working system for the prevention and control of student bullying and a working system for the prevention of sexual assault and sexual harassment of children, and require schools, teachers and other staff to report relevant cases in accordance with the law when they discover them.

It is necessary to point out that for school bullying, under the guidance of *the Law of the People's Republic of China on the Protection of Minors (2021)*, the Ministry of Education of the People's Republic of China has specially issued the Provisions of *the People's Republic of China on the Protection of Minors in Schools (2021)*, which summarizes five types of bullying behaviors, including physical infringement, humiliation of personality, infringement of property, malicious exclusion, online defamation or dissemination of privacy, including: (1) beating, kicking, slapping, scratching, biting, pushing;(2) Infringing on the personal dignity of others by means of insults, ridicule, mockery, sarcasm, or insulting nicknames; (3) Snatching, forcibly taking, or intentionally destroying others' property; (4) Maliciously excluding or isolating others, influencing others' participation in school activities or social interactions; (5) Fabricating facts to slander others, spreading rumors or misinformation to slander others, or maliciously disseminating others' privacy through the Internet or other information dissemination methods.

In the management of school bullying incidents:

For schools, on the one hand, schools should establish student bullying governance organizations, responsible for the prevention, publicity, and education of student bullying, organizing identification, implementing corrections, providing assistance, and so forth. On the other hand, schools shall educate and guide students to establish equal, friendly, and mutually supportive peer relationships, organize teachers and staff to learn policies, measures, and methods related to the prevention and handling of student bullying, carry out corresponding special education for students, and provide necessary family education guidance to the parents of relevant students based on the circumstances.

Faculty and staff, faculty and staff should pay attention to students who may be in a vulnerable or special position due to physical conditions, family backgrounds, academic performance, etc., and where it is discovered that students are isolated or excluded, they shall intervene in a timely manner. Where it is discovered that students have obvious emotional abnormalities, physical injuries, or other such circumstances, they shall promptly communicate and understand the situation, and where there may be circumstances of being bullied or it has already been discovered that students have been bullied, they shall promptly stop it and report it to the school.

For students, schools should educate and support students to take the initiative and promptly report bullying situations they discover, and protect the lawful rights and interests of themselves and others.

About campus sexual assault injury:

The Civil Code of the People's Republic of China and the Criminal Law of the People's Republic of China both make special protection provisions, of which the Law of the People's Republic of China on the Protection of Minors (2021) pays more attention to the prevention of sexual assault on campus. On the basis of this Law, schools shall employ necessary measures to prevent and stop faculty, staff, and others from entering campuses, and establish a work system for preventing sexual assault and sexual harassment of children.

On the one hand, schools should establish systems such as codes of conduct for faculty and staff interactions with students, regulations on the safety management of student dormitories, and regulations on the management of video surveillance, and establish working mechanisms for preventing, reporting, and addressing sexual assault and sexual harassment. Schools shall take necessary measures to prevent and stop faculty, staff, and other persons entering the campus from committing the following acts: (1) engaging in romantic or sexual relations with students, (2) touching or intentionally touching specific parts of students' bodies, or other obscene acts, (3) making teasing, or sexually suggestive words or deeds toward students, (4) showing or disseminating information, books, periodicals, films, audio-visuals, pictures, or other obscene materials containing pornographic or obscene content to students, (5) possessing audio-visual or audiovisual materials containing pornographic or pornographic content, (6) engaging in other illegal and criminal acts that constitute sexual harassment or sexual assault.

On the other hand, schools shall carry out age-appropriate sex education for minor students, and increase children's awareness and ability to protect themselves against sexual assault and harassment. Schools shall promptly employ relevant protective measures for children who have been sexually assaulted or harassed, providing children with professional psychological counseling to help them get out of the psychological shadow in a timely manner, and at the same time shall protect children's privacy and prevent the dissemination of sexual assault and information on sexual harassment, so that children who have suffered sexual assault or sexual harassment do not suffer secondary harm.

For the legislative provisions of the foregoing, please refer to Articles 39 and 40 of *the Law of the People's Republic of China on the Protection of Minor (2021)*:

Article 39
Schools shall establish work systems for the prevention and control of student bullying, and carry out education and training on the prevention and control of student bullying for faculty, staff, students, and so forth.

Schools shall immediately stop students' bullying conduct, notify the parents or other guardians of the minor students who have been bullied and the minor students who have been bullied to participate in the identification and handling of the bullying conduct;

Schools shall strengthen discipline of minor students who carry out bullying in accordance with the law based on the nature and extent of the bullying conduct. Schools must not conceal serious bullying conduct, and shall promptly report it to the public security organs and administrative departments for education, and cooperate with the relevant departments to handle it in accordance with the law.

Article 40
Schools and kindergartens shall establish work systems for preventing sexual assault and sexual harassment of minors.

Schools and kindergartens must not conceal illegal and criminal conduct such as sexual assault or sexual harassment of minors, and shall promptly report it to the public security organs and administrative departments for education, and cooperate with the relevant departments to handle it in accordance with law.

Schools and kindergartens shall carry out sex education appropriate to minors for their age, increasing minors' awareness and ability to protect themselves from sexual assault and harassment. Schools and kindergartens shall promptly employ relevant protective measures for minors who have suffered sexual assault or sexual harassment.

Finally, special provisions are made to strengthen the main responsibility of teachers. Faculty and staff are an important body responsible for the protection of schools, and the Provisions of *the People's Republic of China on the Protection of Minors in Schools (2021)* issued by the Ministry of Education of the People's Republic of China specifically set out requirements for the management of the behavior of teachers and staff.

On the one hand, schools shall strictly implement the system of reporting and inquiring about entry, and shall not employ persons with the following circumstances: (1) those who have been deprived of their political rights or have received a criminal punishment of fixed-term imprisonment or higher for intentional crimes,

(2) those who have been punished by the administration of public security for illegal acts such as prostitution, prostitution, drug abuse, or gambling, (3) those who have been expelled or dismissed for abuse, sexual harassment, corporal punishment, or humiliation of students, and (4) those who have carried out other acts that are included in the scope of professional prohibitions in the field of education.

On the other hand, schools should strengthen the management of faculty and staff, and prevent and stop faculty and staff from carrying out acts prohibited by laws, regulations, rules, and teacher ethics norms. Schools and faculty members shall not carry out the following acts: (1) taking advantage of the convenience of their positions in managing students or opportunities such as admissions examinations, awards, and evaluations, or recommendation evaluations to solicit or accept property, banquets, or other benefits from students and their parents in any form; (2) Selling to students or requesting or designating students to purchase specific tutoring books, workbooks, and other teaching and auxiliary materials or other goods and services for the purpose of profit; (3) Organizing or requiring students to participate in off-campus paid make-up classes, or cooperating with off-campus institutions, (4) Inducing, organizing, or requiring students and their parents to log on to specific commercial websites to participate in activities such as live video broadcasts, online shopping, online voting, and vote swiping, illegally providing or leaking student information, or using the student information in their possession to seek benefits, and (5) other acts of using the authority to manage students to seek improper benefits.

The Law of the People's Republic of China on the Protection of Minor (2021) stipulates the obligation of schools to protect their students from the "impart knowledge and educate" and "safety guarantee", laying the most fundamental foundation for improving the "school protection" system in the "six protection systems" for the child. It can be said that the rights of Chinese minor students on campus such as equality, life, health and freedom, personality rights, privacy rights, education rights, rest rights, property rights, portrait rights, intellectual property rights, participation rights, and the right to appeal are all strongly protected by law.

4.2.2.3 Social Protection Under the Six Protection Systems (Articles 42–63 of the Act)

In accordance with the purpose of the United Nations Convention on the Rights of the Child to protect the legitimate rights and interests of children, all social organizations should take various measures to help children grow up healthily. In the "six protection systems" for the child established by *the Law of the People's Republic of China on the Protection of Minor (2021)*, this law requires all types of social entities to provide corresponding social protection for children, and divides the responsibilities of each type of entity, creating a favorable social environment for the healthy growth of children.

Social protection means that all sectors of society, as the main body of protection responsibility, should protect children in an all-round way in all aspects in a form and measures suited to the characteristics of children (Guo, 2021). *The Law of the People's Republic of China on the Protection of Minor (2021)* clearly states that the whole society should establish a good habit of caring for and caring for children. Under the guidance of this Law, China has promulgated a number of legal documents that give the whole society the responsibility to protect children at the legal level, including:

(1) Urban and rural grassroots mass autonomous organizations need to bear supplementary responsibility for the protection of children;
(2) Relevant organizations should allocate favorable resources to children and provide more welfare and convenient services;
(3) Provisions on the proper and prohibited behaviors of child protection entities such as medical care, media, transportation, urban construction, public resources, and hotels are proposed, emphasizing the obligation to ensure the safety of public places;
(4) All types of organizations should create a positive social atmosphere for children and purify the social environment in accordance with the law;
(5) Prevent children from actively coming into contact with places and activities that are not conducive to their physical and mental health development;
(6) Create a system for inquiring about and prohibiting industries that have close contact with children in order to prevent them from being subjected to sexual assault, abuse, violence, trafficking, and other harms.

For specific provisions, see Article 42 of this Law:

> **Article 42**
> ***The whole society shall establish a good practice of caring for and caring for children. The State encourages, supports, and guides people's organizations, enterprises, public institutions, social organizations, and other organizations and individuals to carry out social activities and services conducive to the healthy growth of children.***

Children are guarded by parents or other guardians at home, protected by teachers and other teachers at school, and protected by third-party organizations when children are not supervised by school or home. *The Law of the People's Republic of China on the Protection of Minors (2021)* requires that residents' committees and villagers' committees shall set up special personnel and posts to be responsible for child protection efforts and perform corresponding functions, as detailed in article 43 of this Law:

> **Article 43**
> ***Residents' committees and villagers' committees shall set up special personnel and posts responsible for efforts on the protection of minors, assist relevant government departments in publicizing laws and regulations on the protection***

of minors, guide, assist, and supervise minors' parents or other guardians in performing guardianship duties in accordance with law, establish information archives for left-behind minors and minors in difficulty, and give care and support.

Residents' committees and villagers' committees shall assist relevant government departments in overseeing the entrusted care of minors, and where it is discovered that the entrusted person lacks the ability to care or is negligent in performing care duties, they shall promptly report it to the relevant government departments, and inform the minors' parents or other guardians, to help and urge the entrusted person to perform their care duties.

On this basis, *the Law of the People's Republic of China on the Protection of Minors (2021)* puts forward more requirements for child protection from the perspective of "social protection", mainly in four aspects.

Firstly, organizations should allocate favorable resources to children and provide more welfare facilities and services. *The Law of the People's Republic of China on the Protection of Minor (2021)* clarifies the scope of children's welfare in terms of their enjoyment of care or preferential treatment, the provision of targeted services, and the establishment of convenient facilities.

On the one hand, the organizations concerned should provide free services to children. Patriotic education bases, libraries, youth palaces, children's activity centers, and children's homes shall be open to children free of charge. Museums, memorial halls, science and technology museums, exhibition halls, art galleries, cultural centers, community public interest Internet access service venues, as well as theaters, stadiums, zoos, botanical gardens, parks, and other such venues, shall be open to children free of charge or at a discounted rate in accordance with relevant provisions. Urban public transportation, as well as highways, railways, waterways, air passenger transport, and so forth, shall implement free or discounted fares for children in accordance with relevant provisions. On the other hand, the State encourages various organizations to actively carry out activities to provide convenient services for children. Patriotic education bases, museums, science and technology museums, art galleries, and other public venues may set up special sessions for children to provide targeted services for children. All kinds of enterprises and institutions can develop their educational resources, set up children's open days, and provide support for children's theme education, social practice, and vocational experience. All kinds of scientific research institutions and scientific and technological social organizations may carry out activities to popularize science among children. All kinds of large public places, public transportation, tourist attractions, and so forth shall set up maternal and infant rooms, infant care tables, toilets, handwashing stations, and other sanitary facilities that are convenient for young children to use, to provide convenience for children. At the same time, *the Law of the People's Republic of China on the Protection of Minors (2021)* emphasizes that no organization or individual may violate relevant provisions by restricting the care or preferential treatment that children should enjoy.

The legislative provisions of the above are set out in articles 44–47 of this Law:

Article 44

Patriotic education bases, libraries, youth palaces, children's activity centers, and children's homes shall be open to minors free of charge, and museums, memorial halls, science and technology museums, exhibition halls, art galleries, cultural centers, community public interest Internet access service venues, as well as theaters, stadiums, zoos, botanical gardens, parks, and other such venues, shall be open to minors free of charge or at a discounted rate in accordance with relevant provisions.

The State encourages patriotic education bases, museums, science and technology museums, art galleries, and other public venues to set up special sessions for minors, to provide targeted services for minors.

The state encourages state organs, enterprises, public institutions, military units, and so forth to develop their educational resources and establish open days for minors, to provide support for minors in thematic education, social practice, professional experience, and so forth.

The state encourages scientific research institutions and scientific and technological social organizations to carry out science popularization activities for minors.

Article 45

Urban public transportation, as well as highways, railways, waterways, air passenger transport, etc., shall implement free or discounted fares for minors in accordance with relevant provisions.

Article 46

The State encourages large public venues, public transportation, tourist attractions, and so forth to set up maternal and infant rooms, infant care tables, toilets, wash basins, and other sanitary facilities that are convenient for young children, to provide convenience for minors.

Article 47

Relevant provisions must not be violated by any organization or individual to restrict the care or preferential treatment that minors should enjoy.

Secondly, organizations should create a good social atmosphere for children and contribute to the development of children's mental health. *The Law of the People's Republic of China on the Protection of Minor (2021)*sets forth requirements for various social organizations such as news media, advertisers, publishing houses, and film and television companies, encouraging them to create, publish, produce, and disseminate books, newspapers, periodicals, films, radio and television programs, stage arts, audio-visual products, electronic publications, and online information that are conducive to the healthy growth of children, and at the same time strengthen publicity on child protection, so as to fully protect the legitimate rights and interests of children. Specifically, there are the following five contents:(1) The news media should strengthen publicity on child protection, and conduct public opinion supervision of acts that violate children's lawful rights and interests. When incidents involving children, the news media should adopt an objective, prudent, and proportionate approach to cover and report on them, and must not infringe upon the children's reputation, privacy, and other lawful rights and interests. (2) For other social organizations or individuals, books, newspapers and periodicals, films, radio and television programs, stage art works, audio-visual products, electronic publications, or online information that are published, published, or disseminated must not contain content that endangers children's physical and psychological health, such as advocating obscenity, pornography, violence, cults, superstition, gambling, suicide, terrorism, separatism, or extremism, and if it contains other content that might impact children's physical and psychological health, a warning shall be made in a conspicuous manner. (3) Advertisements containing content that endangers children's physical and mental health must not be published, broadcast, posted, or distributed by any organization or individual; (4) China has always adopted a zero-tolerance attitude towards pornographic materials and information, and in particular, prohibits all organizations or individuals from using children to engage in pornographic activities. Obscene pornographic materials and online information about children must not be produced, reproduced, published, disseminated, or possessed by any organization or individual. (5) Children's right to privacy in communications should be protected. Children's letters, diaries, e-mails, or other online communications must not be opened, consulted, concealed, destroyed, or illegally deleted by any organization or individual.

For details, please refer to Articles 48–53 and 63 of the Law of the People's Republic of China on the Protection of Minors (2021).

Article 48
The State encourages the creation, publication, production, and dissemination of books, newspapers, periodicals, films, radio and television programs, stage art works, audio-visual products, electronic publications, and online information that are conducive to the healthy growth of minors.

Article 49
The news media shall strengthen publicity on the protection of minors, and conduct public opinion supervision of acts that infringe upon the lawful rights and interests of minors. News media coverage and reporting of incidents involving minors shall be objective, prudent, and proportionate, and must not infringe upon minors' reputation, privacy, or other lawful rights and interests.

Article 50
It is prohibited to produce, reproduce, publish, publish, or disseminate books, newspapers, periodicals, films, radio and television programs, stage art works, audio-visual products, electronic publications, and online information that contains content that promotes obscenity, pornography, violence, cults, superstition, gambling, suicide, terrorism, separatism, extremism, and other content that endangers the physical and mental health of minors.

Article 51
Where any organization or individual publishes, publishes, or disseminates books, newspapers, periodicals, films, radio and television programs, stage art works, audio-visual products, electronic publications, or online information, and contains content that might impact minors' physical and psychological health, a notice shall be given in a conspicuous manner.

Article 52
It is forbidden to produce, reproduce, publish, disseminate, or possess obscene pornographic materials and online information about minors.

Article 53
Advertisements containing content endangering the physical and psychological health of minors must not be published, broadcast, posted, or distributed by any organization or individual.

Article 63
No organization or individual may conceal, destroy, or illegally delete the content of minors' letters, diaries, e-mails, or other online communications. Except in the following circumstances, minors' letters, diaries, e-mails, or other online communication contents must not be opened or accessed by any organization or individual: (1) the parents or other guardians of minors who lack the capacity for civil conduct open or inspect them on behalf of minors; (2) conduct inspections in accordance with law for national security or the investigation of criminal offenses; (3) in emergency situations to protect the minors' personal safety.

Thirdly, a good social atmosphere is inseparable from strong social security, and while working with families and schools to protect children's mental health, "social protection" also includes the protection of children's personal safety. *The Law of the People's Republic of China on the Protection of Minors (2021)* emphasizes that all types of social organizations should create a safe and healthy environment conducive to the growth of children, and puts forward requirements for different entities, mainly involving child injury protection and daily life.

On the one hand, because children are inferior to adults in terms of physical fitness and ideological cognition, and are often the targets of criminals, *the Law of the People's Republic of China on the Protection of Minors (2021)* strictly prohibits any organization or individual from committing any illegal or criminal acts against children, and clearly states that no organization or individual shall carry out acts such as abduction, kidnapping, abuse, illegal adoption, sexual assault, or sexual harassment against children, and shall not coerce, entice, instigate, or use children to engage in illegal and criminal activities, otherwise they will bear legal responsibility. On the other hand, in order to fully ensure the safe growth of children, the Law of *the People's Republic of China on the Protection of Minors (2021)* clarifies the responsibilities of different entities: (1) the obligation of manufacturers and sellers of various daily necessities to ensure quality, (2) the obligation of operators of public places to provide safety measures, and (3) the obligation of accommodation operators to verify the situation of children.

For details, please refer to Articles 54–57 of the Law of the People's Republic of China on the Protection of Minors (2021):

Article 54
It is forbidden to abduct, kidnap, abuse, or illegally adopt minors, and to sexually assault or harass minors. It is prohibited to coerce, entice, or instigate minors to participate in underworld criminal organizations or engage in illegal or criminal activities. It is forbidden to coerce, deceive, or exploit minors to beg.

Article 55
The production and sale of food, medicines, toys, utensils, game and amusement equipment, amusement facilities, and so forth for minors shall comply with national or industry standards, and must not endanger minors' physical safety and physical and mental health. The producer of the above-mentioned products shall indicate the precautions in a conspicuous position and those that do not indicate the precautions shall not be sold.

Article 56
Public venues where minors gather for concentrated activities shall comply with national or industry security standards, and employ corresponding security protection measures. Facilities that may have safety risks shall be regularly maintained, safety warning signs shall be set up in conspicuous places, and the appropriate age range and precautions shall be indicated; Large-scale shopping malls, supermarkets, hospitals, libraries, museums, science and technology museums, amusement parks, stations, docks, airports, tourist attractions, and other such venues shall set up security alert systems for searching for lost minors. After receiving a request for help, the site operating unit shall immediately activate the security alarm system, organize

personnel to conduct a search and report to the public security organs. When emergencies occur in public places, priority shall be given to the rescue of minors.

Article 57

When hostels, guesthouses, hotels, and other lodging operators accept minors to stay in the hotel, or when they accept minors and adults to stay together, they shall inquire about the contact information of their parents or other guardians, the identity and relationship of the occupants, and other relevant information.

Finally, through the two major measures of avoiding children's contact with special activities and purifying the team of practitioners who have close contact with children, the "social protection" has been further improved, and the "six protection systems" for the children have been strengthened.

The first measure is to avoid children's active contact with places and activities that are not conducive to their physical and mental development. On the one hand, *the Law of the People's Republic of China on the Protection of Minors (2021)* prohibits any organization or individual from opening commercial entertainment venues or providing products harmful to the physical and mental health of children. For-profit entertainment venues, bars, Internet cafes, tobacco, alcohol, and lottery ticket sales outlets, etc., have a special environment and complex personnel, which have many negative impacts on children's physical and mental health and are not suitable for children's activities. The operators of the above-mentioned establishments shall not provide services to children under the age of 18, and shall not set up business premises in the vicinity of schools and kindergartens. At the same time, it is forbidden for any organization or individual to provide or sell controlled knives or other equipment that may cause serious injury to children. Business operators shall set up signs in conspicuous places prohibiting or restricting children under the age of 18, and where it is difficult to determine whether they are over the age of 18, they shall be required to present their identity documents. On the other hand, except as specifically provided by law, no organization or individual may recruit children under the age of 16 when recruiting. China has responded positively to the United Nations Convention on the Rights of the Child and has always taken a negative attitude towards the use of child labor. In 2002, the State Council of China promulgated the Provisions of the People's Republic of China on the Prohibition of Child Labor, which stipulates that no unit or individual may recruit or introduce children under the age of 16 to employment, and then *the Law of the People's Republic of China on the Protection of Minors (2021)* and *the Labor Law of the People's Republic of China* and other prohibitive provisions are made at the legal level, and when an employer recruits a person, it must verify the ID card of the recruited person; Children under the age of 16 are not allowed to be hired. At the same time, employers may recruit children who have reached the age of 16 but are not yet 18 years old, provided that they have the consent of the children and their guardians, and shall strictly implement the provisions of the State in terms of types of work, working hours, labor intensity and protective measures, and shall not arrange for them to engage in excessively heavy, toxic, harmful or other work or dangerous work that endangers the physical and mental health of children. In special circumstances, employers may recruit children under the age of 16, for example, literary and sports units may, with the consent of the children's parents or other guardians, recruit professional literary and artistic workers or athletes under the age of 16, but shall ensure the physical and mental health of the children and their right to receive compulsory education, and must not organize children to perform performances or other activities that endanger their physical and mental health.

For details, please refer to Articles 58–61 of the Law of the People's Republic of China on the Protection of Minors (2021):

Article 58
For-profit entertainment venues, bars, Internet access service business sites, and other venues unsuitable for minors must not be set up in the vicinity of schools and kindergartens.

Operators of for-profit singing and dancing entertainment venues, bars, internet access service business sites, and other venues for activities that are not suitable for minors must not allow minors to enter;

Business operators shall set up signs in conspicuous locations prohibiting or restricting minors from entering, and where it is difficult to determine whether they are minors, they shall be required to present their identity documents.

Article 59
Cigarettes, alcohol, and lottery sales outlets shall not be set up around schools and kindergartens. It is forbidden to sell cigarettes, alcohol, or lottery tickets to minors, or to redeem lottery prizes.

Tobacco, alcohol, and lottery operators shall set up signs in conspicuous places that do not sell tobacco, alcohol, or lottery tickets to minors;

No one is allowed to smoke or drink alcohol in schools, kindergartens, and other public places where minors gather for activities.

Article 60
It is forbidden to provide or sell controlled knives or other equipment that may cause serious injury to minors. Where it is difficult for business operators to determine whether the purchaser is a minor, they shall be required to present their identity documents.

Article 61
Minors under the age of 16 must not be recruited by any organization or individual, except as otherwise provided by the State.

For-profit entertainment venues, bars, internet access service business sites, and other venues that are not suitable for minors must not recruit minors who are already 16 years old.

Units and individuals employing minors who have reached the age of 16 shall implement state provisions on the type of work, working hours, labor intensity, and protective measures, and must not arrange for them to engage in excessively heavy, toxic, harmful, or other labor or dangerous work that endangers the minors' physical and psychological health.

Minors must not be organized by any organization or individual to carry out performances or other activities that endanger their physical and psychological health. With the consent of minors' parents or other guardians, where minors participate in performances, program productions, and other such activities, the organizers of the activities shall protect the lawful rights and interests of minors in accordance with relevant state provisions.

The second measure is to clarify the provisions of the employment inquiry system. *The Law of the People's Republic of China on the Protection of Minors (2021)* clarifies the obligation to inquire into units with close contact with children, requiring units with close contact with children to regularly check whether their staff have serious criminal records every year.

Units that have close contact with children refer to enterprises, public institutions, and social organizations that have responsibilities for children's education, training, guardianship, rescue, care, medical care, and so forth, mainly including (1) schools, kindergartens, and other educational institutions, and off-campus training institutions; (2) child aid and protection institutions, child welfare establishments, and other child placement and aid institutions; (3) infant and child care service establishments and early education service establishments; (4) off-campus childcare, temporary care and domestic service establishments; (5) Medical institutions that provide medical services for children, etc. When recruiting staff, the above-mentioned units shall inquire with the public security organs and people's procuratorates whether the applicant has a record of serious violations or crimes, and if it is discovered that the applicant has a record of sexual assault, abuse, trafficking, violent injury, or other violations or crimes, they must not be hired, and as far as possible isolate unfavorable factors that might affect the healthy growth of children. For details, please refer to Article 62 of *the Law of the People's Republic of China on the Protection of Minors (2021)*:

Article 62

When recruiting staff for units that have close contact with minors, they shall inquire with the public security organs and people's procuratorates whether the applicants have a record of sexual assault, abuse, trafficking, violent injury, or other violations or crimes; Units that have close contact with minors shall periodically conduct annual inquiries into whether staff members have

the illegal or criminal records described above. Where it is discovered through inquiries or other means that their staff members have the conduct described above, they shall be promptly dismissed.

In summary, social protection is ultimately about creating a social environment conducive to the healthy growth of children, specifically for the safety and physical health of children, and for children's mental and mental health. It is conducive to the social and cultural protection of children, labor protection, and other aspects. *The Law of the People's Republic of China on the Protection of Minor (2021)* fully integrates the responsibilities and obligations of all parties in society to promote the all-round development of children and stipulates that the main bodies responsible for child protection work include individuals, grassroots autonomous organizations, enterprises and institutions, etc., which is of significance for promoting the formation of a social consensus on child protection.

4.2.2.4 Network Protection Under the Six Protection Systems (Articles 64–80 of the Act)

In the Internet era, cyberspace, as an extension of the real world such as family, school, and society, has become a new environment for children's growth. As an important part of "six protection systems" for the child, Network protection requires the cooperation of all entities, requiring the state, society, schools, and families to perform their respective duties to protect the security of children's personal information. *The Law of the People's Republic of China on the Protection of Minor (2021)*, comprehensively regulates the concept of online protection, online environment management, related corporate responsibility, online information management, personal online information protection, and prevention and control of online addiction. It should be pointed out that the Regulations of the People's Republic of China on the Protection of Minors Online, promulgated by the State Council of China on January 1, 2024, make more detailed and clear provisions for the protection of children online, protecting children's rights to use the Internet in accordance with the law, while ensuring and guiding children's safe and reasonable use of the Internet, in an effort to achieve all-round protection for children online and offline ("Structural Cultivation of Youth Internet Literacy," 2022).

The most important thing for children's online protection is to cultivate and enhance children's Internet literacy. Cyber literacy refers to an individual's ability to use the Internet correctly and effectively, including cognition of online media, information identification, cyber security, cyber ethics, application of cyber technology, cyber participation and collaboration, and the use of cyber for self-development (Central Committee of the Communist Youth League & China Internet Information Center, 2021).

The Law of the People's Republic of China on the Protection of Minor (2021), clearly states that the state, society, schools, and families should work together to cultivate and improve children's cyber literacy, enhance children's awareness and ability to use the Internet in a scientific, civilized, safe, and rational manner, and protect children's lawful rights and interests in cyberspace. On the one hand, the state encourages and supports the research and development, production, and use of network protection software, smart terminal products, children's models, children's zones, and other network technologies, products, and services that specifically target children and adapt to the laws and characteristics of children's physical and mental health development, strengthening the establishment and transformation of an accessible online environment, and promoting minors to broaden their horizons, cultivate their sentiments, and improve their quality. On the other hand, the state encourages and supports the production, reproduction, publication, and dissemination of online information that carries forward the Core Socialist Values and advanced socialist culture, revolutionary culture, and excellent traditional Chinese culture, forging a strong sense of community for the Chinese nation, cultivating children's feelings for the country and good moral character, guiding children to develop good living habits and behavioral habits, and creating a clear cyberspace and a positive online ecology conducive to the healthy growth of minors.

For details, please refer to Articles 64 and 65 of the Law of the People's Republic of China on the Protection of Minors (2021):

Article 64

The state, society, schools, and families shall strengthen publicity and education on minors' online literacy, cultivating and increasing minors' online literacy, enhancing minors' awareness and ability to use the internet in a scientific, civilized, safe, and reasonable manner, and safeguarding minors' lawful rights and interests in cyberspace.

Article 65

The State encourages and supports the creation and dissemination of online content that is conducive to the healthy growth of minors, and encourages and supports the research and development, production, and use of online technologies, products, and services that specifically target minors and are suitable for minors' physical and psychological health.

In recent years, government departments, schools, families, and all sectors of society have paid more and more attention to the cultivation of children's Internet literacy, and have adopted a series of measures. *The Law of the People's Republic of China on the Protection of Minors (2021)* puts forward separate requirements for all parties in terms of protecting children's privacy and personal information, increasing the prevention and control of online addiction, standardizing the management of online live streaming, and prohibiting cyberbullying, so as to ensure the effective operation of children's online protection mechanisms. On this basis, government departments at all levels have continuously introduced and improved policies and regulations on children's Internet use and safety; schools in many places have set up independent courses for Internet literacy education; more and more parents are paying more and more attention to improving their own Internet literacy and setting an example for their children in terms of learning Internet knowledge and skills; social organizations have integrated resources from all walks of life to carefully plan a variety of public welfare projects and series of activities; and Internet companies have actively undertaken social responsibilities and made use of technological advantages to promote child protection work (Tong, 2021).

Regarding the government's responsibilities in "online protection", *the Law of the People's Republic of China on the Protection of Minors (2021)* proposes that local people's governments at the county level or above and their relevant departments shall do a good job of protecting children online in accordance with their respective duties. The government shall make scientific plans and rational distributions, promote the balanced and coordinated development of public-interest online services, strengthen the establishment of public cultural facilities that provide public-interest online services, and improve the conditions for children to access the Internet. Among them, the state internet information department is responsible for overall planning and coordination, and the state press and publication and film departments, as well as the State Council's relevant departments such as for education, telecommunications, public security, civil affairs, culture and tourism, health, market supervision and management, and radio and television, are to cooperate on the basis of their respective duties.

For the national cyberspace administration, *the Law of the People's Republic of China on the Protection of Minors (2021)* puts forward three macro requirements: First, strengthen supervision and inspection of children's online protection efforts, punish the use of the Internet to engage in activities that endanger children's physical and mental health, and provide children with a safe and healthy online environment. For example, clarify the relevant technical standards or requirements for children's online protection software and smart terminal products specifically intended for use by children, and guide and supervise network-related industry organizations to assess the effectiveness of the use of smart terminal products in accordance with relevant technical standards and requirements. Second, with the assistance of departments such as public security, culture and tourism, press and publication, film, radio, and television, and based on the need to protect children of different ages, determine the type, scope, and criteria for judging online information that may impact children's physical and mental health. Third, regularly carry out publicity and education on the prevention of children's internet addiction, supervising the performance of online product and service providers in their obligations to prevent children's internet addiction, and at the same time guiding families, schools, and social organizations to cooperate with each other to adopt scientific and reasonable methods to prevent and intervene in children's internet addiction.

For the government education department, according to *the Law of the People's Republic of China on the Protection of Minors (2021)*, on the one hand, online literacy education should be included in the content of school quality education, and the national cyberspace administration should formulate children's online literacy assessment indicators. On the other hand, schools should be guided and supported in carrying out children's online literacy education, cultivating children's awareness of cyber security, civility, behavioral habits, and protection skills around the formation of awareness of online ethics, the cultivation of online rule of law concepts, the capacity building of online use, and the protection of personal and property security. For example, by assigning primary and secondary school with instructors with corresponding professional competence, purchasing services from the government, or encouraging primary and secondary schools to procure relevant services on their own, we can provide students with high-quality online literacy education courses.

While the above-mentioned departments provide "online protection", *the Law of the People's Republic of China on the Protection of Minors (2021)* also clearly requires relevant government departments such as press and publication, education, health, culture and tourism, public security, and market supervision and management to do a good job of protecting children online in accordance with their respective duties, to carry out supervision and management of institutions engaged in the prevention and intervention of children's Internet addiction, and to regularly carry out publicity and education on the prevention of minors' Internet addiction, and to assist the national internet information department in providing children with safe, Healthy online environment.

For details, please refer to Articles 66–68 of the Law of the People's Republic of China on the Protection of Minors (2021):

Article 66

Internet information departments and other relevant departments shall strengthen oversight and inspections of efforts to protect minors online, lawfully punish the use of the internet to engage in activities that endanger minors' physical and psychological health, and provide a safe and healthy online environment for minors.

Article 67

Internet information departments, in conjunction with departments such as for public security, culture and tourism, press and publication, film, and radio and television, are to determine the type, scope, and criteria for judging online information that might impact minors' physical and psychological health, based on the needs of protecting minors at different ages.

Article 68

Departments such as for press and publication, education, health, culture and tourism, and internet information shall periodically carry out publicity and education on preventing minors from becoming addicted to the internet, supervise the performance of online product and service providers in their obligations to prevent minors from becoming addicted to the internet, and guide families, schools, and social organizations to cooperate with each other and employ scientific and reasonable methods to prevent and intervene in

minors' addiction to the internet. Minors' addiction to the internet must not be interfered with by any organization or individual in a manner that harms minors' physical and psychological health.

While the government is leading, families and schools should also assist in "online protection" in accordance with relevant laws and policies, and schools and families should educate and guide children to participate in activities that are beneficial to their physical and mental health, use the Internet scientifically, civilly, safely, and rationally, and prevent and intervene in children's Internet addiction.

With regard to the family's responsibilities in "online protection", according to *the Law of the People's Republic of China on the Protection of Minors (2021)*, children's parents and other guardians should strengthen the establishment of family education and family style, improve their own online literacy, regulate their own use of the Internet, and strengthen education, demonstration, guidance, and supervision of children's use of the Internet. Specifically, it can be implemented in the following aspects:

Firstly, parents should avoid excessive use of the Internet by their children. Parents and children can work together to create a set of Internet rules as early as possible and adjust them as their child's age and needs change. At the same time, they should understand the real needs of their child. Pay attention to how children are online and what they do online, and through observation, listening, and communication, understand the needs behind children's relevant behaviors, so as to carry out targeted regulation and guidance.

Secondly, parents should help their children reject cyberbullying, parents should guide children to be civilized online, they can discuss with their children the possible negative effects and serious consequences of bullying others, encourage children to manage their emotions, control their impulses, and solve interpersonal conflicts between peers. At the same time, pay attention to children's daily state. Pay close attention to changes in the child's online and offline social status and daily emotional behavior, take the initiative to inquire, and intervene in a timely manner once it is discovered that children have encountered or committed cyberbullying behavior, and if illegal or criminal conduct is involved, reporting the incident to the public security organs and seek assistance.

Thirdly, parents should guide their children to protect their personal information. Advise children to pay attention to the account privacy settings of online social platforms, and think twice before sharing information that involves personal privacy, such as name, address, school, personal photo, contact information, etc. Guide children to learn to identify suspicious links and web pages, and pay attention to the confidentiality of account passwords and payment information.

Fourthly, parents should avoid their children's exposure to inappropriate online information. Parents can work with their children to find and filter content on the Internet that is appropriate for their children's age and stage of physical and mental development, and can also consider installing content-blocking and filtering software on electronic devices to help children learn to use auxiliary tools. In short, the premise of guiding children's growth is to lead by example, parents and other family members should regulate their own use of the Internet, set a good example for children, and try their best to create a good environment for their children to grow up.

With regard to schools' responsibilities in "network protection", minor students will also be exposed to the internet during their study and life at school, and in order to help students develop healthily, schools shall include content such as improving students' online literacy in education and teaching activities, and reasonably use the internet to carry out teaching activities.

First of all, establish and improve the management system for students to access the Internet during school, standardize the management of smart terminal products brought into school by minor students in accordance with the law, and help students develop good Internet habits. When schools provide internet access service facilities for minor students, they shall install children's online protection software or employ other technical measures for security protection. Secondly, cultivate students' awareness of network security and network rule of law, and enhances students' ability to obtain, analyze, and judge network information. If schools discover that minor students are addicted to the internet, they shall promptly inform their parents or other guardians, jointly educate and guide the minor students, and help them return to normal study and life. Finally, schools should strengthen guidance and training for teachers, and improve teachers' ability to identify and intervene early in the internet use of minor students.

For details, please refer to Articles 69–71 of the Law of the People's Republic of China on the Protection of Minors (2021):

Article 69
Internet access service facilities provided to minors in schools, communities, libraries, cultural centers, youth palaces, and other such venues shall install software for the protection of minors or employ other technical measures for security protection.

Article 70
Schools shall make reasonable use of the Internet to carry out teaching activities. Without the permission of the school, minor students must not bring mobile phones and other smart terminal products into the classroom, and those brought into the school shall be uniformly managed. Where schools discover that minor students are addicted to the internet, they shall promptly inform their parents or other guardians, jointly educate and guide the minor students, and help them return to normal study and life.

Article 71
Minors' parents or other guardians shall increase their internet literacy, regulate their own use of the internet, and strengthen guidance and oversight of minors' use of the internet. Minors' parents or other guardians shall avoid

minors' exposure to online information that is harmful or might impact their physical and psychological health through methods such as installing software for the protection of minors' networks on smart terminal products, selecting service models and management functions suitable for minors, and reasonably arranging the time minors spend using the internet, to effectively prevent minors from becoming addicted to the internet.

With regard to society's role in "cyber protection", when cyberspace is a new environment for children to grow up in, then the scope of the functions of various social organizations to protect children should also be extended to the Internet. In "Network protection", the state places special emphasis on the responsibilities of cyber-related industry organizations. In order to effectively advance efforts to "protect children online", providers of online products and services, personal information processors, and manufacturers and sellers of smart terminal products shall comply with laws, administrative regulations, and relevant state provisions, respect social mores, abide by business ethics, be honest and trustworthy, perform obligations to protect children online and assume social responsibility. At the same time, news media, social groups, and other organizations in the internet-related industry shall lawfully complete efforts to protect children online within the scope of their operations.

For online information processors, children's privacy and personal information shall be protected. According to *the Law of the People's Republic of China on the Protection of Minors (2021)*, online information processors shall follow the principles of legality, legitimacy, and necessity when processing children's personal information online, and at the same time, when processing the personal information of children under the age of 14, they shall obtain the consent of the child's parents or other guardians. The "Provisions of the People's Republic of China on the Online Protection of Children's Personal Information" make detailed provisions on this basis: First, personal information processors shall strictly set the access rights of information to their staff based on the principle of minimum authorization, and control the scope of children's personal information. Second, where leaks, alterations, or losses of children's personal information occur or might occur, personal information handlers shall immediately initiate an emergency response plan for personal information security incidents, employ remedial measures, promptly report to departments such as for internet information, and inform the affected children and their guardians of the incident. Third, personal information handlers shall conduct annual compliance audits of their handling of children's personal information in compliance with laws and administrative regulations, either on their own or by retaining a professional body, and promptly report the audit to departments such as for internet information.

For providers of online products and services, children must not be provided with products and services that induce them to become addicted. *The Law of the People's Republic of China on the Protection of Minors (2021)* requires that if an internet service provider discovers that a child has published private information online, it shall promptly alert and take necessary protective measures. Manufacturers and sellers of smart terminal products of network products and service providers shall install children's online protection software on their products, or inform users in a conspicuous manner of the channels and methods for installing children's online protection software. Online service providers such as online games, online livestreams, online audio and video, and online social networking shall set up corresponding functions such as time management, authority management, and consumption management for children's use of their services. Online education network products and services that target children shall follow laws, administrative regulations, and relevant state provisions, and provide corresponding products and services on the basis of the characteristics of children's physical and mental development and cognitive abilities at different ages, and must not insert links to online games, and must not push advertisements or other information unrelated to teaching.

For online gaming service providers, according to "*the Law of the People's Republic of China on the Protection of Minors" (2021)*, first, they should classify game products in accordance with relevant national provisions and standards, make age-appropriate prompts, and establish and improve game rules to prevent children from becoming addicted to the Internet. Children must not be allowed to come into contact with inappropriate games or game functions, and online games that have not been approved in accordance with law must not be operated. Second, children should be required to register and log in to online games with real identity information, and establish a unified electronic identity authentication system for children's online games.

Online live streaming service providers must not provide online live streaming publisher account registration services for children under the age of 16, and when providing online live streaming publisher account registration services to children between the ages of 16 and 18, their identity information shall be verified, and the consent of their parents or other guardians shall be obtained.

For details, please refer to Articles 72–76 of the Law of the People's Republic of China on the Protection of Minors (2021):

Article 72
Where information processors process minors' personal information online, they shall follow the principles of legality, legitimacy, and necessity.

Where the personal information of minors under the age of 14 is handled, the consent of the minors' parents or other guardians shall be obtained, except as otherwise provided by laws and administrative regulations.

Where minors, parents, or other guardians request that information handlers correct or delete minors' personal information, the information handlers shall promptly employ measures to correct or delete it, except as otherwise provided by laws and administrative regulations.

Article 73
Where network service providers discover that minors have published private information online, they shall promptly give a reminder and employ necessary protective measures.

Article 74
Providers of online products and services must not provide minors with products and services that induce them to become addicted.

Online service providers such as online games, online live streaming, online audio and video, and online social networking shall set up functions such as time management, authority management, and consumption management for minors' use of their services.

Online education network products and services that target minors must not insert links to online games, and must not push advertisements or other information unrelated to teaching.

Article 75
Online games may only be operated after approval in accordance with law. The state is to establish a uniform electronic identity authentication system for minors in online games.

Online gaming service providers shall require minors to register and log in to online games with their real identity information.

Online gaming service providers shall follow relevant state provisions and standards to categorize game products, make age-appropriate reminders, employ technical measures, and must not allow minors to come into contact with inappropriate games or game functions.

Online gaming service providers must not provide online gaming services to minors between 10 p.m. and 8 p.m. the next day.

Article 76
Online live streaming service providers must not provide online live streaming publisher account registration services for minors under the age of 16, and when providing online live streaming publisher account registration services for minors who are at least 16 years old, they shall verify their identity information and obtain the consent of their parents or other guardians.

In addition to the above-mentioned specific measures, *the Law of the People's Republic of China on the Protection of Minors (2021)* clearly requires those in the online industry to participate in the governance of "cyberbullying". No organization or individual must use text, pictures, audio, video, or other forms of online bullying to carry out cyberbullying such as insulting, defaming, threatening, or maliciously damaging the image of children. Specifically, there are the following requirements:(1) Providers of online products and services shall establish convenient, reasonable, and effective channels for complaints and reports, disclose information such as the methods for complaints and reports, and promptly accept and handle complaints and reports involving children. (2) Network product and service providers shall establish and complete mechanisms for early warning, prevention, identification, monitoring, and disposition of cyberbullying, set up functions and channels to facilitate children and their guardians to preserve records of cyberbullying and exercise their right to notify, and provide cyberbullying information protection options that facilitate children to set up blocks of unfamiliar users, the visibility of information posted by themselves, prohibit the reproduction or comment of information posted by themselves, and prohibit sending messages to themselves. (3) Where network service providers discover that users have published or transmitted information that contains content that endangers children's physical and psychological health, they shall immediately stop the transmission of the relevant information, employ measures to address it such as deleting, blocking, or disconnecting links, store relevant records, and report it to departments such as for internet information and public security. (4) Where network service providers discover that users are using their network services to commit illegal or criminal acts against minors, they shall immediately stop providing network services to the users, store relevant records, and report to the public security organs.

For details, please refer to Articles 77–80 of the Law of the People's Republic of China on the Protection of Minors (2021):

Article 77
Minors who have been cyberbullied, as well as their parents or other guardians, must not be notified by any organization or individual through the Internet in the form of text, pictures, audio, or video, and their parents or other guardians to notify the network service provider to take measures such as deleting, blocking, or disconnecting links. After receiving the notice, network service providers shall promptly employ necessary measures to stop cyberbullying and prevent the spread of information.

Article 78
Providers of online products and services shall establish convenient, reasonable, and effective channels for complaints and reports, disclose information such as the methods for complaints and reports, and promptly accept and handle complaints and reports involving minors.

Article 79
Any organization or individual discovers that online products or services contain information that endangers the physical and psychological health of minors, and has the right to make a complaint or report to the provider of the network product or service, or the internet information and public security departments.

Article 80

Where network service providers discover that users have published or disseminated information that might impact minors' physical and psychological health, and have not made a conspicuous reminder, they shall make a reminder or notify the user to give a reminder.

Where network service providers discover that users have published or disseminated information that contains content that endangers minors' physical and psychological health, they shall immediately stop transmitting the relevant information, employ measures to address it such as deleting, blocking, or disconnecting links, store relevant records, and report it to departments such as for internet information and public security.

Where network service providers discover that users are using their network services to commit illegal or criminal conduct against minors, they shall immediately stop providing network services to the users, store relevant records, and report to the public security organs.

In addition to the Internet-related industries, the Regulations of the People's Republic of China on the Protection of Minors Online, issued by the State Council of China, provide that social groups, such as the Communist Youth League, the Women's Federation, the Trade Union, the Disabled Persons' Federation, the Working Committee for the Care of the Next Generation, the Youth Federation, the Student Federation, the Young Pioneers, and other people's organizations, relevant social organizations, and grassroots mass autonomous organizations, shall assist the relevant departments in efforts to protect children online and protect the lawful rights and interests of children. Units that have close contact with children, such as communities, libraries, cultural centers, youth palaces, and other venues, shall install children's online protection software or employ other technical security measures for Internet access service facilities provided to children. For news media, they shall use methods such as news reports, special columns (programs), and public interest advertisements to carry out publicity on laws, regulations, policy measures, typical cases, and relevant knowledge on the protection of minors online, conduct public opinion oversight of conduct that violates the lawful rights and interests of minors, and guide the entire society to participate in the protection of minors online.

Network protection work of the child should adhere to the "Principle in the Best Interests of the Child", adapt to the laws and characteristics of children's healthy physical and mental development and cyberspace, and implement social co-governance, providing a pure land for child protection. Among them, the cultivation of children's Internet literacy is a long-term project, that aims to cultivate children with noble character, mature cognition, and strong creativity, promote children's all-round development, and help children achieve self-service, self-shaping, and self-improvement in the Internet.

4.2.2.5 Government Protection Under the Six Protection Systems (Articles 81–99 of the Act)

Articles 42–45 of *the United Nations Convention on the Rights of the Child (CRC)* clearly require all countries to actively implement the Convention, to carry out the protection of children's rights under the guidance of the principles of the Convention, to provide the most favorable guarantee for the realization of children's rights in various environments such as the family, school, and society through the executive power, and to enable the public to understand the responsibilities of various government organs. *The Law of the People's Republic of China on the Protection of Minors (2021)* establishes "Government protection" at the legal level, and identifies the state (government) as the main body responsible for the protection of children, providing a strong guarantee for safeguarding the legitimate rights and interests of children.

Government protection refers to the protection of children's rights by governments at all levels through their administrative powers within the scope of their duties, and the provision of maximum support for the healthy growth of children. In particular, when children are not effectively guarded for various reasons, the relevant functional departments of the government will take care of and rescue them, so government protection can also be understood as state guardianship. As an important part of the "six protection systems" for the child, *the Law of the People's Republic of China on the Protection of Minors (2021)* specifically stipulates the government child protection institutions and coordination mechanisms established in the "General Provisions". First, the office system of the coordination mechanism is stipulated; secondly, the objects and contents of the coordination mechanism are stipulated, mainly including the support and guarantee of the natural and prohibited behaviors in "family protection, school protection, social protection, and network protection"; thirdly, the state guardianship responsibilities undertaken by the civil affairs departments are stipulated; and finally, a series of specific systems are established to safeguard the legitimate rights and interests of children.

The Law of the People's Republic of China on the Protection of Minors (2021) emphasizes the responsibility of the state (government) to protect in the general provisions and makes a top-level design for the government to carry out child protection work, requiring the government to establish special child protection institutions and coordination mechanisms. At the same time, in accordance with the principle of the best interests of the child, when the primary responsible person in the family, school, society, the Internet, and other environments cannot provide adequate protection to the child, the state (government), as the main body responsible for child protection, is responsible for regulating, supervising, guiding, rewarding and punishing the child protection behavior of the primary responsible entity in the aforementioned different environments. At the macro level, in April 2021, the State Council established the "State Council Leading Group for Child Protection" as the State Council's deliberative and coordinating body, and set up its office in the Ministry of Civil Affairs, which is mainly responsible for the following duties: (1) to coordinate the national child protection work, and to study and deliberate on major child protection issues, (2) to coordinate and promote the formulation and implementation of child protection plans, policies, measures, and standards by relevant units, and (3) to supervise and inspect the implementation of the Law on the Protection of Minors and other relevant laws, regulations, and systems. (4) Guide all regions and relevant units to do a good job of child protection efforts in accordance with their legally-prescribed duties, and strengthen oversight and accountability of units or regions that fail to perform their duties and cause a negative impact; (5) Summarize and promote work experience in child protection, organize and carry out statistical surveys, publicity, education, and commendation and reward work; and complete other matters assigned by the Party Central Committee and the State Council. At the micro level, township people's governments and neighborhood offices are to set up child protection workstations or designate specialized personnel to handle child-related matters in a timely manner, and support residents' committees and villagers' committees in setting up special personnel and posts to do a good job in child protection work. At the same time, on the basis of the predominance of specialized institutions for child protection, this Law sets out in detail the duties and obligations of other government departments, such as the education department and the civil affairs department, and each department cooperates with each other to play the role of "government protection" in areas such as education guarantees, safety guarantees, health care, and social assistance, so as to safeguard the legitimate rights and interests of children.

For details, please refer to Articles 9 and 81 of this Law:

Article 9

People's governments at the county level or above shall establish coordination mechanisms for child protection efforts, to plan, coordinate, supervise, and guide relevant departments to do a good job of child protection efforts within the scope of their respective duties.

Article 81

The functional departments of people's governments at the county level or above undertaking specific work on coordination mechanisms for the protection of minors shall clarify the relevant internal bodies or specialized personnel responsible for undertaking efforts on the protection of minors. Township people's governments and neighborhood offices shall establish work stations for the protection of minors or designate specialized personnel to promptly handle matters related to minors.

Under the guidance of the Child Protection Coordination Mechanism, the first emphasis on "government protection" is the family education of children. *The Law of the People's Republic of China on the Protection of Minors (2021)* includes the government as the main body of responsibility for family education and requires the government to actively carry out family education guidance services, so as to ensure that children have a good family education environment. Family education guidance services refer to the educational guidance and support provided by professional institutions or professionals for families to help parents better understand their children's growth needs, and provide scientific educational methods and strategies to promote the all-round development of children. Parents shall learn about family education, accept guidance on family education, and create a good, harmonious, and civilized family environment. Under the promotion of multiple organizations led by the government's education department, family education is no longer just the responsibility of the "family", but also the common responsibility of multiple organizations dominated by the government. For details, see Article 82 of this Law:

> **Article 82**
> ***All levels of government are to include family education guidance services in the urban and rural public service system, carry out publicity on family education knowledge, and encourage and support relevant people's organizations, enterprises, public institutions, and social organizations to carry out family education guidance services.***

Under the guidance of the Child Protection Coordination Mechanism, the second emphasis of "government protection" is on the education and protection of children in schools. *The Law of the People's Republic of China on the Protection of Minors (2021)* emphasizes that the government should develop all types of education, encourage and support schools to fulfill their responsibilities, and protect children's right to education as well as their personal safety.

On the one hand, government departments, mainly the education sector, should ensure that children receive an educational environment. Children's right to education is enshrined in *the Constitution of the People's Republic of China*, and *the United Nations Convention on the Rights of the Child* calls on States to guarantee children's right to education. *The Law of the People's Republic of China on the Protection of Minors* puts forward clear requirements for the government: people's governments at all levels shall take various measures to ensure that children enter schools to receive education, and to protect the right to education of all children, including left-behind children, children with disabilities, and children in difficulty, and the education administrative departments shall bear the primary responsibility. Relevant government departments, mainly administrative departments for education, shall ensure children's right to education in the following aspects: (1) Employ measures to ensure that left-behind children, children in difficult circumstances, and children with disabilities receive pre-school, compulsory, and vocational education. (2) Develop childcare and preschool education, run infant care service institutions and kindergartens, and support social forces to set up maternal and infant rooms, infant care service institutions, and kindergartens in accordance with the law. (3) Cultivate and train the education personnel of infant and child care service institutions and kindergartens, and improve their professional ethics and professional ability. (4) Develop vocational education, ensure that children receive vocational education or vocational skills training, and encourage and support people's organizations, enterprises, public institutions, and social organizations to provide vocational skills training services for minors. (5) Employ various measures to ensure that children with disabilities who have the ability to receive ordinary education and are able to adapt to campus life receive education in the nearest ordinary schools and kindergartens, and ensure that children with disabilities who do not have the ability to receive ordinary education receive education in special education schools and kindergartens. At the same time, ensure the conditions for running and running special education schools and kindergartens, and encourage and support social forces to set up special education schools and kindergartens.

For details, please refer to Articles 83–86 of the Law of the People's Republic of China on the Protection of Minors (2021):

Article 83
People's governments at all levels shall safeguard minors' right to receive education, and take measures to ensure that left-behind minors, minors in difficult circumstances, and minors with disabilities receive compulsory education. The administrative departments for education shall order their parents or other guardians to send minor students who have dropped out of school to receive compulsory education for minor students who have not yet completed compulsory education.

Article 84
People's governments at all levels shall develop childcare and pre-school education, run infant and child care service institutions and kindergartens, and support social forces in establishing maternal and infant rooms, infant and child care service establishments, and kindergartens in accordance with the law. Local people's governments at the county level or above and their relevant departments shall cultivate and train the personnel of infant and child care service establishments and kindergartens, and increase their professional ethics and professional ability.

Article 85
People's governments at all levels shall develop vocational education, ensure that minors receive vocational education or vocational skills training, and encourage and support people's organizations, enterprises, public institutions, and social organizations in providing vocational skills training services for minors.

Article 86
People's governments at all levels shall ensure that minors with disabilities who have the ability to receive ordinary education and are able to adapt to campus life receive education in the nearest ordinary schools and kindergartens,

and ensure that minors with disabilities who do not have the ability to receive ordinary education receive pre-school, compulsory education, and vocational education in special education schools and kindergartens. All levels of the people's government shall ensure the conditions for running and operating special education schools and kindergartens, and encourage and support social forces in establishing special education schools and kindergartens.

On the other hand, government departments, mainly public security organs, should ensure campus safety and maintain public order and traffic order around campuses. *The Law of the People's Republic of China on the Protection of Minors (2021)* stipulates that local people's governments and their relevant departments shall ensure campus safety, supervise and guide schools, kindergartens, and other units in implementing campus safety responsibilities, and establish mechanisms for reporting, handling, and coordinating emergencies. Public security organs and other relevant departments shall lawfully ensure public security and traffic order around campuses, set up monitoring equipment and traffic safety facilities, and prevent and stop illegal and criminal acts against children. At the same time, public places fulfill their safety and security obligations, and give priority to the rescue of children in emergencies, so as to provide a legal basis for handling all kinds of cases in which children are injured in public places.

For details, see Articles 87–88 of this Law:

Article 87

Local people's governments and their relevant departments shall ensure campus security, supervise and guide schools, kindergartens, and other units in implementing campus security responsibilities, and establish mechanisms for reporting, handling, and coordinating emergencies.

Article 88

Public security organs and other relevant departments shall maintain public security and traffic order around campuses in accordance with law, set up monitoring equipment and traffic safety facilities, and prevent and stop illegal and criminal acts against minors.

Under the guidance of the Child Protection Coordination Mechanism, the third emphasis of "Government Protection" is the protection of children in the social environment. *The Law of the People's Republic of China on the Protection of Minors (2021)* clarifies that governments at all levels shall perform the following duties: (1) The government shall establish and improve venues and facilities suitable for children, and support schools to open cultural and sports facilities to children free of charge or at a discounted rate during the student holidays, and prevent any organization or individual from encroaching on or destroying the venues and facilities of children's activity venues. (2) In terms of children's physical health, government health departments shall provide health care and nutrition guidance to children, provide health care services, strengthen the prevention and management of infectious diseases, do a good job in injury prevention and intervention, and guide and supervise schools, kindergartens, and infant and child care service establishments in carrying out health care work. (3) In the area of children's mental health, government health departments shall conduct efforts such as children's psychological treatment, psychological crisis intervention, and early identification, diagnosis, and treatment of mental disorders. Government administrative departments for education shall strengthen children's mental health education, and establish mechanisms for early detection and prompt intervention of children's psychological problems.

For details, please refer to Articles 89 and 90 of this Law:

Article 89

Local people's governments shall establish and improve activity venues and facilities suitable for minors, support the construction and operation of public interest activity venues and facilities for minors, encourage social forces to establish activity venues and facilities suitable for minors, and strengthen management.

Local people's governments shall employ measures to encourage and support schools in opening cultural and sports facilities to minors free of charge or on a preferential basis during legally-prescribed national holidays, rest days, and winter and summer vacations.

Local people's governments shall employ measures to prevent any organization or individual from encroaching upon or destroying the venues, houses, and facilities of schools, kindergartens, infant and child care service establishments, and other activity venues for minors.

Article 90

People's governments at all levels and their relevant departments shall provide guidance on health care and nutrition for minors, and provide health care services.

Health departments shall regulate vaccine vaccination for minors in accordance with law, prevent and treat common and frequently occurring diseases among minors, strengthen the prevention and management of infectious diseases, do a good job of harm prevention and intervention, and guide and supervise schools, kindergartens, and infant and child care service establishments in carrying out health care work.

The administrative departments for education shall strengthen mental health education for minors, establishing mechanisms for early discovery and prompt intervention of minors' psychological problems. Health departments shall do a good job of efforts such as psychological treatment for minors, psychological crisis intervention, and early identification, diagnosis, and treatment of mental disorders.

Under the guidance of the Child Protection Coordination Mechanism, the fourth aspect of "government protection" emphasizes the protection of children from the family, school, society, and other environments, that is, government departments directly take measures to rescue children in need, and assume the responsibility of guardianship. *The Law of the People's Republic of China on the Protection of Minors (2021)* requires that people's governments at all levels and their relevant departments shall implement categorical safeguards for children in difficult circumstances, and take measures to meet their basic needs in areas such as life, education, safety, medical rehabilitation, and housing.

For details, see Article 91 of this Law:

Article 91

All levels of people's government and their relevant departments are to implement categorical safeguards for minors in difficulty, and take measures to meet their basic needs in areas such as life, education, security, medical rehabilitation, and housing.

When the government provides assistance to children in difficulty, there are cases where children who are left uncared for or who are separated from the family environment lack guardianship. *The Law of the People's Republic of China on the Protection of Minors (2021)* focuses on the establishment of temporary and long-term entrusted care systems, as well as temporary and long-term national (government) guardianship systems. Parents or other guardians are the first responsible persons for guardianship, but it is difficult for traditional family guardianship to achieve comprehensive guardianship of children. When the parents or other guardians of the children are unable to perform their guardianship duties, and the entrusted care mentioned in the "Family Protection" mentioned above cannot be realized, *the Law of the People's Republic of China on the Protection of Minors (2021)* proposes that the civil affairs department of the government shall carry out temporary or long-term guardianship of children separated from the family environment on behalf of the state. Other departments such as finance, education, health, and public security have cooperated with civil affairs departments to assume temporary or long-term guardianship duties, effectively avoiding the dilemma of some children falling into the predicament of no one to take care of them due to a lack of guardians.

Temporary guardianship refers to the fact that when a dispute arises over the determination of a guardian, it is necessary to initiate a guardianship dispute resolution procedure, and the residents' committee, villagers' committee, civil affairs department, or people's court appoints the guardian. However, the guardianship dispute resolution procedure takes a certain amount of time, and the ward's personal rights, property rights, and other lawful rights and interests may be unprotected until a guardian is appointed. For example, if a person with guardianship qualifications is unwilling to serve as a guardian because of each other's prevarication, in this case, in order to protect the lawful rights and interests of the ward, it is necessary to designate a temporary guardian for the ward, and the temporary guardian shall exercise all the duties of guardian until the guardian is appointed, and the temporary guardian will not be relieved of his position.

Temporary guardians are appointed by the residents' committee, villagers' committee, relevant organizations provided for by law, or civil affairs departments for the ward's residence. When any of the following 7 circumstances occur, the civil affairs departments are to conduct temporary guardianship of the children in accordance with the law. Including: (1) Children are vagrant and begging or their identities are unknown, and their parents or other guardians cannot be found temporarily; (2) The whereabouts of the guardian are unknown and no one else can serve as the guardian; (3) Guardians are unable to perform guardianship duties due to their own objective reasons or due to the occurrence of natural disasters, accidents, public health incidents, and other emergencies, resulting in the lack of guardianship of children; (4) The guardian refuses or neglects to perform guardianship duties, resulting in the child being left uncared for; (5) Guardians instigate or exploit children to commit illegal or criminal acts, and the children need to be taken out of the placement; (6) Children who have been seriously injured by their guardians or face threats to their personal safety need to be placed urgently; (7) Other circumstances stipulated by law.

For children in temporary custody, the civil affairs departments may place children in temporary custody through methods such as entrusting relatives to raise them or foster them at home, and may also transfer them to child aid and protection establishments or child welfare establishments to take them in and raise them. If the guardian regains the capacity to perform guardianship duties, the civil affairs department may, after assessment, return the child to the guardian for care.

Long-term guardianship refers to the fact that where a person does not have guardianship qualifications in accordance with law, the civil affairs department is to serve as the guardian, and may also be served by the residents' committee or villagers' committee of the ward's domicile that has the capacity to perform guardianship duties. In any of the following circumstances, the civil affairs departments shall conduct long-term guardianship of minors in accordance with law: (1) The child's parents or other guardians cannot be found; (2) The guardian dies or is declared dead and no one else can serve as a guardian; (3) The guardian loses the ability to guardianship and no one else can serve as a guardian; (4) The people's court decides to revoke the guardian's qualifications And designate the civil affairs department as the guardian; (5) Other situations stipulated by law. After the civil affairs department conducts an adoption assessment, it can legally hand over children under its long-term custody to qualified applicants for adoption. After the adoption relationship is established, the custody relationship between the civil affairs department and the child is terminated. If the civil affairs department assumes the responsibility of temporary guardianship or long-term guardianship, the finance, education, health, public security, and other departments shall provide cooperation according to their respective responsibilities.

For the above content, please refer to Articles 92–96 of the Law of the People's Republic of China on the Protection of Minors (2021):

Article 92
Under any of the following circumstances, the civil affairs department shall provide temporary custody of minors in accordance with the law: (1) The minor is wandering and begging or his identity is unknown, and his parents or other guardians cannot be found temporarily; (2) The whereabouts of the guardian are unknown. And no one else can serve as a guardian; (3) The guardian is unable to perform guardianship duties due to his own objective reasons or due to emergencies such as natural disasters, accidents, public health emergencies, etc., resulting in a lack of guardianship of the minor; (4) The guardian refuses or Neglect to perform guardianship duties, resulting in minors being left without care; (5) Guardians instigate and use minors to commit illegal and criminal acts, and minors need to be removed from their homes; (6) Minors are seriously injured by their guardian's Injury or facing threats to personal safety and need to be urgently resettled; (7) Other situations stipulated by law.

Article 93
For minors under temporary guardianship, the Civil Affairs department may adopt methods such as entrusting relatives to raise them, fostering them in families, or handing them over to minors rescue and protection agencies or child welfare agencies for shelter and care. During the period of temporary guardianship, if the civil affairs department assesses that the guardian is again qualified to perform guardianship duties, the civil affairs department may return the minor to the custody of the guardian.

Article 94
Under any of the following circumstances, the civil affairs department shall provide long-term custody of the minor in accordance with the law: (1) The minor's parents or other guardians cannot be found; (2) The guardian dies or is declared dead and there is no other A person can serve as a guardian; (3) the guardian loses the ability to guardianship and there is no other person who can serve as a guardian; (4) the people's court decides to revoke the guardian's qualifications and appoints the civil affairs department to serve as the guardian; (5) other circumstances stipulated by law.

Article 95
After the civil affairs department conducts an adoption assessment, it may legally hand over the minor under its long-term custody to a qualified applicant for adoption. After the adoption relationship is established, the guardianship relationship between the civil affairs department and the minor is terminated.

Article 96
If the civil affairs department assumes the responsibility of temporary guardianship or long-term guardianship, the finance, education, health, public security, and other departments shall cooperate according to their respective responsibilities. People's governments at or above the county level and their civil affairs departments shall establish minors' rescue and protection institutions and child welfare institutions as necessary, and be responsible for taking in and raising minors under the custody of the civil affairs departments.

In order to provide adequate and strong support for the protection of children's rights, the "Government Protection" has clearly established a series of systems to ensure the protection of children, on the basis of emphasizing the responsibilities of various departments in different environments.

The Law of the People's Republic of China on the Protection of Minor (2021) proposes the following measures for which the government should take the lead and be responsible: First, the government should establish an all-media child protection service with hotlines as the mainstay, People's governments at the county level or above should open a unified national child protection hotline to promptly accept and refer complaints and reports of violations of children's lawful rights and interests. Second, the government shall establish an information inquiry system for persons who committed offenses such as sexual assault, abuse, trafficking, and violent injury, and provide free inquiry services to units that have close contact with children. Third, the government should cultivate, guide, and regulate the participation of relevant social organizations and social workers in child protection efforts, carry out family education guidance services, and provide professional services for children's psychological counseling, rehabilitation assistance, guardianship, and adoption assessments. For details, please refer to articles 97–99 of this Law:

Article 97
People's governments at the county level or above shall open a unified national hotline for the protection of minors, promptly accepting and referring complaints and reports of violations of minors' lawful rights and interests, and encouraging and supporting people's organizations, enterprises, public institutions, and social organizations to participate in the establishment of service platforms, service hotlines, and service sites for the protection of minors, and providing consultation and assistance on the protection of minors.

Article 98
The State is to establish a system for inquiring into information on persons who have violated the law or committed crimes such as sexual assault, abuse, trafficking, or violent harm, and provide free inquiry services to units that have close contact with minors.

Article 99
Local people's governments shall cultivate, guide, and regulate the participation of relevant social organizations and social workers in efforts to protect minors, carry out family education and guidance services, and provide professional services for minors such as psychological counseling, rehabilitation assistance, guardianship, and adoption assessments.

Government protection reflects the improvement of the government's social governance capacity, and is an inevitable requirement for China to build a social governance pattern of co-construction, co-governance and sharing in the new era, and conveys the support attitude of the Party and the state towards child protection work. State guardianship should not only assume the responsibility of raising children when they are in danger, but should also make every effort to prevent children from being in a state of crisis; not only to ensure the growth of children, but also to create a good environment to achieve the all-round development of children's morality, intelligence, physical fitness, aesthetics, and labor. State guardianship should not only be given materially, but should also be emotionally cared for like parents, so that the protection of the child can be warmer.

4.2.2.6 Judicial Protection Under the Six Protection Systems (Articles 100–116 of the Act)

In recent years, with the rapid development of the economy and the increasing diversification of society, child crime has increased in countries around the world, and the age of the child has increased. How to protect children's basic human rights and protect their legitimate rights and interests when handling cases of child violations and crimes and violations against children has led to the emergence of children's judicial protection (Liu, 2023).

Judicial protection refers to the necessary protective measures taken by the judicial organs to adapt to the physical and mental characteristics of the children and to protect the children's rights and interests from harm after the children enter the judicial process. According to *the Law of the People's Republic of China on the Protection of Minor (2021)*, judicial organs mainly include public security organs, people's courts, people's procuratorates and judicial-administrative organs, collectively referred to as judicial organs. In "judicial protection", judicial organs shall establish specialized bodies or designate specialized personnel to be responsible for handling cases involving children, with specialized teams composed of persons familiar with the physical and psychological characteristics of children, and having professional background knowledge such as psychology, education, sociology, etc., to perform their duties in accordance with law and protect children's lawful rights and interests. On the one hand, it is necessary to persist in giving priority to education and supplemented by punishment to save children involved in crimes to the greatest extent, and on the other hand, it is necessary to adhere to a "zero tolerance" attitude and severely punish crimes against children. Under this concept, we adhere to the comprehensive protection of multiple systems, comprehensively protect the legitimate rights and interests of children, and establish a final line of defense for the "six protection systems" for the child (Liu, 2022).

When it comes to judicial protection, *the Law of the People's Republic of China on the Protection of Minors (2021)* first clarifies the general rules that judicial authorities should follow when handling cases involving children. (1) Judicial organs shall ensure that a certain proportion of female staff is included among specialized institutions or specialized personnel, and conduct special evaluations and training for these entities or individuals; (2) When judicial organs handle cases involving children, they should consider the physical and mental characteristics of children and their needs for healthy development, use language and expressions that children can understand, and listen to the children's opinions. (3) Judicial organs, as well as other organizations and individuals, must not disclose the names, images, residences, schools, and other information that might identify children in cases, except in situations such as searching for missing or trafficked children. (4) Judicial organs or other legal aid institutions shall provide assistance to children in need of legal aid or judicial assistance, and provide them with legal aid or judicial aid in accordance with law. For details, see Articles 100–104 of this Law:

Article 100
Public security organs, people's procuratorates, people's courts, and judicial administrative departments shall perform their duties in accordance with law to protect the lawful rights and interests of minors.

Article 101
Public security organs, people's procuratorates, people's courts, and judicial administrative departments shall designate specialized agencies or designate specialized personnel to be responsible for handling cases involving minors. Personnel handling cases involving minors shall undergo special training and be familiar with the physical and psychological characteristics of minors. Specialized agencies or specialized personnel shall have female staff. Public security organs, people's procuratorates, people's courts, and judicial administrative departments shall carry out evaluation and evaluation standards for the above-mentioned institutions and personnel that are appropriate to efforts on the protection of minors.

Article 102
Public security organs, people's procuratorates, people's courts, and judicial administrative departments handling cases involving minors shall consider the physical and psychological characteristics of minors and the needs of their healthy growth, use language and expressions that minors can understand, and hear the opinions of minors.

Article 103
Public security organs, people's procuratorates, people's courts, judicial administrative departments, and other organizations and individuals must not disclose the names, images, residences, schools, and other information that might identify minors in cases, except in situations such as searching for missing or trafficked minors.

Article 104
Legal aid institutions or public security organs, people's procuratorates, people's courts, and judicial administrative departments shall provide assistance to minors in need of legal aid or judicial assistance, and provide them with legal aid or judicial aid in accordance with law. Legal aid institutions shall appoint lawyers familiar with the physical and psychological characteristics of minors to provide legal aid services to minors. Legal aid institutions and lawyers associations shall conduct guidance and training for lawyers handling juvenile legal aid cases.

Meanwhile, *the Law of the People's Republic of China on the Protection of Minors (2021)* emphasizes the special protection of children by the people's procuratorates and people's courts, after clarifying the general provisions of the judiciary on children's judicial activities. People's procuratorates have the right to initiate public interest litigation where they are lawfully supervised by litigation activities involving children, and where the public interest is involved. People's courts hearing cases involving children such as inheritance and divorce shall respect the true wishes of the children and protect the lawful rights and interests of the children such as their inheritance rights and the right to receive bequests.

People's procuratorates participate in the judicial protection of children through the exercise of prosecutorial power throughout the entire process, and conduct oversight of litigation activities involving children in accordance with law. According to *the Law of the People's Republic of China on the Protection of Minors (2021)*, where the lawful rights and interests of children are violated and relevant organizations and individuals fail to initiate litigation on their behalf, the people's procuratorate may urge and support them to initiate litigation, and where the public interest is involved, the people's procuratorate has the right to initiate public interest litigation. Through the channel of public interest litigation, it is possible to speak out for children who lack the means to protect their rights, arouse widespread public attention and public opinion, and gradually form a consensus that the problem should be solved in the process of continuous discussion.

When people's courts handle cases involving children, they shall follow the "principle of the best interests of children". In order to maximize the protection of the legitimate rights and interests of children, courts at all levels in China have set up juvenile courts to hear cases that may have an impact on the rights and interests of children, and the Opinions of the Supreme People's Court of the People's Republic of China on Strengthening the Trial of Juveniles in the New Era issued by the Supreme People's Court have clarified the scope of cases accepted by juvenile courts, and respectively stipulate the circumstances under which civil cases and criminal cases involving child protection may be accepted, among which the following civil cases shall be heard by juvenile courts:

(1) Marriage and family dispute cases involving child support, guardianship, visitation, etc., as well as divorce cases suitable for trial by juvenile courts;
(2) Cases of personality rights disputes in which one or both parties are children;
(3) Cases of tort liability disputes where the infringer is a child, and cases where the infringed party is a child, and where the juvenile court hears more appropriate tort liability disputes;
(4) Personal safety protection order cases involving children;
(5) Other civil cases involving the protection of children's rights and interests.

The following criminal cases shall also be heard by the Juvenile Court:

(1) Cases of crimes committed by students who were under the age of 22 at the time of filing the case by the People's Court;
(2) Cases of rape, indecency a
(3) Cases of killing, injuring, kidnapping, abducting, abducting, absolving, abandoning, and other crimes that seriously violate children's personal rights;
(4) Cases of modification of criminal punishment such as commutation, parole, temporary service of sentence outside of prison, revocation of suspended sentence, and other criminal punishment modifications in the criminal cases
(5) Other criminal cases involving children that are more appropriate for the juvenile court to hear.

According to *the Law of the People's Republic of China on the Protection of Minors (2021)*, on the one hand, courts hearing inheritance cases should protect children's inheritance rights and bequest rights in accordance with the law. When people's courts hearing divorce cases involve the issue of raising minor children, they shall respect the true wishes of the minor children who have reached the age of 8, and handle them in accordance with the law in accordance with the principle of the best interests of the minor children on the basis of the specific circumstances of both parties. *The Civil Code of the People's Republic of China* also provides relevant provisions in this regard. On the other hand, where a child's parents or other guardians do not perform guardianship duties in accordance with law or seriously infringe upon the lawful rights and interests of the child under guardianship, the people's court may, on the basis of an application by relevant persons or units, issue a personal safety protection order or revoke guardianship qualifications in accordance with law. Parents or other guardians whose guardianship qualifications have been revoked shall continue to bear the cost of child support in accordance with the law. *The Anti-Domestic Violence Law of the People's Republic of China* has set up a special system to provide detailed provisions for personal safety protection orders. In addition, where people's courts hear cases such as divorce, custody, adoption, guardianship, or visitation involving children, they may conduct a social investigation of the children's circumstances on their own or by entrusting a social organization, and carry out extended work such as social care, psychological counseling, court education, family education, judicial assistance, and return visits to help and educate, to increase the legal and social effects of case handling. For details, please refer to Articles 105–109 of *the Law of the People's Republic of China on the Protection of Minors (2021)*:

Article 105
The people's procuratorate shall supervise litigation activities involving minors in accordance with the law through the exercise of prosecutorial power.

Article 106
Where the lawful rights and interests of minors are violated and relevant organizations or individuals fail to initiate litigation on their behalf, the people's procuratorate may urge and support them to initiate litigation.

Article 107
The people's courts hearing inheritance cases shall protect the inheritance rights and bequest rights of minors in accordance with law. Where people's courts hearing divorce cases involve the issue of raising minor children, they shall respect the true wishes of the minor children who have reached the age of 8, and handle them in accordance with law in accordance with the principle of the best interests of the minor children on the basis of the specific circumstances of both parties.

Article 108
Where minors' parents or other guardians do not perform guardianship duties in accordance with law, or seriously infringe upon the lawful rights and interests of minors under guardianship, the people's courts may, on the basis of an application by relevant persons or units, lawfully issue a personal safety protection order or revoke guardianship qualifications. Parents or other guardians whose guardianship qualifications have been revoked shall continue to bear the cost of child support in accordance with law.

Article 109
Where a people's court hears a case involving minors such as divorce, custody, adoption, guardianship, or visitation, it may conduct a social investigation of the minors' circumstances on its own or by entrusting a social organization.

In the course of handling cases involving children, the public security organs file and investigate, the procuratorates review and prosecute, and the courts hear and make judgments, and the three organs divide labor and cooperate with each other to severely punish crimes against children such as killing, injuring, sexual assault, trafficking, and abuse in accordance with law, and jointly safeguard the lawful rights and interests of children. According to *the Law of the People's Republic of China on the Protection of Minors (2021)*, the following requirements are put forward for public security organs, people's procuratorates and people's courts:

Interrogations of juvenile criminal suspects or defendants, or questioning juvenile victims or witnesses, shall lawfully notify their legally-designated representatives, adult relatives, representatives of their schools, and other appropriate adults to appear, and employ appropriate methods and conduct them in appropriate venues, to protect minors' rights to reputation, privacy, and other lawful rights and interests.

Where people's courts hold in-court proceedings to hear cases involving children, minor victims and witnesses generally do not appear in court to testify. For minor witnesses who must appear in court, protective measures such as the use of technology to protect their privacy and psychological interventions should be taken.

Public security organs, people's procuratorates, and people's courts shall cooperate with other relevant government departments, people's organizations, and social organizations to carry out necessary protective measures such as psychological intervention, economic assistance, legal aid, and school transfer placements for minor victims of sexual offense or violence and their families.

When handling cases of sexual or violent harm to children, measures such as simultaneous audio and video recordings shall be employed when questioning minor victims or witnesses, and should be completed as soon as possible. If the minor victim or witness is female, the procedure should be conducted by female staff.

For details, please refer to Articles 110–112 of the Law of the People's Republic of China on the Protection of Minors (2021):

Article 110

Public security organs, people's procuratorates, and people's courts interrogating juvenile criminal suspects or defendants, or questioning juvenile victims or witnesses, shall notify their legally-designated representatives, adult relatives, school representatives, and other appropriate adults to appear, and employ appropriate methods and venues to ensure minors' right to reputation, privacy, and other lawful rights and interests.

People's courts hold in-court proceedings in cases involving minors, and minor victims and witnesses generally do not appear in court to testify.

Article 111

Public security organs, people's procuratorates, and people's courts shall cooperate with other relevant government departments, people's organizations, and social organizations to carry out necessary psychological intervention, economic assistance, legal aid, school transfer, and other protective measures for minor victims of sexual offense or violence and their families.

Article 112

When public security organs, people's procuratorates, and people's courts handling cases of sexual or violent harm to minors, they shall employ measures such as simultaneous audio and video recordings when questioning minor victims or witnesses, and try to complete it all at once. If the minor victims and witnesses are female, they shall be carried out by the female staff members.

In view of the immature mentality and unformed personality of the criminally involved children, *the Law of the People's Republic of China on the Protection of Minors (2021)* proposes to implement the policy of education, reform, and rescue for children who have violated the law and committed crimes, and adhere to the principle of education first, supplemented by punishment. After children who have violated the law or committed crimes are punished in accordance with law, they must not be discriminated against in areas such as advancement to higher education or employment. (1) Where judicial organs discover that relevant units have failed to perform their duties to protect children, such as education, management, rescue, and care, they shall make a recommendation to that unit. (2) Judicial organs shall consider actual conditions and carry out publicity and education efforts on the rule of law for minors on the basis of the characteristics of cases involving minors. (3) The state encourages and supports social organizations and social workers to participate in psychological intervention, legal aid, social investigation, social care, education and corrections, community corrections, and other such efforts for minors in cases involving children.

Judicial organs should save children involved in crime to the greatest extent possible. Implement the principles of education, reform, and rescue, not only persisting in punishment in accordance with law, but also emphasizing education and transformation, vigorously urging people to learn their way back and prevent recidivism. For children whose subjective malice is not great and the circumstances of the crime are relatively minor, coordinate the implementation of the criminal justice policy of blending leniency and severity and the criminal justice policy of fewer arrests, careful prosecution and careful detention, and persist in the direction of decriminalization, non-criminalization, and non-incarceration. Resolutely punish children with deep subjective malice, cruel criminal methods, and serious consequences, resolutely punish them in accordance with law, never blindly conniving, and implement measures of "protection, education, and control" in an integrated manner, not only to let children involved in crimes feel the majesty of the rule of law, but also to warn and educate society.

For details, please refer to Articles 113–116 of the Law of the People's Republic of China on the Protection of Minors (2021):

Article 113

Implement the policy of education, reform, and rescue for juveniles who have violated the law and committed crimes, and adhere to the principle of education first, supplemented by punishment. After juveniles who have violated the law or committed crimes are punished in accordance with law, they must not be discriminated against in areas such as advancement to higher education or employment.

Article 114
Where public security organs, people's procuratorates, people's courts, and judicial administrative departments discover that relevant units have failed to perform their duties to protect minors, such as education, management, rescue, and care, they shall make recommendations to that unit. The unit to be suggested shall make a written reply within one month.

Article 115
Public security organs, people's procuratorates, people's courts, and judicial administrative departments shall carry out publicity and education on the rule of law for minors in light of actual conditions and on the basis of the characteristics of cases involving minors.

Article 116
The State encourages and supports social organizations and social workers to participate in psychological intervention, legal aid, social investigation, social care, education and corrections, community corrections, and other such work as for minors in cases involving minors.

In the "six protection systems" for the child, judicial protection is the last line of defense for the protection of children's rights and interests, and compared with other protections, judicial protection will involve more issues of convergence with other laws, and strengthening judicial protection of children is not only related to the healthy growth of children, but also carries the historical mission of realizing the Chinese dream of the great rejuvenation of the Chinese nation. T*he Law of the People's Republic of China on the Protection of Minor (2021)* strives to provide strong judicial services and safeguards for the healthy growth of children, and to create an environment for children to thrive, grow up healthily and grow safely.

4.2.3 Legal Liability Under the Law of the People's Republic of China on the Protection of Minors (2021) (Articles 117–129)

The law is holy and solemn, and all organizations and individuals should abide by the law, otherwise they should bear the corresponding consequences. Incorporating child protection into law, establishing a series of systems, and setting corresponding consequences for violating the law, is the most powerful weapon in child protection work to protect children's rights and interests. The Law of the People's Republic of China on the Protection of Minors (2021) establishes six protection systems of "family, school, society, network, government, and justice" on the basis of the general principles and basic systems set out in the General Provisions. In the section on legal responsibility, this law reaffirms the responsible entities in the "six major protections" system for children, refines the legal responsibilities of various entities in the family, school, society, online and other environments following "violating the law", and also stipulates the supervision duties of the procuratorate in the judicial system and the overall system for the protection of minors outside the judicial system. For violations of children's rights and interests, the relevant responsible entities will face different legal liabilities, including civil liability, administrative liability, and criminal liability.

In terms of basic systems, *the Law of the People's Republic of China on the Protection of Minor (2021)* establishes a mandatory reporting system for crimes against children in the general provisions, and sets forth requirements for various types of responsible entities in the "six protections" system. Where failure to perform reporting obligations causes serious consequences, the competent department at the level above or the unit to which they belong is to give sanctions to the directly responsible managers and other directly responsible personnel in accordance with law.

From the perspective of family protection, the child's parents or other guardians should perform their guardianship duties in accordance with the law to ensure the healthy growth of the child. According to *the Law of the People's Republic of China on the Protection of Minors (2021)*, if a child fails to perform guardianship duties in accordance with the law or violates the lawful rights and interests of a child, the residents' committee or villagers' committee at the place of residence shall admonish and stop it; Where public security organs receive reports, or where public security organs, people's procuratorates, or people's courts discover in the course of handling a case that the child's parents or other guardians have the circumstances described above, they shall give them a reprimand and may order them to accept family education guidance.

From the perspective of school protection, schools undertake the tasks of "impart knowledge and educate" and "safety guarantee", and *the Law of the People's Republic of China on the Protection of Minors (2021)* clearly states that if the following circumstances occur, the relevant subjects will be punished, and criminal responsibility will be investigated if the circumstances are serious. (1) Corporal punishment or disguised corporal punishment or other acts that insult human dignity by school teachers and staff. (2) The school expels or indirectly expels minor students in violation of state regulations. (3) The school's practice of passively responding to campus bullying, resulting in harm to students' rights and interests.

From the perspective of social protection, relevant social organizations shall actively provide welfare and amenities to children, ensure children's personal safety in social activities, and operate a positive social and cultural environment. *The Law of the People's Republic of China on the Protection of Minors (2021)* provides for the following:

(1) Where children are not given free or preferential treatment, the departments for market regulation, culture and tourism, and transportation are to order correc-

tions to be made within a set period of time in accordance with their duties and division of labor, and give warnings or even fines.

(2) The production, reproduction, publication, distribution or dissemination of books, newspapers and periodicals, films, radio and television programs, stage works, audiovisual products, electronic publications and Internet information that endanger children's physical and mental health shall be ordered by the departments of press and publication, radio and television, film, Internet and information technology to make corrections within a time limit in accordance with their respective duties; They shall be given punishments such as warning, fine, suspension of production or suspension of business or revocation of business license.

(3) Where a safety alarm system for searching for lost children is not set up in public places, and where inns, guesthouses, hotels, and other lodging operators fail to verify the identity and relationship of the occupants when receiving children, the departments for market regulation, emergency management, public security, and so forth, in accordance with their duties and division of labor, are to order corrections to be made within a set period of time, and give warnings, fines, revocation of business licenses, and other punishments.

(4) Operators of for-profit singing and dancing entertainment venues, bars, Internet cafes, and other places that are not suitable for children provide services to children; amusement and entertainment venues provide electronic game equipment to children in violation of regulations; or where business operators sell cigarettes, alcohol, or lottery tickets to children, or redeem lottery prizes, the departments of culture and tourism, market supervision and management, tobacco monopoly, and public security shall, in accordance with their duties and division of labor, order corrections to be made within a set period of time, and give warnings, fines, revocation of business licenses, and other punishments.

(5) Individual who smokes or drinks alcohol in schools, kindergartens or other public places where children are concentrated shall be ordered by the departments of public health, education, market supervision and administration according to their respective functions and duties to make corrections, give a warning, or even impose a fine.

(6) Where the relevant business operators employ child labor in violation of the regulations and violate the provisions on the prohibition of employment, the departments of culture and tourism, human resources and social security, market supervision and administration shall, in accordance with the division of responsibilities, order corrections within a time limit, issue warnings, impose fines, revoke business licenses and administer other punishments.

From the perspective of Internet protection, online product and service providers, personal information processors, manufacturers and sellers of smart terminal products, and other network-related industry organizations shall actively preserve the online environment, protect children's personal privacy and information, implement systems for the prevention and control of online addiction, and assume their due duties. According to the Law of the People's Republic of China on the Protection of

Minors (2021), relevant departments such as public security, internet information, telecommunications, press and publication, radio and television, culture and tourism, and other relevant departments are to order corrections in accordance with their duties and division of labor, and impose penalties such as warnings, fines, and revocation of business licenses.

From the perspective of government protection and judicial protection, the staff of government departments and judicial organs should strictly enforce the law in accordance with the principle of fairness and justice. *The Law of the People's Republic of China on the Protection of Minors (2021)* clearly stipulates that if a staff member of a state organ neglects his duties, abuses his power, or engages in irregularities for personal gain, thereby harming the lawful rights and interests of children, he shall be punished in accordance with the law.

In the "Six Protections system" of the child, *the Law of the People's Republic of China on the Protection of Minors (2021)* sets administrative responsibilities for the relevant responsible subjects, on this basis, any organization or individual that infringes on the legitimate rights and interests of children and causes personal, property or other damage shall bear civil liability in accordance with *the Code of the People's Republic of China* on the Minor People; If the act constitutes a violation of the administration of public security, penalties for the administration of public security shall be imposed in accordance with *the Law of the People's Republic of China on Penalties for the Administration of Public Security for Minors*; If the case constitutes a crime, criminal responsibility shall be investigated in accordance with *the Criminal Law of the People's Republic of China* on Minors.

For details, please refer to Articles 117–129 of the Law of the People's Republic of China on the Protection of Minors (2021):

Article 117
Where the provisions of paragraph 2 of Article 11 of this Law are violated by failing to perform the reporting obligation and causing serious consequences, the competent department at the level above or the unit to which they belong shall give sanctions to the directly responsible managers and other directly responsible personnel in accordance with law.

Article 118
Where the parents or other guardians of minors fail to perform their guardianship duties in accordance with the law or infringe upon the lawful rights and interests of minors, the residents' committee or villagers' committee at their place of residence shall admonish and stop them;

Where public security organs receive a report, or where the public security organs, people's procuratorates, or people's courts discover in the course of handling a case that minors' parents or other guardians have the circumstances described above, they shall reprimand them and may order them to accept family education guidance.

Article 119
Where schools, kindergartens, infant care services and other institutions and their teaching and staff violate the provisions of Articles 27, 28 and 39 of this Law, the departments of public security, education, public health, market supervision and administration shall order them to make corrections in accordance with their respective duties; If the offender refuses to make corrections or the circumstances are serious, the person directly in charge and other persons directly responsible shall be given sanctions according to law.

Article 120
Where the provisions of Articles 44, 45, or 47 of this Law are violated by failing to give minors free or preferential treatment, the departments for market regulation, culture and tourism, and transportation are to order corrections to be made within a set period of time and give warnings in accordance with their duties and division of labor, and where corrections are refused, a fine of between 10,000 and 100,000 RMB is to be given.

Article 121
Where the provisions of Articles 50 and 51 of this Law are violated, the departments of press and publication, radio and television, film, internet information, and other departments shall, in accordance with their duties and division of labor, order corrections to be made within a set period of time, give warnings, confiscate unlawful gains, and may concurrently impose a fine of up to 100,000 RMB; Where relevant permits are revoked, and unlawful gains are to be 1 million RMB or more, a concurrent fine of between 1 and 10 times the amount of unlawful gains is to be given, and where there are no unlawful gains or the unlawful gains are less than 1 million RMB, a concurrent fine of between 100,000 and 1,000,000 RMB is to be given.

Article 122
Where the premises operation unit violates the provisions of paragraph 2 of Article 56 of this Law, or the accommodation operator violates the provisions of Article 57 of this Law, the market supervision and management, emergency management, public security and other departments shall order rectification within a time limit and give a warning according to the division of duties; If the party refuses to make corrections or has caused serious consequences, it shall be ordered to suspend business for rectification or its business license or relevant license shall be revoked and a fine of not less than 10,000 yuan but not more than 100,000 yuan shall be imposed.

Article 123

Where the relevant business operator violates the provisions of Article 58, paragraph 1 of Article 59 and Article 60 of this Law, the departments for culture and tourism, market supervision and administration, tobacco monopoly and public security shall, in accordance with their respective duties, order correction within a time limit, give a warning, confiscate the illegal gains and may concurrently impose a fine of not more than 50,000 yuan; If the party refuses to make corrections or the circumstances are serious, it shall be ordered to suspend business for rectification or its business license or relevant license shall be revoked, and a fine of not less than 50,000 yuan but not more than 500,000 yuan may also be imposed.

Article 124

Whoever, in violation of the provisions of paragraph 2 of Article 59 of this Law, smokes or drinks alcohol in schools, kindergartens or other public places where minors are concentrated shall be ordered by the departments of public health, education, market supervision and administration according to their respective functions and duties to make corrections, give them a warning and may concurrently be fined not more than 500 yuan; If the place manager fails to stop it in time, the public health, education, market supervision and administration departments shall give a warning and impose a fine of not more than 10,000 yuan in accordance with the division of duties.

Article 125

If anyone violates the provisions of Article 61 of this Law, the departments of culture and tourism, human resources and social security, and market supervision and administration shall, in accordance with their respective duties, order him to make corrections within a time limit, give him a warning, confiscate his illegal gains, and may concurrently impose a fine of not more than 100,000 yuan; If the party refuses to make corrections or the circumstances are serious, it shall be ordered to suspend production or business or revoke its business license or relevant licenses, and be fined not less than 100,000 yuan but not more than one million yuan.

Article 126

Where a unit that has close contact with minors, in violation of the provisions of Article 62 of this Law, fails to fulfill its obligation of inquiry, or recruits or continues to employ persons with relevant criminal records, the departments of education, human resources and social security, market supervision and administration shall, in accordance with the division of duties, order correction within a time limit, give a warning, and impose a fine of not more than 50,000

yuan; If the party refuses to make corrections or has caused serious consequences, it shall be ordered to suspend business for rectification or revoke its business license or relevant licenses, and shall be fined not less than 50,000 yuan but not more than 500,000 yuan, and the persons in charge directly responsible and other persons directly responsible shall be given sanctions according to law.

Article 127

Where an information processor violates the provisions of Article 72 of this Law, or an Internet product or service provider violates the provisions of Article 73, 74, 75, 76, 77 and 80 of this Law, the relevant departments of public security, Internet and information technology, telecommunications, press and publication, radio and television, culture and tourism shall, in accordance with their respective duties, order correction and give a warning. If the illegal gains are not less than one million yuan, a fine of not less than one time but not more than ten times the illegal gains shall be confiscated; if there are no illegal gains or the illegal gains are less than one million yuan, a fine of not less than one million yuan shall also be imposed; the persons directly in charge and other responsible persons shall be imposed a fine of not less than ten thousand yuan but not more than one hundred thousand yuan; If it refuses to make corrections or the circumstances are serious, it may be ordered to suspend the relevant business, suspend business for rectification, close the website, revoke the business license or revoke the relevant license.

Article 128

Where employees of state organs neglect their duties, abuse their powers, or twist the law for personal gain, harming the lawful rights and interests of minors, they shall be given sanctions in accordance with the law.

Article 129

Whoever violates the provisions of this Law by infringing upon the lawful rights and interests of minors, causing harm to persons, property, or other harms, shall bear civil liability in accordance with the law. Anyone who violates the provisions of this Law and constitutes an act violating the administration of public security shall be punished for the administration of public security according to law; If the case constitutes a crime, criminal responsibility shall be investigated according to law.

4.3 Summary

The work of child protection is beneficial for the present and for the future. As a state party to *the United Nations Convention on the Rights of the Child*, China has made great efforts to protect children. Under the guidance of *the Convention on the Rights of the Child* and *the Constitution of the People's Republic of China*, China has been actively promoting the protection of children. The implementation of the Law of the People's Republic of China on the Protection of Minors is one of the best answers to China's child protection work in the past decades (Xi, n.d.).

The Law of the People's Republic of China on the Protection of Minors is the first basic law to comprehensively protect the rights and interests of children. The six protection systems of the child established by the law, including family, school, society, Internet, government, and judiciary - represent significant progress in China's legislation on child protection, and the implementation of the Law marks a new era of child protection in China. This chapter introduces in detail *the Law of the People's Republic of China on the Protection of Minor (2021)*, which can present China's distinct international vision and local awareness, and demonstrate China's determination to build a legal system for the protection of children's rights and interests in China and to promote child protection.

Spring breeze turns rain, moisturizing things silently. In general, *the Law of the People's Republic of China on the Protection of Minors (2021)* provides a sufficient legal basis for the healthy growth of children, clarifies the legal responsibilities of all sectors of society to protect children, and creates a good social atmosphere for the healthy growth of children. Under the guidance of the Law, China will continue to promote child protection and make concerted efforts at home, school, society and government to promote the all-round development of children's moral, intellectual, physical, aesthetic and labor skills, cultivate idealistic, moral, educated and disciplined socialist builders and successors, protect children's legitimate rights and interests from infringement, and promote social stability and family happiness (Chui & Jordan, 2018).

References

Annan, K. A. (2000). *World Status of Children.*

Chen, Y., & Zhang, A. (2023). Reflection and optimization of the compulsory reporting system of juvenile infringement cases and its application. *Journal of Sichuan Police College, 5*, 64–74.

Chui, C. H. K., & Jordan, L. (2018). Child protection in China: Threats and opportunities. *Asia Pacific Journal of Social Work and Development, 2*, 84–96.

Guo, L. (2021). *Law of the People's Republic of China on the Protection of Minors M* (p. 138). Law Press.

Hämäläinen, J., Wu, S., & Zhao, F. (2023). The Chinese View of the Rights of the Child: An analysis of the law of the protection of minors. *The International Journal of Children's Rights, 1*, 167–189. https://doi.org/10.1163/15718182-31010004

Li, J. Current trend and hotspot of juvenile protection research in China. *Journal of South-South University for Nationalities (Humanities and Social Sciences Edition)*
Liu M. The Interpretation of the Law on the Protection of Minors. Changzhou Saluo Lane Hong'an Kindergarten.
Liu, X. (2023). *Building a strong fortress for the judicial protection of minors*. People's Court Daily.
Liu, Y. (2022). Analysis of the construction of the juvenile protection system in China. *Youth Exploration, 1*, 60–70.
Ma, Z., & Bo, L. (2023). Evolution, hot spots, and prospects of the Minor Protection Law in China—Visual analysis of the research literature based on CNKI (1981-2022). *Research on Juvenile Crime Prevention, 6*, 83–90.
Structural Cultivation of Youth Internet Literacy September, 2022. China Cyberspace Technology 5.
The Central Committee of the Communist Youth League protects the youth Rights and Interests Department, China Internet Information Center. (2021). The 2020 National Research Report on the Internet Use of Minors.
Tong, X. (2021). Interpretation of the newly revised Law of the People's Republic of China on the Protection of Minors (based on the perspective of civil affairs). *Social Welfare, 5*, 26–28.
Wang, R. (1994). The school protection of minors. *Juvenile Delinquency Problem, 2*, 15.
Xu, L., Li, P., Ni, H., Wang, B., Zheng, S., & Zhu, D. (2023). Analysis of the family protection mechanism of minors in the construction of a harmonious society. *New West, 4*, 113–115.
Yao, J., & Chen, Z. (2021a). Amendments, advances, and prospects of the Protection of Minors Act. *Youth Exploration, 5*, 5–17.
Yao, J., & Chen, Z. (2021b). Revision, progress, and prospects of the law on the protection of minors. *Youth Exploration, 5*.
You, W., & Li, T. (2021). "Six major protections" under the perspective of the Protection of Minors. *Ethnic Education in China, 6*, 8–10.

Chapter 5
The Law on the Prevention of Juvenile Delinquency (2021): Constructing a Child-Centered Prevention System

5.1 Introduction

Article 36 of *the United Nations Convention on the Rights of the Child* provides that States Parties shall protect the child against all other forms of exploitation prejudicial to any aspects of the child's welfare. But it is a social problem that child crime harms their welfare seriously, which receives a universal concern in the world. Prevention is a positive, efficient, low-cost means of crime management. Therefore, the prevention of child crime is a significant task in the process of building a harmonious society in China (Zhou, 2022).

The Law of the People's Republic of China on the Protection of Minors (2021) and The Law of the People's Republic of China on the Prevention of Juvenile Delinquency (2021) are important supports for the protection of children and the management of child crimes in the new era. The two laws complement each other with their unique charm and influence. The Law of the People's Republic of China on the Protection of Minors (2021) focuses on protecting the legitimate rights and interests of children. The Law of the People's Republic of China on the Prevention of Juvenile Delinquency (2021) has better filled the legal gap in the critical prevention of children at fault in China. A more scientific classification of the behavior of the guilty children has been carried out, and a professional education system for the guilty children has been established (Yao, 2019).

The Law of the People's Republic of China on the Prevention of Juvenile Delinquency was first promulgated in 1999 and specifically deals with the criminal misdemeanor of minors. The law was revised to meet the latest needs of social development in 2012 and 2020. The law is consistent with the criminal law of the People's Republic of China and the law of the People's Republic of China on penalties for the administration of public security, and it further clarifies the legal relationship and orientation of the three, ensuring the core position of educational

© The Author(s), under exclusive license to Springer Nature Singapore Pte Ltd. 2026

H. Li, P. Liang, *The Legal System for the Protection of Children's Rights in China*, Resilient and Friendly Living Environments,
https://doi.org/10.1007/978-981-95-9925-7_5

correction in the prevention of Children's crime, and is conducive to creating a healthy social environment for their growth.

As a "Rule of law gift" given to children by Chinese mothers, *The Law of the People's Republic of China on the Prevention of Juvenile Delinquency (2021)* has 7 chapters and 68 articles. Based on education and protection, the minors' bad behavior should be prevented and corrected in time. The act consists of general provisions, education for the Prevention of crime, the prevention of undesirable behavior, the correction of serious undesirable behavior, the prevention of recidivism, legal liability, and chapter 7 of the By-laws. The relevant rights and obligations of the parents or other guardians of minors, schools, educational executive branch, Public Security Bureau, Judiciary, and judicial organs of society are stipulated respectively.

The Law of the People's Republic of China on the Prevention of Juvenile Delinquency (2021) is an important component of the legal system for the protection of children's rights and interests. It is a vivid chapter in the practice of judicial protection of children, responding positively to the current public opinion. This chapter provides a detailed interpretation of *the juvenile delinquency prevention Law of the People's Republic of China (2021).*

5.2 Core System Design of The Law of the People's Republic of China on the Prevention of Juvenile Delinquency

The Law of the People's Republic of China on the Prevention of Juvenile Delinquency (2021) is structured according to the "Three-level prevention"' model in criminological theory. Based on the urgency of crime occurrence, crime prevention is divided into general prevention, critical prevention, and recidivism prevention. The "Education of Preventive Juvenile Delinquency" in Articles 15–27 of the act reflects the idea that primary prevention is general prevention; The "Prevention of Minors' Misbehavior" in Articles 28–37 and "Correction of Minors' serious misbehavior" in article 38–49 of the law embody the content of secondary prevention, that is, critical prevention; "The Prevention of juvenile recidivism" in article 50–60 focuses on three levels of prevention that is recidivism prevention. Among them, critical prevention is the core content of the law, creatively put forward the concept of "Bad behavior" and "Serious bad behavior", and made an enumerative provision for them, this is great progress in China's children's legislation.

5.2.1 General Provisions on Legislative Objectives and Principles

The fundamental issues relating to the prevention of child crime are laid down in the general part, including the objectives of the legislation, working principles, the subjects and responsibilities of participation, the strengthening of scientific research, and measures of recognition and reward.

1. Legislative Objectives

The Law of the People's Republic of China on the Prevention of Juvenile Delinquency (2021) aims to better protect the rights and interests of minors through law, while also preventing and reducing their harm to society and others. A crime is an act that endangers society and should be punished according to law. Crime is the unity of form characteristic of criminal illegality and essence characteristic of serious social harmfulness. What's more, child crime behavior has the characteristics of low age, serious violence, gang-related crimes, harmful behavior, and bad habits continue to worsen. The child is at an important stage of physical and mental development., and their brains and nervous systems are highly developed during puberty. Due to a lack of self-discipline and the ability to distinguish right from wrong, the child is highly susceptible to outside negative influence and acquires bad behavior. It is possible to prevent children from committing crimes if they are properly directed to correct their bad behavior. See Article 1 of this law:

Article 1
This law is enacted in order to protect the physical and mental health of minors, to cultivate their good conduct, and to effectively prevent them from breaking the law and committing crimes.

2. Principles

The working principles of preventing child crime include (1) a combination of education and protection; (2) hierarchical prevention, intervention, and correction; (3) respect for the human dignity of children and protection of their legitimate rights and interests; and (4) comprehensive treatment.

(1) Principles of education and protection. The principles are based on the characteristics of the child, and the analysis of subjective and objective causes of child crime. First of all, the stage of children is a weak self-resistance period and a need to shape, educate, train, and protection of the period. Secondly, article 3 of the UN Convention on the Rights of the Child states: "The best interests of the child shall be a primary consideration in all acts concerning children, whether carried out by public or private social welfare agencies, courts, administrative authorities or legislative bodies." The principle of protection is the overarching principle of safeguarding the rights and interests of the child, and it directs the work of child protection in all fields of society. Therefore, the prevention of child crime should also focus on the protection of children's interests. The key is to fully protect the rights and interests of the child, to achieve their fair and balanced development, to be able to develop a rational attitude and outlook on life by engaging in lawful and beneficial social activities, and to finally form a non-criminal attitude. See Article 2 of the Juvenile Delinquency Prevention Law of the People's Republic of China (2021) for details:

Article 2
The Juvenile delinquency prevention should be based on the combination of education and protection of minors, and should focus on prevention and intervention in advance, the minor's bad behavior and serious bad behavior timely hierarchical prevention, intervention and correction.

(2) Principle of hierarchical prevention, intervention, and correction. According to the degree of the child's fault, the step-by-step multi-entity treatment measures are set up to realize the hierarchical, pluralistic, and targeted educational correction, ensuring the desired results are achieved. It is not only the inherent requirement of the law of judicature but also the inevitable choice of the fine administration of judicature. As the object of intervention of the hierarchical intervention mechanism, the two ends of the "Axis of conduct" represent the general bad conduct and the most serious criminal conduct. And, occupying the center position of the axis is a serious bad behavior. The ultimate goal of scientific evaluation and grading of the application of the grading intervention mechanism is to select appropriate intervention measures for the guilty children and to maximize the effect of educational correction. At the same time, the process of hierarchical prevention of child crime is not a linear flow, but based on the effectiveness of interventions and the status of children. It can link the family, school, educational administration, government, social between the realization of regression and recycling, to avoid the loss of control of children.

Article 12 of *the UN Convention on the Rights of the Child* states: "The child who is capable of forming his or her views shall have the right to express them freely in all matters affecting him or her, and the views of the child shall be given due weight in accordance with the age and maturity of the child." This article mainly emphasizes the role of the child as a promoter and active participant and practically establishes the child as the main body in the protection of their interests. On the one hand, scientific grading is based on an accurate assessment of the degree of the child's deviance. On the other hand, in the daily operation of the hierarchical intervention mechanism, the guilty child is not only the object of Intervention but also the main force in achieving their own education correction. Therefore, when handling children's cases, the case-handling organs should give full play to the child's subjective initiative, pay attention to children's opinions and needs, and encourage the child's active and effective participation in various interventions with more than two options available where possible, in order to achieve the desired effect of the intervention. See Article 2 of *the Juvenile Delinquency Prevention Law of the People's Republic of China (2021)* for details:

Article 2
Juvenile delinquency prevention should be based on the combination of education and protection of minors, and should focus on prevention and intervention in advance, the minor's bad behavior and serious bad behavior timely hierarchical prevention, intervention, and correction.

(3) The principle of respecting the human dignity of the child and protecting their legitimate rights and interests. This principle insists the child is right-based, highlighting the most advantageous child principle. The child includes not only individual children but also specific groups of the child and the child as a whole. The protection of the child is not given in a one-way street but in a mutual interaction in which child participation is an important component. In dealing with matters involving the unspecified children, the voice of the child should not be ignored. Firstly, taking into account the specific circumstances and special needs of the child in question is essential. Secondly, the interests of children are given special and preferential consideration when the interests of all parties are weighed. See Article 3 of *the Juvenile Delinquency Prevention Law of the People's Republic of China (2021)* for details:

Article 3
In carrying out preventive juvenile delinquency work, the human dignity of minors shall be respected, and their legitimate rights and interests such as the right to reputation, privacy, and personal information shall be protected.

(4) The principle of comprehensive management. In order to strengthen the responsibility of the main body of society, this principle is based on the complexity and comprehensiveness of the reasons for the child's crimes. The system of child crime prevention is characterized by the diversity of subjects and the interactivity of contents. From the state organs of public power to the party and league organizations, and then to social organizations, China's child crime prevention system participates in a wide range of the main body and embodies the comprehensive meaning of comprehensive management. The main bodies involved in the prevention of child crime include state organs, people's organizations, social organizations, enterprises and institutions, residents' committees, villagers' committees, schools, families, and children. The interaction of the work system and work content reflects the meaning of integration in comprehensive management (Yin & Huang, 2022). The participants of the prevention work should take various measures to prevent children's crimes from different angles and save lost children through education, thus forming a big pattern of the whole society working together. See Article 4 of *the Juvenile Delinquency Prevention Law of the People's Republic of China (2021)* for details:

Article 4
The Preventive Juvenile Delinquency shall be dealt with comprehensively under the Government of the People's Republic of China organizations at all levels. The state organs, people's organizations, social organizations, enterprises and institutions, residents' committees, villagers' committees, schools, families, etc. shall take their respective responsibilities and cooperate with each other, we will work together to prevent juvenile delinquency, eliminate all negative factors that breed juvenile delinquency in a timely manner, and create a good social environment for the healthy development of minors.

The prevention of child crime is a systematic project. *The law of the People's Republic of China on the prevention of juvenile delinquency crime (2021)* specifies in detail the responsible parties and their corresponding duties. First of all, based on the national parental rights principle, the government is undoubtedly the main participant in the prevention of child crime, taking on the policy-making, supervision and management and other aspects of work. The government should strengthen supervision over the prevention management of the administrative departments, pay attention to strengthening supervision over the work on the child, and require the functional departments to carry out prevention work on the child under the rule of law and to detail their responsibilities, so as to guarantee the effect of legal education. Secondly, it is particularly important to point out that one of the core duties of state organs to prevent the child from committing crimes is to strengthen the construction of specialized schools and develop specialized education. Special education is intended for the child with serious misconduct. Special Education has dual attributes. On the one hand, it belongs to the national education system, which is an educational system with its own laws. On the other hand, it belongs to the system of measures of child protection, which is a compulsory correction system. It also provides for a number of important safeguards, namely, (1) the incorporation of economic and social development planning; (2) the establishment of a special education steering committee; (3) the establishment of special schools in a rational manner according to needs; (4) the State Council is authorized to formulate specific measures for the construction of specialized schools and specialized education. Finally, *The Law of the People's Republic of China on the Prevention of Juvenile Delinquency (2021)* stipulates the duties of the Public Security Bureau, People's Procuratorates, People's Court, Ministry of Justice, Young Communist League, women's federations, trade unions, federations of persons with disabilities, work committees concerned with the next generation, youth federations, student federations, Pioneer movement, relevant social organizations, and individual children. See Articles 5–11 of the juvenile delinquency prevention law of the People's Republic of China (2021) for details:

Article 5

The duties and responsibilities of the Government of the People's Republic of China at all levels in the field of juvenile delinquency prevention shall be as follows:

(1) to formulate a work plan for the prevention of juvenile delinquency;
(2) to organize the relevant departments of Public Security, education, civil affairs, Culture and Tourism, Market Supervision and administration, Internet Information, health, press and publication, film, radio and television, administration of justice, etc. to carry out preventive juvenile delinquency work;
(3) to provide policy support and financial security for the prevention of juvenile delinquency;
(4) to conduct inspections of the implementation of this law and the implementation of work plans;

(5) to organize and carry out juvenile delinquency education;
(6) other juvenile delinquency duties.

Article 6
The State shall strengthen the construction of special schools to provide special education to minors who have committed serious misconduct. Specialized education is an integral part of the national education system and an important protective measure for educating and rectifying minors who have serious bad behavior.

Provincial Government of the People's Republic of China should integrate the development of specialized education and the construction of specialized schools into their economic and social development plans. Local Government of the People's Republic of China at or above the county level shall set up special education steering committees and set up special schools according to needs.

The Special Education Steering Committee is composed of education, civil affairs, finance, human resources, Social Security, public security, judicial administration, People's Procuratorate, People's Court, Young Communist League, Women's Federation, Working Committee on Caring for the next generation, special schools, etc., as well as lawyers, social workers, and other personnel, to study and determine the special school teaching, management, and other related work.

Specific measures for the construction of special schools and special education shall be formulated by the State Council.

Article 7
The Public Security Bureau, People's procuratorates, People's Court, and Ministry of Justice Departments shall be in charge of the prevention of juvenile delinquency by special institutions or specialized personnel who have received professional training and are familiar with the physical and mental characteristics of minors.

Article 8
The Young Communist League, women's federations, trade unions, disabled persons' federations, working committees concerned with the next generation, youth federations, student federations, Pioneer movement and related social organizations, the Government of the People's Republic of China at all levels and their relevant departments, people's procuratorates and People's Court should be assisted in carrying out preventive juvenile delinquency work, so as to nurture social forces and provide support services for preventive juvenile delinquency.

Article 9
The state shall encourage, support, and guide social organizations such as social work service agencies to participate in the work related to juvenile delinquency prevention and strengthen supervision.

Article 10
No organization or individual may abet, coerce, or induce a minor to commit a bad act or a serious bad act, or provide conditions for a minor to commit such an act.

Article 11
Minors shall abide by laws and regulations and social and public moral norms, build up self-esteem, self-discipline, and self-strengthening consciousness, and enhance their ability to distinguish right from wrong and to protect themselves, consciously resist all kinds of bad behavior as well as illegal and criminal acts of temptation and infringement.

The Law of the People's Republic of China on the prevention of juvenile delinquency crimes (2021) also provides for the strengthening of scientific research on the prevention of child crime, as well as commendation and incentive measures. See Articles 12–14 of this law for details:

Article 12
The Prevention of Juvenile Delinquency shall take into account the physiological and psychological characteristics of minors of different ages, and strengthen the research on adolescent education, psychological care, psychological correction, and crime prevention countermeasures.

Article 13
The state encourages and supports the development of juvenile delinquency-related disciplines, professional establishment, personnel training, and scientific research, and conducts international exchanges and cooperation.

Article 14
The state shall commend and reward organizations and individuals who have made notable achievements in the prevention of juvenile delinquency.

5.2.2 *Mechanism of General Prevention*

General prevention refers to the identification and determination of the natural and social environment that provides an opportunity for or contributes to the commission of a crime and the conditions that prevent and eliminate the commission of a crime (Yuan, 2021). The problem of child crime is a complex crime problem composed of many external and internal factors. In order to achieve a good prevention and control effect, we must base on the existing legal norms and the physical and mental characteristics of children, carry out accurate prevention, and give play to the role of the social support system to achieve the whole process of prevention. The prevention of child crime is a systematic project with long-term relationships and influence the future development. Effective prevention of delinquent children to reduce crime is a shared responsibility of the justice system and the social sphere. To strengthen the prevention and intervention of children's crimes, the child should be educated in crime prevention through school education, community correction, child discipline, and other means, so as to reduce the risk of children's crimes.

Crime prevention education revolves around the responsibilities of the parties involved in general prevention.

Firstly, the state, society, schools, and families should carry out crime prevention education to enhance children's awareness and ability to prevent crimes. See Article 15 of the Juvenile Delinquency Prevention Law of the People's Republic of China (2021) for details:

> **Article 15**
> ***The state, society, schools, and families shall strengthen the education of minors in the core socialist values, carry out education in crime prevention, and strengthen minors' concept of the rule of law, to enable minors to establish a sense of discipline and law-abiding and prevent crimes, improve self-control ability.***

Secondly, parents or other guardians are the first responsible subjects in the prevention of children's crimes. They should fully perform their guardianship duties in accordance with the law, cultivate children's good character, and give timely education, guidance, and advice. The family is the primary place of contact for children and the first step in educating them. Child discipline is the foundation and the cornerstone of all education. As a child's first teacher, parents often have a direct impact on children's character, quality, and so on, and will accompany them through a long period of growth. Article 26(1) of the civil code states: "Parents shall have the obligation to bring up, educate and protect their minor children." Parents of children shall have direct responsibility for the education of children to prevent crimes, which naturally includes the contents of upbringing and education. As legal guardians of children, parents should: (1) strengthen the discipline and education of the child, maintain communication and exchange with their children, master their ideological trends, and guide the child to establish correct values and outlook on life, to strengthen the capacity for self-control and a sense of responsibility; (2) while at the same time setting an example of positive role models for children through their own normative behavior; (3) providing appropriate education on the rule of law, to make children understand the harm and consequences of crime, so that children have a sense of awe of the law, away from the Red Line of the law. See Article 16 of *The Law of the People's Republic of China on the Prevention of Juvenile Delinquency (2021)* for details:

Article 16

The parents or other guardians of minors shall bear direct responsibility for the crime prevention education of minors, and shall perform their guardianship duties in accordance with the law, establish good family customs, and cultivate the good conduct of minors; If a minor is found to be abnormal in psychology or behavior, he shall be informed of the situation and given education, guidance and advice in a timely manner, and shall not refuse or neglect his guardianship duties.

Thirdly, schools are the main battleground for the prevention of child crime. Specific measures should be taken to carry out targeted education on crime prevention, the rule of law, mental health education, establish a system for preventing and controlling bullying among students, introduce social workers in school, contact and cooperation between home and school, and assess work effect. The school is the first socialized environment after the child jumps out of the family and is the child's main education place. School education is the main front for the provision of a specialized system of education, which is further extended and strengthened on a child discipline basis. Faced with the reality that the child's outlook and personality have not been formed yet, the school undertakes the educational responsibilities of concept shaping and personality shaping. The school enjoys a relatively complete and independent main body responsibility and is a special place for providing systematic scientific knowledge and developing professional teaching activities for children (Su & Chen, 2022). Schools develop programs and rules for the prevention of crime against the child, and clarify the responsibilities of the various departments of the school in the area of crime prevention for children, so as to ensure that crime prevention education for the child is truly put in place. The school should report to the parents the first time the child who is at the first sign of a mistake, and correct the mistakes by way of labor education, so as to relieve their bad psychology. Schools should strengthen legal education on the child's crimes, to make them aware of the dangers and consequences of crimes and enhance their legal awareness and sense of responsibility. What's more, schools should create a good atmosphere through mock courts in which you can not commit, dare not commit, and are unwilling to commit. The construction of schools can not only reserve a way for the children to return to society but also carry out the judicial policy of "Less arrest, less prosecution, and less detention". See article 17–23 of *the Juvenile Delinquency Prevention Law of the People's Republic of China (2021)* for details:

Article 17

The Administrative Departments of Education and Schools shall incorporate crime prevention education into school teaching plans, and guide the teaching staff to take into account the characteristics of minors, and adopt a variety of ways to juvenile students targeted crime prevention education.

Article 18

A school shall employ full-time or part-time teachers engaged in legal education, and from the judicial and law enforcement agencies, legal education

and legal services, and other units to hire rule of law vice-principals, off-campus rule of law counselors.

Article 19
Schools shall provide full-time or part-time mental health education teachers to carry out mental health education. According to the actual situation, the school can cooperate with professional mental health organizations to establish mental health screening and early intervention mechanisms to prevent and solve students' abnormal psychological and behavioral problems.

The school shall strengthen communication with the parents or other guardians of the underage students and jointly carry out mental health education for the underage students; if it is found that the underage students may suffer from mental disorders, the parent or other guardian shall be informed immediately and sent to the relevant professional institution for medical treatment.

Article 20
The Administrative Department of Education shall, in conjunction with the relevant departments, establish a system for preventing and controlling student bullying. The school should strengthen the daily safety management, perfect the workflow of the detection and disposal of students' bullying, and strictly investigate and timely eliminate all kinds of hidden dangers that may lead to students' bullying behavior.

Article 21
The Administrative Department of Education encourages and supports schools to employ social workers to stay in schools for a long time or on a regular basis to assist in the development of moral education, rule of law education, life education, and mental health education, participate in the prevention and handling of bullying.

Article 22
Educational Administrative Departments and schools shall introduce scientific and reasonable educational methods by holding lectures, symposiums, training, and other activities, and instruct staff, parents, or other guardians of underage students to effectively prevent juvenile delinquency.

Schools shall inform the parents or other guardians of minor students of their plans for crime prevention education. The parents or other guardians of the minor students shall cooperate with the school to carry out targeted crime prevention education for the minor students.

Article 23
The Administrative Department of Education shall incorporate the effectiveness of crime prevention education into the annual assessment of schools.

Finally, the Government of the People's Republic of China and relevant departments, judiciary, mass organizations, villagers' committees, venues for off-campus activities, vocational training institutions, and employers should carry out publicity activities and training on the prevention of child crime. Society is another important place for the child's education. All sectors of society should strengthen the publicity and education for the prevention of children's crimes, so that children can understand the harmfulness and consequences of crimes and, at the same time provide relevant legal knowledge and legal aid services. Social education is a broader platform to complement child discipline and school education. We should give full play to the role of social organizations, and form a situation of joint efforts, mass prevention, and control. The community should serve as a comprehensive platform, social organizations as the carrier, and social work professionals as the supporting force, focusing on educating, managing, and serving dropout children, idle children, left-behind children, and other groups, while timely understanding and grasping their psychological trends. See article 24–27 of *the Juvenile Delinquency Prevention Law of the People's Republic of China (2021)* for details:

Article 24
Government of the People's Republic of China at all levels and their relevant departments, people's procuratorates, People's Court, Young Communist League, Pioneer movement, women's federations, disabled persons' federations, working committees for the care of the next generation, etc. shall combine with practice, to organize and organize various forms of publicity and educational activities on preventive juvenile delinquency. Where conditions permit, bases may be set up for the rule of law education of young people and legal education for minors.

Article 25
The Residents' Committee and the Villagers' Committee shall actively carry out targeted publicity activities on preventive juvenile delinquency and assist the Public Security Bureau in maintaining law and order around the school, to keep track of the guardianship, schooling, and employment situation of minors in their respective jurisdictions in a timely manner, and to organize and guide community and social organizations to participate in juvenile delinquency prevention work.

Article 26
Places for out-of-school activities such as youth palaces and children's activity centers shall take crime prevention education as an important part of their work and carry out various forms of publicity and education activities.

Article 27
When vocational training institutions and employing units provide vocational training to minors who have reached the age of 16 and are preparing for employment, they shall include crime prevention education in the training contents.

Children who grow up in the new age have more possibilities, but they also face many temptations. To achieve effective crime prevention, we need to pay attention to the whole society, to avoid the child going astray only after regret. The prevention of child crime should be based on the healthy growth and social development needs of children. On the one hand, we should improve the endogenous environment of child discipline through the child discipline guidance service system. On the other hand, we should encourage the participation of social forces to establish a home-school-community collaborative education mechanism to provide a good external environment for juvenile delinquency prevention. All parties need to work together to build a comprehensive social prevention and protection system, and jointly create a good environment for the child's healthy growth so that the child's life is in self-realization of development.

5.2.3 Critical Prevention

Critical prevention refers to the intervention and correction during the prevention window for some abnormal behaviors of the child that have not yet constituted crimes so that the child with abnormal behaviors can return to their normal life trajectories. Critical prevention advances the process of prevention to the evolution of bad behavior, concretizes the objective of the system, classifies and rationalizes the system measures, and forms a normative and complete system of child crime prevention. In contrast to the post-mortem punishment of "closing the barn door after the horse has bolted", critical prevention through strict standards to frame the child who may be in violation of the law groups, to take an intervention, corrective measures to prevent crime in the bud. In order to construct the mechanism of critical preventive treatment of children at fault, we should adhere to the principles of "National parental power", "Children's best interests" and "Differential treatment". The child who is at fault should be dealt with quickly in procedure and leniently in substance on the basis of helping them return to society in the future (He & Pei, 2021).

5.2.3.1 General Misconduct Intervention

General Misconduct Intervention is based on three core issues, first, how to define bad behavior, second, how to intervene in bad behavior by family, community, and school, and third how to intervene in common bad behavior.

First of all, *the Law of the People's Republic of China on the Prevention of Juvenile Delinquency (2021)* defines the undesirable behavior of children in terms of child protection by means of definitions and enumerations. The common feature of bad behavior is being "Not conducive to the healthy growth of minors", and its focus is from social order to the physical and mental health of the child, reflecting China's criminal policy on children from punishment to protection. Bad behavior is a kind of behavior that is harmful to the child's physical and mental health, but not harmful to society. Bad behavior is characterized by "what adults can do, children cannot", representing the lowest level of criminal behavior, such as children smoking, drinking truancy, and other detailed, life-oriented behavior. The bad behavior belongs to the child's "Identity crime behavior", which is usually rebellious and overstepping behavior in a specific period, and has strong self-healing properties. Therefore, we should focus on discipline and disciplinary intervention, of which child discipline and school education are the most important.

Bad behavior is the starting point of a hierarchical intervention system. Although the general bad behaviors only affect the child's conduct and do not appear to show a high risk of the perpetrator, traditional Chinese culture believes that "no evil is too small". Looking closely at the past experiences of child suspects, it can be found that the misdeeds of children are usually aggravated and aggravated by adverse environmental factors. Therefor the prevention of child crime should be fully covered, early Intervention and systemic correction. See Article 28 of *the Juvenile Delinquency Prevention Law of the People's Republic of China (2021)* for details:

Article 28

For the purpose of this law, the term "Bad behavior" refers to the following behaviors committed by minors that are detrimental to their healthy growth:

(1) smoking and drinking;
(2) repeated truancy and truancy;
(3) staying out at night or running away from home for no reason;
(4) indulging in the internet;
(5) associating with people with bad habits in society, organizing or participating in gangs that commit bad acts;
(6) entering places that are not suitable for minors according to laws and regulations;
(7) participating in gambling or gambling in disguised forms, or participating in activities such as feudal superstitions and cults;
(8) reading, watching, or listening to books, audio-visual products, or internet information that propagate obscenity, pornography, violence, terror, extremism, etc.;
(9) other bad behaviors that are harmful to the healthy growth of minors.

Secondly, the intervention for bad behavior is carried out by the family, the community, and the school on the basis of their respective duties: (1) the Guardian on the basis of his duties to discipline the child for bad behavior; (2) the community stops the child from behaving badly and urges the guardian to perform his or her duties; (3) the school can apply six kinds of management education measures to the students' bad behavior based on the educational duty. Although the system of critical prevention is one of the levels in the treatment of children's crimes, there are levels in the system itself. After the bad behavior is classified as the target behavior of critical prevention, in the selection of intervention measures, rather, judiciary intervention should be avoided and relatively light measures should be considered, with an emphasis on disciplinary and disciplinary interventions and using the least invasive intervention to achieve the best preventive effect. Measures for the prevention, education, and protection of undesirable behavior are mainly social and non-judicial in nature and do not impose administrative punishment or compulsory educational correction on children in any form, they will not be held criminally responsible. Parents or other guardians should be alert to their children who have committed minor offenses and strictly control their bad behavior. Social organizations need to grasp the mentality of such children in a timely manner, and actively communicate with families, schools, and jointly help the child who commits minor violations to return to the right track. Schools discipline children for minor offenses, require them to attend school services, order them to make guarantees, give warnings, and so on. See Articles 29–32 of *the Juvenile Delinquency Prevention Law of the People's Republic of China (2021)* for details:

Article 29
If the parents or other guardians of a minor discover that the minor has bad behavior, they shall stop it in a timely manner and strengthen discipline.

Article 30
Where a Public Security Bureau, a residents' committee, or a villagers' Committee discovers that a minor under its jurisdiction has committed any improper act, it shall stop it in a timely manner and urge his parents or other guardians to fulfill their duties of guardianship in accordance with the law.

Article 31
Schools shall strengthen management education and shall not discriminate against minors who have misbehaved; if they refuse to correct or the circumstances are serious, the school may, as the case may be, discipline or adopt the following measures of Management and education:

(1) discipline;
(2) requirements for compliance with specific codes of conduct;
(3) requirements for participation in specific topics of education;
(4) requirements for participation in school service activities;
(5) requiring psychological and behavioral intervention by social workers or other professionals;
(6) other appropriate management education measures.

Article 32

Schools and families shall strengthen communication and establish a home-school cooperation mechanism. If the school decides to adopt management education measures for minor students, it shall promptly inform its parents or other guardians; the parents or other guardians of minor students shall support and cooperate with the school in carrying out management education.

Finally, for bullying, truancy, staying out overnight, running away from home, and other more common situations, this law stipulates the school, family, public security organs, and relevant units of specific intervention duties.

Bullying on campus. Schools can take the following measures to prevent bullying in schools. (1) formulate an emergency response plan for student bullying incidents; (2) provide professional psychological counseling to the victims in a timely manner; (3) improve the campus security system, and strengthen inspection; (4) contact the parents of the victims in time and help the parents to enlighten and cure the victims.

Truancy. If a child is absent from school or plays truant, the school shall promptly contact his or her parents or other guardians to find out the underlying reasons for such absenteeism and provide the appropriate measures to solve the child's difficult problems.

Staying out overnight and running away from home. In order to prevent children from staying out at night and running away from home without reason, we should take relevant measures: (1) families and schools work together to build a responsibility mechanism; (2) improve children's safety consciousness and self-protection ability; (3) to carry out cultural and recreational activities and strengthen the management effect. The school should vigorously advocate civilized life, and polite exchanges, and create a harmonious and orderly campus atmosphere.

See Articles 33–37 of the Juvenile Delinquency Prevention Law of the People's Republic of China (2021) for details:

Article 33

Where a minor student steals a small amount of property or bullies a student by beating, abusing, intimidating, or forcibly demanding property, the circumstances are minor, schools may take corresponding management and education measures in accordance with article zero of this law.

Article 34

Where an underage student is absent from school or plays truant, the school shall promptly contact his parents or other guardians to find out about the relevant situation; if there is no justifiable reason, the school and the parents or other guardians of the underage students shall urge them to return to school to study.

Article 35
If a minor does not return home at night or runs away from home without reason, his or her parents or other guardians, or the boarding school where he or she resides, shall promptly search for him or her and report to the Public Security Bureau if necessary.

Those who take in minors who stay out late or run away from home shall contact their parents, guardians, or schools in a timely manner, and those who are unable to do so shall report to the Public Security Bureau in a timely manner.

Article 36
For minors who stay out at night, run away from home, or live on the streets, the Public Security Bureau and public places management agencies shall take effective protection measures in a timely manner after finding or receiving reports, and notify his parents or other guardians or the boarding school where he resides, and shall escort him back to his residence or school if necessary; if he is unable to contact his parents or other guardians or the school, minors shall be escorted to rescue and protection institutions to receive assistance.

Article 37
Where the parents or other guardians of a minor or a school discover that a minor has organized or joined a gang that commits a bad act, they shall stop it in a timely manner; if they discover that the gang is suspected of breaking the law or committing a crime, should be reported to the Public Security Bureau immediately.

5.2.3.2 Rehabilitation of Serious Misconduct

To deconstruct the different levels of children's misdeeds from a systematic perspective, the ones in the central position should be considered serious misdeeds. Grasping this central point plays a vital role in the critical prevention and recidivism prevention of child crime. There are two core problems in the treatment of serious misconduct, one is how to define serious misconduct, and the other is how to design a system of treatment measures.

Based on the consideration of linking up and coordinating with *the Law on Punishment of Public Security Administration* and the Criminal Law, a serious misdemeanor is a harmful act committed by children against society, including two types: one is the act of violating Public Security Administration, the other is the act that violates the Criminal Law but is not criminally punished because it has not reached the age of criminal responsibility. The common feature of seriously bad behavior is described as "Serious harm to society". See Article 38 of *The Law of the People's Republic of China on the Prevention of Juvenile Delinquency (2021)* for details:

Article 38

The term "Serious undesirable acts" as used in this law refers to acts committed by minors that are provided for in the criminal law and are not subject to criminal punishment because they are under the age of legal criminal responsibility, as well as the following serious harm to society:

(1) gang fights, chasing, intercepting others, forced or arbitrary damage, occupation of public and private property, and other acts of provocation and trouble;
(2) illegal carrying of firearms, ammunition, crossbows, daggers, and other state-prescribed control devices;
(3) beating, insulting, intimidating, or intentionally harming another person's body;
(4) theft, robbery, robbery, or intentional destruction of public or private property;
(5) dissemination of obscene books, audio-visual products, or information, etc.;
(6) prostitution, solicitation of prostitution, or performing obscene performances;
(7) taking or injecting drugs, or to provide drugs to others;
(8) participate in gambling for more money, (9) other serious harm to society behavior.

The intervention of serious bad behavior is an important node in the prevention of children's first offense, but also the core of the hierarchical intervention mechanism. The ultimate goal of scientific evaluation and accurate grading of the application target and scope of the grading intervention mechanism is to select the most suitable intervention measures for the guilty children and to realize the maximum effect of educational correction. Serious misconduct uses more severe measures than bad behavior, including informal interventions such as home discipline and school education, as well as formal interventions of an administrative nature. There are three types of measures for serious malpractice, the first is nine kinds of educational measures, the second is special educational measures, the third is special educational measures, and the intensity of the three types of measures is constantly upgrading.

The hierarchical treatment of the child at fault is an inevitable requirement for the further improvement and fine development of the child justice system. We should make use of the social security system under the guidance of the United Nations Convention on the Rights of the Child, and fully mobilize judiciary and other resources to enrich and improve protective measures. Distinguishing between the place where the intervention is carried out and the extent of the restriction on the rights and freedoms of children at fault, interventions can be classified from light to heavy: socialized treatment, semi-institutional treatment, institutional treatment, and criminal treatment (Song & Qian, 2022).

First, 9 kinds of corrective educational measures belong to socialized treatment measures. Socialized treatment measures, also known as family, school, and socio-educational measures, generally do not change the life and learning environment of minors. They are not administrative or criminal punishments but a kind of educational measure of "teaching instead of punishment". Therefore, in the practice of hierarchical intervention, the implementer may decide to apply it alone or in combination with other measures according to the actual needs. See Articles 39–42 of *the Juvenile Delinquency Prevention law of the People's Republic of China (2021)* for details:

Article 39
If the parents or other guardians, schools, residents' committees or villagers' committees of a minor discover that someone abets, coerces, or lures a minor to commit a serious misdeed, should be reported to the Public Security Bureau immediately. If the public security organ receives a report or discovers the above-mentioned situation, it shall promptly investigate and deal with the case in accordance with the law.

Article 40
Where a Public Security Bureau receives a report or discovers that a minor has serious misconduct, it shall stop it in a timely manner, investigate and deal with it according to law, and may order his parents or other guardians to eliminate or mitigate the consequences of the violation, take measures to exercise strict discipline.

Article 41
The Public Security Bureau may, depending on the specific circumstances, take the following corrective and educational measures with respect to minors who have committed serious misconduct:

(1) admonish them;
(2) order them to apologize and compensate for losses;
(3) order them to make amends;
(4) ordering regular reporting of activities;
(5) ordering compliance with specific codes of conduct and not to carry out specific acts, contact with specific persons, or enter specific places;
(6) ordering psychological counseling and behavior correction;
(7) ordering them to take part in social service activities;
(8) ordering them to receive social observation and have them educated, supervised, and restrained by social organizations and relevant institutions in appropriate places;
(9) other appropriate corrective and educational measures.

Article 42
The Public Security Bureau May, as necessary, invite social organizations such as schools, residents' committees, villagers' committees, and social work service agencies to participate in corrective education for minors.

The parents or other guardians of minors shall actively cooperate with the implementation of corrective and educational measures, and shall not obstruct or leave unattended.

Second, special educational measures are semi-institutional treatment measures. Semi-institutionalized treatment measures, which fall between socialization and institutionalization measures, are mainly applied to the child who have committed more serious crimes and misdemeanors and cannot be effectively corrected by socialized treatment measures alone. There is a clear difference between specialized schools and juvenile detention centers: (1) From the legal nature, the special school is a kind of educational correction for children who do not meet the conditions of general education. Juvenile detention is a form of Re-education through labor for children who have committed serious misconduct or are already at risk. (2) From the point of view of its purpose, the special school is set up to prevent crimes and to educate minors correction, rather than restrict personal freedom. The purpose of juvenile detention centers is to punish and rehabilitate minors who have serious bad behavior or have a certain personal danger. (3) As far as the foundation is concerned, the foundation for the establishment of special schools is *the Law of the People's Republic of China on the Prevention of Juvenile Delinquency (2021)*, juvenile detention centers are based on *the Prison Law of the People's Republic of China* and *the Criminal Procedure Law of the People's Republic of China*. At the same time, semi-institutional treatment measures, although involving specialized schools, still require the cooperation of parents and families and do not remove children from the social support system. See Articles 43 and 44 of *the Juvenile Delinquency Prevention Law of the People's Republic of China (2021)* for details:

Article 43
Where the parents or other guardians of a minor who has committed a serious misdemeanor, or the school in which the minor resides is unable to exercise discipline or the discipline is ineffective, an application may be filed with the administrative department of Education, after being assessed and approved by the Special Education Steering Committee, the educational administration department decides to send them to special schools for special education.

Article 44
If a minor has one of the following circumstances, the minor shall be assessed and approved by the Special Education Steering Committee, and the educational administration, in conjunction with the Public Security Bureau, may decide to enroll him in a special school for special education:

(1) to commit an act of serious danger to society, in a serious manner or with serious consequences;

(2) repeatedly commit acts that seriously endanger society
(3) refusing to accept or cooperate with the corrective and educational measures provided for in article forty-one of this law;
(4) other circumstances as prescribed by laws and administrative regulations.

Third, the special corrective educational measures are institutional treatment measures. The institutionalization treatment measure is a kind of measure in the system of non-penalty treatment, which has the character of taking in and restricting personal freedom for a long time. *The Law of the People's Republic of China on the Prevention of Juvenile Delinquency (2021)* provides for the establishment of special places by the government for the child who has committed serious offenses but cannot yet apply criminal treatment measures. And those children shall be subjected to compulsory isolation, compulsory treatment, and compulsory education. Such institutional treatment measures are different from criminal treatment measures and do not have the function of penalty enforcement. The application of corrective educational measures is determined by the Public Security Bureau. The application of special educational measures can be classified into two types: application for admission and compulsory admission. See Articles 45–49 of *the Juvenile Delinquency Prevention law of the People's Republic of China (2021)* for details:

Article 45
If a minor commits an act specified in the criminal law and is not subject to criminal punishment because he or she is under the age of legal criminal responsibility, he or she shall be assessed and approved by a special education steering committee, the educational administration, in conjunction with the Public Security Bureau, may decide to provide special corrective education.

The provincial-level Government of the People's Republic of China should, taking into account local conditions, determine at least one special school to set up special places in accordance with different school districts, classes, and other means to provide special corrective education for minors as stipulated in the preceding paragraph.

The special places specified in the preceding paragraph shall be managed in a closed loop, and the Public Security Bureau and Ministry of Justice Departments shall be responsible for the correction of minors, while the administrative departments of education shall be responsible for the education of minors.

Article 46
A special school shall, in due course of each semester, submit to the Special Education Steering Committee for an assessment of the situation of minors receiving special education. If, after evaluation, it is appropriate to transfer minors back to ordinary schools, the Special Education Steering Committee shall make a written recommendation to the original decision-making

authority, which shall decide whether to transfer minors back to ordinary schools.

If the original decision-making organ decides to transfer minor students back to an ordinary school, the original school may not refuse to accept them; if, due to special circumstances, it is not suitable to transfer them back to the original school, the Education Administrative Department shall arrange for the transfer.

Article 47
Special schools shall educate and correct minors who receive special education in a classified way, and carry out moral, legal, and mental health education in a targeted manner, minors who have not completed their compulsory education should be guaranteed continued compulsory education.

The status of minor students of specialized schools shall be retained in the original school, and the original school shall issue a graduation certificate if the students meet the graduation requirements.

Article 48
The specialized school shall strengthen its contact with the parents or other guardians of minors receiving specialized education and regularly report to them on the treatment and education of minors, to provide convenience for parents or other guardians, relatives, etc. to visit minors.

Article 49
If a minor or his parents or other guardians are not satisfied with the administrative decision stipulated in this chapter, they may file an administrative reconsideration or an administrative lawsuit in accordance with the law.

5.2.4 Juvenile Recidivism Prevention System

Prevention of recidivism refers to the punishment and corrective education of the child who has committed crimes so that they will not commit crimes again. Article 40 of *the United Nations Convention on the Rights of the Child* provides that, "States Parties recognize the right of children alleged, accused or believed to have infringed criminal law to be treated in a manner that promotes their dignity and worth and enhances their respect for the human rights and fundamental freedoms of others. Such treatment should take into account their age and their desire to promote their reintegration into society and play an active role in society." *The Law of the People's Republic of China on the Prevention of Juvenile Delinquency (2021)* places greater emphasis on the prevention of child crime, and it also pays attention to the protection of the development of children after their release from prison or after receiving community correction, so as to reduce the possibility of the child re-committing crimes, which is beneficial to the protection of children. The prevention of recidivism is oriented to return to the good and to bridge the gap from evil. Crime prevention at this level is largely within the criminal justice system.

The prevention of recidivism revolves around how to better help and promote the return of the child who has committed crimes to society. It integrates with the criminal procedure law, community correction law, and prison law, proposing measures such as: strengthening education on the rule of law in handling cases; further standardizing the system of social investigation and psychological assessment; establishing a system of suitable guarantors and a system of social observation and care; and strengthening measures such as separate detention, management, and education; and community correction, ensuring the compulsory education, legal education and vocational and technical education of minors serving prison terms, and implementing measures for the placement of the child who has been released from prison and receive community correction, the relevant measures and the system of sealing criminal records shall be applied to minors, and the people's procuratorates shall exercise legal supervision over the prevention of recidivism.

First of all, in the process of handling the case, we should strengthen the rule of law education, further standardize the social investigation and psychological evaluation system, and establish a suitable guarantor system and social observation system. After the occurrence of child crime, timely intervention and education should be carried out to prevent their re-offending. The return of a child will affect a family, a school, but also the whole of society to form a trend of thought of self-reflection, and fundamentally promote the overall effect of crime prevention (Zhou & Wang, 2020). The prevention of recidivism has become more focused on targeted education, and specific provisions have been added to the Public Security Bureau, prosecutors' offices, and courts when dealing with criminal cases involving children. Social investigation and psychological assessment of child suspects and defendants are provided as a reference for handling cases and educating children. Among them, on the one hand, social investigation should be entrusted to a social investigation institution with corresponding qualifications. A juvenile delinquency criminal suspect or a defendant may, when necessary, entrust the work of a judicial office, a juvenile protection organization, a psychological counselor, or other qualified personnel with psychological counseling. On the other hand, social surveys should focus on the child's family situation, growth experience, guardianship and education and social interaction, etc. We should analyze the child's bad behavior, serious bad behavior and criminal behavior according to their needs, and propose educational and corrective suggestions. See article 50–52 of *the Juvenile Delinquency Prevention Law of the People's Republic of China (2021)* for details:

Article 50

In handling criminal cases involving minors, the Public Security Bureau, People's procuratorates and People's Court shall, in light of the physiological and psychological characteristics of minors and the circumstances of their crimes, carry out law education targeted at them.

To educate minors involved in criminal cases, where the participation of adult relatives other than their legal representatives or teachers, counselors, etc. is conducive to the reform and rescue of minors, the Public Security Bureau, People's Procuratorates and People's Court shall invite them to participate in relevant activities.

Article 51

The Public Security Bureau, People's procuratorates and People's Court shall handle criminal cases involving minors, they may, on their own, or entrust relevant social organizations and institutions to conduct social investigations into the growth experience, reasons for committing crimes, guardianship, education, etc. of the defendants of juvenile delinquency criminal suspects; The psychological assessment of a juvenile delinquency suspect, the defendant and his legal representative may be carried out as required and with the consent of the juvenile delinquency suspect, the defendant and his legal representative.

The reports of social investigation and psychological assessment can be used as references for handling cases and educating minors.

Article 52

Where the Public Security Bureau, People's procuratorates, and People's Court apply to minors who have no fixed domicile and cannot provide guarantors, they shall designate appropriate adults as guarantors, if necessary, minors who are released on bail and awaiting trial may be arranged to receive social observation.

Second, enforcement of measures to strengthen separate detention, management, and education, as well as community correction measures to protect the compulsory education, legal education, and vocational and technical education of juvenile offenders. The child's justice cannot be simply "Done in one go", it must be established in line with the physical and mental characteristics of the child's criminal justice treatment model. Judicial protection does not mean that all cases have to go through the criminal justice process, on the contrary, it should also reflect the care of child justice in other areas. An independent special agency for the prevention and handling of children's crimes and mistakes shall be established, and special departments or special personnel shall be set up in the Public Security Bureau, People's

Procuratorates, and People's Court to handle children's crimes and mistakes. See Articles 53 and 54 of the Juvenile Delinquency Prevention Law of the People's Republic of China (2021) for details:

Article 53
Minors who are detained, arrested, or whose sentences are to be carried out in juvenile correctional institutions shall be detained, managed, and educated separately from adults. Community correction for minors shall be carried out separately from that for adults.

The Public Security Bureau, People's procuratorates, People's Court, and Ministry of Justice Departments shall cooperate with the educational administrative departments for minors who have the above-mentioned circumstances and have not completed compulsory education, to ensure that they continue to be in compulsory education.

Article 54
Juvenile correctional institutions and community correction institutions shall strengthen rule of law education for juvenile offenders and objects of juvenile community correction and provide them with vocational education according to the actual situation.

Lastly, following the completion of the implementation of the measures, measures for the placement and rehabilitation of the child who has been released from prison and who has received community correction are being implemented, and the relevant measures and the system of sealing criminal records are being applied to minors, the People's Procuratorates exercise legal supervision over the prevention of reoffending.

The implementation of placement and education measures is conducive to the smooth return of the guilty child to society. For the guilty children instead of simply "letting them go" or "punishing them", the state departments and social organizations should establish corresponding auxiliary measures, such as placement and education measures, to help the children return to the right track smoothly. In the process of implementing the measures of placement and education, we should help the children in accordance with their individual characteristics, and not take blunt measures.

A system of sealing records of children's misdeeds. Article 40 of *the UN Convention on the Rights of the Child* stresses that "The privacy of children shall be fully respected at all stages of the proceedings". The principle of privacy protection should be applied throughout all stages of the handling of children's critical behavior, such that (1) investigations of children are generally not made public; (2) decisions on and implementation of relevant handling measures should be made in private; (3) files on children's cases must be kept strictly confidential and must not be made known or used by third parties. The system of keeping records of children's misdeeds is beneficial to weakening children's psychological labels and helping the child to go back to school, further, their studies, get jobs, and return to society smoothly. The critical file of a child who has committed a critical act is kept for a legal period of time, while the child's mental health is assessed and assessed annually, and the seal may be terminated if serious misconduct or risk factors are found. For the implementation of critical behavior of children, in their school, further education, employment, and other aspects of their implementation of critical behavior will not be adversely affected. In addition, relevant departments and media should also pay attention to the protection of privacy, anonymity, and silencing when reporting on children's cases.

The people's procuratorates exercise legal supervision over the prevention ore offending it. It is also the inherent requirement to promote the modernization of the national governance system and governance capacity that promoting the establishment and improvement of a prevention framework for the prevention of Children's crimes. The supervision system of the People's Procuratorate also conforms to the development trend of our country's children's governance work (Zhang & Feng, 2022). Moreover, this is advantageous to the "Catfish effect" of legal supervision, and solves realistic problems such as the loss of control, to eliminate the hidden dangers of children's crimes and form a resultant force of child protection. The prosecutorial organs should promote the extension of the rule of law and enhance the effectiveness of social governance. They should make use of all kinds of media resources and platforms to reinforce the strength of propaganda guidance and supervision by public opinion and broaden the channels of clue discovery. We will improve the reporting mechanism and reward system, encouraging the public to report crimes that infringe on the child's rights and interests and improve cooperation mechanisms with judicial administration, social organizations, and volunteers. We will give full play to the role of public interest litigation prosecutorial function, promote the protection of the child's legitimate rights and interests, and safeguard public interests to coordinate and promote.

See article 55–60 of the Juvenile Delinquency Prevention Law of the People's Republic of China (2021) for details:

Article 55

A community correction institution shall inform the juvenile community correction objects of the relevant provisions on the placement of help and education, and with the placement of help and education work departments to implement or solve the problem of juvenile community correction objects, such as school, and employment.

Article 56
For minors who have been released after serving their sentences, juvenile correctional institutions shall notify their parents or other guardians in advance of their timely recovery, and shall assist in the implementation of measures for placement and rehabilitation. If there are no parents or other guardians, or it is impossible to ascertain the identity of their parents or other guardians, the juvenile correctional institution shall notify in advance the Ministry of Justice of the place where the juvenile's household registration was held or where he lives to arrange for the personnel to pick him up on time, the Department of Civil Affairs or the residents' committee or the villagers' Committee shall exercise guardianship over them in accordance with law.

Article 57
The parents or other guardians of minors, as well as schools, residents' committees, and Villagers' committees, shall take effective measures to help and educate minors who have received community correction and been released after serving their sentences, to assist the judiciary and relevant departments in the placement and teaching work.

The Residents' Committee or the Villagers' Committee may employ retirees, volunteers, or other persons who are of good moral character, have a decent style of work, and are enthusiastic about the work of minors to assist in the resettlement and education work as stipulated in the preceding paragraph.

Article 58
Minors who have been released after serving their sentences and receive community correction shall enjoy the same rights as other minors in terms of resuming their studies, pursuing further studies, and obtaining employment in accordance with the law, and no unit or individual may discriminate against them.

Article 59
Where the criminal records of minors are sealed up according to law, the Public Security Bureau, People's procuratorates, People's Court, and Ministry of Justice Offices shall not provide them to any unit or individual, except where the judiciary is required for handling cases or the unit concerned makes inquiries in accordance with the relevant provisions of the state. Units and individuals conducting inquiries according to law shall keep confidential the relevant recorded information.

The provisions of the preceding paragraph shall apply to the records of minors receiving specialized corrective education and specialized education, as well as records of administrative punishment, criminal coercive measures, and non-prosecution.

Article 60
The People's Procuratorate shall exercise prosecutorial power in accordance with law to supervise the prevention of juvenile delinquency.

5.2.5 Legal Responsibility

Legal liability is the legal consequence that the subject concerned should bear if he violates the provisions of *the Law of the People's Republic of China on Juvenile Delinquency Prevention (2021)* and fails to fulfill the corresponding obligations. The compulsion of law is one of the important characteristics of law, and also an important guarantee for the implementation of legal norms. *The People's Republic of China Law on Juvenile Delinquency Prevention (2021)* has its own unique requirements, which aim to control criminal acts in their infancy. The operation of such laws relies on in-depth research into the patterns of occurrence and development of criminal phenomena, as well as scientific assessment of the possibility of future criminal outcomes. Under such a premise, the establishment of legal liability will not be as clear and rigid as the traditional law, but pay more attention to the effect of preventive measures and the actual impact. *The Law of the People's Republic of China on the Prevention of Juvenile Delinquency (2021)* specifies the duty of parents or other guardians, schools, educational administrative departments, governments, social organizations, etc. to strengthen the education, management, and protection of children, and to prevent their crimes. It is clear that these legal responsibilities are primarily requirements and restraints on adults. And that the conscious observance and enforcement of these legal norms is the hope of the state, which otherwise has the right to impose sanctions for acts of resistance, breach, or destruction, to ensure the implementation of legal norms. See Articles 61–67 of *the Juvenile Delinquency Prevention Law of the People's Republic of China (2021)* for details:

Article 61
If the Public Security Bureau, People's Procuratorate, or People's Court, in the course of handling a case, discovers that the parents or other guardians of a minor who has committed a serious misdeed have not performed their duties of guardianship in accordance with the law, they should be admonished and may be ordered to accept child discipline instruction.

Article 62
If a school or its teaching staff violates the provisions of this law, fails to perform their duty to prevent juvenile delinquency, or mistreats or discriminates against minors concerned, the education administration and other departments

shall order them to make corrections and notify them of criticism; If the circumstances are serious, the directly responsible person-in-charge and other directly responsible persons shall be punished according to law. If the Act constitutes a violation of the administration of public security, the Public Security Bureau shall, in accordance with the law, impose a public security administration penalty.

Teaching and administrative staff instigate, coerce, or induce minors to commit bad acts or serious bad acts, as well as those with bad conduct or bad influence, the educational administrative department and the school shall be dismissed or dismissed according to law.

Article 63
Where, in violation of the provisions of this law, the relevant minors are discriminated against in terms of resuming their studies, further studies, employment, etc., the unit in which they work or the departments of education, human resources, Social Security, etc. shall order them to make corrections; if they refuse to make corrections, the directly responsible person-in-charge or other directly responsible persons shall be punished according to law.

Article 64
Where a social organization, institution, or its staff maltreat or discriminate against a minor under social care, or issue a false social survey or psychological evaluation report, if the Department of Civil Affairs, Judicial Administration, or other departments impose sanctions on the person in charge or other persons directly responsible in accordance with the law, constituting a violation of Public Security Administration, the Public Security Bureau shall impose public security administration penalties.

Article 65
Whoever abets, coerces, or entices a minor to commit a bad act or a serious bad act, which constitutes a violation of the administration of public security, shall be punished by the Public Security Bureau for Public Security Administration according to law.

Article 66
In the prevention of juvenile delinquency Abuse of authority, dereliction of duty, favoritism, and malpractice, state organs and their functionaries shall, in the case of the persons in charge and other persons directly responsible, the punishment shall be given according to law.

Article 67

Whoever violates the provisions of this law and constitutes a crime shall be investigated for criminal responsibility according to law.

At the same time, it should be noted that *the Law of the People's Republic of China on the Prevention of Juvenile Delinquency (2021)* is not a punishment law for child misconduct, but a special child protection law. It clearly defines child misconduct, as serious misconduct, but for children is mainly education and guidance, but does not provide for the child to violate the law's legal responsibility. However, this does not mean that a child can violate this law without any responsibility. The purpose of this law is to educate, protect the healthy growth of the child, and actively prevent the child from breaking the law and committing crimes. However, what should we do if the child has committed bad acts and serious bad acts or even criminal acts? China's law has a unified and complete system. We can apply other relevant laws to deal with it, such as civil law, public security administrative regulations, and criminal law can adjust and deal with these acts. *The Law of the People's Republic of China on Penalties for the Administration of Public Security, the Criminal Law of the People's Republic of China*, etc., put more emphasis on ex post facto punishment, while *the Law of the People's Republic of China on the Prevention of Juvenile Delinquency (2021)*, focuses on the prevention in advance. For the sake of the child's healthy growth and social progress and development, children themselves should study *the Law of the People's Republic of China on the Prevention of Juvenile Delinquency (2021)* carefully at the dawn of the new millennium, to comprehensively improve their own qualities, including the quality of law and the concept of the rule of law. Then they can make their due contribution to the building of a great, prosperous, and powerful motherland with Chinese characteristics in the twenty-first century.

5.3 Summary

The development of a country depends on the unremitting struggle of generations. The so-called "The youth outshines the blue" and "The waves behind the Yangtze River push forward the waves" all express the infinite potential and possibility of young life. And children as the rising sun, not only shoulder the mission of contributing to the country but also have the right to feel the warmth from the motherland's nourishment. Therefore, China has always been committed to exploring good ways to protect the child and has established a complete legal system to protect the child's rights and interests. *The Law of the People's Republic of China on the Prevention of Juvenile Delinquency (2021)* is an important part of the legal system for the protection of children's rights and interests, to provide a solid institutional guarantee for the prevention of child crime and the protection of healthy growth of children.

The prevention and intervention of children's wrong behavior is not only the need for social governance but also the need to protect children's rights interests and development. The promulgation and implementation of *the Law of the People's Republic of China on the Prevention of Juvenile Delinquency (2021)* establishes a mechanism for graded intervention and correction of children at fault, which is in line with the national conditions, and forms a good atmosphere of care and love for children has in the whole society. This chapter takes the grade prevention, intervention, and correction of children's crime as the main content, and expounds on the general prevention, critical prevention, and recidivism prevention system of children's crime in detail. This chapter describes the responsibilities and corresponding legal responsibilities of family, school, government, and related social organizations are clearly defined. Only when the subject and the responsibility of the subject are clear, the system of hierarchical prevention and intervention can be effectively implemented. The two-way theory-practice approach to justice for children with Chinese characteristics ensures that *the Law of the People's Republic of China on the Prevention of Juvenile Delinquency (2021)* can withstand the test of practice, and it will be further improved and developed in practice.

We will support the healthy growth of children rule of law for a blue sky, and care for more children and a better tomorrow. In the future, China will continue to strengthen the policy-making, system-building, implementation effect, and value evaluation of child crime prevention. We will continue to modernize China's system and capabilities for the prevention and correction of children's crimes, ensuring the healthy development of society and children!

References

He, W., & Pei, Z. (2021). A probe into the mechanism of critical preventive treatment of juvenile delinquents--taking the juvenile care system in Taiwan as a mirror. *People's Procuratorate, 14*, 68–70.

Song, Y., & Qian, W. (2022). A study on the hierarchical intervention mechanism of juvenile delinquents in our country--focusing on specialized education. *Journal of the Yunnan Normal University (Philosophy and Social Sciences), 6*, 56–69.

Su, M., & Chen, X. (2022). Juvenile delinquency prevention and child discipline legislation. *Journal of China Women's University, 2*, 21–26.

Yao, J. (2019). Predicament and outlet of juvenile law. *Social Science Abstracts, 11*, 74–76.

Yin, L., & Huang, J. (2022). Prevention of juvenile delinquency status, problems and solutions. *Journal of Wuhan Public Security Cadre College, 4*, 57–61.

Yuan, N. (2021). On the legal construction of the juvenile delinquency three-level prevention model--from the perspective of the revision of the law on the prevention of juvenile delinquency. *Study on the Prevention of Juvenile Delinquency, 2*, 42–50.

Zhang, Y., & Feng, Y. (2022). Prevention and control of juvenile delinquency under age in the post-criminal law Amendment XI era. *Journal of the Shihezi University (Philosophy and Social Sciences Edition), 1*, 54–63.

Zhou, S., & Wang, C. (2020). Study on the system of critical prevention of minors. *Juvenile Delinquency, 2*, 46–54.

Zhou, Y. (2022). The trend of special education legislation under the concept of responsive legislation--from the perspective of the revision of the law on the prevention of juvenile delinquency. *Journal of Chinese People's Public Security University Science (Social Sciences), 3*, 11–19.

Chapter 6
The Anti-Domestic Violence Law in China: Protecting Children's Rights Within the Family Sphere

6.1 Introduction

The impact of domestic violence on children has become an important issue facing all countries in the world, the United Nations established November 25 every year as the "International Day for the Elimination of Domestic Violence", all countries and regions in the world have always been very concerned about the issue of domestic violence against children. As a signatory to the United Nations Convention on the Rights of the Child, China has always attached great importance to the survival and development of children, actively fulfilled its obligations under the Convention, and made unremitting efforts to protect the rights and interests of children (Editorial Department of This Journal, 2016).

The harm brought by domestic violence to children is immeasurable, whether it is a personal experience of domestic violence or witnessing domestic violence, whether it involves a single incident or years of abuse. All have negative effects on the healthy growth of children. Research shows that domestic violence will cause children to produce a series of behavioral problems, which may be manifested as aggressive behavior, conduct disorder, etc., in the short term, it easily causes a series of serious social harm consequences, so it is urgent to sanction, stop and prevent domestic violence against minors.

Since ancient times, the Chinese nation has embraced a fine traditional culture of "self-cultivation, family harmony, governance, peace and prosperity" and "family harmony and prosperity". To carry forward Chinese culture, attach importance to family virtues, promote family harmony, love each other, and promote the healthy growth of the next generation has been the pursuit of our Chinese nation since ancient times. To effectively protect the rights and interests of all family members, especially women, and children, and strive to make every family happy and

© The Author(s), under exclusive license to Springer Nature Singapore Pte Ltd. 2026
H. Li, P. Liang, *The Legal System for the Protection of Children's Rights in China*, Resilient and Friendly Living Environments,
https://doi.org/10.1007/978-981-95-9925-7_6

harmonious is the driving force for the Chinese government to constantly improve laws and regulations.

In 2015, the 18th session of the Standing Committee of the 12th National People's Congress deliberated and adopted the Anti-Domestic Violence Law of the People's Republic of China, which went into effect on March 1, 2016. The Anti-Domestic Violence Law of the People's Republic of China has made special provisions for the protection of children. In the process of enacting the Law, the perspective of child protection that has been called for by experts and scholars over the years has been actively adopted, and special protection content has been highlighted. The introduction of the Anti-Domestic Violence Law of the People's Republic of China is of great significance, not only providing a strong legal basis and protection for victims of domestic violence but also clarifying the illegal nature of domestic violence by removing erroneous conceptions. In addition, the law stresses the importance of preventing domestic violence and requires the whole society to work together, including the state, groups such as workers and young women, and mass media, to jointly promote family virtues and anti-domestic violence propaganda. The law also focuses on guiding family members to care for each other, promoting family harmony and social stability, with a view to realizing the dialectical unity of governing the country by law and governing the country by virtue.

In accordance with the guiding spirit of the United Nations Convention on the Rights of the Child, this chapter will give a detailed interpretation of the protection of children's rights and interests in the Anti-Domestic Violence Law of the People's Republic of China, and show readers that China has taken positive actions to protect children from domestic violence.

6.2 Special Protection of Children from Domestic Violence

Family should be a happy harbor for everyone, but the problem of domestic violence has become an obstacle to the happiness of some children. Domestic violence includes "soft violence" and "hard violence", and children easily become the main victims of domestic violence in the growing process. Therefore, by formulating the Anti-Domestic Violence Law of the People's Republic of China, by giving play to the guiding and promoting role of legislation, and by preventing and reducing the impact of domestic violence on children, it is more conducive to promoting family virtues and promoting family construction, so as to create a good family atmosphere for the healthy growth of children.

From the perspective of chapter content, the Anti-Domestic Violence Law of the People's Republic of China is mainly composed of six chapters: general provisions, prevention of domestic violence, disposal of domestic violence, personal safety protection order, legal responsibility, and supplementary provisions. The general provisions play a leading and guiding effect, while the specific protection content is mainly composed of three parts. They are prevention, disposal, and personal safety protection orders these three chapters, the content of these three chapters occupy the backbone of the entire "People's Republic of China Anti-Domestic Violence Law", and is also the next part we want to focus on interpretation.

6.2.1 Legal Definition of Domestic Violence

There are various forms of domestic violence, and the violent injury suffered by children in the family is not only the physical violence commonly understood, but also more forms of expression, including life health safety, physical health, mental health, personal freedom, and so on, but it is essentially a violation of the personal rights of family members. Theoretically, there are four main types of domestic violence: physical violence, mental violence, sexual violence, and economic control. This Law defines "domestic violence", lists the types and main forms of domestic violence, and includes acts of insult, abuse, slander, invasion of privacy, defamation of personality, intimidation, threat, and harassment of family members into the scope of domestic violence, which is typical mental violence that can cause inferiority, fear, anxiety and depression of the victim (Jin, 2020). Adults who are mentally sound and have independent thinking and discerning abilities can be subjected to mental violence, let alone children, so under the provisions of this law, domestic violence against children is not only reflected in physical violence but also reflected in mental abuse. In the past, most of the violence that the general public paid attention to was physical violence but ignored the psychological harm caused by emotional violence to children, such as emotional indifference, neglect of life, and other "cold violence", which invisibly caused great harm to children's mental health. For example, the negative impact of violence on children manifests itself in mental health problems, interpersonal problems, behavioral problems, learning and growth problems, and self-identity problems. In this regard, the Anti-Domestic Violence Law of the People's Republic of China fulfills the promise of States parties under the Convention on the Rights of the Child to protect children physically and psychologically during their growth and incorporates "mental violence" into the concept of domestic violence. At the end of the concept, the word "etc" is used to leave a specific definition space for law enforcement and judicial departments, which is explained that civil organization experts emphasize the feasibility of targeting "sexual violence" and "economic violence", so as to ensure that people affected by domestic violence seek corresponding relief in an all-round way.

To sum up, it is a wise choice to include mental violence in the scope of domestic violence in an enumerated way in this Law, which is of great significance for the comprehensive protection of the healthy growth of children. The integration of physical and mental, material and spiritual aspects of children's growth cannot be ignored (Luo, 2020). The specific content can be seen in article 2 of the Anti-Domestic Violence Law of the People's Republic of China.

Article 2
The term "domestic violence" as used in this Law refers to physical, mental, and other violations committed between family members by means of beating, binding, mutilation, restriction of personal freedom, frequent verbal abuse, intimidation, etc.

Because most of the words in domestic violence prescribed by law belong to normative elements, which need to be judged by the value of the judge, there is confusion in the identification of domestic violence in judicial practice. For example, after the divorce of parents, whether the violent injury occurred during the unmarried cohabitation of one party and the new partner is domestic violence? Is it domestic violence when a child is left in the care of another person for a long period of time? Is it domestic violence for a foster child to suffer violence while in foster care? Since the Anti-Domestic Violence Law of the People's Republic of China regulates acts of violence between family members, the above issue is based on "whether the violence inflicted by non-family members is domestic violence". Therefore, the supplementary provisions of the Anti-Domestic Violence Law of the People's Republic of China stipulate acts of violence committed by people living together other than family members, are treated it as domestic violence. This is equivalent to expanding the scope of the subject of domestic violence, in addition to family members who have blood relations, people who have close relationships with each other are included in the scope of the Anti-Domestic Violence Law of the People's Republic of China (Dan, 2017). It should be known that in real life, although many people do not belong to the relationship between family members, they have a life relationship and a relationship of rights and obligations similar to that between family members due to their special intimate relationship, and there is a strong personal dependence between them. The more intimate the relationship, the easier it is to produce disputes, and the occurrence of such violence is also highly likely. From the point of view of behavioral characteristics, this is highly similar to domestic violence. The violence suffered by children in the family does not only come from family members, for example, when the guardian and the child under custody do not have a family relationship, there are three typical cases:

The first scenario involves guardianship relationships, such as those with left-behind children in rural areas. When parents work away from home, they may entrust the guardianship responsibility to capable individuals, who could also be close friends. In this case, violence against children will also be regulated by the Anti-Domestic Violence Law of the People's Republic of China; In addition, if a child's parents are deceased and no other guardian is available, the relevant welfare agency will take over the guardianship responsibility, and violence against children will also be regulated by the Anti-Domestic Violence Law of the People's Republic of China.

The second scenario pertains to foster care relationships. Foster care is an important way to settle orphans, abandoned infants, and children who wander and beg. After going through the legal procedures, children under the guardianship of the civil affairs department are entrusted to raise and care in families that meet the conditions of foster care, which not only allows children to harvest love and care in a normal family environment but also enables children to have basic material life security. Foster families are important places for children to live and grow up. In order to fully protect the legitimate rights and interests of children, the violence they suffer in foster families should be adjusted by the Anti-Domestic Violence Law of the People's Republic of China.

The third kind is cohabitation, which is very common in practice. Many divorced parents will start cohabitation before marriage when they find a new partner, and children who experience the divorce of their parents have also become a part of the unmarried cohabitation family relationship. Children in a cohabitation relationship are in a special position and may suffer psychological damage from the divorce. When entering a new cohabitation relationship, children have a large degree of rejection. At this time, both biological parents and new partners can not completely avoid this harm. Moreover, under the influence of traditional concepts, "a hindrance" and "no blood relationship" will put children in a more embarrassing situation, and the partner is often more indifferent to the violence against children. Children also suffer more injuries.

It is undeniable that the intimate relationships generated based on the above circumstances have been largely indistinguishable from family relationships, but they have not been recognized by the law. However, this does not mean that the law connived at it. Children's legitimate rights should still be protected and regulated by the Anti-Domestic Violence Law of the People's Republic of China. All of the above proceed from the actual situation, taking into account the particularity of children and the complexity of the actual situation, and give protection from the legislative level, so as to make the anti-domestic violence protection system for children more thorough. The specific content can be seen in article 37 of the Anti-Domestic Violence Law of the People's Republic of China.

Article 37
Acts of violence committed between persons living together other than family members shall be enforced by reference to the provisions of this Law.

The importance of defining domestic violence as child protection is manifested in a number of ways. First, a clear definition of domestic violence helps children identify and understand domestic violence. Children, as family members, are often indirect victims of domestic violence. A clear definition of domestic violence can help them better understand the issue and take appropriate measures to protect themselves. Second, define domestic abuse as helping children seek help and support. When children clearly are aware that they are experiencing domestic violence, they are more likely to seek help and support. In addition, the definition of domestic violence can also help to promote social awareness and attention to child protection. When domestic violence is clearly defined and widely disseminated, the public will be more aware of the harm and impact of domestic violence on children. This will encourage more institutions and individuals to participate in child protection work and form a broader social support network. This kind of social support is a great encouragement and helps children to better cope with the difficulties and challenges brought about by domestic violence. Finally, the definition of domestic violence is helpful in promoting the improvement of the relevant legal system. By clarifying the definition of domestic violence, the legal system can more accurately define the nature and scope of domestic violence, and thus develop more effective legal measures to protect the rights and interests of children. Together, these functions create a safer, harmonious, and healthy environment for children to grow up in.

6.2.2 *Principles of Protecting Children's Rights in Domestic Violence*

The General provisions of this Law provide for the protection of children's rights and interests in general terms, of which Article 1 clarifies the legislative purpose and expected implementation effect of the Anti-Domestic Violence Law of the People's Republic of China. Article 2 clearly defines the concept of domestic violence and outlines the types and main forms of domestic violence. Article 3 clearly defines the family relations advocated by our country and the responsibility of the State, society, and the family to combat domestic violence. Article 4 provides that the relevant departments and units should be given the main position in the anti-domestic violence and the anti-domestic violence work fund guarantee. Article 5 makes it clear that the anti-domestic violence work should follow the principle of combining education, correction, and punishment, pay attention to protecting the privacy of the parties, and give special protection to special groups. These general provisions have established the basic institutional framework, which is implemented throughout the legal provisions, and also has a guiding role for specific legal provisions. It can be said that the anti-domestic violence protection for children in the general provisions has laid the tone for the subsequent content. The specific content can be seen in articles 1-5 of *the Anti-Domestic Violence Law of the People's Republic of China*.

Article 1
This Law is enacted for the purpose of preventing and suppressing domestic violence, protecting the lawful rights and interests of family members, maintaining equal, harmonious, and civilized family relations, and promoting family harmony and social stability.

Article 2
The term "domestic violence" as used in this Law refers to physical, mental, and other violations committed between family members by means of beating, binding, mutilation, restriction of personal freedom, frequent verbal abuse, intimidation, etc.

Article 3
Family members shall help each other, care for each other, live in harmony, and fulfill family obligations.

Anti-domestic violence is the joint responsibility of the country, society, and every family.

The state prohibits all forms of domestic violence.

Article 4
The organs responsible for women and children's work under the people's governments at or above the county level shall be responsible for organizing, coordinating, guiding, and urging relevant departments to do a good job in combating domestic violence.

Relevant departments of the people's governments at or above the county level, judicial organs, people's organizations, social organizations, residents' committees, villagers' committees, enterprises, and institutions shall, in accordance with this Law and relevant laws, do a good job in combating domestic violence.

People's governments at all levels shall provide necessary financial guarantees for the anti-domestic violence work.

Article 5
Anti-domestic violence work follows the principle of prevention first, education, correction, and punishment combined.

Anti-domestic violence work should respect the true will of the victims and protect the privacy of the parties.

Minors, the elderly, the disabled, women during pregnancy and breastfeeding, and seriously ill patients who suffer domestic violence shall be given special protection.

The general provisions of the Anti-Domestic Violence Law of the People's Republic of China, located at the beginning of this Law, dominate the content of the entire law and have the function of outlining. Its status and function are self-evident. The development of subsequent legal provisions cannot be separated from the core contained in the General provisions, and its legislative purpose will be realized through specific systems, and the basic principles of this law will be implemented into specific legal texts and institutional measures, so that the content of the general provisions and specific provisions will be integrated and coordinated, providing a thorough and solid legal system will be provided for the protection of children's rights and interests.

6.2.3 Domestic Violence Prevention Mechanism

Domestic violence is the result of many factors, such as culture, customs, and so on. It has the characteristics of concealment, complexity, comprehensiveness, and circularity. To manage such a social disease, prevention before the event is always more important than punishment after the event. In reality, many domestic violence lasts a long time, and there are many people who know about it, but it is often taken seriously by society after serious consequences have occurred. Domestic violence occurs in the family, the causes of which are also extremely complex and diverse, and it is often difficult to establish specific preventive measures in advance. In order to show the legislative attitude of firm opposition to domestic violence, the Anti-Domestic Violence Law of the People's Republic of China has set up the second chapter specifically stipulating preventive measures for domestic violence. The prevention of domestic violence is a systematic project that requires the intervention of many agencies and organizations within their respective spheres of competence to address the complexity of domestic violence. This kind of prevention in advance is also the most beneficial way to completely kill and eliminate domestic violence before its formation or germination, which undoubtedly protects children from the harm of domestic violence at the root and maximizes the healthy growth environment for children (Xue, 2012). From the content of the legal text, the legislative preventive measures are mainly reflected in the following two aspects:

The first is publicity and education. The state and social organizations have the obligation to carry out anti-domestic violence publicity and education and popularize the knowledge of anti-domestic violence to enhance the awareness of anti-domestic violence at the level of the whole society. On this basis, it is also necessary to rely on government departments, grass-roots organizations, social institutions and other relevant departments and their staff to actively guide the government, social organizations, and individual citizens to change traditional outdated concepts. Both government departments, social organizations, and individual citizens should face up to the illegality and harm of domestic violence through business training, publicity and education.

Why does the Anti-Domestic Violence Law of the People's Republic of China attach so much importance to the publicity and education of domestic violence? From the reasons for the frequent occurrence of children's domestic violence, the difficulty of preventing it beforehand, the difficulty of finding it afterwards, and the difficulty of judicial intervention, the most fundamental and deepest influencing factor lies in the cognitive deviation at the level of consciousness. Some parents hold traditional educational concepts such as "spare the rod and spoil the rod" and "filial children emerge under strict discipline", so they cannot understand the harm of domestic violence to children's growth; Some judicial organs and staff think that the problem of domestic violence against children is "internal disputes" and "children's education problem"; Children themselves blindly pay attention to the recognition of "100 good filial piety first", lack of awareness of rights and self-protection consciousness become the victims of blindly "stupid filial piety". Therefore, in the Anti-Domestic Violence Law of the People's Republic of China, special emphasis is placed on correcting and improving people's outdated ideas about domestic violence.

Domestic violence is often identified as a private matter, and even judicial law enforcement officers believe that it is not appropriate to intervene too much, after all, it is difficult to judge family matters. However, it is also important to carry out publicity and education. The staff of the judicial and law enforcement agencies should also participate in the training, get out of the ideological shackles, deal with the problem of domestic violence with a positive attitude, and protect children from family harm with a more proactive attitude. When handling domestic violence cases, government departments and their staff should abandon the concept that domestic violence is a family matter and public power should not be involved. Proper performance of responsibilities by relevant departments plays an important role in curbing domestic violence and preventing the occurrence and expansion of damage. Only in this way can perpetrators realize the country's zero-tolerance attitude towards domestic violence. Children can thrive in a harmonious, civilized and healthy family environment.

In addition, the legislation clarifies that social organizations, such as kindergartens, schools, and grass-roots organizations, should assume the responsibility of publicity and education, popularize knowledge about domestic violence and educate parents and children about the illegality of domestic violence, face up to the importance of the illegality of domestic violence and children's rights and interests, guide everyone from the level of consciousness, and improve the legal quality of family members. It also specifically emphasized that schools and kindergartens should carry out family virtue and anti-domestic violence education. Schools and kindergartens, as typical places of learning, not only need to teach children knowledge from books, but also have the responsibility to make children grow up healthily and form a correct concept of right and wrong, and improve their ability to protect themselves. Schools and kindergartens should face not only children, but also parents, helping them fully understand the illegality and harm of domestic violence is the premise of effective prevention of domestic violence and the basis for correct treatment of domestic violence. The most effective way to protect children is to start from an early age, cultivating small citizens with legal awareness and civilized quality, and also letting them children understand what is domestic violence and how to deal with domestic violence. Schools and kindergartens carry out family virtue education and anti-domestic violence publicity, correctly guide parents to take correct ways to teach and manage children, and perform guardianship duties according to law. Every person belongs or will belong to one or more family units, so that when an individual is a member of a family, he or she has the rights and duties of a family member. This kind of publicity and education should not only make children realize the illegality of domestic violence and the seriousness of consequences, but also make it clear that domestic violence is not only a moral evaluation, but also enhance the awareness of "human rights" and self-protection of children under the premise of making clear its illegality, and help them improve their ability and willingness to defend their rights. Everyone has to grow up slowly from the role of the child in the family unit, that is, the vulnerable party, the victim of domestic violence, the bystander who witnessed domestic violence, etc. One day, they will also grow into the "potentate" in the family relationship, and eventually they may use their own advantages to commit violence against the vulnerable party. There are new child victims or child bystanders. Therefore, if we cannot do a good job of publicity and education in advance, it may eventually lead to the tragic cycle of "dragon slayer youth eventually become a dragon". Therefore, personal legal awareness and correct concepts are the top priority of anti-domestic violence. Educate family members to deal with family conflicts in a non-violent way, especially for the perpetrators, guide and educate them, change their traditional education concept of "good people come out of the stick", communicate calmly with children, patiently listen to understand the needs of children, adopt scientific and advanced education methods to nurture children, and pay attention to the physical and mental health of children. It can be seen that only by completely eliminating the traditional outdated ideas and concepts from the consciousness level, can the prevention of domestic violence achieve its original legislative purpose, achieve the ideal effect, and protect the rights and interests of children to the fullest extent. Therefore, the Anti-Domestic Violence Law of the People's Republic of China attaches great importance to the publicity and education measures at the consciousness level. The specific content can be seen in articles 6 to 9 of *the Anti-Domestic Violence Law of the People's Republic of China*.

Article 6
The State shall carry out publicity and education on family virtues, popularize anti-domestic violence knowledge, and enhance citizens' awareness of anti-domestic violence.

Trade unions, Communist Youth Leagues, Women's Federations and Disabled persons' Federations shall, within the scope of their respective work, organize propaganda and education on family virtues and anti-domestic violence.

Radio, television, newspapers and the Internet should carry out propaganda on family virtues and anti-domestic violence.

Schools and kindergartens shall carry out education on family virtue and anti-domestic violence.

Article 7
The relevant departments, judicial organs and women's federations of the people's governments at or above the county level shall include the prevention and suppression of domestic violence in their professional training and statistical work.

Medical institutions shall keep records of the diagnosis and treatment of victims of domestic violence.

Article 8
Township people's governments and sub-district offices shall organize and carry out domestic violence prevention work, and residents' committees, villagers' committees, and social work service agencies shall provide cooperation and assistance.

Article 9
People's governments at all levels shall support social work service agencies and other social organizations to carry out services such as mental health consultation, family relationship guidance, and knowledge education on the prevention of domestic violence.

The second is to focus on the mediation of family disputes. Before the emergence of domestic violence, there are often some family disputes, and it is precisely some small family disputes after a certain period of time, if not properly solved and eliminated, it may become more and more intense and eventually become the fuse of domestic violence, causing great physical and even psychological harm to children when domestic violence breaks out. Even if the long-term family disputes do not evolve into domestic violence, the damage of family disputes to the good family atmosphere is inevitable. Children living in a disharmonious family environment for a long time are also a potential infringement, so it is necessary to mediate the conflict in time when the family conflict occurs, so that domestic violence is stifled in the cradle. Considering that family disputes occur within the family and between relatives, it is necessary not only to safeguard the legitimate rights and interests of the parties, but also to maintain the harmony and unity of marriage and family relations and parent-child relations, and to follow the concept of gender equality and the priority protection of children's interests in mediation. It is worth noting that the mediation responsibility of this law does not only belong to people's mediation organizations, but also gives employers the social responsibility of mediation. The employer is an important part of China's social support system. The powerful party in the family relationship mostly controls the economic power through stable work, while children are attached to their parents in the family relationship and have no economic source and independent living ability. At this time, the imbalance in economic strength and the imbalance of family economic income and expenditure will easily become the potential factor of domestic violence. The employer has a working bond with the employee, and also has a strong influence on the employee. This personal jurisdiction makes the employer have a significant advantage in preventing domestic violence. Therefore, the Anti-Domestic Violence Law of the People's Republic of China sets the duty of mediating family disputes for the employer, in order to create a good family atmosphere for the growth of children. The specific content can be seen in articles 10 and 11 of the Anti-Domestic Violence Law of the People's Republic of China.

Article 10
People's mediation organizations shall mediate family disputes according to law to prevent and reduce the occurrence of domestic violence.

Article 11
Where the employing unit finds that its personnel have domestic violence, it shall give criticism and education, and do a good job in the mediation and resolution of family conflicts.

In addition, this chapter also specifically stipulates that guardians of minors shall conduct family education in a civilized manner, perform their duties of guardianship and education according to law, and shall not commit domestic violence. This answers the question of what kind of family education and family supervision the state requires and advocates for children to receive—in a civilized way. This way is gentle, non-violent, and conducive to the healthy physical and mental development of children. The specific content mainly includes the following four aspects:

First, family education should have the concept of civilization, upholding the core socialist values such as freedom, equality, and justice, recognizing the principle of the greatest interests of children established by the Convention on the Rights of the Child, the principle of priority protection of children and other legal concepts, abandoning the traditional "patriarchal" old habits, and also avoid overindulgence without principle.

Second, a civilized attitude is essential; this means respecting the rights of children, communicating with them on an equal basis, listening to their needs to understand the development of their mentality, and letting children understand the consequences of their actions. Requirements should be presented gently and firmly without projecting one's own emotions onto the children or forcing them to be "obedient."

Third is to have civilized language, pointing out the mistakes of children on the matter. Criticizing children can be serious or even severe, but cannot be rude, sarcastic, blaming, insulting, ridicule, abuse or derogatory intimidation, hurting the child's self-esteem, while not in front of children derogatory, abuse others.

Finally, civilized behavior involves spending quality time with children, such as outdoor activities, visits, shopping, and entertainment, which cultivate a harmonious parent-child relationship, and encourage educational yet enjoyable interactions. And guardians should require children to do things on their own first, setting a good example of children's behavior habits, and demonstrating "zero" tolerance for all violent behavior.

Children's family education is the "beginning of human" education, which plays a fundamental role in children's life, and the purpose of education is to make children's physical and mental healthy development. Therefore, parents should establish correct educational concepts, master scientific educational methods, respect the healthy taste of children, on this basis, comply with the progress of social civilization, and correct the misunderstanding in the traditional concept. *The Anti-Domestic Violence Law of the People's Republic of China* not only provides for the adoption of civilized education methods, but also specifies prohibitions against the use of violence in family education and guardianship relationships, which is conducive to breaking the vicious cycle of domestic violence and preventing children from using domestic violence against their own families and children when they become adults. In other words, the law provides for the protection of children from both positive and negative aspects. The specific content can be seen in article 12 of *the Anti-Domestic Violence Law of the People's Republic of China.*

Article 12
Guardians of minors shall conduct family education in a civilized manner, perform their duties of guardianship and education according to law, and shall not commit domestic violence.

To sum up, the prevention of domestic violence and the protection of children is a systematic project that requires the joint efforts of the whole society. By strengthening the legal system, raising public awareness, and strengthening publicity and education and other measures, we can effectively prevent and reduce the occurrence of domestic violence, and provide a safe and healthy environment for children to grow up. The Anti-Domestic Violence Law of the People's Republic of China has made relatively comprehensive provisions on the prevention of domestic violence before it occurs, including the setting of multi-party responsibility subjects for prevention and publicity and education, the adjustment mechanism of family disputes, and the advocacy of civilized family education methods, so as to create a positive and positive family atmosphere and social atmosphere for the healthy growth of children.

6.2.4 Institutional Response Mechanisms to Domestic Violence

In order to avoid children who have witnessed or suffered domestic violence, want to seek help but cannot find any, resulting in the emergence of rampant domestic violence, and finally aggravate the helplessness and hesitation of children as victims. Therefore, in *the Anti-Domestic Violence Law of the People's Republic of China*, clearly stipulates the contents of separate chapters as measures to deal with domestic violence, which can prevent the recurrence of domestic violence and prevent the victims from being affected by domestic violence again. To a certain extent, it can also guide potential perpetrators of domestic violence to realize the illegality of their own behavior and bear the corresponding responsibility, so as to give up the possible behavior of domestic violence, and achieve the implementation effect of special prevention and general prevention.

The highest priority in this chapter is the measures that can be taken to complain or seek help after the occurrence of domestic violence. *The Anti-Domestic Violence Law of the People's Republic of China* clarifies that after a child has suffered or witnessed domestic violence, the child himself or her legal representative, close relatives or responsible departments have the right to complain to the relevant departments, report, and seek help, and the relevant departments shall deal with it after receiving the relevant information. This answers the way of seeking help after experiencing domestic violence from the legislation, as well as the subject and object of seeking help. It is precisely this provision that makes the victims of domestic violence not only isolated victims, they can also take heart to protect themselves with legal weapons, and at this time must let the victims know that they have the right to complain and seek help. The individual victim may be weak, so the exercise of this power also needs to rely on the power of the relevant units to make it work.

In addition, it has also clarified the mandatory reporting system for domestic violence, which is actually based on Article 13 of the Anti-Domestic Violence Law of the People's Republic of China, and provides a more mandatory and special system on this basis, which is an extension of complaints, responses and help for domestic violence. The target of mandatory reporting is not all victims of domestic violence, but a specific group of people, that is, people without civil capacity and people with limited civil capacity, including children under the age of 18 (Du & Cao, 2022). The establishment of this system takes into account the special situation of children to a great extent, so mandatory reporting can effectively stop and intervene in violence against children. The relevant departments shall report to the public security organs when they find that children have suffered domestic violence or are suspected of having suffered domestic violence (Yang, 2017). Through the mandatory reporting system, a large number of domestic violence cases involving children and other vulnerable groups hidden within the family can be revealed. This slanted protection system makes up for the vulnerable characteristics of children, enables children to receive help and protection in time to avoid re-harm, and fixes evidence in time to enable children to finally get adequate judicial relief (Chen, 2014).Children are in a vulnerable position in family relations, and the long-term family lifestyle and family education mode will make children unable to correctly understand the illegality of domestic violence, coupled with the lack of age and experience, so that they do not have enough awareness and ability to protect themselves. In addition, for such vulnerable groups, the relevant departments should shoulder the corresponding responsibility, even if there is no concrete evidence of children suffering domestic violence, they can initiate mandatory reporting procedures, that is, the relevant departments do not require that there are sufficient qualitative requirements for children suffering domestic violence, as long as they meet the criteria of possibility. At present, the child protection mandatory reporting system is the most effective and direct way to detect and prevent child abuse. The inclusion of the mandatory reporting system in *the Anti-Domestic Violence Law of the People's Republic of China* also demonstrates the "zero tolerance" attitude of the state and society towards domestic violence and the concept of full and comprehensive protection of children. The specific content can be seen in articles 13 and 14 of *the Anti-Domestic Violence Law of the People's Republic of China.*

Article 13
Victims of domestic violence, their legal representatives and close relatives may complain, report or seek help from the units to which the perpetrator or the victim belongs, the residents' committee, the villagers' committee, the women's Federation and other units. After receiving a complaint, response or request for help about domestic violence, the relevant unit shall give help and handle it.

Article 14
Schools, kindergartens, medical institutions, residents' committees, villagers' committees, social work service agencies, rescue management agencies, welfare agencies and their staff in the course of their work found that people without civil capacity, limited capacity for civil conduct suffered or suspected to have suffered domestic violence, shall promptly report to the public security organ. The public security organ shall keep confidential the information of the informant.

The mandatory reporting system mentioned above is to enable those domestic violence cases to be discovered in time, so as to enable the public security organs to intervene smoothly. As for how the public security organs should act after receiving the report, it is a matter in another category, which involves the responsibilities and obligations of the public security organs in handling domestic violence cases. Before properly dealing with the matter in accordance with the provisions of the law and legal procedures, the public security organ shall not only perform its own duties of sending police, searching, collecting evidence, assisting the victim in seeking medical treatment, and identifying the injury but also notify and assist the civil affairs department to relocate the person without civil capacity or with limited civil capacity in need of living care to a temporary shelter, rescue management institution or welfare institution. In this case, children can be protected to a greater extent during the investigation and handling of domestic violence cases to have normal learning and living conditions, so as to avoid children in an isolated situation after the incident of domestic violence. This temporary shelter, rescue management agency, or welfare agency is to fully consider the risk of domestic violence and the particularity of minor victims in domestic violence cases, according to the actual situation of the classification of regional assistance. Compared with other family members, children are more vulnerable to domestic violence in the family, and it is difficult to obtain legal protection through their own ability. Children rely on the care and protection of the family in all aspects of clothing, food, housing, and transportation., because of this, children are likely to be persuaded, misled, controlled, and even threatened by guardians or caregivers after domestic violence, which makes children provide false statements to help the abuser escape punishment. In addition, other family members have negative emotions such as anger and sadness after the abuser is held accountable, they neglect to take care of children or deliberately insult, abuse, and blame children, causing secondary harm to children, so they set up corresponding rescue agencies responsible subjects. The establishment of this article shows that China provides comprehensive protection to vulnerable parties in domestic violence as far as possible. Therefore, protecting the health and safety of children after the incident, taking them away from their families, arranging emergency assistance and placement, providing psychological counseling and care services, and considering whether to return them to their families after the danger is eliminated is also a reflection of the protection of children's rights and interests. The specific content can be seen in Article 15 of *the Anti-Domestic Violence Law of the People's Republic of China*:

> **Article 15**
> ***After receiving a domestic violence report, the public security organ shall promptly send out the police to stop domestic violence, investigate and collect evidence in accordance with the relevant provisions, and assist the victim to seek medical treatment and identify the injury.***
>
> ***Where a person with no capacity for civil conduct or a person with limited capacity for civil conduct is seriously injured by domestic violence, faces a threat to personal safety, or is in a dangerous state without care, the public security organ shall notify and assist the civil affairs department to relocate him to a temporary shelter, a rescue management institution or a welfare institution.***

After the public security organs have completed the work of the above routines, the case has been smoothly promoted to the disposal link. At this time, it should be noted that such cases cannot be handled in a "try to reconcile differences" way. Even in cases of relatively minor domestic violence cases must also be reasonable and rational, so the warning system has emerged. The family itself is a community of interests, both prosper and lose, we can't just impose heavy penalties. Because there are unique personal dependence, emotional connections, common interests, and identity relations between parents and children in family relations, if a domestic violence incident occurs, it will not only have adverse effects on the parties and their families but also make the child victims face difficulties, so that the child victims may instead protect and shield the perpetrators. Therefore, a warning system has been specially set up for minor domestic violence, which can be stopped by means of criticism, education, and monitory issued by public security organs, which not only helps to resolve the plight of child victims but also protects the long-term stability of family relations and children's physical and mental health. The warning system can not only stop domestic violence to a certain extent but also fix evidence. And prevent violence from happening again. Through regular visits and supervision of relevant organs and units, check the implementation of the monitory, and supervise the perpetrators no longer commit domestic violence. To some extent, it is also a preventive measure for the possible recurrence of domestic violence, which is conducive to the timely elimination of potential factors of domestic violence. The specific content can be seen in articles 16 to 17 of *the Anti-Domestic Violence Law of the People's Republic of China*:

Article 16
Where the circumstances of domestic violence are relatively minor and public security administration penalties are not given according to law, the public security organ shall criticize and educate the perpetrator or issue a monitory.

The monitory shall include the identity information of the perpetrator, the statement of the facts of domestic violence, and the content of prohibiting the perpetrator from committing domestic violence.

Article 17
The public security organ shall deliver the monitory to the offender and the victim, and notify the residents committee and the villagers committee.

The residents' committee, the villagers' committee and the public security police station shall visit the perpetrators and victims who have received the monitory and supervise the perpetrators to refrain from committing domestic violence.

When a child is subjected to domestic violence, if the level of violence is serious and cannot be resolved by the mediation and warning system, and there are legal proceedings involved, the child victim will receive free legal services from a legal aid agency. At the same time, the People's Court will also defer the charge, and reduce or waive the charge for child victims in accordance with the law. Considering that children do not have stable economic income and independent sources of property if children in domestic violence cases are caught in litigation, the opposing party is often their parents and relatives, and children are in a vulnerable position in age, mentality, and property. In order to fully protect the equality of the status of both parties in litigation and the full exercise of legal rights, China has set up a relatively perfect legal aid system. In addition, the Anti-Domestic Violence Law of the People's Republic of China also provides for the suspension, reduction, and exemption of litigation costs, which reflects strong humanistic care and special protection. For the problem that it is difficult for child victims to prove that they have suffered domestic violence during litigation, it is further stipulated that the people's court can use the police records, monitory, and injury appraisal opinions of the public security organs as evidence to identify domestic violence, which solves the difficult dilemma of children to prove evidence to a certain extent. The specific content can be seen in Articles 19 and 20 of *the Anti-Domestic Violence Law of the People's Republic of China*:

> **Article 19**
> ***Legal aid agencies shall provide legal aid to victims of domestic violence in accordance with the law.***
>
> ***The People's Court shall, according to law, refer, reduce, or waive litigation costs for victims of domestic violence.***
>
> **Article 20**
> ***In handling cases involving domestic violence, the people's court may determine the facts of domestic violence on the basis of evidence such as police records, monitory, and injury appraisal opinions of public security organs.***

After a domestic violence case has experienced the intervention of the public security organ or the court's trial and judgment, considering the relationship between the perpetrator and the victim, the harm caused by the perpetrator's domestic violence, and the possibility of the perpetrator committing domestic violence again, we should carefully consider the guardianship in the family. The relationship between the guardian and people under guardianship must exist in the family relationship, but if the guardian commits domestic violence and seriously infringes the legitimate rights and interests of the people under guardianship, it is necessary to consider the withdrawal and transfer of guardianship. The occurrence of this kind of domestic violence deviates from the purpose of the establishment of the guardianship system, and the corresponding conditions and circumstances are clearly and completely stipulated in the Civil Code. *The Anti-Domestic Violence Law of the People's Republic of China* further stipulates that serious domestic violence is one of the circumstances under which custody is revoked according to law. After the guardian's guardianship is revoked, the court will appoint a new guardian for the child in order to protect the child's guardianship to continue to receive due care and protection, based on other factors such as the will of the subject entitled to guardianship, character, physical condition, economic conditions, and emotional connection with the child. The rescission of guardianship is due to the fact that he has committed domestic violence against the child, violated the legitimate rights and interests of the child, and violated the duties of the guardian, who is no longer suitable to serve as the guardian, but this does not affect the original guardian to continue to pay the child maintenance fee to the victim, and the perpetrator who has the maintenance obligation must still perform the maintenance obligation and pay the maintenance fee. The specific content can be seen in Article 21 of *the Anti-Domestic Violence Law of the People's Republic of China*:

Article 21
Where a guardian commits domestic violence and seriously infringes upon the lawful rights and interests of his ward, the people's court may, upon the application of the ward's close relatives, the residents' committee, the villagers' committee, the civil affairs department of the county people's government and other relevant personnel or units, revoke his guardianship and appoint another guardian according to law.

The offender whose guardianship is revoked shall continue to bear the corresponding maintenance, maintenance and rearing expenses.

Punishment and warning measures should be taken for the perpetrators of domestic violence, and protection measures and corresponding comfort measures should be taken for the victims to make up for the harm they have suffered as much as possible. The psychological trauma of child victims after suffering domestic violence is manifested as low self-esteem, habitual helplessness, and even derived from depression, anxiety, and other emotional disorders. Such psychological damage is often not fully compensated by economic compensation and punishment afterward. In order to heal their psychological trauma, it is important to provide targeted psychological counseling to child victims. This kind of healing psychological counseling focuses on the function of psychological therapy so that the injured children can re-establish their confidence in life, step out of the shadows, and timely repair and reconstruct the harmonious relationship between family members, which is an extension of the treatment of domestic violence. It can also effectively prevent the recurrence of domestic violence. At present, there are professional psychiatrists, psychological counselors, and others responsible for children's psychological counseling. When conducting psychological counseling for children, professional work programs can be formulated according to specific circumstances to improve pertinence and effectiveness. The specific content can be seen in Article 22 of *the Anti-Domestic Violence Law of the People's Republic of China:*

Article 22
Trade unions, Communist Youth League, women's federations, disabled persons' federations, residents' committees, villagers' committees, etc. shall provide legal education to perpetrators of domestic violence, and may provide psychological counseling to perpetrators and victims when necessary.

In short, the disposal chapter of the Anti-Domestic Violence Law of the People's Republic of China has made comprehensive provisions for child protection, such as a mandatory reporting system, warning system, temporary asylum measures, withdrawal of custody, etc., to ensure that children can receive timely and effective assistance and protection when they are subjected to domestic violence. This helps to establish a safe and harmonious family environment and promotes the healthy growth and development of children.

6.2.5 *Personal Protection Order (PPO) Regime (Protective Order)*

Personal safety protection order system originated in the United Kingdom and is an important measure of domestic violence relief, it is like a "barrier", that separates the perpetrator and the victim separated. The formulation and implementation of this system have greatly reduced the severity and frequency of domestic violence suffered by children and has played a solid protective role. The personal safety protection order is also a legal measure stipulated in the special chapter of *the Anti-Domestic Violence Law of the People's Republic of China*, which aims to enhance the intensity of judicial intervention in domestic violence, and change the protection of child victims from the after-action punishment of the abuser to the punishment and prevention of the victim in advance, strengthening the function of judicial human rights protection. The specific content can be seen in articles 23 to 32 of *the Anti-Domestic Violence Law of the People's Republic of China*.

The personal safety protection order system provides in more detail the subject and object of the application for protection order, the situation of applying on behalf of the application, the way of filing the application, jurisdiction, specific conditions, acceptance, measures, time limit, reconsideration, execution and assistance in execution. Taking into account the lack of age and experience of child victims, the lack of ability to identify and control their own behavior, and most importantly, the lack of appropriate legal capacity, the law sets the subject for them to apply for personal safety protection order when they are victims of domestic violence, Their close relatives, public security organs, women's federations, residents' committees, villagers' committee, and rescue management agencies may apply to the court for personal safety protection orders on behalf of children who have suffered domestic violence. In addition, if the child victim is afraid or unwilling to apply for a protection order due to coercion or intimidation by the abuser, the above subject who knows this can also apply for a personal safety protection order on his behalf. The physical or psychological harm caused to the child victims of domestic violence, because of fear and surrender to the control of the perpetrator, patience, and compromise, over time will inevitably aggravate the harm brought to children by domestic violence, at this time, the timely intervention of close relatives and related organizations is extremely important. The specific content can be seen in Article 23 of *the Anti-Domestic Violence Law of the People's Republic of China*:

> **Article 23**
> ***Where a party applies to a People's Court for a personal safety protection order due to domestic violence or the actual danger of domestic violence, the People's Court shall accept it.***
>
> ***If the party concerned is a person without or with limited capacity for civil conduct or is unable to apply for a personal safety protection order due to coercion or intimidation, its close relatives, public security organs, women's federations, residents' committees, villagers' committees, and rescue management institutions may apply on their behalf.***

In terms of the specific measures of personal safety protection orders, *the Anti-Domestic Violence Law of the People's Republic of China* stipulates three specific prohibitions and one backstop clause, which provides relatively comprehensive protection for victims of domestic violence. From the perspective of children, the protection of children is mainly reflected by prohibiting or restricting the behavior of the perpetrator. First of all, the abuser is prohibited from committing domestic violence, so as to prevent children from being subjected to or suffering from domestic violence again. Its content is not criticism, education, or advocacy, but the content of judicial rulings with mandatory force. Once the personal safety protection order prohibits the use of violence, it will not only violate the rights of the child victims but also challenge the authority of the state's public power. Secondly, abusers are prohibited from harassing, stalking, or contacting child victims and their close relatives. Although harassment, stalking, contact, and other acts do not belong to the traditional sense of violence in essence, or even have no personal danger. However, on the one hand, these acts may bring fear and anxiety to the child victims and their close relatives and cause mental damage, affecting the child victims to return to normal study, family, and life. On the other hand, these acts are likely to be regarded as a prelude to future violent acts and escalate into physical violence with serious harm. In addition, children are protected from domestic violence by ordering the perpetrator to move out of the child's place of residence. Co-housing makes child victims more vulnerable to abuse, and ordering abusers to move away from their homes not only protects the legitimate rights of child victims but also reflects the spirit of imposing adverse consequences on the abuser. Finally, there are other measures to protect the personal safety of child victims as a backstop, which often need to be grasped by the people's court in accordance with the actual situation. For example, keeping a distance from the school of the child victim, paying the child's maintenance and living expenses during the protection order, it is forbidden to consult the child victim's household registration, school records, sources of income, and other relevant information, restricting or prohibiting meetings with child victims, etc. The specific content can be seen in Articles 28 and 29 of *the Anti-Domestic Violence Law of the People's Republic of China*.

Article 28
After accepting an application, the People's Court shall, within 72 hours, make a personal safety protection order or reject the application; If the case is urgent, it shall be done within 24 hours.

Article 29
A personal protection order may include the following measures:

(1) Prohibit the respondent from committing domestic violence;
(2) The respondent is prohibited from harassing, tracking, or contacting the applicant and his/her close relatives;
(3) order the respondent to move out of the applicant's residence;
(4) Other measures to protect the personal safety of the applicant.

To sum up, the personal safety protection order system of *the Anti-Domestic Violence Law of the People's Republic of China* plays a crucial role in this law, especially in providing all-round protection for children. It not only provides a safe haven for child victims to ensure that they are safe from the harm of domestic violence but also provides a clear legal recourse for children to help them seek legal aid and defend their rights and interests. In addition, the personal safety protection order has a preventive effect, which can deter the abuser and reduce the probability of domestic violence.

6.2.6 Legal Liability

Any perpetrator of domestic violence should not retreat completely after committing acts of violence against children, because the damage caused by domestic violence is multifaceted, which will not only violate the legitimate rights and interests of children but also have certain social harm. Therefore, the perpetrator of domestic violence may not only bear administrative punishment, but also involve a crime if the means and results of domestic violence are serious, and should bear the corresponding criminal punishment. For example, beating, binding, mutilation, detention, abuse, intimidation, and other acts against children will generally be punished with detention or fines according to *the Law on Public Security Administration*. In addition, if the domestic violence is serious and causes serious results, involving intentional homicide, intentional injury, negligent death, negligent serious injury, illegal detention, compulsory indecency, insult, insult, libel, etc., will bear the corresponding criminal punishment.

For measures that violate the personal safety protection order, they shall also bear the corresponding civil or criminal punishment. The personal safety protection order itself is an important system in the anti-domestic violence system. For child victims, it plays an important role in soothing their hearts and protecting their life safety. After the People's Court has issued the personal safety protection order, the perpetrators should strictly follow its contents. The violation of the personal safety protection order is not only a violation of the physical safety and mental health of the child victim but also a challenge to the judicial authority.

The Anti-Domestic Violence Law of the People's Republic of China stipulates the mandatory reporting system and clarifies the mandatory reporting obligations of relevant subjects. If the relevant subject violates the mandatory reporting obligation, finds that the child has suffered or is suspected to have suffered domestic violence in the work, but fails to timely report to the public security organ, thereby causing serious consequences, it shall also bear the corresponding punishment. This punishment, which undoubtedly requires the staff of various departments and organizations to actively carry out their punishment, is not an advocacy requirement, but a legal obligation, that is, failure to do so carries adverse legal consequences. The specific content can be seen in Articles 33-36 of *the Anti-Domestic Violence Law of the People's Republic of China*:

Article 33
Where the perpetrator commits domestic violence and constitutes an act violating the administration of public security, he shall be punished for the administration of public security according to law; If the case constitutes a crime, criminal punishment shall be investigated according to law.

Article 34
If the respondent violates the personal safety protection order and constitutes a crime, he shall be investigated for criminal punishment according to law; If the case does not constitute a crime, the people's court shall give him a reprimand and may, in light of the seriousness of the case, impose a fine of not more than 1,000 yuan or a detention of not more than 15 days.

Article 35
Where schools, kindergartens, medical institutions, residents' committees, villagers' committees, social work service organizations, rescue management organizations, welfare organizations, and their staff fail to report to the public security organs in accordance with the provisions of Article 14 of this Law, resulting in serious consequences, the competent department at a higher level or the unit shall impose sanctions on the persons directly in charge and other persons directly responsible according to law.

Article 36
State functionaries responsible for combating domestic violence who neglect their duties, abuse their power, or engage in malpractices for personal gain shall be punished according to law; If the case constitutes a crime, criminal punishment shall be investigated according to law.

To sum up, the legal punishment of *the Anti-Domestic Violence Law of the People's Republic of China* has played a positive role in the protection of children. By punishing abusers, urging relevant agencies to perform their duties, and providing legal aid and judicial relief, the law provides a comprehensive protection system for children, ensuring that their rights and interests are fully protected, and becoming a solid backing for the protection of children's rights and interests.

6.3 Summary

The family is the cornerstone of society, and children deserve to be exposed to the sun and thrive. However, domestic violence makes many children live in a haze. The introduction of *the Anti-Domestic Violence Law of the People's Republic of China* emphasizes that children are not attached to family members such as parents but are independent individuals enjoying basic rights, and their personal rights are protected by law (Rights Department of the All-China Women's Federation, 2016).

As an important part of the legal system to protect children's rights and interests, *the Anti-Domestic Violence Law of the People's Republic of China* plays a vital role in protecting children's rights and interests. By explicitly prohibiting any form of domestic violence against children, it strives to create a social atmosphere against domestic violence, tries to reduce the occurrence of this behavior at its root, and tries to provide a solid legal barrier for children to ensure that their physical safety and mental health are duly protected. The implementation of *the Anti-Domestic Violence Law of the People's Republic of China* marks a new step in the prevention and treatment of domestic violence in China. At the same time, *the Anti-Domestic Violence Law of the People's Republic of China* also protects children's rights and interests, and better protects children from domestic violence through legal measures such as clear definitions, detailed institutional rules, increased penalties, strengthened publicity, and changed educational concepts. However, the perfection of the legal text is only the first step, and the more critical thing is how to ensure the enforcement and implementation of the law. In order to protect children from domestic violence, in addition to the relevant authorities and individuals, we should also work together to publicize and educate the dangers of domestic violence, so as to ensure the effective implementation of *the Anti-Domestic Violence Law of the People's Republic of China* and create a safe and harmonious family environment for children. Only in this way can we maximize the protection of children's rights and interests and provide them with a carefree space to grow (Kan & Tan, n.d.).

The formulation and implementation of *the Anti-Domestic Violence Law of the People's Republic of China* is to better fulfill the promise of *the Convention on the Rights of the Child* and to build a comprehensive protection of children's rights and interests together with other laws protecting children's rights and interests in China. The Convention emphasizes the right of the child to survival, development, and participation in social, cultural, and educational activities while opposing all forms of violence and discrimination. *The Anti-Domestic Violence Law of the People's Republic of China* specifies the rights and protection measures that children should enjoy in the family, as well as the punishment and relief mechanisms for domestic violence. These two laws, one is a global declaration on the rights of the child, and the other is a specific implementation plan at the national level, complement each other, and together form a strong protection of children's rights and interests. This not only shows that China attaches great importance to the rights of children, but also shows that the society cares deeply for every individual, especially for the vulnerable groups (National People's Congress, n.d.).

"There are laws to be followed, laws must be followed, law enforcement must be strict, and violations must be investigated" are the requirements of our laws from enactment to implementation. Therefore, in the construction of the legal system for the protection of children's rights and interests, China has been abiding by its promise to *the Convention on the Rights of the Child*, constantly improving the legal system for the protection of children's rights and interests, and in the process of the implementation of the legal system, making corresponding adjustments according to the actual situation, in order to protect the rights and interests of children in all aspects from both physical and procedural aspects. It is believed that with the increasing perfection of the legal system and the continuous implementation of the corresponding system, the future of children will be better. However, the law is only the beginning of the protection of rights, not the end. Each and every one of us has the responsibility and obligation to publicize, to practice, and to defend the rights and interests of children. Only when every child can grow up in an equal, safe, and harmonious environment can we say that this society is progressive and full of hope. So together, let us work for the future of our children, speak up for their rights, and defend their well-being.

References

Chen, Y.'e. (2014). *Social welfare services Taipei: Taiwan*. Qianhua Digital Culture Corporation.

Dan, S. (2017). Quasi-subject of Domestic violence: Interpretation and identification of Article 37 of the Anti-Domestic Violence Law of the People's Republic of China "People living together other than family members". *Journal of Women's Studies, 4*, 31–37.

Du, Y., & Cao, Y. (2022). "See" or "not see", the harm is there: a perspective on the current situation of child protection mandatory reporting in China. *Research on Children and Adolescents, 1*, 22–30.

Editorial Department of this journal. (2016). Focusing on the highlights of the Anti-Domestic Violence Law of the People's Republic of China to further Promote the implementation of the Expert Symposium on the Anti-Domestic Violence Law of the People's Republic of China. *Journal of Women's Studies, 1*, 5–20.

Jin, X. (2020). *Legal dilemma and system improvement of child domestic violence relief in China*. Qingdao University.

Kan, K., & Tan, L. (n.d.). *Interpretation of the Anti-Domestic Violence Law of the People's Republic of China*. China Legal Publishing House.

Luo, Q. (2020). Triple narrative in the birth of the Anti-Domestic Violence Law of the People's Republic of China. *Legal and Social Development, 1*, 188–206.

National People's Congress. (n.d.). *Anti-Domestic Violence Law of the People's Republic of China*. Law Press.

Rights Department of the All-China Women's Federation. (2016). *Practical questions and answers on the anti-domestic violence law and typical cases*. China Legal Publishing House.

Xue, N. (2012). Multi-agency cooperative intervention model in domestic violence prevention law. *Women's Studies Review, 3*, 36.

Yang, Z. (2017). An analysis of the characteristics of the mandatory reporting system for child protection from the perspective of comparative law. *Science of Law (Journal of Northwest University of Political Science and Law), 1*.

Chapter 7
The Family Education Promotion Law in China: Institutionalizing Family Responsibility for Child Development

7.1 Introduction

China is an ancient civilization with a long history of five thousand years. Since ancient times, China has attached great importance to family education work represented by the "family instruction culture", which has left a profound influence on the later generations. On October 23rd, 2021, The 31st session of the Standing Committee of the 13th National People's Congress of the People's Republic of China voted through *the Family Education Promotion Law of the People's Republic of China*, With the legislation to define the orientation of family education, Make the fine tradition of the Chinese nation attaching importance to family education be consolidated by law, "Organic integration of the existing legal and policy content, fully absorbing the experience of local legislation, it stipulates the principle that the family education work should adhere to, from "who will teach", "how to teach", "what to teach" and "who will manage it", responded to the main problems restricting the development of family education in China, describes the legal picture of family education from the dimensions of family responsibility, state support, and social cooperation" (Deng, 2021).

The healthy growth of the child cannot be separated from a good family environment and the proper guidance of family education. According to the spirit of the Convention on the Rights of the Child and *the Constitution of the People's Republic of China, the Family Education Promotion Law of the People's Republic of China* as China's first special legislation about family education has an important position in the children's rights protection legal system, the legislative appeal is universal improve family education ability, regulating the behavior of family education. As a law that to carry forward the Chinese nation attaches great importance to the family, family education, and family style, promoting the whole society to pay attention to family tradition, cultivating morality, intelligence, physique, aesthetic and labor education comprehensive development of socialist successors, *the Family Education*

© The Author(s), under exclusive license to Springer Nature Singapore Pte Ltd. 2026
H. Li, P. Liang, *The Legal System for the Protection of Children's Rights in China*, Resilient and Friendly Living Environments,
https://doi.org/10.1007/978-981-95-9925-7_7

Promotion Law of the People's Republic of China not only embodies the CPC and the state attaches great importance to family education, carry forward the will of the Chinese nation family virtue, but also the legal guarantee to promote the healthy growth and all-round development of the child.

The full text of the Family Education Promotion Law of the People's Republic of China consists of 6 chapters and 55 articles, including general provisions, family responsibility, state support, social coordination, legal responsibility, and supplementary provisions, basically covering all fields of family education and building a comprehensive protection system for children's right to education.

7.2 The Content of the Family Education Promotion Law of the People's Republic of China

The thought of "Jia Guo Tian Xia" is deeply rooted in the cultural heritage of the Chinese nation. General Secretary Xi Jinping general secretary also repeatedly stressed paying attention to family, pay attention to the family education, pay attention to the importance of family traits: "The Chinese nation's traditional family virtues, remember in the hearts of the Chinese people, into the Chinese blood, is to support the Chinese nation, the important spiritual strength, is the precious spiritual wealth of family civilization construction" (Xi, 2017, p. 353). In a sociological sense, family is the smallest social unit formed based on the connection between marriage and blood. It is a collection of "the relationship between husband and wife and the relationship between parents and children" (Marx & Engels, 2009, p. 532). It is the cell of society and has a profound impact on the operation of society, and then affects the future of a nation and a country (An, 2017).

The children are the future of the motherland and the hope of the nation. Throughout the nations of the world, the success of education for the next generation often determines the prosperity and fall of a country. The Chinese people have a tradition of attaching importance to family education. In the continuation and accumulation of five thousand years of history, many family rules, family instructions, and family letter letters have been handed down, enriching the vast and colorful spiritual treasure house of Chinese civilization. The Family Education Promotion Law of the People's Republic of China makes it clear from the perspective of legislation that family education is not only a "family matter", but also a "state matter". At the same time, this law provides legal guidance for the cooperative education of families, schools, and society, which is of milestone significance for improving the ability of family education and implementing the fundamental task of moral education, and provides a legal guarantee for the construction of all-round guarantee of family education.

7.2.1 General Provisions

Article 1

This Law is enacted for the purposes of carrying forward the Chinese nation's fine tradition of attaching importance to family education, guiding the whole society to pay attention to family, family education, and family tradition, enhancing family happiness and social harmony, and cultivating socialist builders and successors who are fully developed in morals, intelligence, physical fitness, aesthetics, and labor education.

As special legislation for family education, the Family Education Promotion Law of the People's Republic of China is to guide the whole society to pay attention to the important influence of family education as a crucial part of the construction of spiritual civilization (family, family style and family education) on children's growth. This law has changed the shackles of traditional ideas, and raised the development of the child from family affairs in the private field to state affairs related to the national movement, reflecting the simple feelings of traditional Chinese culture that "the home is the smallest country, and the country is thousands of families".

In the long course of human history, private teaching has been the main form of education, and the family has been the main place of educational activities for a long time. Taking ancient China as an example, the traditional practice is to invite "Jiao Shu Xian Sheng" (A private teacher, with independent teaching forms and materials) to teach in the family, or to establish a home school—"A grass-roots educational institution set up by folk individuals to undertake the responsibility of cultural inheritance of the Chinese nation". Parents or other elders in the family also play an important role in educating the next generation of children (Hao & Wang, 2005). But with the beginning of the industrialization revolution, the traditional family education mode became difficult to adapt to the needs of the times, the modern school system gradually appeared, and in the form of standardized (normal) unified to student education, family as the main or even only traditional education mode is broken, education subject gradually transferred to the school and other social institutions, began the social transformation, namely education diversified development.

However, the diversified development of educational places should not go against the objective laws of human growth and cognitive development. Childhood, especially ages 0–7 years old, is the critical period of children's physical and mental development—brain development fastest, learning the most intensive, that is to say, the child before entering school, "children's self-consciousness, such as self-evaluation, self-concept, and self-control, self-control gradually formed and further development", therefore, family education for children's personality value and the cultivation of psychological character has irreplaceable important value (Jing, 2006).

Family education is "in family life, with parent-child relationship as the center, to cultivate the needs of social education activities", it includes moral, intellectual, physical, aesthetic, labor, and other aspects (Guan, 1994), for parents and other guardians actively guide to develop family education—family education should pay more attention to children's physical health, quality, life skills, behavior and the cultivation of culture, highlight the characteristics of family education, further clarify the boundaries of family education and school education. Article 2 of the Family Education Promotion Law of the People's Republic of China stipulates this:

Article 2
For the purpose of this Law, "family education" means cultivation, guidance, and influence conducted by parents or other guardians in moral quality, physical quality, life skills, cultural accomplishments, and behavior habits. and other respects for promoting the comprehensive and healthy growth of minors.

In order to ensure the smooth development and sustainable role of family education, the Family Education Promotion Law of the People's Republic of China on Family Education takes the responsibility subject, main principles, main contents, and methods of family education as the logical context, and draws a legal blueprint to comprehensively guarantee and support family education.

The Family Education Promotion Law of the People's Republic of China in "**promote**" is "in the form of promoting legislation to reduce the intervention of the family", its core is for parents can assign and adapt and respect family education autonomy (Deng, 2021), through clear state, society and other related main body responsibility to provide support and assistance for family education, improve the ability of parents to carry out the family education and quality. Considering the actual needs of family education of most families in China and maximizing the protection of children's rights and interests, clarify the duties of parents and other guardians for family education from the legal level, stipulate the consequences of failing to perform relevant duties, and help parents and other guardians to improve the awareness and ability of family education from the perspective of public service supply. At the same time, the law encourages national staff to play a good leading role in the field of family education, promote the whole with the few people, organically combine the civil servant's integrity education with the family education of the masses, "drive the practical action to worship the whole society to be good", and jointly promote the social atmosphere to be good (Xi, 2020a, p. 168). For details, see Article 4 of the Family Education Promotion Law of the People's Republic of China:

Article 4
Parents or other guardians of minors shall be responsible for the implementation of family education.

The state and society shall provide guidance, support, and services for family education.

State functionaries shall take the lead in establishing sound family traditions and fulfilling the responsibilities of family education.

"Family education as the starting point of life education, is directly related to the healthy growth of a person's life and has a lifelong impact". It must be given priority to family position (Zhai, 2016), correct value guidance for children, break the thought of "Only school education has value", value the value of family education, through the parents in daily life affect the growth of the child, carry forward the Chinese excellent traditional culture and advanced socialist culture, build friendly harmonious family relationship, create a good atmosphere of family environment and learning places. Therefore, the Family Education Promotion Law of the People's Republic of China establishes: (1) moral education is the fundamental task of family education; (2) the foundation of family education is family construction; (3) the essence of family education is life education. The unique status of family education in the education system is clarified, and the road is planned for the family education activities in detail. Article 3 and 15 of the Family Education Promotion Law of the People's Republic of China stipulate the above contents:

Article 3
Cultivating morality and cultivating people shall be the fundamental task of family education. through which, the core values of socialism shall be cultivated and practiced, the excellent traditional culture, revolutionary culture, and advanced socialist culture of the Chinese nation shall be advocated, and the healthy growth of minors shall be promoted.

Article 15
Parents or other guardians of minors and other family members shall pay attention to family building, cultivate a positive and healthy family culture, establish and inherit sound family tradition, carry forward the family virtues of the Chinese nation, jointly build civilized and harmonious family relationships, and create a sound family environment for the healthy growth of minors.

In order to ensure the real implementation and effective role of family education, the Family Education Promotion Law of the People's Republic of China stipulates five basic principles for the implementation of family education:

First, we should respect the law of children's physical and mental development and their individual differences. Rousseau once said: "Education of children must conform to the law of children's physical and mental development and age characteristics, otherwise it will lead to adverse consequences. In the order of all things, man has his place; in the order of life, childhood has his place: adults should be regarded as adults, and children as children." The growth of children presents the law of stage and difference. Only under the premise of respecting the objective law to give full play to people's subjective initiative, and fully grasp the unique personality of children and the universality of educational work, can we achieve good educational results.

Second, we should respect children's personal dignity and protect their personal privacy and information. "Everyone says that children are small, who knows that small thinking is not small", being respected is the most important psychological need of human beings (Tao, 1930), children's heart is eager for equality and respect. In family education, parents should listen to the opinions of the child, avoiding taking adults above children. We should respect children's privacy, protect their legitimate rights and interests, and cultivate their sound personality. This with ***the Personal Information Protection Law of the People's Republic of China, article 28***: "sensitive personal information is once leaked or illegal use, easy to lead to a natural person personal dignity or personal, property safety of personal information, including biometric, religious beliefs, specific identity, health, financial account, whereabouts track information, and under the age of fourteen minors."

Third, we should follow the characteristics of family education and implement the scientific educational concept. Family education has its own unique characteristics, not the reappearance of school education, also should not become a vassal of school education and "second class", the fundamental task of family education, is through life education for the child to accept school education experience foundation, is through the influence of parents own example subtle, silently to children education. Therefore, the way of family education is to use every opportunity to teach, teach through practice, and complete the education of children in daily life.

Fourth, family education, school education, and social education are closely integrated. If family education wants to achieve good results, it cannot be separated from the cooperation and complementarity with school education and social education, make full use of various educational resources, strengthen the benign interaction between family, school, and society, and jointly build an environment conducive to the healthy growth of the child.

Fifth, flexible educational measures should be adapted to the actual situation. Family education is a process in which children perceive and learn from the external world through life. It is a process of accumulating life experience and understanding the truth, and it is also a necessary process for the child to develop and mature with their wisdom. Family education has no fixed teaching materials or standard unified syllabus curriculum, is full of uncertainty. Different families have different educational environments, different children have different personality characteristics, and different stages have different education methods, so family education should have full flexibility.

Article 5 of the Family Education Promotion Law of the People's Republic of China explains this:

Article 5
Family education shall satisfy the following requirements:

(1) Respecting the law of physical and mental development of minors and individual differences.
(2) Respecting the personal dignity of minors, protecting the privacy and personal information of minors, and protecting the lawful rights and interests of minors.
(3) Following the characteristics of family education and implementing scientific concepts and methods of family education.
(4) Family education, school education, and social education are closely integrated and coordinated.
(5) Adopting flexible and diverse measures in light of the reality.

Family education, of course, is not only by family can fully be implemented, it is the front of social education, its education form, and school education, social education is mutually reinforcing, and presents privacy and public synchronization, so if we want to implement the family education, cannot leave the national power and the social from all walks of life.

After *the Family Education Promotion Law of the People's Republic of China* established the status of family education in the education system and clarified the obligations of parents and other guardians on family education, it also standardizes the responsibilities of the government, schools and society to promote family education (in the law, setting up special chapters on "state support" and "social coordination"), the China's State Council, the People's Governments at various levels, the administrative departments of education and the Women's Federation are clarified (Article 6), Trade unions, the Communist Youth League and other organizations (Article 9), Residents 'committees and Villagers' committees (article 38), Primary and secondary schools and kindergartens (Article 39), Public security unit(A kind of Chinese police officer), People's Procuratorates and People's Courts (Article 8, Article 49, etc.), Civil affairs, health and market regulators, Family education guidance institutions (article 28, etc.), marriage registration agencies and adoption registration agencies (article 32), child welfare institutions and assistance and protection agencies for minors (article 33), Infant and child care services, early education services (article 44). Health care institutions (article 45), Libraries, youth palaces, science and technology museums, gymnasiums and patriotism education bases and other cultural and sports institutions. The responsibilities and obligations of television, newspapers and other news media (article 46) in family education.

In addition, the Family Education Promotion Law of the People's Republic of China also stipulates the relevant incentive measures (article 12) and commemorative date (article 13), strengthens its connotation and value through institutional means, forms the joint compulsory measures to protect children's family education, and mobilizes the whole society to do a good job in family education.

See Article 6, 8, 9, 12 and 13 of the Family Education Promotion Law of the People's Republic of China:

Article 6

The people's governments at all levels shall guide the family education work and establish and improve the education mechanism under which families, schools, and society cooperate. The institutions of the people's governments at or above the county level in charge of women's and children's work shall organize, coordinate, guide, and urge relevant departments to effectively complete family education.

The education administrative departments and the women's unions shall make overall plans for and coordinate social resources, promote the building of a family education guidance service system covering urban and rural areas in a corporative manner, and undertake the routine affairs of family education work in accordance with the division of duties.

The spiritual civilization construction departments at or above the county level and the public security, civil affairs, judicial administration, human resources and social security, culture and tourism, health, market regulation, radio and television, sports, press and publication, cyberspace and other relevant departments of the people's governments at or above the county level shall effectively complete the family education work within the scope of their respective duties.

Article 8

The people's courts and people's procuratorates shall maximize their functional role, cooperate with the people's governments at the same level and their relevant departments in establishing an interactive mechanism for the family education work, and jointly and effectively complete the family education work.

Article 9

The trade unions, the communist youth leagues, the disabled persons' federations, the science and technology associations, the working committees for the care of the next generation, the residents' committees, and the villagers' committees, among others, shall, in consideration of their own work, actively carry out the family education work and provide social support for family education.

Article 12

The state shall encourage and support natural persons, legal persons, and unincorporated organizations in donating for or providing voluntary services for family education, and grant tax incentives in accordance with the law where the conditions are met.

The state shall commend and reward organizations and individuals who have made outstanding contributions to family education in accordance with the relevant provisions.

Article 13
The week of International Family Day on May 15th is the National Family Education Promotion Week.

The law also stipulates that the government should actively fulfill its responsibilities, encourage the participation of social organizations and individuals to provide professional guidance and services for family education and implement technical support. It should be noted that the government should ensure that a sufficient financial budget is invested in the guidance of family education. At the same time, these services should emphasize their public welfare nature, requiring that all families should be covered as far as possible so that families with difficulties in developing family education can have the opportunity to find help. For details, see Articles 7 and 10 of *the Family Education Promotion Law of the People's Republic of China*:

Article 7
The people's governments at or above the county level shall develop special plans for the family education work, incorporate family education guidance services into the urban and rural public service system and the catalogue of government purchased services, include relevant funds in the fiscal budget, and encourage and support the provision of family education and guidance by government purchase of services.

Article 10
The state shall encourage and support enterprises, public institutions, social organizations, and individuals in carrying out public welfare family education service activities in accordance with the law.

In addition, this law specifically requires institutions of colleges and universities to conduct scientific research on family education by setting up family education subjects. A notable focus within this mandate is the emerging discipline of family pedagogy—which mainly studies the rules, contents, and methods of cultivating talents in the family environment, involving many disciplines such as physiology, psychology, pedagogy, etc., which lays a good foundation for the professional construction of family education. See Article 11 of *the Family Education Promotion Law of the People's Republic of China* for the above content:

Article 11
The state shall encourage the development of family education research, encourage institutions of higher education to offer provide professional family education courses, support normal colleges and schools and qualified institutions of higher education in strengthening family education discipline development, train family education service professionals, and provide training of family education service personnel.

In summary, *the Family Education Promotion Law of the People's Republic of China* accurately positioning the background of socialism with Chinese characteristics into the new era, the task of family education, objectives, content, principles and methods. This law plays a crucial role in guiding the whole society attaches great importance to family, family education, and construction in the field of the spiritual civilization, strengthening family education work, cultivating the all-round development of new era. To some extent, the Family Education Promotion Law of the People's Republic of China is not only a law on family education, but also a law with moral education as the main line, a law to promote the comprehensive and healthy growth of children, but also a textbook for family education and a family education instruction book.

7.2.2 System of Family Responsibilities

"The hand that promotes the world is the hand that shakes the cradle, and the quality of the mother determines the future of the nation." Parents, as the main person responsible for carrying out family education activities (Wang, 2010, p. 109), undertake the important mission and sacred responsibility of guiding children's positive progress and ensuring the healthy development of children. The aim of *the Family Education Promotion Law of the People's Republic of China* is through the guardian to carry out science and system of family education, promote the healthy growth of children, the second chapter "Responsibilities of Families" with ten provisions, detailed guide guardian how to undertake the implementation of family education responsibility, at the same time clear the family education should not be what behavior, delimit the bottom line for family education activities.

7.2.2.1 Guardians' Primary Duty in Family Education

The quality of family education depends largely on the competence of the guardians (mainly of the parents and primary caregivers. The guardian bears the main responsibility of raising and educating the child. Only when the guardian has the scientific concept of family education and grasps the correct method of family education, can they lay a solid foundation for the education of children. This is consistent with the international concept of protecting children's rights and interests.

To ensure effective family education, it is essential first to cultivate qualified guardians who are aware of their legal responsibilities, establish scientific concepts of family education, master correct methods, and enhance their ability to educate. The Family Education Promotion Law of the People's Republic of China strengthens the status of guardians as the subject of responsibility for the child and warns guardians not to fulfill their legal obligations because of entrusting others. For details, see Articles 14 and 21 of *the Family Education Promotion Law of the People's Republic of China*:

Article 14
Parents or other guardians shall establish a sense of responsibility that family is the first classroom and parents are the first teachers, assume the primary responsibility for the implementation of family education for minors, and use correct thoughts, methods, and behaviors to educate minors on developing good thoughts, conduct and habits.

Other family members with full capacity for civil conduct who live together shall assist and cooperate with parents or other guardians of minors in carrying out family education.

Article 21
Parents or other guardians of minors entrusting others to take care of minors in accordance with the law shall keep in touch with the entrusted persons and the minors, learn about minors' study, life and psychological conditions on a regular basis, and jointly perform family education responsibilities with the entrusted persons.

7.2.2.2 Content and Methods of Family Education

As for the content of family education, this law emphasizes six main aspects, implementing the socialist core values into family education, affirming the importance of family education for the cultivation of children's moral character, physical and mental health and good habits, and once again emphasizes the uniqueness of family education which is different from school education.

First, to cultivate the feelings of family and country. Guardians should always regulate their own words and deeds, in order to guide children to establish a correct and healthy values, outlook on life, world outlook. "To promote patriotism, we should start with children, and patriotism should run through the whole process of education and spiritual civilization construction." Loving the motherlands vast landscapes, its people, and national culture is the most essential emotion that every Chinese citizen with conscience and patriotism should have, it is to test a person the touchstone of loyalty to the motherland, but also the legal parents should perform family education duties (Xi, 2018, p. 183). It clearly stipulates that when parents carry out family education, they should love the CPC, love the people, love the country and the collective, establish the organic unity of safeguarding national unity and forging the sense of community of the Chinese nation, and always play an example role in family life.

Second, to cultivate good moral character. Moral education is the fundamental task of education, with family being the starting point and basis point for a person to receive education. Guardians should educate the child to worship virtue, respect the elderly and protect the weak, love family, thrift, unity and mutual assistance, integrity and friendship, abide by discipline and law, and cultivate their good social morality, family virtues, personal morality and awareness of the rule of law. "Should be good moral ideas to children, guide them to have human integrity and backbone, help them to form a good heart, promote their healthy growth, grow up to be useful to the country and the people", guardians need to pay attention to children's moral education, from the dribs and drabs in the daily life, gradually cultivate children's moral character (Xi, 2020b, p. 282), as Sima Guang said "people of virtue always value the smallest frugality", noble moral character is not simply through discipline can form, but constantly develop in practice. This point especially emphasizes the family education to play to its unique advantages to cultivate children.

Third, set up a correct view of success. The report to the 20th National Congress of the Communist Party of China said, must adhere to the "science and technology is the first productive force, talent is the first resource, innovation is the first power, further implement the strategy of science and education, talent strategy, innovation driven development strategy", reflected in the family education, as "to promote science and education, sow the seeds of science, stimulate curiosity, imagination, desire. Parents in the family need to create an innovative atmosphere to help children to develop a wide range of interests, and enhance the development of scientific exploration spirit, innovation consciousness and ability, scientific enlightenment education for children". At the same time, parents should abandon the biased educational concept, to establish the consciousness of "There are three hundred and sixty trades, and every trade has its master", according to the children's talent and personality, family situation, to help the cultivation of highly skilled talents and "great country craftsman".

Fourth, to promote the physical health of the child. Guardians should ensure that children's balanced nutrition, scientific exercise, adequate sleep, physical and mental pleasure, and guide them to develop good living habits and behavior habits. "Be a person with a mind like saint and a body like a barbarian", in recent years, many guardians only pay attention to the learning of children's knowledge, but ignore the cultivation of physical fitness; some children fail to develop good living habits, such as excessive reliance on electronic products, unlimited use of electronic products, resulting in physical decline and cause other physical health problems. Guardians have the responsibility to guide them to develop good living and behavior habits. Only in this way, the small saplings of the motherland can grow into the towering trees of the Chinese nation.

Fifth, to promote children's mental health. The child is in the period of rapid development of mental health. With the acceleration of the pace of life in modern society, the pressure caused by the external environment such as family, school and society and the deviation of children's cognitive, emotional and behavioral development will cause psychological problems in children. Guardians are adults who have the most contact with children, they should pay attention to children's mental health as they care about physical health. In daily life, they should pay attention to the subtle changes in children's moods and behaviors, give timely and correct guidance, and actively pay attention to them. At the same time, with the rapid development of society and the traditional and new events that harm children, guardians should help the child master safety knowledge and skills, and enhance their awareness and ability of self-protection.

Sixth, to cultivate children's labor habits. Labor is an important concept in the Marxist ideological system, the fundamental force to promote the progress of human society, and the necessary process of human self-creation and self-improvement. Helping the child to set up the correct labor concept, improving the self-care ability and independent living ability, developing the excellent character of enduring hardships and standing hard work and the good habits of loving labor, are not only the righteousness of family education, but also integral to the holistic development encompassing "moral, intellectual, physical, aesthetic, and labor education". This is directly related to whether the great socialist cause has a successor. Comrade Mao Zedong once said "Labor can transform thoughts and transform people", family education from school education and social education of the most significant feature is through the practice of labor education children, children in labor following the example of guardians, gradually learning knowledge and skills, complete the social exploration, "cultivate generation after generation of high-quality workers who love labor, are diligent in labor, and are good at labor".

In addition to detailing the content of family education, to guide guardians, this law also provides the family education methods, for the Angle of the most beneficial to children, the Family Education Promotion Law of the People's Republic of China detailed the nine methods of family education for children, encouraging for guardians, especially children's parents, hand to guide them how to carry out family education:

First, personal involvement and strengthening parent-child companionship. "What children rely on their parents is not a part of life, but all." Parent-child parenting and strengthening parent-child companionship are the first essence of family education (Fei, 2019, p. 78). Guardians (especially children's parents) are the primary and responsible person for children's growth, and accompanying the child through a short childhood should be an important mission of parents. If the guardian has to entrust others to take care of the children, he must also maintain close contact with the children, timely contact with schools, communities and other organizations, and cannot be absent in the family education.

Second, joint participation and the roles of both parents. "Nurturing or not teaching is a father's fault", the Chinese traditional education thought early to realize the importance of parents for children's education, but affected by the long unbalanced inadequate economic development reality, lead to a family main education responsibility is often the mother, father's role in the education is absent, it is bad for the growth of the child. The Family Education Promotion Law of the People's Republic of China clearly states that both parents should play a joint role in family education. Even in separated and divorced families, both parents should fulfill their obligation to educate their children (see Article 20 of the Law later).

Third, seize every educational opportunity in daily life. "Reasonable life is reasonable education". The biggest characteristic of family education is to take life as textbooks and guardians as teachers (Tao, 1930). "Normal life in the family is the most basic way of life of human beings", which is full of educational resources and opportunities (Lin, 2019). Guardians should seize all kinds of opportunities to educate and influence their children with their life itself. "Everyone's life is composed of small things, and only by raising a small virtue can it become a great virtue" (Xi, 2018, p. 183).

Fourth, the unconsciously influenced, combining words and examples. What is education? It should be "enjoy the breeze among the rain altars, and return home singing", it should not be reprimanded and blame, also should not be empty talk and vanity, but in a relaxed atmosphere of sharing knowledge process, is a experience "like spring breeze". Guardians should educate their children by words and deeds, slowly influencing their children's cognition and behavior habits, preventing the emergence of "classroom" education mode, and transform family education into another kind of school education.

Fifth, balance strictness with kindness and mutual assistance. According to the theory of parenting mode, due to the children's poor self-control and discrimination, blindly love and care may evolve to spoil the children (Baumrind, 1996, p. 410), which is not conducive to the growth of children. Guardians need to have certain authority, for children's education to have rules, need certain rewards and punishment measures, "not blindly spoil or indulge, but on the basis of understanding of children, give appropriate guidance and encouragement", so as to the correct education, give the child principle, wisdom, the bottom line of love (Nelsen, 2016, p. 5).

Sixth, respect differences and give scientific guidance according to age and personality characteristics. Children are not lifeless items, they have their own personality and interests, so the family education for the child is not to copy the "other people's children", but to try their best to explore the possibility of children, make a tree stand tall and upright, let a flower emit its fragrance. Therefore, respecting children's differences, tapping children's potential, "according to the children's age characteristics, gender characteristics and personality differences for targeted education", are things that family education should pay special attention to the problem (Zhu, 2021, p. 22).

Seventh, foster equal communication, and offer respect, understanding, and encouragement. "It is very common in the families to adopt a domineering attitude towards children, which can suppress their personalities even in affectionate environments." In the family education, guardian need to pay attention to and children always maintain respect and open attitude to communicate (Montessori, 2012), understand the needs of the child, answer the child's doubts, make the child feel respected and recognized, it helps to cultivate children independent sound personality.

Eighth, promote mutual growth; guardians and children should grow together. Family education has the characteristics of interactive and timing, guardian should be in the process of family education learning to improve their education way, "between high quality, high state of family life, company and get along, can establish close feelings between parents and children, communication and interaction, acquire the corresponding social ability and moral value". The Chinese people have always emphasized that it is never too old to learn. Family education is not so much an education for the child, but more like a process of guardian' self-education and self-growth (Zhang & Liu, 2021).

Ninth, it is necessary to adopt the ways and methods most conducive to the healthy growth of the child according to the actual situation. "Water has no constant shape, and people have no constant norm", guardians should realize the true meaning of family education, to avoid making family education lose its original intention, cannot play a real effect. At the same time, guardians need to master the law of children's development, educate children according to different stages and different scenarios, and give full play to their own subjective initiative (Zhang & Chen, 2021).

Article 16 of *the Family Education Promotion Law of the People's Republic of China* lists 6 main contents of carrying out family education, and Article 17 lists 9 ways and methods of family education. The specific contents are as follows:

Article 16

Parents or other guardians of minors shall carry out family education based on the physical and mental development characteristics of minors of different ages and with the following contents as the guidelines:

Educating minors to love the Party, the state, the people, the collectives, and socialism, establishes the concept of safeguarding national unity, building a sense of the Chinese nation's community, and cultivating family and country feelings.

Educating minors to respect morality and do good turns, respect the old and love the young, love families, be diligent and thrifty, work in unity and help one another, be faithfully and friendly, observe law and discipline, and cultivate their favorable social ethics, family virtues, personal morality.

Helping minors establish a correct outlook on becoming talents, guiding them to cultivate a wide range of hobbies, healthy aesthetic pursuits, and sound study habits, and enhancing scientific exploration spirit, and innovative consciousness and ability.

Ensuring that minors have balanced nutrition, scientific exercise, adequate sleep, and physical and mental pleasure, guiding them to develop sound living and behavioral habits, and promoting their physical and mental health.

Paying attention to the mental health of minors, teaching them to cherish their lives, and providing safety knowledge education on transportation, healthy Internet access, anti-bullying, anti-drowning, anti-fraud, anti-trafficking, anti-sexual assault, and other respects for them, and helping them master safety knowledge and skills to enhance their awareness and ability of self-protection.

Helping minors establish correct labor concepts, participate in labor within their capacity, improve their self-care ability and independent living ability, and develop excellent characters of bearing hardships and standing hard work and sound habit of loving labor.

Article 17
Parents or other guardians of minors who implement family education shall pay attention to minors' physical, psychological, and intellectual development status, respect their rights to participate in relevant family affairs and express opinions, and reasonably use the following methods:

Raising minors personally and strengthening parent-child companionship.

Jointly participating in education and playing the role of both parents.

Watching for opportunities to teach minors and educating minors in daily life.

Exerting a subtle influence on minors' character and combining teaching by personal example and verbal instruction.

Combining strictness and kindness, and paying equal attention to care and strict requirement.

Respecting differences and conducting scientific guidance based on age and personality characteristics.

Conducting exchanges on an equal footing, and respecting, and encouraging minors.

Conducting mutual promotion, and jointly growing up with children.

Other ways and methods that are beneficial to minors' all-round development and healthy growth.

7.2.2.3 Parents' Responsibility for Developing Family Education

For the better implementation of family education, the law not only positively encourages guardians to implement family education, but also establishing a correct concept of family education. To urge the parents to perform their duties, Including following the rules of children's growth, and Setting up the correct concept of family education; Second, it should cooperate closely with primary and secondary schools, kindergarten infant care service institutions and communities, Actively participate in family education guidance and practice activities; Third, if their parents are separated or divorced, Should cooperate with each other to fulfill their family education responsibilities, Do not refuse or neglect their performance; Fourth, to entrust others to take care of children according to law, Should be regularly informed of the children's living and learning conditions, Fulfill the responsibility of family education (see the quotation of article 21 for details); Fifth, the reasonable arrangement of children's study, rest, entertainment and exercise time. For details, see Articles 18–20 and 22 of the Family Education Promotion Law of the People's Republic of China:

Article 18
Parents or other guardians of minors shall establish a correct concept of family education, consciously learn the knowledge on family education, conduct targeted learning during pregnancy and important periods when minors enter into infant and child care service institutions, kindergartens, and primary and secondary schools, master scientific family education methods, and improve their ability of family education.

Article 19
Parents or other guardians of minors shall closely cooperate with primary and secondary schools, kindergartens, infant and child care service institutions, and communities, actively participate in the public welfare guidance for family education and practical activities provided by them, and jointly promote minors' healthy growth.

Article 20
Parents of minors who are separated or divorced shall cooperate with each other in fulfilling their family education responsibilities, and neither party shall refuse or neglect to fulfill responsibilities; and any party shall not hinder the other party from carrying out family education, unless as otherwise prescribed by law.

Article 22
Parents or other guardians of minors shall reasonably arrange time for minors to study, rest, entertain and do physical exercises, avoid increasing minors' learning burden, and prevent minors from indulging in the Internet.

At the same time, *the Family Education Promotion Law of the People's Republic of China* requires that no one is allowed to infringe on children's rights, such as discrimination against the child by gender, physical condition, and intelligence, and clearly requires that domestic violence should not be allowed, along with any coercion, induce, abet, connivance or use children to engage in bad activities. Among them, the prohibition of domestic violence does not mean the prohibition of educational punishment but refers to the prohibition of violence to restrict children's personal freedom or infringe on children's physical and mental acts, which causes damage to children's right to life health, and personal dignity. The provisions for the prohibition of sexual activities are reflected in Article 23 of *the Family Education Promotion Law of the People's Republic of China*:

Article 23
Parents or other guardians of minors shall not discriminate against minors due to gender, physical condition, and intelligence, among others, commit domestic violence, or force, induce, incite, or use minors to carry out activities in violation of laws and regulations and social ethics, or indulge them with such activities.

According to *the Family Education Promotion Law of the People's Republic of China*, if the parents or other guardians refused, idle in the family education responsibility, or illegally hinder other guardians implement family education, will bear adverse consequences, will be criticized education, exhortation to stop, when necessary, it will be required to accept family education guidance. The detailed rules are elaborated in the "Legal Liabilities" chapter.

7.2.3 National Support

China's constitution requires the state to protect children's rights and interests in education. In view of the situation that some parents "raise but do not teach" and "teach improperly", the state has the right and responsibility to intervene moderately in family education from the perspective of putting children first. At the same time, in the face of the problem of unbalanced education resources, the state has an obligation to provide guidance and help to family education. This involvement is crucial not only for social stability and sustainable development but also helps protect children interests from being compromised, inheriting the Chinese nation attaches great importance to the education and care of children, highlighting the country under the socialist system of special care and special protection of the child.

7.2.3.1 Relevant Functions and Duties of the People's Governments at All Levels

The Family Education Promotion Law of the People's Republic of China to family education from "family" to "state", from "government can do 'to' government must do", the administrative organ to promote family education responsibilities (Cong, 2021), and combined with the advantages of administrative organs at all levels detailed classification, respectively, planning the national, provincial and county level government family education work system:

As a central administrative organ, China's State Council, on behalf of the will of the state, undertakes the responsibility of timely formulating the national family education guidance outline, organizes and guides the implementation of family education nationwide, and leads the development of family education nationwide.

Since China is a large and populous country, different regions and nationalities have different special conditions. Because China is a developing country with unbalanced development, local administrative authorities under the guidance and guidance of the local government, such as writing in minority languages and setting standards according to the regional economic development. See Article 24 of *the Family Education Promotion Law of the People's Republic of China*:

Article 24
The State Council shall organize relevant departments to develop, revise and timely enact the National Family Education Guidelines.

Provincial people's governments or qualified people's governments at the districted city level shall organize relevant departments to compile or adopt family education guidance textbooks suitable for local conditions, and develop corresponding work standards and evaluation standards for family education guidance services.

Considering the economic cost and transportation factors, the penetration rate of offline family education guidance is restricted to some extent, the law requires administrative organs at or above the provincial level to provide information technology platform for family education, open a service hotline, break through the restriction of space and time on family education, and guarantee the guidance service; See Article 25 of *the Family Education Promotion Law of the People's Republic of China*:

Article 25
People's governments at or above the provincial level shall organize relevant departments to coordinate the construction of a shared service platform for family education information, set up public welfare online parent schools and online courses, launch service hotlines, and provide online family education guidance services.

As a county administrative organ with close contact with the majority of families, it needs to implement eight measures: (1) to ensure the implementation of the policy of reducing the homework burden and off-campus training burden for students in compulsory education; (2) Determine the guidance institutions for family education, Carry out relevant work in accordance with actual conditions (see articles 28 and 29 of the law quoted later); (3) Establish a family education service team, Training of professional talents; (4) Carry out research work on family education; (5) Provide family education services; (6) Create conditions for carrying out family education; (7) To care for children in difficulties and left-behind children; (8) To ensure the funds for the work related to family education, Adhere to the nature of public welfare.

For details, see Articles 26,36 and 52 of the Family Education Promotion Law of the People's Republic of China:

Article 26
Local people's governments at or above the county level shall strengthen supervision and administration, reduce students' burden on homework and off-campus training during the compulsory education period, smooth the communication channels between schools and families, and promote mutual cooperation between school education and family education.

Article 36
Paragraph 3 Relevant departments of education, civil affairs, health, and market regulation, among others, shall, within the scope of their respective responsibilities, guide and supervise family education service institutions and employees in accordance with the law.

Article 52
Family education guidance institutions falling under any of the following circumstances shall be ordered by the competent departments to take corrective action within a prescribed time limit, and institutions refusing to take corrective action or falling under serious circumstances shall be ordered by the competent departments to cease business for rectification, and be subject to revocation of business license or revocation of registration:

(1) Failing to undergo the formalities for formation in accordance with the law.
(2) Engaging in behaviors beyond the permitted business scope or conducting false or misleading publicity, thus resulting in adverse outcome.
(3) Infringing upon the lawful rights and interests of minors, and their parents or other guardians.

In order to carry out the guidance work of family education scientifically, the people's government at the county level should set up professional guidance and service teams, and encourage social workers and volunteers to devote themselves to family education guidance and service. With special attention must be paid to troubled children and left-behind children, the administrative organ to assume greater responsibility, and give more care, not only to provide life support to protect the rights and interests of children, and actively create employment opportunities, for related children's guardians can stay in the local work, guarantee their work and life, to create a good family education atmosphere for the child. Education administrative departments and the Women's Federation, as the main departments to protect the rights and interests of children in difficulties and left-behind children, play the main responsibility in this process. Article 27 and Article 30 of *the Family Education Promotion Law of the People's Republic of China* reflect the above contents:

Article 27
Local people's governments at or above the county level and relevant departments shall organize the formation of professional teams for family education guidance services, strengthen the training of professionals, and encourage social workers and volunteers to participate in family education guidance services.

Article 30
The people's governments of districted cities, counties, and townships shall, in light of local reality, adopt measures, establish files for left-behind minors and families of minors in distress, provide support for life, entrepreneurship, employment, and other care services, and create conditions for parents or other guardians of left-behind minors and minors in distress to implement family education.

Educational administrative departments and women's unions shall adopt targeted measures to provide services for the implementation of family education by parents or other guardians of left-behind minors and minors in distress, and guide them to actively pay attention to the physical and mental health of minors and strengthen family care.

The administrative departments of education and the Women's Federation shall take targeted measures to provide services for the family education of parents or other guardians of left-behind minors and minors in distress, and guide them to actively pay attention to the physical and mental health of minors and strengthen family care.

It has also made clear provisions on the work of other relevant government departments at the same level, and emphasized that relevant departments have the supervision responsibility for family education through listing, so as to prevent the phenomenon of not performing the duties such as "kicking the ball" between departments.

See Article 6, paragraph 3, of the Family Education Promotion Law of the People's Republic of China.

Article 6, paragraph 3
The spiritual civilization construction departments at or above the county level and the public security, civil affairs, judicial administration, human resources and social security, culture and tourism, health, market regulation, radio and television, sports, press and publication, cyberspace and other relevant departments of the people's governments at or above the county level shall effectively complete the family education work within the scope of their respective duties.

7.2.3.2 Family Education Guidance Institutions

Family education is related to the future of the society, the nation and the country. The construction of the family education guidance and service system is an inevitable trend to improve the basic public service system in the new era, and also an inevitable requirement for realizing the modernization of the national governance system and governance capacity. According to the Family Education Promotion Law of the People's Republic of China, the main body of family education guidance in China is the "Family Education Guidance Institution" established by the county administrative organs, which is responsible for the relevant work in the region. So set because there is no government agency is full-time in family education guidance, if you want to set up a function responsible for, not only difficult to solve the adjustment of the upper organizational framework, the grassroots government is difficult to actual operation, Thus, it is specified that "administrative organs at the county level to establish family education guidance institutions", allowing regions the flexibility to adapt as needed.

The family education guidance service system has the purpose of "educational extension" and improving guardians' educational ability and level (Hu, 2011), which needs to be guided by social organizations or relevant departments outside the family. At the same time, the existing family education guidance service content in the society is scattered and lacks systematicness, and "the service content of commercial training institutions for family education guidance focuses on the cultivation of children's interests, and the guidance of parent-child communication skills is less than 10%". Therefore, it is necessary to integrate market resources and government forces, set up or confirm professional institutions for family education guidance and related research work, train a high-quality family education guidance team, highlight its public welfare attribute, ensure the maximum area to cover the families in the jurisdiction, and become the core force to promote family education.

In the process of confirmation and construction of family education guidance institutions, there needs to be pay attention to play the role of schools, and community organizations, using parents and parents committees, parents schools, and community schools, to provide guidance for family education ability of family, build "home-community-school" linkage mechanism, promote the government functional departments, social organizations, schools, education institutions and the participation in cooperation between families. However, it should be noted that in this process, schools, communities and other organizations only play a supporting role. Family education guidance institutions should perform their duties in accordance with the law, ensuring they do not outsource their core duties or fail to perform due to negligence.

Family education guidance institutions in the process of executing, shall not organize or disguise organization for-profit education training, to the guidance service universal and public welfare, adhere to the people as the center, timely service to the family with demand, "improve the social security system, strengthen the basic public services, take in the bottom line of the people's livelihood, solve the problem of the people anxious sorrow hope, make modernization achievements more fair benefit all the people".

Articles 28, 29, and 31 of the Family Education Promotion Law of the People's Republic of China reflect the above contents:

Article 28

Local people's governments at or above the county level may determine family education guidance institutions through a variety of ways and methods in light of local reality and needs.

Family education guidance institutions shall provide guidance for parent schools in communities, parent schools in schools, and other family education guidance service sites within their jurisdictions, and concurrently carry out research on family education, building and training of service personnel teams, and research and development of public service products.

Article 29
Family education guidance institutions shall provide services for families in need in a timely manner.

For families whose parents or other guardians have certain difficulties in fulfilling their family education responsibilities, the family education guidance institutions shall, in light of the specific circumstances, cooperate with relevant departments in providing targeted services.

Article 31
Family education guidance institutions shall not organize for-profit education and training directly or in a disguised manner when carrying out family education and guidance service activities.

7.2.3.3 The Women's Federation

General Secretary Xi Jinping stressed that in the implementation of the family education promotion law, we should pay attention to give play to the unique role of the Women's Federations, "give play to the unique role of women in promoting the family virtues of the Chinese nation and establishing a good family style...... Help them (referring to the child) to form a good heart and promote their healthy growth." Since the founding of the Communist Party of China has been committed to the women's liberation movement. Under the leadership of the CPC, as a mass organization of women of all ethnic groups and all walks of life united for the liberation of women, the Women's Federation has a wide range of mass and social characteristics, with one of its basic tasks is to serve women and the child.

The top leading body of the Women's Federation is the National Women's Congress and the executive Committee of the All-China Women's Federation. At present, the Women's Federation of National organizations, local organizations, grassroots organizations, and group members of the organization system, including local organizations and grassroots organizations of Women's Federation by the region, the unit of women's congress or congress elected, group members are mainly the female worker committee, and mainly women all kinds of social society, service for women's social groups. The state supports the cause of women's liberation, adheres to the basic state policy of equality between men and women, protects the legitimate rights and interests of women and children, and supports the work of Women's Federations. Their administrative funds, operational activities and career development funds are mainly funded by the government.

The Family Education Promotion Law of the People's Republic of China clearly stipulates that Women's Federations shall coordinate social resources, jointly promote the construction of a family education guidance and service system covering both urban and rural areas, and undertake the daily affairs of family education according to the division of responsibilities. At the same time, specify the women's federation should play women in carrying forward the family virtues of the Chinese nation, set up the unique role of good family trait, make good use of close ties with the women, popularize knowledge of family education, through family education guidance institutions, community parents, civilized family construction and other channels to carry out the family education practice, provide family education guidance services.

See articles 6, 30 and 35 of the Family Education Promotion Law of the People's Republic of China:

> **Article 6, paragraph 2**
> ***The education administrative departments and the women's unions shall make overall plans for and coordinate social resources, promote the building of a family education guidance service system covering urban and rural areas in a corporative manner, and undertake the routine affairs of family education work in accordance with the division of duties.***
>
> **Article 30, paragraph 2**
> ***Educational administrative departments and women's unions shall adopt targeted measures to provide services for the implementation of family education by parents or other guardians of left-behind minors and minors in distress, and guide them to actively pay attention to the physical and mental health of minors and strengthen family care.***
>
> **Article 35**
> ***The women's unions shall maximize the unique role of women in carrying forward the family virtues of the Chinese nation, establishing a sound family tradition, and other respects, publicize knowledge on family education, organize and carry out family education practice activities through various channels such as family education guidance institutions, parent schools in communities, and civilized family building, among others, and provide family education guidance services.***

7.2.3.4 Other Institutions

Other involving the child to improve family education support institutions, such as marriage registration agencies and adoption registration agencies, child welfare institutions, minor relief agencies, the People's Court, and the Women's Federation (about the Women's Federation, see above), etc., should family education work into their work content, and combined with the specific content of their own responsibilities to carry out the implementation.

Specifically, the marriage registration agency and adoption registration agency—in China, is responsible for such affairs of the civil affairs department, according to the relevant laws and regulations, in the relevant formalities should be to the parties to promote family education-related knowledge, including legal knowledge, life knowledge, psychological knowledge, etc., spread safeguard children's development, promote the concept of family education.

In the process of performing their duties, child welfare institutions and juvenile assistance and protection institutions should strictly examine the conditions of relevant personnel, earnestly provide family education guidance, and ensure that the rights and interests of children can be protected.

The People's Courts have played an important role in promoting the protection of children's rights and interests. In addition to the specific guidance, the court in the process of trial to the party propaganda family education knowledge, especially in the divorce case, need to emphasize after divorce parents still bear the responsibility of family education, not absence, this is because "family basic structure changes on the quality of family education greatly, the judicial organ is necessary to give moderate intervention, to buffer may cause negative effects on minors" (Qiu & Niu, 2022). That is, the content of article 20 of the law quoted above.

In addition, state organs, enterprises and institutions, mass organizations and social organizations should combine the construction of family traditions with the characteristics of the unit, guarantee and support workers to participate in family education service activities, and help more families to receive family education guidance. In the process of the construction of socialist spiritual civilization, we should also pay attention to the family construction as an important part of the investigation, and promote the social atmosphere with the family style, so as to influence the appearance of the country and carry forward the core socialist values.

Article 32, 33, 34 and 37 of the Family Education Promotion Law of the People's Republic of China embody the above spirit:

Article 32
Marriage registration institutions and adoption registration institutions shall, by on-site consultation and counseling, broadcasting promotional and educational videos, and other methods, publicize knowledge on family education among and provide family education guidance for parties who handle marriage registration and adoption registration.

Article 33
Child welfare institutions and minor rescue and protection institutions shall provide family education guidance for foster families arranged by them, and parents or other guardians of minors receiving rescue and protection.

Article 34
When hearing divorce cases, the people's courts shall provide family education and guidance for both spouses with minor children.

Article 37
State authorities, enterprises and public institutions, group organizations, and social organizations shall incorporate family tradition construction into cultural construction of entities, and support employees in participating in related family education service activities.

In the activities of creating civilized cities, civilized villages and towns, civilized entities, civilized communities, civilized schools, and civilized families, family education shall be regarded as an important content.

7.2.4 Social Cooperation

"The family, the school, the government and the society are all responsible for the success of education. No one is a bystander, and no one can stay out of it" (Xi, 2019, p. 280). *The Law on the Protection of Minors of the People's Republic of China* puts forward the requirements for the social protection of the child, while *the Family Education Promotion Law of the People's Republic of China* further emphasizes the importance of social coordination, and makes it clear that family education guidance and service is the responsibility of the whole society. At present, China is trying to build a "collaborative education mechanism with schools actively leading, families actively responsible and effective social support". Among them, social forces will play a key role in supplementing and coordinating, and coordinate all forces to support the development of family education. Starting from different subjects, the law explains what responsibilities the society needs to undertake in the field of family education, and basically covers the aspects of family education at the social level.

7.2.4.1 Grassroots Mass Self-Governing Organizations

Residents' committees and villagers' committees are autonomous grassroots organizations established in urban and rural areas under the Chinese Constitution. They represent a crucial aspect of the development of socialist democratic politics in China, embodying the practice where the people are the most direct and profound masters of their domain. These committees are intimately connected to people's daily lives, have a deep understanding of children's family environments, and are closely associated with parents. They play an irreplaceable role in dispute mediation, propaganda, and mobilization within their communities.

This chapter uses "communities" collectively referred to as the residents 'committees and villagers' committees. The concept of "community" originated from tenness' book "Community and Civil Society" (Gemeinschaft und Gesellschaft: Grundbegriffe der reinen Soziologie), he thinks "community is lasting, real life (Tennis, 2019, p. 71), namely "a acquaintance society and kinship ties the emotional social community" (Fei, 2001), "occupied in a is more or less explicitly defined the regional crowd together" (Park et al., 2012, p. 104). In the 1930s, intellectuals led by Fei Xiaotong first translated "community" into Chinese "she' qu", introducing the concept of community to China. With the reform of China's market economy and the gradual disintegration of the unit courtyard, the community has played an increasingly prominent role in the field of grassroots governance in China, and has gradually become a "big family" composed of multiple families. An excellent community will inevitably affect the happy life of every family in the community and the successful development of family education.

The Family Education Promotion Law of the People's Republic of China to build relying on the urban and rural community as the core of the family education public service system, the grass-roots autonomous organizations with family education guidance institutions in the field of knowledge guidance, to help family education guidance, provide guardians parental education and child peer education and other services, "to safeguard and improve people's livelihood, do a good job in the people's livelihood, focusing on the concern of the people think." the service to the door, the family education to the jurisdiction of every family, every child. See Article 38 of *the Family Education Promotion Law of the People's Republic of China*:

Article 38
Residents' committees and villagers' committees may, by relying on public service facilities in urban and rural communities, set up parent schools in communities and other family education guidance service sites, cooperate with family education guidance institutions in publicizing knowledge on family education among residents and villagers, and provide family education guidance services for parents or other guardians of minors.

7.2.4.2 Educational Services

Article 39
Primary and secondary schools and kindergartens shall incorporate family education guidance services into their work plans as the content of professional training of teachers.

Emphasizing the difference between family education and school education does not mean that educational organizations such as schools should be excluded from the category of family education activities. *The Family Education Promotion Law of the People's Republic of China* notes that at this stage because the education level and education skills of the majority of guardians are not high, it stipulates that primary and secondary schools and kindergartens should provide family education guidance in the work plan to train teachers to master this skill.

Teachers have a high status and irreplaceable influence value in the hearts of the children, in China also have "A day as a teacher and a lifetime as a father", therefore the development of family education work cannot be separated from the participation of teachers group, and teachers can deeply influence the family education, "when children in the family cannot get good parents education and close parent-child relationship, good teacher behavior and close relationship between teachers and students can make up and replace the role" (Deng, 2013), so the guidance of family education must absorb teachers, especially the participation of the front-line teachers.

At the same time, primary and secondary schools and other organizations should pay attention to the integrity of education effect, adhere to the school education and family education, social education, strengthen the "home, school, community" collaboration, promote the construction of parents school, parents committee, promote family education experience, promote family education knowledge (Wu et al., 2014), can invite social organizations to conduct cooperation and communication, strengthen external education theory study. Educational organizations also enhance the public welfare of after-school education, actively carry out family education publicity and lectures in communities and other places, and help the development of family education guidance and service institutions such as community schools.

See Article 40, Article 41, and Article 42 of the Family Education Promotion Law of the People's Republic of China:

Article 40
Primary and secondary schools and kindergartens may, by forming parent schools and other methods, regularly organize non-profit family education guidance services and practical activities according to the characteristics of minors of different ages, and contact minors' parents or other guardians and urge them to participate therein.

Article 41
Primary and secondary schools and kindergartens shall, according to the needs of parents, invite relevant personnel to impart family education concepts, knowledge, and methods, organize and carry out family education guidance services and practical activities, and promote joint education by families and schools.

Article 42
Qualified primary and secondary schools and kindergartens shall, under the guidance of the education administrative department, provide support for family education guidance service sites' activities of providing public welfare family education guidance services.

According to the bioecological theory (Bronfenbrenner, 1979), "the environment has an important impact on individual behavior and psychological development" (Che et al., 2007). Behind every problem child is a family with many problems. "Family education has a profound impact on children's personality formation, emotional needs, values, social skills, etc." If there are mistakes in family education, it may lead to psychological problems for the child, thus increasing the risk of children engaging in bad behavior. Therefore, school education should work closely with family education to regulate children's behavior, and avoid the bad family environment leading to children's bad behavior. If the child has bad behaviors, such as school violence. it is crucial to communicate with their guardians promptly. Schools should adhere to the principle of prioritizing education over punishment and offer family education guidance services. These services aim to educate and rehabilitate the child, fostering improvement through a supportive and corrective approach.

For those suspected of illegal crimes, the educational organization shall report to the relevant departments in time and govern according to law. For details, see Article 43 of *the Family Education Promotion Law of the People's Republic of China*:

Article 43
Primary and secondary schools finding that minor students have seriously violated school rules and disciplines shall stop and discipline them in a timely manner, notify their parents or other guardians, and provide targeted family education guidance services for their parents or other guardians; and primary and secondary schools finding that minor students have bad behaviors or serious bad behavior shall handle it in accordance with the relevant laws and regulations.

7.2.4.3 Cultural and Health Institutions

"Society is a big classroom, and life is a textbook." Not only in schools, families and community common places of the child live needs to popularize family education and related guidance, in order to maximize the interests of the child, as long as the child will appear in the place and the work involving the child, such as pregnancy health care, vaccination, early education, etc., should be according to its own advantages to provide scientific family education guidance services, such as health care institutions can be for children's nutrition diet guidance, sports institutions can provide guidance for children's physical exercise and physical health, cultural institutions can provide scientific literacy and cultural education services. Strive to ensure the comprehensive coverage of all children's activity space, do no dead corners of the protection system. The news media should also extensively publicize family education, spread scientific ideas and advanced knowledge, and create a good social atmosphere that attaches importance to family education.

For details, see Article 44–46 of the Family Education Promotion Law of the People's Republic of China:

Article 44
Infant and child care service institutions and early educational service institutions shall provide scientific parenting guidance and other family education guidance services for parents or other guardians of minors.

Article 45
When providing services such as pre-marital health care, pregnancy and childbirth health care, child health care, and vaccination, medical and health care institutions shall carry out publicity of and guidance for knowledge on scientific parenting and early development of infants and young children, for relevant adults, and parents or other guardians of minors.

Article 46
Libraries, museums, cultural centers, memorials, art galleries, science and technology centers, stadiums, youth palaces, children's activity centers, and other public cultural service institutions and patriotic education bases shall carry out publicity of public welfare family education, family education guidance services, and practical activities on a regular basis every year, and develop public cultural service products of family education.

News media such as radio, television, newspapers, and the Internet shall publicize correct family education knowledge, disseminate scientific family education concepts and methods, and create a favorable social atmosphere that values family education.

7.2.4.4 Social Services Organization

To promote family education, we should not only rely on the power of the government but also actively absorb the participation of social forces. *The Family Education Promotion Law of the People's Republic of China* and *the Interim Regulations on the Registration of Private Non-enterprise Units* and other relevant laws and regulations for social forces into the family education services provide legal support, relevant social service organizations shall strengthen their own management, standardize the industry environment, strengthen staff training, improve the service level. The government can provide financial subsidies, incentives, purchase of services, and other means to encourage their development. At the same time, the relevant functional departments of the government should do a good job of supervising and guiding the work of social service organizations.

According to the principle of maximizing the interests of the child, these service organizations should adhere to the non-profit principle and ensure that more families can receive relevant services. This approach is critical given the relatively high proportion of family spending on child education in recent years in our country. Implementing a non-profit principle helps to mitigate the risk of excessive economic burdens on families and ensures the effective use of social resources. Moreover, controlling the influx of capital in the family education sector is essential to prevent imbalances in service development that could exacerbate regional disparities, and the socioeconomic gaps between urban and rural areas, as well as between different economic classes. As a national public service product, family education guidance service should highlight the function of universal benefit and public welfare service. For details, see Articles 36 and 47 of *the Family Education Promotion Law of the People's Republic of China*:

Article 36
Natural persons, legal persons, and unincorporated organizations may form non-profit family education service institutions in accordance with the law.

Local people's governments at or above the county level and relevant departments may adopt supportive measures such as government subsidies, rewards and incentives, and purchase of services to cultivate family education service institutions.

Relevant departments of education, civil affairs, health, and market regulation, among others, shall, within the scope of their respective responsibilities, guide and supervise family education service institutions and employees in accordance with the law.

Article 47
Family education service institutions shall strengthen self-discipline management, develop family education service standards, organize training of employees, and improve the professional quality and ability of employees.

7.2.5 Legal Liability

The Family Education Promotion Law of the People's Republic of China empowers guardians through legislation and mobilizes the resources of all parties in society to ensure the progress of family education activities. Chapter 5 of this law "Legal Liability" for the series of activities defined the bottom's line requirements, and made clear about the family education implementation shall not when or family education service shall not be when individuals or organizations should bear what legal consequences, answered the guardians (parents) should perform what obligations in accordance with the law, the government and society should play what role.

The Family Education Promotion Law of the People's Republic of China better distinguishes the guardians who do not perform family education responsibility accountability scale, to arouse public awareness of children's rights, family education consciousness has a positive role, and fully considers China's national conditions, although the chapter five only seven laws, the relevant regulations not only take into account the reality of the majority of urban and rural families, but also take into account the combination of advocacy principles and operability.

Relevant functional departments have the responsibility to intervene in family education according to the law. This intervention is divided into two aspects—One is the active intervention, that is, when guardians encounter difficulties in the process of fulfilling the family education responsibility, they can seek help from the functional departments or administrative agencies; the second is the negative intervention, that is, when guardians do not perform the duties of family education, or wrong to perform family education, serious dereliction of duty, such as, the child engage in illegal crimes, serious bad behavior, the relevant departments can force guardians to accept the relevant family education guidance, to correct the adverse effects, or even make them face legal punishment.

It needs to be emphasized that the core of this law is the word "promotion", whose purpose is to encourage guardians to actively and correctly carry out family education activities. If relatively tough punitive measures are applied to them, it may strike the enthusiasm and initiative of guardians and fail to achieve the purpose of this law. Therefore, although in the first draft of this law, punitive measures such as "fine and detention" were stipulated for the situation of parents' refusal to fulfill their responsibilities, they were changed to "soft" measures such as "critical education of parents, exhortation and admonish" in the subsequent process.

At the same time, the law also stipulates which functional departments can punish incompetent guardians according to law, as well as the means of punishment, adhering to the principle of maximum interest protection of the child and the implementation of appropriate punishment. For details, see articles 48 and 49 of *the Family Education Promotion Law of the People's Republic of China*:

Article 48

Residents' committees, villagers' committees, women's unions at minors' domiciles, entities where minors' parents or other guardians work, as well as primary and secondary schools, kindergartens and other entities that have close contact with minors finding that parents or other guardians refuse or neglect to perform family education responsibilities or illegally hinder other guardians from implementing family education shall be criticized and educated, admonished and stopped, and urge them to accept family education guidance, if necessary.

Parents or other guardians of minors entrusting others to take care of minors in accordance with the law, and relevant entities finding that entrusted persons do not perform family education responsibilities in accordance with the law, the provisions of the preceding paragraph shall apply.

Article 49
During the process of handling cases, public security organs, people's procuratorates, and people's courts find that minors have committed seriously bad or criminal behaviors or that minors' parents or other guardians have inappropriately implemented family education and have therefore infringed upon the lawful rights and interests of minors shall admonish the parents or other guardians according to the situation, and may order them to accept family education and guidance.

At the same time, the law also stipulates which functional departments can punish incompetent guardians according to law, as well as the means of punishment, adhering to the principle of maximum interest protection of the child and the implementation of appropriate punishment. Simultaneously, the law also makes clear other subjects involving family education responsibilities except for guardians. Due to the family education responsibilities of government departments, institutions to promote family education to play a leading role or key role, so in accordance with the government and perform the relevant functions of the government institutions not role, illegally occupy family education work funds and other abuse of power will be ordered to correct and disciplinary punishment. Similarly, public service institutions and primary and secondary schools that fail to perform their duties or do so inadequately are subject to oversight by competent departments, which can demand corrections; in serious cases, the direct persons in charge may face legal penalties. For example, article 50 and Article 51 of *the Family Education Promotion Law of the People's Republic of China*:

Article 50
Where a government department or institution being responsible for family education falls under any of the following circumstances, it's superior authority or competent entity shall order it to make corrections within a prescribed time limit; under serious circumstances, directly liable persons in charge and other directly liable persons shall be given penalties in accordance with the law:

(1) Failing to perform the responsibilities of family education.
(2) Withholding, occupying, misappropriating, falsely reporting, or fraudulently obtaining family education funds.
(3) Other circumstances of abusing powers, neglecting duties, or making falsification for private gain.

Article 51
Family education guidance institutions, primary and secondary schools, kindergartens, infant and child care service institutions, and early education service institutions failing to perform or incorrectly performing responsibilities for family education guidance services in violation of the provisions of this Law shall be ordered by competent departments to take corrective action within a prescribed time limit; and under serious circumstances, directly liable persons in charge and other directly liable persons shall be given penalties in accordance with the law.

This Law shall be connected with other legal documents safeguarding the rights of the child. Those who seriously infringe on the rights and interests of the child shall be investigated for their illegal responsibility and criminal responsibility according to law. For details, please see the other relevant chapters of the book.

For details, see Articles 53 and 54 of the Family Education Promotion Law of the People's Republic of China:

Article 53
Parents or other guardians of minors who commit domestic violence against minors in the process of family education shall be held legally liable in accordance with the provisions of the Law of the People's Republic of China on the Protection of Minors, the Anti-domestic Violence Law of the People's Republic of China and other laws.

Article 54
Those who constitute any violation of public security administration in violation of the provisions of this Law shall be given public security administrative punishment by the public security authorities according to the law; and shall be held criminally liable in accordance with the law, where a crime is constituted.

7.3 Summary

General Secretary Xi Jinping has pointed out that "no matter how much the change in the times, no matter how much the life pattern changes, we should pay attention to family construction, pay attention to family, family education and family style." If a man in the morning hears the right way, he may die in the evening without regret", education is a lifelong exploration of the cause which requires that our children are trained to be healthy, complete, noble, free people, to achieve the comprehensive development of "moral, intellectual, physical, aesthetic and labor", and to realize their great leap "from the kingdom of necessity to the kingdom of freedom".

The Family Education Promotion Law of the People's Republic of China focuses on the child, highlighting the value orientation of "putting morality first", raising e the traditional Chinese virtue of attaching importance to family education to a legal level, promoting guardians to shoulder the primary responsibility of family education, implement the statutory responsibility of the state to support family education, coordinating and mobilizing all sectors of society, So that the country, society, schools and the family have rules and laws to follow, Form a "family, country, and society" family education security system, let the child "button up the first button of life", So that the fundamental goal of quality education and the fundamental task of cultivating people have been implemented in the field of family education, It has laid a solid legal foundation for the healthy growth of the child.

The Family Education Promotion Law of the People's Republic of China has pushed the cause of family education in China to a new height. In the future, China will continue to promote the implementation of family education, gradually improve the relevant legal system, strengthen the construction of socialist spiritual civilization, and strive to build China into a prosperous, democratic, civilized, harmonious, and beautiful modern socialist country!

References

An, L. (2017). Engels' view of the family and its enlightenment to the construction of family style in contemporary China — An analysis based on "The Origin of the Family, Private Property and the State" as the main text. *Journal of Socialist Core Values*, 2.

Baumrind, D. (1996). The discipline controversy revisited. *Family Relations, 4*, 410.

Bronfenbrenner, U. (1979). *The ecology of human development: Experiences by nature and design*. Harvard University Press.

Che, G., Ding, Y., & Ming, X. (2007). On the construction of a moral education system integrating school, family and social education — You Brown Fen, Bioecological Theory. *Journal of Northeast Normal University (Philosophy and Social Science Edition)*, 4.

Cong, Z. (2021). *Accelerating the development of family education guidance services in China — Expert interpretation of the family education promotion law*. China Women's News.

Deng, J. (2021). The constitutional logic of the family education promotion law. *Journal of Soochow University (Educational Science Edition)*, 4.

Deng, X. (2013). *A study on the relationship between teacher behavior, parent-child interaction, and preschool children's creativity*. Northeast Normal University.

Fei, X. (2001). China's modernization: Rethinking urban community construction. *Jiangsu Social Sciences*, 1.

Fei, X. (2019). *Fertility system* (p. 78). CITIC Publishing Group, CITIC Publishing House.

German Ideology. (2009). *Collected works of Marx and Engels* (Vol. 1, p. 532). People's Publishing House.

Guan, Y. (1994). Family education methods and child socialization. *Tianjin Social Sciences*, 4.

Hao, J., & Wang, X. (2005). On the cultural status of rural private schools in China in the early 20th century. *Journal of Zhejiang University (Humanities and Social Sciences Edition)*, 1.

Hu, J. (2011). *A study on incorporating family education guidance into the government's public service system*. Shanghai Jiao Tong University.

Jing, J. (2006). Cognitive development of children and adolescents. *Chinese Journal of School Health*, 2.

Lin, J. (2019). The logical development of the concept of children's right to family life from the perspective of international human rights conventions. *Human Rights*, 6.

Montessori, M. (translated by Jinghao Guo and Yan Zheng). (2012). *The child in the family*. China Development Press.

Nelsen, J. (translated by Bing Yu). (2016). *Positive discipline*. Beijing United Publishing Company, 5.

Park, E., Burgess, E. N., & McKenzie, R. D. (translated by Junling Song and Yefu Zheng). (2012). *Urban sociology — Chicago school urban studies*. Commercial Press, 104.

Qiu, G., & Niu, Z. (2022). On the role orientation of judicial organs in family education. *Issues on Juvenile Crimes*, 6.

Tao, X. (1930). *Life is education* (p. 9). Published in Village Teachers.

Tennis, F. (translated by Zhang Weichao). (2019). *Community and civil society*. The Commercial Press, 71.

Wang, D. (2010). *Discovering mother* (p. 109). Jiangxi People's Publishing House.

Wu, C., Zhang, J., & Wang, M. (2014). The power of parent involvement — Family capital, home-school cooperation, and child development. *Educational Research Monthly*, 3.

Xi, J. (2017). *Pay attention to family, family education, and family style* (Vol. 2, p. 353). The Governance of China, Foreign Languages Press.

Xi, J. (2019). *On adhering to the party's leadership over all work* (p. 280). Central Literature Press.

Xi, J. (2018). *Actively cultivating and practicing core socialist values since childhood* (Vol. 1, p. 183). The Governance of China, Foreign Languages Press.

Xi, J. (2020a). *On adhering to the comprehensive rule of law* (p. 168). Central Academic Press.

Xi, J. (2020b). On the party's propaganda and ideological work. *Central Academic Press*, 282.

Zhai, B. (2016). Establishing family education values in the new era. *Educational Research*, 3.

Zhang, Y., & Chen, X. (2021). The realistic dilemmas and solutions for minors to realize the right to participate in family affairs. *Journal of Liaoning Administrators College of Police and Justice*, 5.

Zhang, Z., & Liu, L. (2021). *Establishing the professional role of parents in family education — The significant meaning of the family education promotion law legislation* (p. 22). People's Education.

Zhu, Y. (2021). *A — Interpretation <Law of the People's Republic of China on Family Education Promotion>* (p. 22). Published in People's Education.

Chapter 8
The Compulsory Education Law in China: Ensuring the Child's Right to Education and Development

8.1 Introduction

Convention on the Rights of the Child stipulates that States parties should fully protect the child's Development Rights. The Development Right is a comprehensive right that covers the right to education, the right to entertainment, the right to participate in cultural and social life, the freedom of thought and religion, and the right to development of personality, which is beneficial to the child. The right to education is the core power of the Development Right. As a state party of Coall-round development invention on the Rights of the Child (Li, 2022), China is always devoted to promote the development of right to education of the child comprehensively. And China has actively formulated a series of laws and regulations to ensure the overall improvement of the child's quality. President Xi Jinping has also emphasized that: "When education flourishes, the country flourishes; when education is strong, the country is strong. The world's strongest countries are all strong in education, and education has always been a key factor in the rise of strong nations" (Xi, 2023).

Article 46 of Constitution of the People's Republic of China stipulates that: "Citizens of the People's Republic of China have the duty and right to receive education. The State promotes the all-round development of the child and young people, morally, intellectually and physically". Receiving Education is not only a basic right enjoyed by Chinese child, but also a basic obligation they must fulfill. In China's legal system for the protection of child's rights, the Compulsory Education Law of the People's Republic of China plays a crucial role in ensuring child's right to education. By means of legislation, the educational concepts and goals of education in the Compulsory Education Law of the People's Republic of China are highly consistent with the Convention on the Rights of the Child. The provisions of the Convention on the Rights of the Child that guarantee the right of the child to education, such as the principle of the best interests of the child and the recognition of the

© The Author(s), under exclusive license to Springer Nature Singapore Pte Ltd. 2026

H. Li, P. Liang, *The Legal System for the Protection of Children's Rights in China*, Resilient and Friendly Living Environments,
https://doi.org/10.1007/978-981-95-9925-7_8

right of the child to education and the progressive realization of that right on the basis of equal opportunity, are all reflected in the Compulsory Education Law of the People's Republic of China.

The Compulsory Education Law of the People's Republic of China is a legal norm integrating public welfare, unity and obligation. Public welfare means that compulsory education is not for profit, but a cause with public interests, which benefits citizens' well-being, and all the school-age child can receive free education (Liu & Lei, 2023). Unity requires that all compulsory education schools in China must follow the same standard, and the setting of teaching materials, teaching standards and teaching courses should be reasonable. It is to ensure that all the child receive equal compulsory education. Compulsory, means that all the school-age child must receive compulsory education, which is a basic obligation that citizens need to fulfill. The state, society, schools and families have the responsibility to ensure the implementation of the education system.

The three basic features of the Compulsory Education Law of the People's Republic of China, namely, "public welfare, uniformity, and obligatory nature", have been present throughout the Law, laying the foundation for China's education of its children. In addition, the Education Law of the People's Republic of China also stipulates some other basic principles such as the principle of public education, the principle of democracy, the principle of combining the unity and diversity of education, and the principle of adapting education to lifelong learning. The principle of public education means that education is a public undertaking of the whole country, nation and society, ensuring that every citizen has the opportunity and right to receive education. The principle of democratic emphasizes that every citizen can get equal opportunity to education and eliminate all forms of discrimination and unfair treatment. For vulnerable groups, special support should be provided according to the actual situation. The "principle of unity and diversity in education" refers to the harmonization of educational standards and teaching methods throughout the country. Unity of education refers to the unified educational standards. Diversity of education means adopt flexible and diverse teaching methods and contents according to the needs of the different child from different regions and cultural backgrounds. The principle of adapting education to lifelong learning means that education should meet the needs of citizens at different levels in different periods, and education at different levels should be interrelated to form a complete and flexible education system. The Compulsory Education Law of the People's Republic of China starts from the all-round development of the child and the protection of their right to education. It adheres to the basic principles of education, and is committed to ensuring the equality and quality of education for children in an all-round way.

The Compulsory Education Law of People's Republic of China consists of 8 chapters and 63 clauses, including General Provisions, Students, Schools, Teachers, Education and Teaching, Funding Guarantee, Legal Responsibility and Supplementary Provisions. In the subject of rights, the Compulsory Education Law of People's Republic of China not only pays attention to the ordinary school-age child to receive compulsory education, but also pays special attention to the special child, including disabled child, criminal child and minority child in remote areas. In the subject of duty, it also stipulates the responsibilities and obligations of schools, teachers, legal guardians of child, educational administrative departments, and the education content. This chapter will interpret the above related contents one by one according to the codification logic of the Compulsory Education Law of People's Republic of China.

8.2 Specific Stipulations of Compulsory Education Law for the Child Receiving Compulsory Education

Among China's education systems, the Compulsory Education Law of the People's Republic of China is one of the most closely related to the child's right to education, and can be regarded as a compass for the child's education. The Compulsory Education Law of the People's Republic of China is logically rigorous, unfolding from the perspectives of the holders of rights and the subject of duties (Ren, 2022), and making different provisions for the child receiving compulsory education. The General Principles, the first chapter of the Compulsory Education Law of the People's Republic of China, makes general provisions from a macroscopic point of view, including China's compulsory education system, eligible subjects of compulsory education, safeguard measures for compulsory education, its supervision and accountability rules. In the subsequent chapters 2–7 of the Compulsory Education Law of the People's Republic of China makes Specific regulations from micro level, which are distinct from the General Principles. These chapters explain in detail the compulsory education system implemented in China, including the rights subjects of compulsory education, the guarantee measures for the normal implementation of compulsory education and the accountability system for the violation of the provisions of compulsory educations. It provides a comprehensive legal guarantee for the child's compulsory education. According to the compilation sequence of the Compulsory Education Law of the People's Republic of China, this chapter introduces the specific contents of the Compulsory Education Law of the People's Republic of China on the protection of the child's rights and interests in education from the general provisions to the specific provisions.

8.2.1 General Provisions (General Principles)

The first chapter of *the Compulsory Education Law of People's Republic of China* takes the overall situation, generally summarizes the legislative purpose, scope of application and other basic principles of this law. Article 1 of *the Compulsory Education Law of People's Republic of China* directly clarifies the legislative purpose of this law, which ensures that school-age child enjoy the right to receive compulsory education, ensures the smooth implementation of compulsory education, and improves the overall quality of the whole nation. Moreover, Article 3 of *the Compulsory Education Law of People's Republic of China* stipulates that compulsory education must implement the state policy on education, improve the quality of education, and provide quality-oriented education. Education not only educates the mind, but also carries out moral education. In this way the school-age child can fully and comprehensively develop their morality, intelligence and physique. This idea is consistent with Articles 28 and 29 of the Convention on the Rights of the Child, which all believe that the child has the right to education and need to be fully developed in their personality, mind and morality. Next, this chapter will make a detailed interpretation of the compulsory education system, the qualified subject of compulsory education, the guarantee measures of compulsory education, the supervision system of compulsory education and the accountability system of compulsory education stipulated in the general principle of the Compulsory Education Law of People's Republic of China.

8.2.1.1 Compulsory Education System

From the legal point of view, the word "obligation" has the meaning of "mandatory." It is something that someone can do and must do for legal reasons. Compulsory education, that is, the education that the child must accept, and their guardians, school teachers and the government should bear corresponding responsibilities to ensure its successful completion (Ren, 2021). The compulsory education system implemented in China is a 9-year compulsory education system, that is, all the school-age child must receive 6-year education in primary school and 3-year education in junior secondary school, totaling 9 years of education. In the final year, the child must obtain a certificate of compulsory education, in this way the child is considered to have completed compulsory education. As mentioned earlier, compulsory education is a public welfare undertaking given by the state to all school-age child. Therefore, tuition and miscellaneous fees are free of charge, it's a free education for all the child. And China also established the corresponding expenditure security system of compulsory education, which effectively alleviates the problem that some family may not afford the spending of the school. This is undoubtedly an important national welfare for families with financial difficulties. In terms of compulsory education system, China not only fully complies with the provisions of the Convention on the Rights of the Child, but also sets up an extra 3-year compulsory education stage, giving more educational support to the child and forming an education system with China characteristics. Article 2 of *the Compulsory Education Law of People's Republic of China* specifically stipulates the compulsory education system implemented in China.

Article 2
The State implements a system of nine-year compulsory education.

Compulsory education means education which is uniformly provided by the State and which all the school-age child and adolescents must receive, and constitutes a public welfare undertaking which must be guaranteed by the State.

No tuition or miscellaneous fees shall be charged for the provision of compulsory education.

The State establishes a mechanism for guaranteeing funds for compulsory education, to ensure implementation of the system of compulsory education.

8.2.1.2 Eligible Subject of the Compulsory Education

Chinese law protects every Chinese citizen equally, and Chinese law also protects every child's right to education. Thus, one of the conditions for being an eligible subject for compulsory education is that one must have Chinese nationality in China, together with the provision that the 9-year compulsory education system, leads to another condition, namely, an age limit. The specific article that defines the eligible subjects for compulsory education is article 4 of *the Compulsory Education Law of the People's Republic of China.*

Article 4
All the school-age child and adolescents of the nationality of the People's Republic of China shall, in accordance with law, enjoy the equal right, and fulfil the obligation, to receive compulsory education, regardless of sex, ethnic status or race, family financial conditions, religious belief, etc.

According to the relevant provisions of *the Nationality Law of the People's Republic of China*, there are four main cases of Chinese nationality. For example, if both or one of the parents is a Chinese citizen and the child was born in China, he or she acquires Chinese nationality. The remaining three cases will not be detailed here, but can refer to *the Nationality Law of the People's Republic of China* for details. In other words, compulsory education is an obligation that China owes to its own child, and China has no obligation to provide compulsory education to foreign nationals. School-age means the age at which one is fit to receive compulsory education. The minimum age for the school-age child to receive compulsory education is generally 6 years old, and in areas where conditions are not met, it is 7 years old. What's more, some families under special circumstances, it can be appropriately postponed. The explanation of "conditions are not met" will be explained later. *Compulsory Education Law of the People's Republic of China* does not specify an upper age limit for the school-age child. In practice, the upper age limit for compulsory primary education is generally 15 years old.

Article 4 also stipulates that the school-age child with Chinese nationality enjoy this right and fulfil this obligation on an equal footing, irrespective of gender, ethnicity or race. That is to say, both male and female, regardless of their ethnicity, race or religious beliefs, and regardless of their family's property, are equally entitled to the right to education, and have the equal opportunity to receive compulsory education. All the child has to fulfill their obligation to receive it, with no preferential treatment being given to anyone. This is consistent with the principle of equality enshrined in the Constitution of the People's Republic of China. The principle of equality is an important basic principle enshrined in the Chinese Constitution. The implementation of the principle of equality in the compulsory education also shows that there shall be no discrimination against different child in compulsory education. At the same time, it is also a concrete manifestation of the public and democratic principles of *the Compulsory Education Law of the People's Republic of China*.

8.2.1.3 Institutional Guarantee of Compulsory Education

The General Provisions of the Compulsory Education Law of the People's Republic of China stipulate the purpose of the law, the compulsory education system, and specific provisions for children eligible for compulsory education, in addition to safeguards, supervision, and a system of accountability to ensure the implementation of children's right to education. Firstly, the safeguard system. In terms of safeguard system, the compulsory education law stipulates different duty of each different subjects, the government, relevant departments and social institutions, which owe the duty to guarantee the child receiving compulsory education from a macro-regulation. For the government, to fulfill its duties to guarantee the actual implementation of the child's right to education. It emphasizes the balanced development of compulsory education in different area, the rationally allocation of educational resources, especially to improve the teaching conditions in the weak areas. It's for the guarantee of the right to education for child in ethnic areas, rural areas, disabled child and other child in difficult circumstances. For parents or guardians, it is necessary to ensure that the child attend school on time, complete compulsory education successfully, and do not drop out of school. For schools, it is necessary to ensure that their teaching quality meets the regulations and complete the teaching tasks. Secondly, the supervision system. Education supervision bodies of the People's Government have the right to supervise the implementation of compulsory education, and to make supervisory reports available to the public, so that compulsory education activities are open and transparent. Thirdly, accountability system. Any social organization or individual may report to a state organ for violation of the Compulsory Education Law of the People's Republic of China. The general provisions on legal protection of compulsory education are reflected in articles 5, 6, 8 and 9 of *the Compulsory Education Law of the People's Republic of China* (Liu, 2004).

Article 5
People's governments at various levels and their departments concerned shall perform the duties provided for in this Law, to ensure the right of school-age child and adolescents to compulsory education.

Parents of school-age children and adolescents or other statutory guardians shall, in accordance with law, guarantee that they start school at the specified age and receive and complete compulsory education.

Schools providing compulsory education according to law shall accomplish the tasks of instruction and teaching in compliance with the prescribed standards and guarantee the quality of instruction and teaching.

Public organizations and individuals shall create a good environment for school-age children and adolescents to receive compulsory education.

Article 6
The State Council and the local people's governments at or above the county level shall rationally allocate educational resources, promote balanced development of compulsory education, help the schools started on weak foundations to improve the conditions for school running, and adopt measures to ensure that compulsory education is provided in rural areas and in areas inhabited by ethnic groups and that the school-age child and adolescents who are from families with financial difficulties or who are disabled receive compulsory education.

The State arranges for and encourages the economically developed areas to support the underdeveloped areas in providing compulsory education.

Article 7
In compulsory education, the system shall be practiced under which the State Council shall provide guidance, the people's governments of provinces, autonomous regions, and municipalities directly under the Central Government shall make overall plans for its provision and the people's governments at the county level shall play the main role in administration.

The administrative departments for education of the people's governments at or above the county level shall be responsible specifically for the provision compulsory education, and the other administrative departments concerned of the said people's governments shall be responsible for the provision of such education within the scope of their respective duties.

Article 8
The authorities of the people's governments for educational supervision shall oversee the observation of laws and regulations in compulsory education, the quality of instruction and teaching, and the balanced development of compulsory education, and announce their supervision reports.

Article 9
All public organizations and individuals shall have the right to inform the State organs concerned of violations of this Law or lodge complaints against such violations with the said organs.

8.2.2 Specific Provisions: Subject of Rights and Subject of Responsibility

The Compulsory Education Law of the People's Republic of China specifically stipulates the responsibilities of the child receiving compulsory education and the subjects closely related to the child from a specific micro-perspective. This is mainly reflected in the subject of rights, i.e. the rights and obligations of the children themselves who are subject to compulsory education, as well as the subject of responsibilities, i.e. the qualifications and behavioral norms of schools and teachers in the stage of compulsory education, as well as the duties of the government and guardians to ensure that children are subject to compulsory education.

8.2.2.1 Subject of Rights

The Compulsory Education Law of the People's Republic of China has made clear and specific provisions on the subjects of compulsory education, which are students, including the age of enrollment, and enrollment policies. The age for the child to receive compulsory education is stipulated in Article 11 of *the Compulsory Education Law of the People's Republic of China* (Huang et al., 2024).

Article 11
When the child has reached the age of six, their parents or other statutory guardians shall send them to school to receive and complete compulsory education. For the child in areas where conditions do not exist for the child to do so, the beginning of their schooling may be postponed to the age of seven.

If, on account of physical conditions, the school-age child or adolescents need to postpone schooling or be suspended from school, their parents or other statutory guardians shall submit an application to such an effect for approval to the local people's governments of the towns or townships or to the administrative departments for education of the people's governments at the county level.

In other words, the child over the age of six should receive compulsory education, whose parents or legal guardians have the obligation to send the child to school to receive compulsory education, and to complete compulsory education. The right to education of the child should not be restricted or deprived because of any subjective factors from the child or their parents. If parents violate this regulation and fail to let the child receive compulsory education, they will bear certain legal responsibilities. However, in terms of objective factors, "the child in areas where conditions are not available" or due to illness and other reasons, enrollment can be delayed. According to the interpretation of this regulation by the Ministry of Education of People's Republic of China, "the child in areas where conditions are not available" means that some families living in China's frontier, poverty-stricken areas and agricultural and pastoral areas face many challenges in the child's education due to the diversity of geographical environment and unbalanced economic development in China. Limited by these unfavorable factors, it is difficult for them to ensure that the child can smoothly enter school for compulsory education when they are 6 years old. To provide more educational opportunities for the child in these areas so that they can have a better future, the school entry age can be relaxed to 7 years old. As for which areas belong to "areas without conditions", the local people's government will determine them according to the actual situation. This is a regulation that meets the actual needs according to the national conditions and local conditions of China.

Where a school-age child needs to postpone enrollment or suspend schooling due to physical conditions, his or her parents or legal guardians shall apply to the local people's government or the administrative department of education at the county level, and the child may postpone enrollment after approval. After approving the postponement of enrollment, the educational department shall not refuse the child entry to school due to child's school status or other issues.

This relaxed rule, adapted to local conditions, is China's unique response to Article 28 of the Convention on the Rights of the Child, which states that "States Parties shall take all appropriate measures to ensure that school discipline is administered in a manner consistent with the child's human dignity and in conformity with the present Convention." And it is the spiritual embodiment of child's equal right to education. It is also the implementation of the democratic principle of education.

The compulsory education enrollment policy for child is stipulated in Article 12 of the Compulsory Education Law of People's Republic of China (Holland, 2008).

Article 12
School-age child and adolescents shall be exempted from the entrance examinations. The local people's governments at various levels shall ensure that school-age child and adolescents enroll in school near the places where their residence is registered.

For school-age child and adolescents whose parents or other statutory guardians work or reside in places other than the places of their registered residence and who have to receive compulsory education in the places where their parents or other statutory guardians work or reside, the local people's governments shall provide equal conditions for them to receive compulsory education. The specific measures in this regard shall be formulated by provinces, autonomous regions, and municipalities directly under the Central Government.

The administrative department for education of the people's government at the county level shall ensure that the children of servicemen within its administrative area receive compulsory education.

Being exempted from the entrance examinations refers to entrance by other means without examination. In China, the child who receive compulsory education can enjoy exemption from entrance exam, which is a concrete manifestation of equal opportunity. It is also the practice of Article 28 in the Convention on the Rights of the Child. The admission policy is principle of enrollment in a nearby school. The principle of enrollment in a nearby school refers to the child should be assigned to the nearest school to their home as far as possible, so as to reduce the economic burden and take comprehensive consideration of the child's physical and mental health. Article 9 of the first Compulsory Education Law of the People's Republic of China promulgated in 1986 stipulates: "Local people's governments at various levels shall establish primary schools and junior middle schools at such locations that the child and adolescents can attend schools near their homes." Article 12 of the Compulsory Education Law of the People's Republic of China, revised in 2006, also clarifies again the "principle of enrollment in a nearby school". These regulations make it clear that the school-age child have the right to attend school nearby, and make it clear that local governments at all levels have the obligation and responsibility to ensure that child attend school near their domicile. Even for the school-age child whose legal guardians work or live in places other than their domicile, if they need to receive compulsory education at their legal guardians' work or place of residence, the local people's government is also responsible for providing them with equal access to compulsory education. In addition, the soldiers' child, who have devoted a lot of time and energy to protecting the country, and the state should care for the child of soldiers.

8.2.2.2 The Responsibility of the School and the Teacher

School is the main place for the child to live besides their home, and it can be said that it is a second home for child. Then teachers are the parents in this second home, and they are very close to the child. *The Compulsory Education Law of People's Republic of China* has made specific provisions on schools, teachers' obligations and quality education. Obligations to schools include the establishment and construction of schools, campus safety, educational equity, boarding system, and the protection of the educational rights of ethnic minorities and special child. The requirements for teachers include teacher behavior, encouraging volunteer teaching, and society's obligation to protect the child's right to education.

For the establishment and construction of schools, Articles 15 and 16 of *the Compulsory Education Law of People's Republic of China* stipulate as follows (Xu, 2025).

Article 15
The local people's government at or above the county level shall, on the basis of such factors as the number of the school-age child and adolescents and the places of their residence within its administrative area and according to relevant State regulations, formulate and adjust the plans for the establishment of schools. Where schools need to be established in new residential communities, schools shall be established simultaneously with the development of the residential communities.

Article 16
Establishment of schools shall be in compliance with the standards for running schools prescribed by the State and meet the need of instruction and teaching, and shall meet the requirements for location and the standard for construction, as are prescribed by the State, in order to ensure safety of the students and the teaching and administrative staff.

As mentioned above, the principle of enrolment of child in compulsory education is the principle of enrollment in a nearby school. For this purpose, the government shall formulate plans for the construction of schools in accordance with such factors as the number of the school-age children and the degree of distribution and density within its administrative area, and the construction of schools shall conform to the standards for running schools prescribed by the State. The Government should also strengthen the allocation of teaching resources, distribution of teaching resources rationally, and increase its support for rural, impoverished and ethnic areas, so as to ensure the development of compulsory education in these areas.

In addition, campus safety is a key concern. Provisions relating to school safety are specified in articles 23 and 24 of the Compulsory Education Law of the People's Republic of China.

Article 23
People's governments at or above the county level and their departments concerned shall, in accordance with law, maintain order in the areas surrounding the schools, protect the legitimate rights and interests of the students, teachers, and schools, and ensure the security of the schools.

Article 24
Schools shall set up a sound security system and a mechanism in response to emergencies, conduct education among students on the importance of security, tighten administration, eliminate hidden hazards in time, and prevent accidents.

People's governments at or above the county level shall regularly inspect school buildings with respect to their safety and have them maintained or renovated in time, where necessary.

Schools shall not employ persons who have been deprived of their political rights for intentional crimes or persons who are not suited to compulsory education.

Campus safety has always been a key focus of attention in the Chinese legal system. For example, *the Civil Code of the People's Republic of China* provides for the allocation of tort liability in relation to campus safety, and similarly. Campus safety is also highlighted in the Compulsory Education Law of the People's Republic of China. In the revised Compulsory Education Law of the People's Republic of China in 2006, campus safety was included to ensure the safety and health of students and the safety of campuses and surroundings. This change reflects the importance that China attaches to the safety of the child in schools, as well as to the educational environment. The school must establish and improve the safety management system, strengthen safety precautions, and ensure the safety of facilities and equipment and the environment on the campus. At the same time, schools need to strengthen safety education for the child and enhance their safety awareness and self-protection abilities. In addition, schools are required to work closely with local governments and relevant departments to jointly maintain a safe environment around the campus. Schools are not allowed to employ people as staff who are not conducive to the child's growth, life and learning, such as criminals related to the child's crimes, or those who have been deprived of political rights according to law for intentional crimes. Because most of those who have been deprived of political rights for intentional crimes are criminals who have seriously endangered the social order. If let these kinds of criminals engage in the work of the child education is undoubtedly to bring great campus security threat, increasing the psychological burden on the child and placing them in a dangerous environment. The inclusion of campus safety in the Compulsory Education Law of the People's Republic of China provides a more comprehensive safeguard for the safety and health of the child. Only in a safe, healthy and harmonious educational environment can child learn and develop better.

In addition to the inclusion of the issue of school safety in the legal norms, which is a major highlight, another noteworthy highlight is the rectification of the education culture, the prohibition of the establishment of key schools, and the safeguarding of fairness in education. In the public's mindset, key schools often represent higher quality of education, and their teachers and teaching facilities are better than those of non-key schools, but this has also led to an uneven distribution of educational resources. To address this problem, the Compulsory Education Law of the People's Republic of China explicitly prohibits the establishment of priority schools. Government departments at all levels should take measures to establish a preferential mechanism for weak schools in terms of financial input and teachers, so as to improve the teaching level and quality of relatively weak schools. Through balanced investment in schools, every school can have good teachers and facilities, and narrow the gap between schools. This regulation improves the overall level of education, and also helps to narrow the education gap between regions and realize the balanced development of education.

For details on the prohibition of key schools, this can be seen in Article 22 of *the Compulsory Education Law of the People's Republic of China.*

Article 22
People's governments at or above the county level and the administrative departments for education shall promote balanced development among schools by narrowing the differences in the conditions for school running, and they shall not divide the schools into key and non-key schools. And the schools shall not divide the classes into key and non-key classes.

People's governments at or above the county level and their administrative departments for education shall not change the nature of government-run schools in any name or in disguised form.

The Compulsory Education law of the People's Republic of China also regulates the boarding school system, the establishment of schools (classes) for ethnic minorities, the education of the handicapped child, and the compulsory education of delinquent child. It is a comprehensive law that takes into account every child with special circumstances. Details of these systems are set out in articles 17–21 of *the Compulsory Education Law of the People's Republic of China*, and each of these systems will be explained in the following paragraphs.

Article 17
People's governments at or above the county level may, in light of need, establish boarding schools to ensure that the school-age children and adolescents who live far from school receive compulsory education.

Ethnic education is an extremely important action in China. Educational resources are often limited in areas where economic development is more backward, and the ethnic minority child may face language, cultural and other barriers in education. The establishment of special schools (classes) in economically developed areas is conducive to solving these problems and allowing ethnic minority child to enjoy the same educational opportunities. At the same time, safeguards for the education of the minority child are also addressed in *the Education Law of the People's Republic of China*, which provides, for example, that the child in minority areas may be taught in bilingualism. Putonghua is the language commonly used in China for the implementation of educational activities. However, in order to respect the language and cultural rights of ethnic minority child and better meet their language learning needs, according to the actual situation and practical needs, *the Education Law of the People's Republic of China* also protects their right to use their own ethnic languages. Schools and educational institutions in ethnic minority areas can actively introduce and develop bilingual education resources, such as compiling bilingual teaching materials, to provide a better teaching environment for the child in ethnic minority areas. This is also in line with *the Convention on the Rights of the Child* with regard to the concept of guaranteeing ethnic child the enjoyment of their own culture and the use of their own national languages. Specific provisions on ethnic education are set out below.

Article 18
The administrative department for education under the State Council and the people's governments of provinces, autonomous regions, and municipalities directly under the Central Government shall, in light of need, establish schools (classes) in economically developed areas to enroll school-age children and adolescents of ethnic groups.

Disabled child belongs to the vulnerable groups of society and are also one of the key subjects of rights. Chinese law therefore pays extra attention to this group. Both the Education Law of the People's Republic of China and the Compulsory Education Law of the People's Republic of China provide legislative guarantees of the right to education for the special child. Disabled child faces many challenges, and physical handicaps and psychological trauma can make it difficult for them to adapt to society. Therefore, the people's government establishes special education schools and employs special education teachers to carry out compulsory education activities for the child with disabilities to prevent them from being discriminated against because of their physical particularities. The rights and interests of the child with special disabilities studying in ordinary schools are also protected, and schools should provide convenient conditions for the study and rehabilitation of the disabled child. For the guarantee of compulsory education for the disabled child, please refer to Article 19 of *the Compulsory Education Law of the People's Republic of China.*

Article 19
People's governments at or above the county level shall, in light of need, establish schools (classes) to provide special education that is appropriate for school-age children and adolescents who are blind, deaf-mute, or mentally retarded to receive compulsory education. Such schools (classes) shall have places and facilities tailored to the special characteristics of the said children and adolescents for the benefit of their study, rehabilitation and daily life.

Regular schools shall admit to the classes corresponding to the levels of the disabled school-age child and adolescents who are capable of receiving regular education and provide them with aid in study and rehabilitation.

What's more, the right to education of delinquent child is still protected. Even if they make a mistake, also having the right to receive education. And it is very important for this kind of child's education. Regarding the protection of the right to education for the criminal child who commit crimes, the details can be seen in Articles 20 and 21 of *the Compulsory Education Law of the People's Republic of China.*

Article 20
The local people's governments at or above the county level shall, in light of need, establish special schools to provide compulsory education to the school-age adolescents who are prone to such serious juvenile misbehaviors as are specified in the law on prevention of juvenile delinquency.

Article 21
The juvenile delinquents and the minors against whom compulsory educational measures are taken, who have not completed compulsory education, shall be provided with such education, and the funds needed in this respect shall be guaranteed by the people's governments.

With regard to child who have broken the law and committed crimes, China has adopted measures that focus on education and supplement punishment, in order to guide them to turn over a new leaf.

Government departments have set up approved school for the delinquent child to implement compulsory education, and are obliged to guarantee funding. "Approved schools" are schools set up specifically for the child with serious delinquent behavior, guaranteeing the part of child's right to education. According to research data from the Ninth Prosecutor's Office of the Supreme Prosecutor's Office, as of May 2022, there were more than 110 approved schools across the country, with 11 approved schools currently under construction or at the site selection stage. The scope of enrolment in approved schools varies from place to place, but the age of enrolment is generally for minors who have reached the age of 12 but are not yet 18 years old. The Chinese Government has made active efforts to safeguard the right to education of the child who have committed crimes, and has provided the child with better educational opportunities through a variety of means, including strengthening supervision, increasing investment and improving quality. The implementation of these measures will not only help to raise the educational level and quality of life of child in conflict with the law, but also, in the long run, promote the harmonious and stable development of society.

Teachers, as guides on the path of the child's development, are strictly regulated by the Compulsory Education Law of the People's Republic of China. Teachers are not only required to obtain a teaching qualification but also to consciously abide by the code of professional ethics and establish a correct concept of education. In teaching activities, teachers must teach according to their aptitude, following the educational laws or regularities and the child's physical and mental development. In school life outside of learning, teachers must care for the child, pay attention to their individual differences, and promote the all-round development of child. They cannot take over the child's art, music and physical education classes. They must not discriminate against child, and they must not impose corporal punishment on child in disguise. Teachers' behavior can be found in article 29 of *the Compulsory Education Law of the People's Republic of China*.

Article 29
Teachers shall treat students equally in instruction and teaching, pay attention to the individual differences of students, teach students in accordance with their aptitude, and promote their full development.

Teachers shall respect the personality of students, and they shall not discriminate against students, punish them physically or in disguised form, or humiliate them, or strip them of their dignity, nor shall they infringe on the students' legitimate rights and interests.

In addition to providing specific protection for the child in physical and mental health, the Compulsory Education Law of the People's Republic of China also encourages teachers to go to remote, underdeveloped, and ethnic areas such as the countryside to take volunteer teaching, so that the child in these areas can also receive quality education. In this way, the child there can enjoy better educational resources, promote their growth and development, and promote fairness in education. No child in remote rural areas will lose out on education, prevents child in remote rural areas from being left behind at the starting line of education, and it also implements the principle of fairness in the Constitution of the People's Republic of China. Article 33 of *the Compulsory Education Law of the People's Republic of China* provides specific guidance on encouraging teachers to support education.

Article 33
The State Council and the local people's governments at various levels shall encourage and support teachers in urban schools and graduates of schools of higher education to go to rural areas and areas inhabited by ethnic groups to engage in compulsory education.

The State encourages graduates of schools of higher education to teach as volunteers in schools in rural areas and in areas inhabited by ethnic groups where teachers are lacking. The administrative departments for education of the people's governments at the county level shall vouch for their qualifications as teachers according to law, and the length of time of their teaching shall be counted in their length of service.

There are also detailed provisions on what kind of compulsory education child should receive, that is, what kind of compulsory education is child need and what is conducive to their healthy physical and mental growth.

Compulsory education adopts quality education, which is consistent with one of the purposes of education recognized in the Convention on the Rights of the Child: "The education of the child shall be directed to the development of the child's personality, talents and mental and physical abilities to their fullest potential". It is also consistent with the right of the child to rest, cultural and artistic development as recognized in article 31 of *the Convention on the Rights of the Child.*

The concept of quality education in the People's Republic of China Compulsory Education Law emphasizes all-round development. In the concept of quality education, compulsory education activities are not only the imparting of knowledge, but also shouldering the heavy responsibility of cultivating the child's moral character, improving their comprehensive quality and promoting personality development. While cultivating cultural knowledge, quality education pays more attention to cultivating the child's moral quality and physical quality, paying more attention to the child's ability to receive different forms of education, and focusing on the child's all-round development in morality, intelligence, physique, beauty and labor. To achieve these goals, the school curriculum covers many fields, including cultural courses, physical education, art, practice and other courses, aiming at cultivating the child's all-round development. The education of the child is no longer satisfied with the teacher's mechanical instillation of knowledge in the classroom, but begins to advocate the child's active inquiry, mobilize the child's enthusiasm, and guide the child to participate in extracurricular practice and study trips. In this way, teaching is put into practice, and the goal of compulsory education is truly realized, so that the child can truly absorb knowledge, explore their potential, cultivate their moral quality, establish a correct outlook on life and values, and lay a solid foundation for their all-round and future life development. This also follows the idea of encouraging the child to actively participate in cultural and artistic activities in the Convention on the Rights of the Child. For detailed provisions on quality education, please refer to Articles 34–37 of *the Compulsory Education Law of the People's Republic of China.*

Article 34
Instruction and teaching shall be carried out in conformity with the pattern of education and the characteristics of students' physical and mental development, be oriented to the needs of all students, and be designed to impart knowledge to them by organically integrating moral, intellectual, physical and aesthetic education in instruction and teaching, with special attention paid to developing their ability of independent thinking, creativity, and practice, in order to enable them to develop in an all-round way.

Article 35
The administrative department for education under the State Council shall, on the basis of the physical and mental development of school-age children and adolescents and the actual conditions, determine the teaching system, the contents of instruction and teaching and curriculums, reform the examination system and improve the method of student enrollment by senior secondary schools, in order to promote qualities-oriented education.

Schools and teachers shall conduct instruction and teaching in accordance with the determined contents of instruction and teaching and curriculums and ensure that the requirements specified by the State with respect to the essential qualities are met.

The State encourages schools and teachers to adopt such methods of instruction and teaching as the elicitation method, in order to improve the quality of instruction and teaching.

Article 36
Schools shall put moral education in the first place and embody moral education in instruction and teaching, carry out social practices that are suited to the ages of the students, thus to form a system for ideological and ethical education in which the school, family, and society cooperate with each other and help students cultivate good ideology and moral character and a good habit of conduct.

Article 37
Schools shall guarantee the students time for extracurricular activities and organize extracurricular cultural and recreation activities, etc. Public cultural and sports facilities shall be made convenient for schools to carry out extracurricular activities.

8.2.3 Specific Protection Provisions: Finance and Legal Protection

The Compulsory Education Law of the People's Republic of China requires governments at all levels to guarantee the funds for the child's compulsory education, and it makes detailed provisions to prevent the child from being unable to go to school because of the trouble of expenses. At the same time, the legal responsibilities of the government, schools, teachers, and legal guardians of the child receiving compulsory education are stipulated when they fail to perform their duties and ensure that children receive compulsory education.

8.2.3.1 Finance-Guaranteeing System

Compulsory education is a national public welfare undertaking. China has fully incorporated compulsory education into the scope of financial security, exempting the expenses of the child's compulsory education stage. China not only includes the funds needed for compulsory education into the financial budgets of governments at all levels but also allocates the required expenses in full and on time according to the per capital public standards of the child. Moreover, this fund is not constant, and it is required to make timely adjustments according to the actual situation to ensure the normal operation of schools. In addition, it also provides stronger protection for the special child. *The Compulsory Education Law of the People's Republic of China* provides that for schools of special education, such as deaf, mute and blind disabled special child, the compulsory education funding standards for such child are higher than those for child in ordinary schools. This is because special needs children often require more human and material resources, allowing funds can comprehensively protect the compulsory education right of the special child, and make the disabled child accept education without worries from many aspects. The provisions of Article 43 are as follows.

Article 43
The basic standard for the average amount of funds per school student for public use shall be formulated by the administrative department for finance under the State Council together with the administrative department for education and be adjusted in time on the basis of economic and social development. When the standard for the average amount of funds per student for public use is formulated or adjusted, attention shall be paid to meeting the basic needs of instruction and teaching.

The people's governments of provinces, autonomous regions, and municipalities directly under the Central Government shall, in light of the realities within their own administrative areas, formulate the standard for the average amount of funds per school student for public use which shall not be lower than the standard formulated by the State.

The standard for the average amount of funds per student for public use of schools (classes) providing special education shall be higher than that for students of regular schools.

In terms of funding guarantee, in addition to providing comprehensive protection for special children, the Compulsory Education Law of the People's Republic of China also pays extra attention to children in rural areas, stipulating that the budget should be appropriately tilted towards the child in rural areas. Articles 44, 45, and 47 of *the Compulsory Education Law of the People's Republic of China* stipulate this system (Xu et al., 2025).

Article 44
Input of funds for compulsory education shall be provided jointly by the State Council and the local people's governments at various levels on the basis of their respective duties, and the people's governments of provinces, autonomous regions, and municipalities directly under the Central Government shall be responsible for establishing a system for overall planning for bringing such provision into effect. The funds needed for compulsory education in rural areas shall be shared by the people's governments at various levels on the basis of the items and proportions as prescribed by the State Council.

People's governments at various levels shall gratuitously provide textbooks for school-age children and adolescents whose families are in financial difficulties, and subsidize resident students in living expenses.

The specific measures for guaranteeing funds for compulsory education shall be formulated by the State Council.

Article 45
The local people's governments at various levels shall separately list the funds for compulsory education in their financial budgets.

When drawing up their budgets, people's governments at the county level shall arrange the funds for compulsory education in a balanced manner, apart from giving preferential consideration to schools in rural areas and schools started on weak foundations.

Article 47
The State Council and the local people's governments at or above the county level shall, in light of actual need, set up special funds to assist the rural areas and the areas inhabited by ethnic groups in providing compulsory education.

In addition to the state's official guarantee of the child's compulsory education funds, China also encourages social organizations and individuals to donate money to compulsory education funds, establishment of compulsory education foundations, encourage citizens to actively participate in compulsory education, and provide financial support for compulsory education. These measures have not only guaranteed the child's right to receive compulsory education but also played a positive role in improving the quality and level of compulsory education. For details on encouraging the public to support education, please see Article 48 of *the Compulsory Education Law of the People's Republic of China.*

Article 48
The State encourages public organizations and individuals to make donations to compulsory education, and encourages the establishment of foundations for compulsory education in accordance with the State regulations governing the administration of foundations.

8.2.3.2 Legal Protection System

The Compulsory Education Law of the People's Republic of China stipulates how each subject can guarantee the realization of the child's right to compulsory education. At the same time, it also stipulates the legal responsibility of these subjects for violating their obligations and guarantees the effective implementation of the child's right to compulsory education by relevant subjects through strictly legal means (Zheng & Zhan, 2024).

The most important obligation of the government is to ensure the implementation of the child's compulsory education funds. Those who fail to perform their duties of ensuring compulsory education funds, or misappropriate or occupy compulsory education funds, if the conditions are minor, will be given a chance to correct within a time limit, and if the conditions are serious, they will be directly given administrative or criminal sanctions. And if the government sets unreasonable school sites, fails to regularly check school safety, or illegally divides schools into key and non-key types, etc., it will be subject to administrative sanctions. In order to protect the child's right to compulsory education, there is no opportunity. The school's violation of duties is mainly reflected in its violation of regulations to charge students, refusal to admit the special child to enter school, unlawfully creating key and non-key classes, and illegal expulsion of the child, which makes them unable to complete compulsory education. Those who violate relevant regulations shall be given a certain time limit to make corrections, and those who are serious shall be directly punished. For details about the school's illegal responsibility, see Article 57.

Article 57
Under one of the following circumstances, a school shall be ordered to make rectifications within a time limit by the administrative department for the education of the people's government at the county level; and if the circumstances are serious, the person directly in charge and the other persons directly responsible shall be punished according to law:

(1) refusing to admit to the classes corresponding to the levels of the disabled school-age children and adolescents who are capable of receiving regular education;
(2) dividing classes into key and non-key ones;
(3) expelling students in violation of the provisions in this Law; or
(4) using textbooks that have not been examined and for which no approval has been obtained.

Guardians who fail to send the school-age child to school in time to receive compulsory education without justifiable reasons shall be criticized and educated by the local education administrative department and given a certain period of correction. See Articles 58–59 for details.

Article 58
The parents or other statutory guardians of school-age children or adolescents who, without justifiable reasons, fail to send them to schools to receive compulsory education according to the provisions of this Law shall be criticized by the local people's government of the town or township or the administrative department for the education of the people's government at the county level and be ordered by the said government or department to make rectification within a time limit.

Article 59
Under one of the following circumstances, an organization or individual shall be punished according to the provisions of relevant laws and administrative regulations:

(1) coercing or cajoling school-age children or adolescents who should receive compulsory education into forfeiting schooling or dropping out of school;
(2) illegally employing school-age children or adolescents who should receive compulsory education; or
(3) publishing textbooks which have not been examined and for which no approval has been obtained according to law.

When the responsible subject violates the law and the circumstances are serious enough to constitute a crime, he will be investigated for criminal responsibility.

Article 60
A violation of the provisions of this Law that constitutes a crime shall be investigated for criminal responsibility according to law.

8.3 Summary

Education is a powerful tool for ensuring the development rights of the child. Every child has the right to education. President Xi Jinping emphasized that "education has a basic, guiding and overall status and role in our country, so we must adhere to the priority of education development in the national strategic position."

This chapter discusses the core right of the child's right to education, and analyzes the relevant provisions of *the Compulsory Education Law of the People's Republic of China* in depth, focusing on the rights and obligations of the educated child, their guardians, teachers, and the government, with the purpose of comprehensively exploring how relevant laws and regulations provide legal guarantee for the child's right to education. The compilation of *the Compulsory Education Law of the People's Republic of China* fully embodies the right to development among the four rights of the child stipulated in *the Convention on the Rights of the Child*, which is highly consistent with the guarantee of the child's right to education and the educational goals of *the Convention on the Rights of the Child* and follows the principles and spirit of *the Convention on the Rights of the Child.*

The Compulsory Education Law of the People's Republic of China provides all-round protection for the child's right to education. Together with the Education Law of the People's Republic of China and the Law on the Promotion of Private Education of the People's Republic of China, it forms the basic legal framework for the protection of the child's education in China, providing a solid legal foundation for the all-round development of the child (Chen et al., 2022). Under the guidance of the Compulsory Education Law of the People's Republic of China, China's compulsory education system has gradually improved. From primary school to junior high school and then to high school, the compulsory education stage covers the child of all ages. In addition, special education and vocational education also have a place in the compulsory education system, providing diversified development paths for students with special needs and preferences. In future development, China will continue to improve relevant laws and regulations, further strengthen the public welfare and unity of compulsory education, improve the quality of education, and ensure that all school-age children and adolescents can enjoy high-quality educational resources. And as soon as possible the senior high school stage will also be included in the scope of compulsory education. Currently, some cities in China, such as Shenzhen and Zhuhai, have begun to pilot the "12-year compulsory education system".

In the future, China will also constantly sum up the experience of the "12-year compulsory education system" in Shenzhen, Zhuhai, and other cities, accelerate the construction of the "12-year compulsory education", and implement the "12-year compulsory education" nationwide as soon as possible, laying a solid foundation for China's talent training and economic and social development.

References

Chen, Z., Zhou, F., Yu, H., Jiuming, S., Xiaoting, D., Xi, T., Mengjie, S., Qian, S. (2022). Analysis of China's basic education policies in 2021. *People's Education, Z1*, 7–32.

Holland, B. (2008). Migrant children, compulsory education and the rule of law in China. *Buffalo Human Rights Law Review, 14*, 209.

Huang, J., Kong, H., Tian, Y., & Zheng, W. (2024). Parental education and children's educational outcomes: Evidence from the compulsory schooling law in China. *Applied Economics*, 1–16.

Li, W. (2022). *Research on minors' right to development China*. University of Political Science and Law Press.

Liu, F. (2004). Basic education in China's rural areas: A legal obligation or an individual choice. *International Journal of Educational Development, 1*, 5–21.

Liu, S., & Lei, P. (2023). Free compulsory education and social mobility: An empirical study based on CGSS data. *Education and Economy, 2*, 30–40.

Ren, H. (2021). The system structure of the general provisions of the education code. *Oriental Law, 6*, 123–140.

Ren, H. (2022). The specific provisions of the education code: Philosophy, system, and content. *Journal of East China Normal University (Educational Sciences), 5*, 63–76.

Xi, J. (2023). Solidly promoting the building of a strong education nation. *Contemporary Guangxi, 18*, 4–6.

Xu, H., Chen, S., & Min, Y. (2025). Basic education and rural common prosperity: The long-term impact of compulsory education law on rural development. *Finance and Economics Science, 1*, 136–148.

Xu, J. (2025). The normative configuration of "schools and other educational institutions" in the general provisions of the education code. *Administrative Law Review, 3*, 78–91.

Zheng, Y., & Zhan, Z. (2024). Reshaping the concept of educational legal responsibility in the context of education code compilation. *Renmin University of China Education Journal, 4*, 115–127.

Chapter 9
The Law on the Protection of Women's Rights and Interests: Equality, Special Safeguards, and the Rights of the Girl Child

9.1 Introduction

In today's world, all countries are promoting the modern concept of equality between men and women. In this global context of caring for women, the protection of women's rights and interests is a responsibility incumbent on all countries. Governments have attached greater importance to safeguarding the rights and interests of the girl, who is defined in this chapter as a woman under the age of 18. Echoing the principles of *the United Nations Convention on the Rights of the Child*, such as maximizing the interests of the child. China has made great efforts to protect women's rights and interests, especially the ones of girls Through the enactment and implementation of the Law on the Protection of Women's Rights and Interests, it has ensured that girl is given special protection and assistance, have access to services such as education and health care and can fully develop their personalities, abilities and talents, and can live in happiness, love and peace (Keith, 1997). They can grow up in a happy, loving, and peaceful environment, and can actively learn about, participate in, and realize their rights without being subjected to any form of discrimination, thus demonstrating a great nation's style (Cao, 2022).

In order to better promote equality between men and women and safeguard women's rights and interests, China first promulgated the Law on the Protection of Women's Rights and Interests in 1992, which was subsequently amended three times, in 2005, 2018 and 2022. The latest version of the Law on the Protection of Women's Rights and Interests came into force on January 1, 2023, emerging as another major revision of the Law in the 30 years since its implementation. The amendment is dedicated to resolving difficult issues in practice in the areas of marriage and childbirth, property distribution and personal rights, emphasizing the concept of equality between men and women, developing a new concept for the

© The Author(s), under exclusive license to Springer Nature Singapore Pte Ltd. 2026

H. Li, P. Liang, *The Legal System for the Protection of Children's Rights in China*, Resilient and Friendly Living Environments,
https://doi.org/10.1007/978-981-95-9925-7_9

protection of women's human rights, and creating a series of new mechanisms to strengthen the protection of women's rights and interests, contributing to the development of women's human rights in the international arena, and is also consistent with the concepts of the International Covenants on Human Rights, enriches the connotation of women's human rights and is in line with global human rights governance.

The Law on the Protection of Women's Rights and Interests plays an indispensable supplementary and emphatic role in China's legal system for the protection of the child, systematizing, concretizing and comprehensively implementing the provisions of the Constitution of the People's Republic of China, the Civil Code of the People's Republic of China and other relevant laws on the protection of women, and embodying throughout the text the State's responsibility to safeguard women's human rights, while at the same time focusing on the protection of the personal, cultural and educational rights and interests of the girl. At the same time, it also emphasizes the protection of the rights and interests of the girl in terms of personal, cultural, and educational rights and interests, demonstrating China's resolute attitude towards the implementation of the concept of equality between men and women, and elevating the protection of women and the child to the level of national will. In short, the Law not only promotes the advancement of the cause of protecting women and the girl in China, and safeguards the basic State policy of equality between men and women, but also harmonizes with international policies on the protection of women and the child.

Based on the physiological and psychological differences of women, this chapter will combine the laws and take the rights-based perspective of women and the girl, from the provisions on women's enjoyment of equality in political rights, rights and interests of the person and personality, rights and interests in culture and education, rights and interests in labor and social security, rights and interests in property, and rights and interests in marriage and the family, to the provisions on the protection measures for the girl child against infringement, the right to education, and so on, and then to the corresponding remedial measures and legal liabilities. Interpretation of the Law on the Protection of Women's Rights and Interests, as a special law of China, explores how to safeguard the rights and interests of women and girls in all aspects of legislation, puts into practice the basic national policy of equality between men and women, advocates and promotes values and norms of conduct conducive to the development of the girl, and examines how to combine it with the United Nations Convention on the Rights of the Child in terms of respect for the rights and dignity of the child, the maximization of the interests of the child, and the rights of the child to education and protection from any form of violence. How to integrate with the principles of *the Convention on the Rights of the Child*, such as respect for the rights and dignity of the child and maximizing the interests of the child, and how to reflect the child's right to education and freedom from all forms of violence.

9.2 Specialized Protection System for Girls (Under 18 Years of Age)

The Law on the Protection of Women's Rights and Interests adheres to and implements the concept of equality between men and women, takes the overall interests of the broadest range of women as its starting and ending point, comprehensively summarizes the successful experiencc of protecting women's rights and interests over the past decade or so, adapts to the needs of the new situation, and makes comprehensive additions and improvements to the equal rights enjoyed by women in all aspects of political, economic, cultural and social, as well as family, life. At the same time, the law is also very comprehensive in safeguarding the rights and interests of the girl, including personality rights and interests, cultural education and other aspects, from ex ante protection to ex post relief, and is committed to combining the four principles of *the Convention on the Rights of the Child*, namely non-discrimination, maximization of the interests of the child, the right to survival and development, and respect for the ideas of the child, including the right to development, the right to protection, so as to ensure that all the girl can receive special protection and assistance and will not be subject to any discrimination, will not be subject to any discrimination. Lastly, *the Law on the Protection of Women's Rights and Interests*, while granting women and the girl their legitimate rights and interests and guaranteeing equality between men and women, also provides adequate relief and safeguards, and seeks to minimize the harm done to women and the girl.

9.2.1 Principle of Gender Equality

As one of the founders of human civilization and one of the driving forces of social progress, women play a crucial role in a country's legal framework, and their legal status is a direct reflection of the country's degree of civilization and social progress. Under the leadership of the Communist Party of China, China has always emphasized the concept of equality between men and women, making the protection of women's rights and interests and the realization of equality between men and women the goal of the country's endeavors, and treating the cause of women as an important part of the Party's work. To this end, China has put forward the basic State policy of equality between men and women. In safeguarding women's rights and interests, China's legal position focuses not only on women, but also on the girl, who are physically and mentally more vulnerable, reflecting society's comprehensive protection of women's and the girl's rights and interests and its concern for the special needs of the child. In terms of equality of rights and interests of persons and personalities, women and men are guaranteed equal rights while women are given special protection. In terms of equality of rights and interests in culture and education, women and men are guaranteed the same right to education and shall not be discriminated against or excluded from education. In terms of equality of rights and interests in labor and social security, special protection is also given to women on the basis of their special characteristics, so as to achieve equality in the substantive sense. In terms of equality in property rights and interests, women are guaranteed community property and inheritance rights. In terms of equality of rights and interests in marriage and family, women's freedom in family life is guaranteed, and efforts are made to establish equal, harmonious and civilized marriage and family relations. The existence of these provisions not only formally safeguards women's legal rights and interests, but also substantively promotes the value of equality between men and women, and is a concrete manifestation of the pursuit of civilization and progress for society as a whole (Wang, 2015).

Under the concept of human rights protection in the Constitution of the People's Republic of China, article 2 of the Law on the Protection of Women's Rights and Interests makes equality between men and women a basic state policy at the legal level and explicitly states that women and men enjoy equal rights in political, economic, cultural, social and family matters, and at the same time enjoy special rights and interests in accordance with the law and that the state must take measures to progressively improve systems to protect the rights and interests of women. The State must take measures to gradually improve the system for safeguarding the rights and interests of women and to eliminate all forms of discrimination against women. This also echoes the "principle of equality between men and women" in Article 48 of the Constitution of the People's Republic of China, which states that women in the People's Republic of China enjoy equal rights with men in all aspects of political, economic, cultural, social and family life. For details, see Article 2 of the Law on the Protection of Women's Rights and Interests:

Article 2

It is a basic state policy to realize equality between men and women. Women shall enjoy equal rights with men in all aspects of political, economic, cultural, social and family life.

The state shall take necessary measures to promote equality between men and women, eliminate all kinds of discrimination against women, and prohibit the rejection of or restrictions on women's lawful enjoyment and exercise of various rights and interests.

The state shall protect the special rights and interests enjoyed by the women under the law.

With regard to equality of political rights, China has always adhered to the basic State policy of equality between men and women, insisting that women enjoy the same broad range of political rights as men and participate in the political life of the country in accordance with the law, and has also been actively training and selecting female cadres. Women have the right to participate in State and social affairs, to put forward their views on the management of the State and society, and to contribute their strength, and State organs at all levels respect and listen to the views of women and women's organizations on the protection of their legitimate rights and interests.

In practice, the power of women cannot be ignored, and China has taken active measures to support the growth of female talent, emphasizing that women are also capable of holding up half of the sky and that women's political wisdom and talent must not be overlooked on the basis of gender. These legal provisions help women to participate in the formulation and implementation of national policies and to influence national decision-making, thus giving women more voice and respect in political life.

Article 34 of the Constitution of the People's Republic of China provides that "All citizens of the People's Republic of China who have reached the age of 18 have the right to vote and stand for election, regardless of ethnic status, race, sex, occupation, family background, religious belief, education, property status or length of residence, except persons deprived of political rights according to law." This basic civil and political right is also reflected in the Law on the Protection of Women's Rights and Interests, which emphasizes in particular that women enjoy the right to vote and to stand for election on an equal footing with men; this is an important political right of women, and also an important way for women to manage the affairs of the State, and their political participation is of great significance to the promotion of the development of the State and the progress of society. Women's equal rights in politics are embodied in articles 12–15 of *the Law on the Protection of Women's Rights and Interests*:

Article 12
The State guarantees that women enjoy political rights on an equal footing with men.

Article 13
Women have the right to participate in the management of State affairs, economic and cultural affairs, and social affairs through various means and forms in accordance with the law.

Women and women's organizations have the right to submit to State organs at all levels opinions and proposals on the protection of women's rights and interests.

Article 14
Women enjoy the right to vote and to stand for election on an equal basis with men.

The National People's Congress and local people's congresses at all levels shall be guaranteed an appropriate number of female deputies. The State takes measures to gradually increase the proportion of female deputies in the National People's Congress and local people's congresses at all levels.

An appropriate number of women members of residents' committees and villagers' committees shall be guaranteed.

Article 15

The State actively trains and selects women cadres, and attaches importance to the training and selection of women cadres from ethnic minorities.

State organs, group organizations, enterprises and institutions shall adhere to the principle of equality between men and women in the training, selection and appointment of cadres, and shall have an appropriate number of women as leading members.

Women's federations and their group members may recommend women cadres to State organs, group organizations, and enterprises.

The State takes measures to support the growth of female talent.

Based on the basic national policy of equality between men and women, in terms of equality of rights and interests of the person and personality, *the Law on the Protection of Women's Rights and Interests* makes it clear that women's personal freedom and human dignity are inviolable, and that their rights to life, body, health, name, portrait, reputation, honor and privacy are not to be infringed upon. This is an emphasis on women's basic rights and an important safeguard, as well as a manifestation of social equality, ensuring that they enjoy the same rights and protective treatment as men under the law. Women's personal and personality rights and interests will not be neglected by the authorities and so on because of their gender, and the standards of protection for men and women are substantially the same, except that because of physiological factors women are more vulnerable to injury to their persons and personalities, and the law emphasizes the rights that women should enjoy to ensure that they can receive timely and effective assistance in the event of infringement. For women, sexual harassment is a serious violation of personal and personality rights and interests and must be cracked down on in the law.

In this regard, the Law on the Protection of Women's Rights and Interests defines the concept of sexual harassment and establishes that going against the will of the woman is the only subjective criterion for judging the situation, so as to prevent the perpetrator from evading his responsibility on the grounds that the circumstances of the harassment are too minor. The Law distinguishes between several types of sexual harassment, including verbal harassment, textual harassment, graphic harassment, physical harassment, and other sexual harassment, and stipulates relief paths for victimized women, striving to safeguard women's right to sexual autonomy, and providing a clear legal basis and a defined relief path for the whole of society to prevent and curb sexual harassment, ranging from ex-ante protection to the provision of relief after the fact, which makes women's protection more comprehensive and more likely to provide women with security. This makes the protection of women more comprehensive and enables women to have a sense of security and live a healthy and safe life, which is also a reflection of social justice and equality, and active care for women. Details can be found in articles 18–22 and 28 of *the Law on the Protection of Women's Rights and Interests*:

Article 18
The State guarantees women equal rights and interests with men in the person and personality.

Article 19
Women's personal freedom shall be inviolable. Unlawful detention or deprivation or restriction of a woman's personal freedom by other unlawful means is prohibited; unlawful searches of a woman's body are prohibited.

Article 20
Women's human dignity shall be inviolable. It is prohibited to damage a woman's human dignity by insulting or slandering her.

Article 21
A woman's right to life, body and health shall be inviolable. Abuse, abandonment, mutilation, sale, and other acts that infringe upon a woman's right to life and health are prohibited.

Article 22
Sexual harassment of women against their will, by words, writing, images, physical behavior, etc., is prohibited.

Victimized women may file complaints with the relevant units and State organs. The relevant unit or State organ that receives the complaint shall deal with it in a timely manner and inform the victim in writing of the outcome.

The victimized woman may report the matter to the public security authorities, or may bring a civil action in the people's court, requesting the perpetrator to assume civil liability in accordance with the law.

Article 28
Women's personality rights and interests, including the right to a name, portrait, reputation, honor, privacy and personal information, are protected by law.

With regard to equality of rights and interests in culture and education, China has also consistently implemented the State policy of equality between men and women, insisting that women have the same right to education as men. It asserts that there should be no gender-specific restrictions on women's advancement to higher education and participation in activities and that no one should deprive women of their right to education. By giving women space for full development on the soil of culture and education without any hindrance, women are better able to develop themselves and achieve self-fulfillment, and to promote a society that is equal, tolerant, and progressive. In addition, the law contains relevant provisions for schools and relevant departments, for example, schools cannot refuse to admit women or raise the admission standards for women on the basis of gender, and people's governments at all levels should take measures to ensure that women enjoy equal rights and opportunities to receive secondary and higher education. Articles 35, 37, and 40 of *the Law on the Protection of Women's Rights and Interests* specifically provide for this:

Article 35
The State guarantees that women enjoy cultural and educational rights equal to those of men.

Article 37
Schools and relevant departments shall implement the relevant State regulations to ensure that women enjoy equal rights with men in such areas as enrolment, advancement to higher education, awarding of degrees, sending of students to study abroad, and employment guidance and services.

In admitting students, schools may not refuse to admit women or raise the admission standards for women on the basis of their gender, except in the case of special specialties prescribed by the State.

People's governments at all levels shall take measures to ensure that women enjoy equal rights and opportunities to receive secondary and higher education.

Article 40
State organs, social organizations and enterprises and institutions shall implement the relevant State regulations to ensure that women enjoy equal rights with men to engage in scientific, technical, literary, artistic and other cultural activities.

Also following the principle of the State policy of equality between men and women, in terms of equality of rights and interests in labor and social security, women enjoy the same rights as men in terms of employment, entitlement to welfare benefits, promotion, etc., while at the same time prohibiting employers from targeting female employees due to special circumstances, such as marriage, pregnancy, maternity leave, breastfeeding and so forth, and from making unequal decisions. In response to the historical and social background, the Law on the Protection of Women's Rights and Interests fully recognizes in the legal system that there are physiological differences between women and men, and under this recognition, rather than simply applying the concept of equality between men and women mechanically to the laws and regulations, the Law pays more detailed attention to and takes care of women's needs at special times and in special situations, so as to achieve equality in the substantive sense. In the legal framework, specific and powerful protective measures are provided for women during special periods, such as pregnancy, childbirth, and breastfeeding, as well as under special circumstances, such as gender discrimination, in order to prevent and rectify gender discrimination in employment, to create a fair employment environment for women, and to provide the necessary support and assistance to women who have difficulty in finding employment.

These legal provisions not only safeguard women's rights and interests but also show respect for women in terms of their physiological differences and special needs. Through these measures, China's legal system seeks to create a social environment that is friendlier and fairer to women and to ensure that women enjoy equal rights and interests at all levels of life. The implementation of this legal concept can, in social practice, prompt people to pay attention to and understand the special needs of women. Such care will not only help women to develop better in their lives but will also help to promote the overall development of society so that each member can prosper together in an environment of equality and respect. By taking gender differences into account and formulating corresponding regulations to eliminate the impact of differences, China has not only made substantial progress in promoting equality between men and women but has also taken a positive and solid step towards building a more just and equal society. Details can be found in articles 41, 42, 45, 46, and 48 of *the Law on the Protection of Women's Rights and Interests*:

Article 41
The State guarantees that women enjoy equal labor and social security rights with men.

Article 42
People's governments at all levels and relevant departments shall improve employment security policies and measures, prevent and rectify gender discrimination in employment, create a fair environment for women's employment and entrepreneurship, and provide the necessary support and assistance to women who have difficulty in finding employment.

Article 45
Equal pay for equal work for men and women shall be implemented. Women enjoy equal rights with men in the enjoyment of welfare benefits.

Article 46
The principle of equality between men and women shall be adhered to in the promotion of posts and grades, the appraisal of professional and technical titles and positions, and training, and there shall be no discrimination against women.

Article 48

Employers may not, on account of marriage, pregnancy, maternity leave, breastfeeding and other circumstances, reduce the wages and benefits of female workers, restrict female workers' access to promotion, advancement, evaluation of professional and technical titles and positions, dismiss female workers, or unilaterally terminate their labor (employment) contracts or service agreements. If a female worker's labor (employment) contract or service agreement expires during her pregnancy and the period of maternity leave she is entitled to under the law, the term of the labor (employment) contract or service agreement shall automatically be extended until the end of the maternity leave. However, unless the employer terminates or suspends the labor (employment) contract or service agreement in accordance with the law, or the female worker requests the termination or suspension of the labor (employment) contract or service agreement in accordance with the law.

Employers may not discriminate against women on the basis of gender when implementing the national retirement system.

With regard to equality in property rights and interests, women enjoy equal property rights with men on the basis of the State policy of equality between men and women; women enjoy equal rights with men in the contracting of rural land, the distribution of the proceeds of collective economic organizations, the use of compensation for land expropriation or requisition, and the use of homesteads, and they also enjoy equal inheritance rights, in accordance with the law and in a reasonable manner. Article 13 of *the Constitution of the People's Republic of China* also stipulates that citizens' lawful property rights are inviolable, and the State protects citizens' right to private property and inheritance in accordance with the provisions of the law. However, because of traditional cultural and ethical relations, women are often discriminated against in families or collective organizations on the basis of their gender, resulting in the deprivation of their lawful property rights and interests or unlawful interference in their property rights and interests, which are divided among men. Therefore, in order to change the old patriarchal concepts of women and to safeguard women's lawful property rights and interests, *the Law of the People's Republic of China on Protection of the Rights and Interests of Women* puts special emphasis on women's equal rights to property rights and interests and stipulates that No one shall interfere with the lawful property rights and interests of women. The introduction of this legal provision was undoubtedly a great shock to the old concepts, emphasizing women's equal rights in property rights and interests and explicitly prohibiting any form of interference and deprivation. In this process, women's organizations, legal institutions, the education sector, and other social forces should all play an active role in promoting the realization of equality between men and women. *The Law on the Protection of Women's Rights and Interests* has made clear provisions and efforts to safeguard women's property rights and interests, emphasizing women's equal rights, details of which can be found in articles 53, 55, 56 and 58:

Article 53
The State guarantees that women enjoy property rights equal to those of men.

Article 55
Women shall enjoy equal rights with men in respect of confirmation of membership in rural collective economic organizations, contracted land management, distribution of proceeds from collective economic organizations, compensation for land acquisition and resettlement or expropriation, and the use of homesteads. When applying for real estate registration of the right to contract for the management of rural land and the right to use homesteads, all members of the family, including women, who are entitled to such rights shall be listed in the real estate registration book and the certificate of ownership. Agreements on compensation and resettlement for expropriation or compensation for expropriation shall include women who are entitled to the relevant rights and interests, and record the content of those rights and interests.

Article 56
Villagers' self-governance statutes, village rules and regulations, decisions of villagers' meetings, meetings of villagers' representatives, and other decisions on matters involving the interests of villagers shall not infringe on the rights and interests of women in rural collective economic organizations on the grounds that they are unmarried, married, divorced, widowed, or have no male members in their households. Where a man settles in a woman's residence as a result of marriage, the man and the child shall enjoy rights and interests equal to those of the members of the rural collective economic organization in which they are located.

Article 58
Women enjoy inheritance rights equal to those of men. Women exercise their inheritance rights in accordance with the law, without discrimination. Widowed women have the right to dispose of inherited property in accordance with the law, and no organization or individual may interfere.

In terms of equality of rights and interests in marriage and the family, women should also enjoy equal rights with men, in accordance with the national policy of equality between men and women, and both parties to a marriage should endeavor to create an atmosphere of equality and harmony in the family, which the law stipulates that the relevant authorities should promote. Within one year after pregnancy or childbirth, or within 6 months after termination of pregnancy, based on the special physiological and psychological situation of women during this period, the law imposes special obligations and restrictions on men, i.e., men are prohibited from filing for divorce, thus providing special protection for women in a disadvantaged position. This is a special right granted by the law to women in accordance with the actual situation, taking into account the physical and psychological vulnerability of women during this period, and guaranteeing that women's basic rights will not be violated, to realize equality between men and women in the true sense of the word, rather than just shouting slogans, which is an important manifestation of the progress of equality in society, as well as caring for women and giving them practical protection.

At the same time, women enjoy equal rights to possess, use, gain, and dispose of the common property of the husband and wife, without being affected by any other subjective or objective factors, which guarantees women's equal status in the marriage and family, as well as the equality of their property. In practice, women's contribution in marriage and family is often neglected, and their legitimate rights and interests are often not fully protected. In enacting the law, the legislator has also fully taken into account the plight of women in practice and has adopted tilted protection in the process of enacting the law, with the aim of emphasizing that women are also contributing to the family and that they are therefore of course entitled to enjoy the common property of the family. Furthermore, women and men enjoy equal rights to custody of minor the child for women and men, which cannot be ignored, are not denied or restricted on the basis of gender. The Law on the Protection of Women's Rights and Interests guarantees equal rights for men and women in respect of marriage and the family, while at the same time providing certain special protection for women's rights and interests in accordance with practice, thus truly realizing the substantive equality of men and women (Xia, 2020). Details can be found in articles 60, 63, 64, 66, and 70 of *the Law on the Protection of Women's Rights and Interests*:

> **Article 60**
> ***The State guarantees that women enjoy equal rights with men in marriage and the family.***
>
> **Article 63**
> ***Marriage registration authorities shall provide marriage and family counselling services and guide the parties concerned to establish equal, harmonious and civilized marriage and family relations.***
>
> **Article 64**
> ***During a woman's pregnancy, within one year after giving birth, or within six months after termination of pregnancy, the man may not file for divorce; however, the woman may file for divorce or the people's court may deem it necessary to accept the man's request for divorce.***
>
> **Article 66**
> ***Women have equal rights with their spouses to possess, use, gain, and dispose of the common property of the couple, regardless of the income status of either party.***

Article 70
Both parents have equal rights to custody of their minor child.

If the father is dead, incapable of guardianship or otherwise unable to act as guardian of his minor the child, no organization or individual may interfere with the mother's right of guardianship.

In short, China recognizes the inequalities that women encounter in practice because of physical and psychological factors, and has therefore always adhered to the concept of equality between men and women, especially in the protection of women's rights and interests. In promoting the protection of women's rights and interests, China has constantly emphasized that the true realization of equality between men and women is not just a matter of words, but also a matter of actions and institutional safeguards. Accordingly, it actively encourages all walks of life to take practical measures to ensure that women enjoy genuine equality and are not discriminated against in terms of their rights and interests in the areas of politics, the person and personality, culture and education, labor and social security, property, marriage and the family, and that special support is provided to meet their needs at different physiological periods. Accordingly, China will always take appropriate measures to realize the basic concept of equality between men and women at both the legal and practical levels, and will continue to encourage all sectors of society as well as individuals to practice equality between men and women, and to contribute their own efforts to safeguarding the legitimate rights and interests of women.

9.2.2 Priority Provisions for the Protection of the Rights and Interests of Women Under 18 Years of Age

The child are the hope and future of national development, and the girl is the mothers of the future; it is international practice, as well as a basic principle established in Chinese law, to give special and priority protection to the child. China has also made clear provisions to safeguard the growth of the girl child; the Law on the Protection of Women's Rights and Interests takes full account of women's physiological and psychological peculiarities, and emphasizes equal protection and special protection for the girl child. It focuses on the Government's responsibility to publicize the idea of equality between men and women, safeguard the rights and interests of persons and personalities, safeguard physiological and psychological health, and protect the right to education, social security, property rights and family rights and interests, and seeks to safeguard the rights and interests of the girl child in all respects and without any gaps.

Articles 42–45 of *the United Nations Convention on the Rights of the Child* stipulate the Government's obligation to protect the child, for example, through the Government's monitoring of the progress of the child's rights, so that the general public can understand and monitor the duties of the various governmental organs.

The Law on the Protection of Women's Rights and Interests fully echoes this (Federle, 2000), and in terms of protecting the rights and interests of the girl child, it indicates that governments at all levels should be deeply involved in the protection of the girl child, and, on the basis of full awareness of the rights and interests of the girl child, should do all they can to strengthen the protection of these rights and interests and put them into practice. The Chinese Government will continue to deepen its understanding of the protection of the rights and interests of the girl child, treating the girl as individuals with rights and dignity rather than as victims, and investing more resources in the education, health, and welfare of the girl in order to improve the environment in which they grow up. Under this working mechanism, the rights and interests of the girl in the areas of person and personality, cultural education, labor and social security, property, marriage, and family have been comprehensively safeguarded, reflecting the Chinese Government's relentless pursuit of the protection of the rights and interests of the girl and its insistence on comprehensively leading the work for the girl, committing itself to soundly perfecting the legal system for safeguarding the rights and interests of the girl and to continually improving the environment in which they grow up, and always placing the rights and interests of the girl in the highest position. The rights and interests of the girl are always given the highest priority. Details can be f*ound in Article 3 of the Law on the Protection of Women's Rights and Interests*:

Article 3

The leadership of the Communist Party of China in safeguarding women's rights and interests shall be upheld, and a working mechanism for safeguarding women's rights and interests shall be established that is government-led, coordinated by all parties, and participated in by society.

People's governments at all levels shall emphasize and strengthen the work of safeguarding women's rights and interests.

Institutions in people's governments at or above the county level that are responsible for the work of women and the child are responsible for organizing, coordinating, guiding, and supervising the work of the relevant departments in safeguarding women's rights and interests.

The relevant departments of the people's governments at or above the county level do a good job of safeguarding women's rights and interests within their respective areas of responsibility.

Governments at all levels should endeavor to fulfill their responsibility to protect the girl within their own spheres of responsibility; in addition to this, it is even more necessary to promote the concept of equality between men and women through education at the basic institutional level, in order to protect the rights and interests of the girl child at the root. China has incorporated this concept into its national education system, and has begun to publicize the basic concept of equality between men and women during childhood; this is an important step in shaping the basic thinking and concepts of its citizens, so as to promote the gradual formation of a correct understanding and appreciation of the concept of equality between men and women as the child grow up. Propaganda is a process of continuous effort. We should implement gender equality and the safeguarding of women's rights and interests throughout the entire process of national education, directing society's attention to the survival and development of women, constantly promoting the concept of gender equality, creating more equal opportunities, and fostering the public's awareness of their concern for women and the girl. This is specified in Article 10 of *the Law on the Protection of Women's Rights and Interests*:

> **Article 10**
> ***The State shall incorporate the basic national policy of equality between men and women into the national education system, carry out publicity and education, enhance the awareness of equality between men and women in society as a whole, and cultivate a social culture of respect and care for women.***

With regard to the physical rights and interests of the child, article 19 of *the United Nations Convention on the Rights of the Child* provides that "States shall protect the child from physical or mental violence, injury or abuse, neglect, maltreatment or exploitation, including sexual abuse." Similarly, with regard to the personal rights and interests of the girl child, China has also cracked down on crimes against the girl. *The Law on the Protection of Women's Rights and Interests* specifically lists a number of rights, and the girls enjoy personal rights and interests on an equal footing with boys, including the right to life, the right to the body, the right to health, and so on, indicating that their personal rights and interests are protected by the law, and endeavor to ensure that the physical and mental health of the girl is not infringed upon. At the same time, more detailed provisions have been made on sexual harassment, which causes the greatest harm to women, clarifying that sexual harassment is defined as the act of harassing a woman against her will by verbal, physical, or written means, and prohibiting anyone from infringing on the right to sexual freedom of women and the girl against their will, thus expanding the channels for defending the right to sexual harassment, and doing a good job of providing relief after the fact.

Moreover, because of the immaturity of the girls' physiological and psychological development, they are more vulnerable to abuse than adult women; China has taken into account the need to utilize national education to provide different gender education at different stages according to the age of the girl child, so as to enhance the girl child's awareness of, and capacity for, self-protection. Schools must contribute by strengthening school management, continuously optimizing school work mechanisms, and increasing their efforts to protect girls. At the same time, the measures taken by different departments to protect the girl from abuse have been stipulated, emphasizing the combination of pre-protection and post-protection work. National education is an important means of raising girls' awareness and ability to protect themselves. The content of education should vary according to the age and stage of the girl child, so as to adapt to her physical and psychological development.

Through education, the girl can learn about their rights and ways to protect themselves and enhance their awareness of self-protection. Secondly, schools are important places for protecting girls from abuse. Schools must contribute by strengthening school management and stepping up their efforts to protect the girls. Schools should formulate a detailed safety management system and conduct regular safety inspections to ensure campus safety. At the same time, schools should strengthen safety education for teachers and students and raise their awareness of safety. In addition, the Government has stipulated the measures to be taken by different departments with regard to the victimization of the girl, while care should be taken at all times to protect their privacy. These policies respond positively to the relevant provisions of *the United Nations Convention on the Rights of the Child* on the right of the child to protection, as specified in articles 19, 21, 23, and 24 of *the Law on the Protection of Women's Rights and Interests*:

Article 19
Women's personal freedom shall be inviolable. Unlawful detention and deprivation or restriction of a woman's personal freedom by other unlawful means are prohibited; unlawful search of a woman's body is prohibited.

Article 21
Women's rights to life, body, and health shall be inviolable. Abuse, abandonment, mutilation, sale, and other acts that infringe upon a woman's right to life and health are prohibited.

Fetal sex determination for non-medical needs and sex-selective artificial termination of pregnancy are prohibited.

Medical institutions shall obtain a woman's consent when performing fertility surgery, special examinations, or special treatments; in the event of disagreement between a woman and her family or relatives, the woman's wishes shall be respected.

Article 23
It is prohibited to sexually harass a woman against her will by means of speech, writing, images, or physical behavior.

Victimized women may file complaints with the relevant units and State organs. The relevant unit or State organ that receives the complaint shall deal with it in a timely manner and inform the victim in writing of the outcome.

The victimized woman may report the matter to the public security authorities, or may bring a civil action in the people's court, requesting the perpetrator to assume civil liability in accordance with the law.

Article 24

Schools shall, in accordance with the age and stage of female students, provide education in physiological hygiene, mental health, and self-protection, and take measures in the areas of education, management, and facilities to raise their awareness and ability to protect themselves against sexual abuse and harassment, and to safeguard the personal safety and healthy physical and mental development of female students.

Schools shall establish a working system for the effective prevention and scientific handling of sexual abuse and harassment. Schools shall not conceal any illegal or criminal acts of sexual abuse or harassment of female students, and shall promptly notify the parents or other guardians of the victimized minor female students, report the case to the public security authorities and the administrative departments of education, and cooperate with the relevant departments to deal with the case in accordance with the law.

Schools, public security organs, education administrative departments and other relevant units and personnel shall protect the privacy and personal information of female students who have been subjected to sexual abuse or harassment, and provide the necessary protective measures.

China has also made corresponding efforts with regard to the personality rights and interests of the girl, such as the right to a name, the right to a portrait, the right to reputation, the right to honor, and the right to privacy and personal information. In current society, media reports often exaggerate or even spread rumors, seriously damaging the personality interests of natural persons, and even more so in the case of minors. In this regard, the Law on the Protection of Women's Rights and Interests specifically stipulates, in article 28, that the news media should exercise caution and due diligence in reporting on news events, verifying the source of the information before releasing it and basing themselves on the authoritative information released by the official authorities, while at the same time paying attention to the protection of the privacy of the girl child, and adhering to the principle of proportionality, and refraining from infringing upon the personality rights and interests of the girl child by exaggerating the facts, over-dramatizing the story and other means. Article 37 of *the United Nations Convention on the Rights of the Child* also mentions that "no child shall be subjected to torture or other forms of cruel, inhuman or degrading treatment or punishment." This shows that there is a worldwide consensus on the protection of the child's rights and interests as human beings.

At the same time, the Chinese Government has always attached great importance to the health of the girl child and has set up a comprehensive healthcare system for this purpose. This initiative focuses not only on the physical health of the girls but also on their mental health, with the aim of providing girls with all-round health protection and promoting their healthy growth. First of all, the popularization of health knowledge is an important part of safeguarding the physical health of the girl. Through various channels, such as schools, communities, and the media, the Government publicizes knowledge about health care, disease prevention, and healthy lifestyles among the girl and their parents, so that the girls can develop good habits and raise their awareness of self-protection from an early age. Secondly, the Government also attaches importance to the treatment of the girls' illnesses, and through the establishment of a comprehensive medical network, provides professional timely, and effective treatment. However, it is not enough to focus only on the girl's physical health. The Government also pays great attention to the girl's mental health and actively provides them with psychological counseling and psychological treatment services to help them solve their psychological problems and promote their mental health development. Overall, the Chinese Government's women's health service system provides a solid guarantee for the healthy and happy growth of the girl. We look forward to more countries and regions learning from China's experience and contributing to the cause of the girl's health. Articles 28, 30, and 31 of *the Law on the Protection of Women's Rights and Interests* specify:

Article 28
Women's personality rights and interests, including the right to name, portrait, reputation, honor, privacy and personal information, are protected by law. Media coverage of events involving women shall be objective and proportionate, and shall not infringe upon women's personality rights and interests through exaggeration or over-exaggeration. It is prohibited to demean and damage women's personalities through the mass media or in other ways. Without one's consent, a woman's portrait may not be used through advertisements, trademarks, exhibition windows, newspapers, periodicals, books, audio-visual products, electronic publications, the Internet, or other forms, unless otherwise provided for by law.

Article 30
The State establishes and improves the system of women's health services, guarantees women's access to basic medical and health services, and carries out the prevention, screening, and treatment of common and frequent diseases among women, so as to raise the level of women's health.

The State takes the necessary measures to popularize health knowledge, health care, and disease prevention and treatment during menstruation, pregnancy, childbirth, breastfeeding, and menopause, to safeguard the health needs of women during their special physiological periods, and to provide support for mental health services for women in need.

Article 31
Local people's governments at or above the county level shall set up maternal and child healthcare institutions to provide women with healthcare and services for the prevention and treatment of common diseases.

The State encourages and supports social forces to participate in the cause of women's health and wellness by way of donations, funding, or the provision of voluntary services in accordance with the law, and to provide safe physiological health supplies or services to meet the diverse and differentiated health needs of women.

Employers shall regularly arrange for female workers to undergo examinations for gynecological and breast diseases, as well as other health examinations for women's special needs.

The Law on the Protection of Women's Rights and Interests is designed to ensure equality between men and women, and it also guarantees equality for girls in terms of their rights and interests in culture and education, which is consistent with *the United Nations Convention on the Rights of the Child* on the right to development; the child has the right to the full development of their intellectual and physical capacities, and the right to education, as part of the right to development, is also a basic right to which the child should be entitled. Education is an important means of improving the social status of girls and promoting equality between men and women, and it is essential to increase investment in girls' education, raise their educational level, and cultivate their self-esteem, self-confidence, self-reliance, and self-improvement, so as to enable them to better integrate into, participate in and contribute to society. Firstly, the responsibilities of guardians and the Government with regard to education have been stipulated. Guardians should fulfill their duties as custodians of the girl and ensure that they receive compulsory education; they may not arbitrarily withdraw them from school or restrict their right to education. The Government shall strengthen its investment in compulsory education, provide the necessary educational resources and conditions, and guarantee the right of girls to receive compulsory education. Secondly, it is stipulated that society shall not discriminate against the girl. All aspects of society shall provide equal cultural and educational opportunities for the girl, and shall not discriminate against or exclude the girl on the basis of gender or other grounds. At the same time, the law also prohibits any organization or individual from infringing on the right of the girl to receive cultural education in any way, including, but not limited to, restricting school enrolment, withdrawing from school, or altering school registration on the basis of gender. Articles 35, 36, and 37 of *the Law on the Protection of Women's Rights and Interests* specifically provide for this:

Article 35

The State guarantees that women enjoy the right to cultural education on an equal basis with men.

Article 36
Parents or other guardians shall fulfill their obligation to ensure that female minors of school age receive and complete compulsory education. Parents or other guardians who fail to send school-age female minors to school without a valid reason shall be criticized and educated by the local township people's government or the educational administrative department of the people's government at the county level, and ordered by law to make corrections within a specified period of time. Residents' committees and villagers' committees shall assist the government in its work. The government and schools shall take effective measures to resolve practical difficulties in schooling for female minors of school age and create conditions to ensure that female minors of school age complete compulsory education.

Article 37
Schools and relevant departments shall implement the relevant State regulations to ensure that females enjoy equal rights with males in such areas as enrolment in schools, advancement to higher education, the awarding of degrees, dispatching students to study abroad, and employment guidance and services. In admitting students, schools may not refuse to admit women or raise the admission standards for women on the basis of their gender, except in the case of special specialties prescribed by the State. People's governments at all levels shall take measures to ensure that women enjoy equal rights and opportunities to receive secondary and higher education.

In China's social security system, the protection of the social rights and interests of the girl has always been a top priority. China has always firmly assumed this responsibility, maintaining social stability, safeguarding the legitimate rights and interests of the girls, and providing them with practical social welfare. These include, for example, the basic medical services and mental health counseling mentioned above, as well as social insurance and social assistance, in order to ensure that they can grow up healthily. In reality, however, there are still some old patriarchal attitudes that often lead to unequal treatment of men and women, one of which is that inheritance is usually assigned to male heirs. In order to address this problem, China has formulated relevant regulations to safeguard the property and inheritance rights of the girl, thereby comprehensively supplementing and improving the rights of the girl in economic terms. The girls have the same right to inheritance as boys and are able to acquire property through family status relationships. We cannot deprive them of this fundamental right because of their gender. Therefore, we must resolutely oppose any form of gender discrimination and prejudice and ensure that girls enjoy equal rights and opportunities in the family and in society. In conclusion, China has always taken the protection of the social rights and interests of the girl child as an inescapable responsibility in terms of social security rights and interests. Through the provision of practical social welfare, the safeguarding of girls' property and inheritance rights, the fight against gender discrimination, and attention to girls' education, China has provided strong safeguards for the healthy growth of girls. We believe that, with the joint efforts of society as a whole, the rights and interests of girls will be better protected and promoted, and gender equality in Chinese society will be further advanced and improved. Articles 41, 50, 53, and 58 of *the Law on the Protection of Women's Rights and Interests* contain specific provisions:

Article 41
The State guarantees that women enjoy equal labor rights and social security rights with men.

Article 50
The State develops social security and guarantees women's rights and interests in social insurance, social assistance, and social welfare. The State promotes and encourages social welfare activities for the benefit of women.

Article 53
The State guarantees that women enjoy property rights equal to those of men.

Article 58
Women enjoy inheritance rights equal to those of men. Women shall exercise their inheritance rights in accordance with the law, without discrimination. Widowed women have the right to dispose of inherited property in accordance with the law, and no organization or individual may interfere.

China has also made considerable efforts to protect the rights and interests of the girls in the family. It has responded to and put into practice Article 19 of the United Nations Convention on the Rights of the Child, which states that "States Parties shall take all appropriate legislative, administrative, social and educational measures to protect the child, while in the care of parent(s), legal guardian(s) or other person(s) responsible for the care of the child, from all forms of physical or mental violence, injury or abuse, neglect or negligent treatment, maltreatment or exploitation, including sexual abuse. sexual assault." The impact of domestic violence on the child's development is incalculable, and the child who has suffered domestic violence is not only physically harmed, but also mentally harmed. China has enacted legislation to strictly prohibit domestic violence, create a harmonious family atmosphere for the growth of girls, and safeguard their physical and mental health. Preventive measures are taken beforehand, and afterward, the relevant departments and organizations must provide timely help and assistance to the girl, so as to minimize the impact of domestic violence. The concept of resolutely opposing domestic violence and providing timely assistance to victims is also reflected in the Law of the People's Republic of China against Domestic Violence. Article 13 of which stipulates that "Victims of domestic violence, their legal representatives, and close relatives may lodge complaints, reflect on the matter, or seek help from the aggressor or the victim's unit, residents' committee, villagers' committee, women's federation, etc.". The relevant units receive complaints, reflections, or requests for assistance from the victim or the victim's unit. Upon receipt of a complaint, reflection or request for assistance in relation to domestic violence, the unit concerned shall provide assistance and deal with the matter. Victims of domestic violence, their legal representatives, and close relatives may also report the case to the public security organs or bring it to the people's courts in accordance with the law. Units and individuals who discover domestic violence in progress have the right to discourage it in a timely manner. This shows that China's protection of the rights and interests of the family is relatively comprehensive and that it is firmly opposed to the undesirable behavior of domestic violence. Article 65 of *the Law on the Protection of Women's Rights and Interests* specifies:

> **Article 65**
> ***Domestic violence against women is prohibited.***
>
> ***The relevant departments of the people's governments at or above the county level, judicial organs, social organizations, enterprises and institutions, grass-roots mass self-governance organizations, and other organizations shall, within their respective spheres of responsibility, prevent and curb domestic violence and, in accordance with the law, provide assistance to female victims.***

As can be seen from the foregoing, the Chinese Government has made great efforts to protect the girl, reflecting the commitment of a great nation. Taking into account the right of the child to protection under the United Nations Convention on the Rights of the Child, it has strengthened national education, promoted the idea of equality between men and women, comprehensively safeguarded the personal and individual rights and interests of the girl child, strengthened the protection of the physical and mental health of the girl child, and safeguarded the girl child's right to education (Wang, 1995), social security, and the right to own property, while at the same time resolutely opposing domestic violence. Overall, the Government plays a crucial role in the protection of the rights and interests of the girl, and through legal safeguards and practical action, it is able to ensure that the girl enjoy equal rights and opportunities. To achieve this goal, the Government needs to overcome many challenges and work together with communities, educational institutions, families, and the public. Only in this way can truly achieve comprehensive protection of the rights and interests of the girl and create a fairer and more inclusive social environment for their future. In response to the issue of protection of the girls' rights and interests, further studies will be conducted in the future on how to further promote the protection of girl's rights and interests through education reform, social and cultural changes, and the enactment of laws. Attention will also need to be paid to how existing problems can be solved in practice and how the working mechanism can be continuously optimized to ensure that the rights and interests of the girl are truly protected.

9.2.3 Remedies and Legal Liability

As an important part of society, the contribution of women in the family, workplace, and society cannot be ignored. However, for a long time, women have been facing various challenges and unequal treatment related to physical differences, mental health, and the plight of social roles. In order to address these issues, the Law of the People's Republic of China on the Protection of Women's Rights and Interests not only grants women their legitimate rights and interests but also provides comprehensive safeguards when their rights and interests are infringed upon. This includes a series of remedies, such as legal proceedings, administrative remedies, mediation, and other means. Moreover, it stipulates the corresponding legal sanctions to be imposed on citizens, legal persons, or other organizations for committing acts of infringing upon the rights and interests of women. The legal responsibilities borne by citizens, legal persons, or other organizations that commit acts that violate women's rights and interests are also stipulated. The existence of these provisions helps to safeguard women's legitimate rights and interests in a timely and effective manner, providing them with legal weapons to defend themselves against unfair treatment. While focusing on women's rights and interests, these provisions also pay special attention to the protection of women under the age of 18, seeking to create, through a comprehensive legal system, a more just, equal, and caring social environment in which women can be fully respected and treated equally at all levels of society.

The Law on the Protection of Women's Rights and Interests provides for a number of measures to give women adequate relief in the event of abuse. One of these remedy states that any organ or organization has the power to stop and report acts that violate the rights and interests of women and girls, including legal aid agencies, the judiciary, women's associations, and township and village people's governments. This provision is designed to emphasize the shared responsibility of society to ensure that women and girls enjoy the protection of their legitimate rights and interests in all areas. By granting organs and organizations the right to stop and report crimes, the law emphasizes the active role of social institutions in safeguarding the rights and interests of women and girls. The involvement of such institutions may include government agencies, social groups, non-profit organizations, etc., thus forming a mechanism for multi-party cooperation to comprehensively promote the suppression and combating of acts that infringe on the rights and interests of women and girls. The core objective is to ensure that women's legitimate rights and interests are effectively safeguarded and respected. The power of organs and organizations does not stop at the follow-up stage of dealing with violations but emphasizes the role of prevention and suppression. By stopping violations in a timely manner, society can prevent potential problems with women's rights and interests, thereby creating a more just and equal social environment. In addition, by clearly stipulating in the law that organs and organizations have the responsibility to stop and report acts of infringement on the rights and interests of women and girls, society will be more sensitive to this topic, thus generating more public discussion and attention to the issue of women's rights and interests. For details, see Article 72 of *the Law on the Protection of Women's Rights and Interests*, which summarizes the full range of remedies and protections available to women and girls, with each step of the process interlocking, from reporting to handling to providing assistance:

> **Article 72**
> ***Any organization or individual has the right to discourage or stop any act that infringes on the lawful rights and interests of women, or to file a complaint or denunciation with the relevant authorities.***
>
> ***Upon receipt of a complaint or denunciation, the relevant authorities shall deal with it promptly in accordance with the law and shall maintain the confidentiality of the complainant or denouncer.***
>
> ***If a woman's lawful rights and interests are infringed upon, she has the right to request the relevant authorities to deal with the matter in accordance with the law, to apply for mediation or arbitration in accordance with the law, or to bring a lawsuit in the people's courts.***
>
> ***For women who meet the conditions, local legal aid organizations or judicial organs shall assist them and provide them with legal aid or judicial assistance in accordance with the law.***

The Women's Union is an important and irreplaceable organization in safeguarding the legitimate rights and interests of women and girls by providing remedies when their rights and interests are violated. First of all, the Women's Union is entrusted with the responsibility of providing support and assistance to women and girls. When their rights and interests are infringed upon, they can seek assistance from the Women's Union in the hope of obtaining professional support to better safeguard their legitimate rights and interests. At the same time, according to the law, the Women's Federation has the right to request the relevant departments and organizations to deal with matters that violate women's rights and interests. This means that the Women's Union can use legal means to compel the relevant parties to take action to stop the infringement and protect their rights and interests.

Of course, under certain circumstances, if the Women's Union finds that the relevant department or unit is not handling matters that violate women's rights and interests properly, the Women's Union has greater autonomy and can play its supervisory role. This means that the Women's Union can take appropriate action to ensure that violations of women's and girl's rights are dealt with fairly and appropriately. Finally, women's federations are often tasked with raising awareness of women's rights issues in society. Through education and publicity activities, women's associations can encourage society to pay more attention to and understand the importance of women's rights and interests, and to promote public awareness of and support for equality between men and women. Overall, the responsibility of the Women's Federation in the protection of women's rights and interests is not only about supporting individual cases but also about positively influencing social structures and perceptions. Through its unique status and rights, the Women's Federation plays an irreplaceable role in promoting gender equality and safeguarding the rights and interests of women and girls. This is stipulated in Article 73 of *the Law on the Protection of Women's Rights and Interests*:

> **Article 73**
> ***Women whose lawful rights and interests have been infringed upon may seek assistance from women's organizations such as women's federations. Women's federations and other women's organizations shall safeguard the lawful rights and interests of infringed women, and have the right to request and assist the relevant departments or units to investigate and deal with the matter. The department or unit concerned shall investigate and deal with the matter in accordance with the law and give a reply; if it fails to do so or does so inappropriately, the agency of the people's government at or above the county level responsible for working with women and the child or the Women's Federation may propose to it that it supervise the handling of the matter, and, if necessary, may request the people's government at the same level to carry out an investigation. If a victimized woman needs assistance in litigation, the Women's Federation shall provide support and assistance.***

In China, the establishment of a nationally unified hotline for the protection of women's rights and interests is also a rapid, timely, and effective relief measure for dealing with violations of the legitimate rights and interests of women and girls. The law stipulates that people's governments at or above the county level should establish a nationally unified hotline for the protection of women's rights and interests, which means that a unified telephone hotline has been set up throughout the country to provide women and girls with advisory, complaint and assistance services. This helps to provide a convenient communication channel for quick access to help and support.

At the same time, the law requires government agencies to take prompt action when they receive reports or complaints of violations of women's and girl's rights and interests. This includes initiating investigation procedures, providing temporary protection measures, and ensuring that they can receive timely help when they are threatened or victimized.

In addition to this, the law encourages members of society and social organizations to actively participate in matters relating to the protection of the rights and interests of women and girls. This can be done by providing advice, reporting violations, and assisting in investigations. The Government has set up a cooperation mechanism to establish partnerships with non-governmental organizations, women's organizations, and others to jointly promote the protection of women's rights and interests.

Similarly, the Government should provide women and girls with the necessary resource support, including legal aid, psychological counseling, and shelters, which will help women and girls recover from violations and rebuild their lives. Lastly, the Government should conduct regular publicity and education campaigns to raise the girl's awareness of the protection of their rights and interests, and at the same time encourage wider social concern and participation in this area. The Chinese Government aims to establish a sound system for protecting the rights and interests of women and girls, not only by providing assistance and support but also by promoting the joint efforts of all parties in society to provide more comprehensive and effective protection for the legitimate rights and interests of women and the girl. Details can be found in article 76 of *the Law on the Protection of Women's Rights and Interests*:

Article 76

The people's governments at or above the county level shall set up a nationally unified hotline for the protection of women's rights and interests, and promptly receive and transfer complaints and reports of infringement of women's lawful rights and interests; after receiving such complaints and reports, the relevant departments or units shall deal with them in a timely manner. Encouragement and support are given to group organizations, enterprises and institutions, social organizations, and individuals to participate in the establishment of hotlines for the protection of women's rights and interests, and to provide advice and assistance in the protection of women's rights and interests.

When the legitimate rights and interests of women and girls are infringed upon, the prosecutorial organs play an important role, aiming to safeguard their rights and interests and to protect the public interest of society. The assistance of the prosecutorial organs is also an important relief measure. The Law on the Protection of Women's Rights and Interests states that when prosecutorial authorities find that the lawful rights and interests of women and girls have been infringed upon and that such infringement affects the public interests of society, they have the right to make prosecutorial recommendations, which means that the prosecutorial authorities can make recommendations to the relevant authorities, prompting action to be taken to resolve the problem and safeguard their rights and interests.

The prosecutorial authorities may also exercise the right to initiate public interest litigation in certain cases provided for by law. Prosecutorial organs can represent the public interests of society and, through legal means, hold those who violate the rights and interests of women and girls accountable, prompting wider social concern and participation in efforts to safeguard women's rights and interests.

At the same time, the law stipulates the duties of the prosecutorial authorities, which include safeguarding the legitimate rights and interests of women and girls. This means that within the framework of the law, the prosecutorial authorities have the responsibility to take action to prevent and combat behavior that infringes on women's rights and interests. The duties of the procuratorate as set out in the law provide solid legal support for women, who, when faced with infringements of their rights and interests, can rely on the intervention of the procuratorate to safeguard their rights using legal means.

Overall, the involvement of the procuratorate emphasizes the importance of safeguarding the legitimate rights and interests of women and girls, providing support for victims through legal means, and prompting society to pay more attention to and value the protection of women's rights and interests. The establishment of this legal framework has provided women and girls with stronger legal safeguards and enhanced their status in the legal system. Moreover, State organs, social organizations, enterprises, and institutions can support the prosecution of women who have been victimized. This can be seen in articles 77 and 78 of *the Law on the Protection of Women's Rights and Interests*:

> **Article 77**
> ***Where infringement of a woman's lawful rights and interests results in damage to the public interest, the prosecutorial organ may issue a prosecutorial recommendation; where one of the following circumstances exists, the prosecutorial organ may institute a public interest litigation in accordance with the law: (1) Infringement of the rights and interests of women when confirming membership of a rural woman's collective economic organization, or infringement of women's rights and interests to contracted rural land and to collective income, to the distribution of compensation for the expropriation and expropriation of land and to the use of homesteads (2) Infringement of women's equal rights and interests in employment; (3) Failure to take reasonable measures to prevent and stop sexual harassment; (4) Degrading and damaging women's personalities through the mass media or in other ways; (5) Other serious infringements of women's rights and interests.***

> **Article 78**
> ***State organs, social organizations, enterprises, and institutions may support women who are victims of infringement of women's rights and interests in taking their cases to the people's courts.***

In order to effectively safeguard the legitimate rights and interests of women, and in particular to ensure the healthy growth of the girl, *the Law of the People's Republic of China on the Protection of Women's Rights and Interests* establishes remedies for violations of women's rights and interests, and at the same time specifies the relevant legal liabilities of various types of subjects, in particular the penalties to be imposed on those who have violated the law and failed to comply with the law. On specific occasions when women's rights and interests are infringed upon, the relevant persons should fulfill their corresponding legal obligations and take certain measures to protect women's legitimate rights and interests. If they fail to take certain measures, they will bear the corresponding legal responsibility. Moreover, under certain circumstances, relevant persons who violate women's rights and interests, such as abusers or discriminators, need to bear legal responsibility. This may include criminal, administrative, or civil liability, depending on the nature and extent of the infringement. The objective of these relevant provisions is to ensure that women and girls are able to enjoy equal rights in society and that when their rights are violated, the law provides a range of means to hold them accountable, provide them with assistance, and ensure that normal social participation is restored. This helps to improve the social status of women and girls, ensure that men and women enjoy the same rights, and promote equality and inclusion in society. Details can be found in articles 79, 80, 82, 84, and 85 of *the Law on the Protection of Women's Rights and Interests*:

Article 79
In the event of a violation of the provisions of Article 22, paragraph 2, of this Law, a person who fails to fulfill his or her reporting obligations shall be punished in accordance with the law by the persons directly in charge and other persons directly responsible.

Article 80
Anyone who engages in sexual harassment against women in violation of the provisions of this Law shall be criticized and educated by the public security authorities or issued a letter of admonition, and shall be punished by his or her employer in accordance with the law.

Article 82
Anyone who, in violation of the provisions of this Law, disparages or damages the personality of a woman through the mass media or by other means shall be ordered by the public security, Internet information, culture, and tourism, radio and television broadcasting, press and publication, or other relevant departments, in accordance with their respective powers and functions, to make corrections, and shall be subject to administrative penalties in accordance with the law.

Article 84
Anyone who, in violation of the provisions of this Law, shirks, delays, suppresses, or fails to investigate or handle complaints, accusations, or denunciations of infringement of women's rights and interests, or who retaliates against those who have lodged such complaints, accusations or denunciations, shall, in accordance with the law, be ordered to rectify the situation and the persons directly responsible and other persons with direct responsibility shall be sentenced to penalties. Where State organs and their personnel fail to perform their duties in accordance with the law or fail to stop in a timely manner acts of infringement of women's rights and interests or fail to provide the necessary assistance to victimized women, resulting in serious consequences, the persons directly responsible and other persons directly in charge shall be given penalties in accordance with the law. Where, in violation of the provisions of this Law, women's rights and interests in person and personality, cultural and educational rights and interests, labor and social security rights and interests, property rights and interests, and the rights and interests of the marriage and family are infringed upon, they shall be ordered to make corrections in accordance with the law, and the persons directly responsible and other persons directly liable shall be given disciplinary measures in accordance with the law if they are State employees.

Article 85
Where violations of the provisions of this Law infringe upon the lawful rights and interests of women, other laws and regulations prescribing administrative penalties shall take precedence over their provisions; where such violations result in property loss or personal injury, civil liability shall be borne in accordance with the law; and where such violations constitute a crime, criminal liability shall be investigated in accordance with the law.

It can be seen from the law that when the rights and interests of women and girls are harmed, the relevant departments or organizations not only have the responsibility and obligation but must also take active action to safeguard the legitimate rights and interests of women. This provision emphasizes that the protection agencies should actively take responsibility for women's rights and interests, and makes it clear that if the relevant departments or organizations fail to fulfill their corresponding obligations, they will be held legally responsible. The establishment of these legal responsibilities ensures that women's equal status in society and the legal system is fully respected, and is of great significance in safeguarding the dignity of the Law on the Protection of Women's Rights and Interests and in educating offenders and citizens to consciously safeguard women's rights and interests.

In summary, *the Law on the Protection of Women's Rights and Interests* regulates in detail the remedial measures and legal responsibilities of women and the girl when their rights and interests are infringed upon. It not only clarifies the rights and obligations of individuals, institutions and social organizations in this context, but also establishes a solid legal basis for safeguarding the legitimate rights and interests of women. The law covers all sectors of society and emphasizes the shared responsibility for safeguarding the rights and interests of women and the girl. Through the relevant provisions, women are able to seek redress in accordance with the law when their rights and interests are violated, ensuring the various social roles are clear about their responsibilities in this regard. The law sets out clear rights and obligations for the protection of women's and the girl's rights and interests, making it easier to pursue responsibility and safeguard women's dignity under the legal framework. The Law on the Protection of Women's Rights and Interests is also consistent with the concept of equality of all persons, as proclaimed in the Constitution of the People's Republic of China, and reflects respect for basic human rights. It provides strong legal support for the realization of social equality and equality between men and women, and ensures that women and the girl enjoy equal status and rights in society.

9.3 Summary

Equality between men and women is China's basic national policy, but because of the physiological and psychological differences between men and women, Chinese law has made special protections and provisions for women in order to fully safeguard the legitimate rights and interests of women and the girl. However, these special provisions are not a privilege, but rather a practical expression of China's care for vulnerable groups, giving women and the girl a legal status of special protection.

The Law on the Protection of Women's Rights and Interests has been carefully crafted to integrate with *the United Nations Convention on the Rights of the Child*, aligning actively with international policy to formulate legal provisions that foster the healthy growth of the girl child. China has also developed its own understanding of the principle of maximizing the interests of the child, such as guaranteeing the right of the girl to education and protecting them from sexual abuse, while at the same time responding to the right of the child to protection and the right of the child to development, and reflecting the comprehensive, equal and priority protection of the child.

This chapter interprets China's current protection policies for women and the girl in the light of *the Law on the Protection of Women's Rights and Interests*. It can be seen from the provisions of the Law that China has actively responded to social concerns, is committed to solving difficult problems in practice, has developed new concepts for the protection of women's human rights, has pioneered a series of new mechanisms to strengthen the protection of equality between men and women, has responded to the new phenomena that have emerged in society, and has a high degree of political responsibility and a sense of mission to safeguard women's rights and interests on an equal footing with those of men, and has made the protection of women's rights and interests one of the country's major responsibilities and obligations. In order to protect the rights and interests of the girl, the Chinese Government and the relevant departments have taken a series of measures, including strengthening publicity and education, raising public awareness, enhancing legal safeguards and providing legal assistance. At the same time, schools and families should also strengthen care and education for the girl, foster their self-respect, self-confidence, self-reliance and self-improvement, and promote their healthy growth. Additionally, corresponding relief measures and responsibilities are stipulated to ensure that the process of protecting women and the girl is interlocked and that effective assistance is provided at all stages. In order to better protect the rights and interests of women and the girl, all members of society should make efforts, and all of them should be responsible for the implementation of the basic national policy of equality between men and women.

The Law on the Protection of Women's Rights and Interests protects the rights and interests of the girl in a multi-faceted, prioritized, and equal manner, reflecting China's great national style of protecting women and the child in the context of global care for women and the child. The Law on the Protection of Women's Rights and Interests emphasizes the complementary and special protection of the girl child, and further clarifies the protection of the girl child under the guidance of *the Constitution of the People's Republic of China, the Civil Code of the People's Republic of China* and other foundational norms and laws, ensuring that the rights and interests of the girl child are also comprehensively protected in the face of the development of the new age and the emergence of new phenomena. The rights and interests of the girl child are also fully protected in the new era of development and new phenomena. On the other hand, this is also China's further response to *the United Nations Convention on the Rights of the Child,* and another powerful answer to the protection of the child. In the future, China will continue to pay attention to the protection of women and the girl, and will respond in a timely manner.

References

Cao, W. (2022). Improving the legislative system for the protection of women's rights and interests in China: Taking the revision of the "Law on the Protection of Women's Rights and Interests" as an opportunity. *Human Rights, 3*, 102–124.

Federle, K. H. (2000). Children's rights and the need for protection. *Family Law Quarterly, 3*, 421–440.

Keith, R. C. (1997). Legislating women's and children's rights and interests in the PRCa. *The China Quarterly, 149*, 29–55.

Wang, L. (1995). Special protection for girls in Chinese law. *Preschool Education, Z2*, 34–35.

Wang, L. (2015). Legal culture from a gender perspective. *Journal of Political Science and Law, 3*, 41–48.

Xia, J. (2020). The best interests of the child principle in residence disputes after parental divorce in China. *International Journal of Law, Policy and the Family, 2*, 105–125.

Chapter 10
Judicial Protection of Children's Civil Rights: The Role of the Civil Code and Civil Litigation Practice

10.1 Introduction

Building a stable growth environment for minors is an important task for the country and society. Although the current focus of protecting the rights and interests of minors in litigation involving minors in China is on traditional criminal proceedings (Xiao, 2019), the protection of minors in China is gradually penetrating into civil litigation, implementing comprehensive protection of their interests. The Civil Code highly protects the interests of minors and has made a series of special provisions to safeguard the rights and interests of minors in China. As a corresponding procedural law, *the Civil Procedure Law of the People's Republic of China* is an important guarantee for the effective implementation of the substantive rights stipulated in the Civil Code in terms of procedures.

The Civil Code highly protects the interests of minors and has made a series of special provisions to safeguard the rights and interests of minors in China. As a corresponding procedural law, *the Civil Procedure Law of the People's Republic of China* is an important guarantee for the effective implementation of the substantive rights stipulated in the Civil Code in terms of procedures. *The Civil Procedure Law of the People's Republic of China* is an important component of China's socialist legal system, serving as the legal basis for courts to hear and execute civil cases in terms of procedures. This law mainly includes four parts of special provisions on general provisions, trial procedures, execution procedures, and foreign-related civil litigation procedures, involving 27 chapters and 306 clauses. With the development and progress of society, the protection of the rights and interests of minors has become an important issue in society. As a country that values the rights and interests of minors, China has made positive efforts in legislation.

This chapter will combine relevant laws and regulations, taking the protection of children's rights as the starting point, and through special provisions of the law and the exercise of judges' own discretion in the trial of specific civil cases, provide

© The Author(s), under exclusive license to Springer Nature Singapore Pte Ltd. 2026

H. Li, P. Liang, *The Legal System for the Protection of Children's Rights in China*, Resilient and Friendly Living Environments,
https://doi.org/10.1007/978-981-95-9925-7_10

special protection for the interests of minors from the pre-trial preparation stage, case trial stage, and execution stage. In the pre-trial preparation stage, the establishment of the interest representative system, the protection of the right to participate in litigation, the establishment of special case trial procedures, and the prohibition of public trial of minor cases ensure the interests of minors in civil litigation, ensure their active participation in litigation and effectively safeguard their legitimate rights and interests, which is conducive to protecting their privacy rights (Chen, 2008). During the court trial stage, special provisions have also been made for minors to testify in court, ensuring their right to testify fairly and objectively. In the implementation stage, the special status of minors was fully considered, and special protection was also provided for minors to ensure their right to survival and development. In addition, from the perspectives of divorce litigation and public interest litigation for minors, this article elaborates on China's special provisions for minors in litigation, both of which reflect the protection of children's rights in China's Civil Procedure Law and maximize the protection of children's rights.

10.2 Child Protection in Civil Procedure

Since the promulgation of the Convention on the Rights of the Child by the United Nations, countries have increasingly focused on protecting children's rights. The right to participation is one of the important rights stipulated in the Convention on the Rights of the Child, which refers to the right of children to participate in family, cultural, and social life. China has also successively promulgated a series of laws related to children to protect their rights and interests. As an important procedural law in China, the Civil Procedure Law of the People's Republic of China has made a series of special provisions on children's participation in litigation, from the pre-trial preparation stage to the trial and execution stage, reflecting the maximum protection of children's participation rights and other rights in China.

10.2.1 Pre-trial Proceedings: Locus Standi and In Camera Hearings

The Civil Code of the People's Republic of China has defined the civil capacity and civil rights capacity of citizens, and there are no children in China without civil capacity or with limited civil capacity. In order to protect the legitimate rights and interests of children, different provisions have been made between the special procedure for identifying citizens with no capacity for civil conduct and the traditional procedure. In cases where this type of procedure applies, there are no plaintiffs or defendants in traditional cases, and both parties only see conflicts without civil rights and interests. The purpose of setting up this procedure is to protect, supervise, and manage the legitimate rights and interests of persons with no capacity for civil conduct and those with limited capacity for civil conduct, and to ensure transaction safety and social order. After determining that a citizen has no capacity for civil conduct, according to legal provisions, if the civil legal act performed by him is invalid or the effectiveness is uncertain, the court may designate a guardian for him/her to perform his/her guardianship duties, exercise civil rights and obligations on his/her behalf, and act on his/her behalf in the litigation process (Liang, 2019).

Litigation capacity, also known as party capacity, refers to the ability to enjoy civil litigation rights and assume civil litigation obligations. Having this ability is the legal qualification as a party to civil litigation. A person with the capacity for litigation rights can act as a party to civil litigation, and a person with the capacity for litigation rights must also have the capacity for litigation behavior when conducting litigation. Litigation capacity, also known as litigation capacity, refers to the ability to exercise litigation rights and fulfill litigation obligations through one's own actions, that is, the ability to personally conduct litigation activities. The litigation capacity of citizens begins in adulthood and ends in death or declaration of incapacity. The litigation capacity of legal persons and other organizations begins with their establishment in accordance with the law and ends with their dissolution or revocation. Litigation capacity and litigation capacity refer to the ability of the litigation subject to safeguard their civil rights and engage in litigation activities. Civil capacity and litigation capacity refer to the ability of the civil subject to exercise their rights and engage in civil activities. There is a distinction between litigation capacity and non-litigation capacity, while civil capacity includes capacity, non-capacity, and limited capacity. For adults and mentally ill individuals, in order to protect their civil rights and interests, the law grants them the qualification of litigation subjects, and their legal representatives act as agents for litigation and response. In order to protect the right of minors to participate in litigation, relevant judicial interpretations stipulate that in litigation, the guardian of a person without civil capacity or with limited civil capacity is their legal representative. If there is no designated guardian in advance, it can be determined through consultation with qualified guardians; If consultation fails, the People's Court shall designate the legal representative in the litigation among them. For specific provisions, please refer to Article 60 of the Civil Procedure Law:

Article 60
A person without legal capacity shall have his guardian act as the legal representative to represent him in litigation. If the legal representatives shift the responsibility of representation to each other, the people's court shall designate one of them to act on their behalf in the lawsuit.

The right to protection is an important right of children, and the United Nations Convention on the Rights of the Child stipulates that children have the right to protection, which refers to the rights of children to be guaranteed in terms of survival, development, health, safety, and other aspects. Specifically. The right of children to protection includes the following aspects: (1) Right to survival: Children have the right to adequate nutrition, healthcare, and health protection to maintain their life and health. (2) The right to development: the Child has the right to education, training, and opportunities to develop their intelligence and abilities. (3) The right to health: the Child has the right to access medical security for disease prevention and treatment to maintain their physical health. (4) Safety rights: Children have the right to receive protection from any form of harm, abuse, and exploitation. Our country's various laws and regulations actively practice the protection of children and their various rights.

Tort liability refers to the responsibility that the perpetrator should bear for infringing on the legitimate rights and interests of others. Tort liability generally has four constituent elements: first, the illegal act of the act; Secondly, the existence of harmful facts; Thirdly, causal relationships; Fourthly, the perpetrator is subjectively at fault. *The Civil Code of the People's Republic of China* has made a series of special provisions for minors to assume liability for infringement, which is conducive to protecting the legitimate rights and interests of minors.

The Civil Code of the People's Republic of China provides detailed provisions on how to remedy the infringement of the rights and interests of others or the infringement of the legitimate rights and interests of minors in the tort liability section (Zhu, 2025). When minors are infringed upon in school, schools or relevant institutions will bear supplementary responsibilities to ensure that their rights are effectively remedied. China has made detailed provisions in substantive law on how to protect the legitimate rights and interests of minors when they are infringed. To ensure the realization of their rights, the Civil Procedure Law of China lists minors and their guardians as co-defendants in the legal relationship of infringement, which is conducive to ensuring that the infringed minors can effectively receive compensation and increasing the channels for the infringed minors to obtain relief. In civil litigation, if a person without civil capacity or with limited civil capacity causes harm to others, the person without civil capacity or with limited civil capacity and their guardian shall be joint defendants. For specific provisions, please refer to Article 60 of the Civil Procedure Law of the People's Republic of China:

Article 60
A person without legal capacity shall have his guardian act as the legal representative to represent him in litigation.

The right to privacy refers to a personal right of citizens to enjoy a peaceful private life and personal information that is protected by law and not illegally disturbed, known, collected, utilized, or disclosed by others. The right to privacy grants the right holder the right to control their personal life, which includes the right to defend against others stealing personal privacy, decide whether to disclose privacy to others, and determine the scope of disclosure. The common types of privacy rights include personal freedom of life, intelligence confidentiality, personal communication confidentiality, and personal privacy utilization. Privacy rights are an important aspect of the personality rights of citizens.

The right to privacy has an important impact on maintaining personal dignity, maintaining personal peace, and enhancing personal security. It is of great significance in safeguarding the legitimate rights and interests of minors and safeguarding their physical and mental health (Liu & Huang, 2025). The right to privacy is not only a fundamental right of children but also a right protected by the Constitution of our country. The Civil Code of the People's Republic of China particularly emphasizes the protection of citizens' privacy rights.

Article 1033 stipulates
Natural persons enjoy the right to privacy. No organization or individual shall infringe upon the privacy rights of others by means of espionage, intrusion, disclosure, or disclosure. Privacy refers to the private space, activities, and information of natural persons who live in peace and do not want others to know.

China attaches great importance to the protection of the privacy of minors. In order to protect the privacy of minors, the Criminal Procedure Law of China stipulates that all cases involving minors shall not be heard in public, and for juvenile offenders, in order to ensure their normal return to society and ensure their physical and mental health, China targets juvenile offenders in the Criminal Procedure Law. A system for sealing criminal records has been established. Regarding the protection of the privacy of minors, *the Civil Procedure Law of the People's Republic of China* has made corresponding provisions, see Article 137 of this Law:

Article 137
The people's court shall hear civil cases in public, except for those involving state secrets, personal privacy, or as otherwise provided by law. Divorce cases and cases involving trade secrets, if the parties apply for a closed trial, may be closed for trial.

Divorce cases usually involve the issue of raising underage children. Therefore, in order to ensure the normal life and survival of minors, China's Civil Procedure Law has made special provisions for the trial of divorce cases, that is, divorce cases can be heard in private according to the application. Therefore, not conducting a public trial also maximizes the protection of the privacy of minors.

10.2.2 Trial Proceedings: Right to Testify and Competency Determination

A witness refers to a person who understands the facts of a case and is summoned by the people's court to testify. The statement made by a witness to the people's court regarding their understanding of the facts of the case is called witness testimony. Witnesses appearing in court to testify is both a right and an obligation. The rights of witnesses include: firstly, the right to security protection. The People's Procuratorate shall ensure the safety of witnesses and their close relatives, and shall hold them legally responsible for threatening, insulting, assaulting or retaliating against them; Secondly, the right to sufficient statement, where witnesses have objective and sufficient conditions to provide evidence, can absorb witness assistance in the investigation; Thirdly, verify the record rights, and witnesses can supplement or correct their records.

In addition, witnesses also have corresponding obligations: firstly, the obligation to testify. Anyone who knows the situation of the case has the obligation to testify in court; Secondly, the obligation to testify truthfully is that witnesses should objectively and impartially provide evidence, and shall not fabricate facts or falsely accuse or frame. Witnesses appearing in court to testify is an important part of litigation activities, and it is also an inevitable requirement of modern prosecution defense trial methods. It is a basic measure to ensure judicial fairness. He played a positive and important role in the timely trial of various cases by the people's courts, clarifying facts, distinguishing right from wrong, correctly applying the law, cracking down on crimes, punishing illegal activities, and protecting the legitimate rights and interests of the parties involved. Witnesses appearing in court to testify and objectively and fairly state the facts of the case is a glorious obligation of Chinese citizens, which is conducive to maintaining judicial fairness and improving judicial efficiency.

The current laws in our country have the following restrictions on witnesses: firstly, witnesses must be natural persons, therefore, legal and non-legal entities cannot be witnesses. The evidence they provide may become documentary evidence, unlicensed, or audio-visual materials, but must not be used as witness testimony; Secondly, people who cannot express their will correctly cannot be witnesses; Thirdly, the litigation agent, legal representative, and representative in the litigation cannot concurrently serve as witnesses in this case. Similarly, the judges, appraisers, investigators, and translators in this case cannot also serve as witnesses in this case. Except for the above-mentioned individuals who cannot testify, anyone who knows the facts of the case can serve as a witness, regardless of their gender, nationality, position, religion, belief, ethnicity, race, political status, educational level, experience, etc. It can be seen that there is no age requirement for witnesses in China, that is, both minors and children have the right and obligation to testify in court. Therefore, China's laws have made special provisions for minors to testify in court. Our country has made special provisions for minors to testify in court. Firstly, it clarifies the qualifications of witnesses to testify in court through legislation and establishes special provisions for minors to testify in court, such as not requiring the signing of a guarantee letter (Yu & Zhang, 2010). The specific regulations are as follows:

Article 119

Article 119 of the Interpretation of the Supreme People's Court on the Application of the Civil Procedure Law of the People's Republic of China: Before a witness appears in court to testify, the people's court shall inform them of their obligation to testify truthfully and the legal consequences of perjury, and order them to sign a guarantee letter, except for those without civil capacity and those with limited civil capacity. The provisions of this interpretation regarding the signing of the guarantee by the parties shall apply to the signing of the guarantee by the witness.

Provisions of the Supreme People's Court on Evidence in Civil Procedures:

Article 67
Article 67 of the Several Provisions of the Supreme People's Court on Evidence in Civil Litigation states that a person who cannot correctly express their intention cannot serve as a witness. Individuals without civil capacity or with limited civil capacity who are suitable for their age, intellectual status, or mental health status, as the facts to be proven, may serve as witnesses.

Article 71
Article 71 of the "Several Provisions of the Supreme People's Court on Evidence in Civil Litigation" states that the people's court shall require witnesses to sign a guarantee letter before giving testimony, and read out the content of the guarantee letter in court. Except for those without civil capacity and those with limited civil capacity as witnesses. If the witness has legitimate reasons to be unable to read the guarantee letter, the clerk shall read it on his behalf and provide an explanation. Witnesses who refuse to sign or read the guarantee shall not testify and shall bear the relevant costs on their own. The content of the witness guarantee shall be subject to the provisions of the party's guarantee.

Article 90
Article 90 of the Several Provisions of the Supreme People's Court on Evidence in Civil Litigation states that the following evidence cannot be used as the sole basis for determining the facts of a case: (1) statements of the parties; (2) Testimonies made by individuals without or with limited capacity for civil conduct that do not correspond to their age, intellectual or mental health status; (3) Testimonies presented by witnesses who have an interest in one party or their agent; (4) Audiovisual materials and electronic data with doubts; (5) Copies and reproductions that cannot be verified with the original or original documents.

10.2.3 Enforcement Stage: Preservation of Costs and Participation of Family Members

The United Nations Convention on the Rights of the Child stipulates that children have the right to life, survival, development, and participation. The right to survival includes the right to life, the right to health, and the right to access healthcare. Article 6 of *the United Nations Convention on the Rights of the Child* states: "Every child has an inherent right to life." The right to survival is the most fundamental right of children. Compared to other rights, it comes first. *The Civil Code of the People's Republic of China* establishes the system of mandatory inheritance as a necessary means to safeguard the right to survival of underage heirs. Prioritizing the preservation of necessary inheritance shares for minors in accordance with the law to safeguard their survival rights and interests. At the same time, elderly care and childcare are also traditional virtues of the Chinese nation and principles advocated and upheld by the entire legal system of our country.

As the legal status and capacity of minors are limited, therefore, special protection should be given to their rights and interests during the compulsory enforcement process. In order to ensure the livelihood of minors, the Civil Procedure Law stipulates that when enforcing the property of the debtor, the livelihood of minors should be maximally protected, and necessary living expenses should be reserved for minors raised by the debtor. This expense not only includes the basic living expenses of minors but also includes the entire stage of their education until adulthood. Please refer to Articles 169 and 254 of *the Civil Procedure Law of the People's Republic of China* for details:

Article 169
The people's court may, on the application of the parties, rule before enforcement in the following cases: (1) recover alimony, upbringing, upbringing, pension, medical expenses, etc.; (2) Claim labor remuneration; (3) Due to emergencies, it is necessary to execute in advance.

Article 254
If the person subject to execution fails to fulfill the obligations determined by the legal document in accordance with the execution notice, the people's court has the right to withhold or extract the income of the part of the obligation that the person subject to execution should fulfill. But the necessary living expenses of the executed person and their dependent family members should be retained. When the people's court detains or withdraws income, it shall make a ruling and issue a notice of assistance in execution. The unit where the debtor is located, banks, credit cooperatives, and other units with savings business must handle it.

The Civil Code of the People's Republic of China has made a series of provisions to protect the residential tranquility of citizens. As an important place for the survival and living of minors, family houses play a crucial role in their growth process. Compulsory measures such as forced eviction from a house may have irreversible effects on the psychological well-being of minors. Therefore, in order to protect the psychological health of minors, *the Civil Procedure Law of the People's Republic of China* stipulates that in the process of forced eviction from a house, adult family members should be present to protect the psychological well-being of minors. When implementing compulsory measures against minors, the executor fully considers their physical and mental development and interests, takes into account their sensitivity, and ensures their legitimate rights and interests. Please refer to Article 261 of this Law for details:

Article 261

Compulsory relocation of a house or forced withdrawal of land shall be announced by the dean, ordering the person subject to execution to perform within a specified period of time. If the person subject to enforcement fails to perform within the prescribed time limit, the enforcement officer shall enforce it. When enforced, if the person subject to enforcement is a citizen, the person subject to enforcement or their adult family members shall be notified to be present; If the person being executed is a legal person or other organization, their legal representative or main person in charge shall be notified to be present. Refusal to be present does not affect execution. If the person subject to execution is a citizen, their workplace or grassroots organization where the house or land is located shall send representatives to participate. The executor shall record the compulsory execution situation in a written record, which shall be signed or stamped by the person present. The property that has been forcibly removed from the house shall be transported by the people's court to the designated place and handed over to the person subject to enforcement. If the person being executed is a citizen, they can also be handed over to their adult family members. The losses caused by refusal to accept shall be borne by the person subject to execution.

10.3 Special Provisions on the Protection of the Rights and Interests of Minors

Although the protection of children's rights in procedural law in China is mainly stipulated in the Criminal Procedure Law of the People's Republic of China, the current Civil Procedure Law in China is gradually penetrating the protection of minors, mainly reflecting in divorce litigation and civil public interest litigation for minors. In divorce proceedings involving dependent minors, the rights of minors should be fully protected, and guardians should be selected based on the principle that is most beneficial to minors, which is completely consistent with the Civil Code of the People's Republic of China. Regarding civil public interest litigation, the relevant organizations stipulated in China's civil litigation regulations should include organizations that protect minors.

10.3.1 Civil Public Interest Litigation of Minors

Minors are the future of a country and the hope of a nation. Public interest litigation for the protection of minors, launched by the Political Research Office of the China Green Development Association on International Children's Day in 2021, refers to the public interest litigation related to the protection of minors. It refers to the lawsuit that relevant authorities and organizations may bring to the people's court to protect the interests of minors when the illegal or inaction of natural persons, legal persons, or other organizations poses risks and infringes on the physical and mental health and legitimate rights and interests of unspecified minors. Please refer to Article 55 of *the Civil Procedure Law of the People's Republic of China* for details:

> **Article 55**
> ***For acts that pollute the environment, infringe upon the legitimate rights and interests of numerous consumers, and harm public interests, the organs and relevant organizations prescribed by law may bring a lawsuit to the people's court.***

Organs and relevant organizations should include the main body of social organizations. "Social organizations for the protection of minors are at the forefront of serving minors, directly dealing with minors and their parents. They have a good understanding of the relevant situation, are easy to gain their trust, have strong professionalism, and have a good foundation for protecting and serving minors. Therefore, social organizations should be able to file public interest lawsuits for situations where the rights and interests of unspecified minors are violated."

Juvenile public interest litigation has its unique personal attributes, and attention should also be paid to distinguishing it from other types of public interest litigation in terms of protection methods. The protection of minors has a minor perspective. According to the relevant provisions of the Law on the Protection of Minors, we must adhere to the principle of being most beneficial to minors, and carry out relevant work in combination with the laws and characteristics of the physical and mental health development of minors. If there is a conflict or contradiction of interests, it is necessary to study and judge from the perspective of minors what is most beneficial to them, in order to make the most favorable decision for them.

Justice is the last line of defense to maintain social fairness and justice. When the rights subject is unable to remedy their rights through private means such as negotiation, they can also file a lawsuit with the court. The judicial protection of minors by courts in civil litigation is mainly reflected in the following aspects: (1) For minors from economically disadvantaged families who are unable to pay litigation fees, the court will delay, reduce or exempt them from paying litigation fees in accordance with the law, ensuring that they can participate in litigation normally and better protect their legitimate rights and interests; (2) For minors from economically disadvantaged families who do not have the money to hire lawyers, if they meet the conditions for applying for legal aid under the Legal Aid Law, not only can their legal representatives actively apply for legal aid from the legal aid center. The court will also provide assistance to minors in need of legal aid and provide legal aid to them in accordance with the law; (3) The court will designate specialized agencies or designated personnel to handle cases involving minors. Personnel handling cases involving minors should undergo specialized training and be familiar with the physical and mental characteristics of minors. There should be female staff members in specialized institutions or personnel; (4) If the defendant is unable to compensate the minor for all their losses after winning the judgment, the court will guide or assist the minor in applying for judicial assistance, and the state will provide appropriate economic assistance to help them overcome their living difficulties.

10.3.2 Special Protection in Divorce Litigation

Family is crucial in the growth process of minors, and parental divorce directly affects the vital interests of their children. Therefore, in the process of handling divorce cases, China pays special attention to the rights and interests of underage children and protects their physical and mental health. In divorce litigation, it usually involves not only the division of property and the transformation of identity between spouses, but also the issue of raising underage children. Therefore, in order to protect underage children, the current Civil Code and Civil Procedure Law of the People's Republic of China have made special provisions.

The Civil Code of the People's Republic of China has made a series of provisions on the custody of underage children after divorce, including the ownership of custody rights for underage children, life security and relief for underage children after divorce, and granting visitation rights to the party who does not directly care for underage children in order to ensure their healthy growth as much as possible.

In the field of civil litigation, the specific circumstances and punishment measures of guardians infringing on the interests of underage children truly maximize the interests of underage children, supplemented by procedural safeguards. China has many years of experience in the reform of family litigation. In 2018, the Supreme People's Court issued the "Opinions on Further Deepening the Reform of Family Trial Methods and Working Mechanisms (Trial)" (hereinafter referred to as the "Opinions on Family Reform") based on summarizing the experience of family litigation reform in various regions. In terms of procedure, the Civil Procedure Law of our country deals with divorce cases by not only striving for the most suitable upbringing conditions and growth environment for underage children, but also preventing secondary harm caused by the exercise of visitation rights, in order to maximize the interests of minors.

In practice, in the specific litigation process, the judicial organs in China have also made their own efforts to protect the interests of minors. Their efforts indicate the biased protection of minors in divorce proceedings in civil litigation. Firstly, the judicial organs are cautious when judging divorce cases. When judging divorce cases, the judicial organs usually carefully examine the main reasons behind the divorce cases and adopt targeted methods to resolve conflicts based on the main reasons of the divorce. Secondly, in the process of determining or changing custody relationships, paying custody fees, and exercising visitation rights, more emphasis is placed on the perspective of minors, respecting the principles that are most beneficial to minors, and implementing them in judgments (Xiang & Guo, 2023). Thirdly, in the process of handling divorce cases, we should actively change our mindset and closely connect with the relevant laws formulated in China to protect minors, such as *the Anti Domestic Violence Law*, *the Law on the Protection of Minors*, *the Law on the Promotion of Family Education*, etc., so that the new concepts in these laws can also be involved in the trial of divorce cases, thus maximizing the protection of the interests of minors.

Every child's growth involves their family. The effective fulfillment of guardianship responsibilities by parents, as well as their care and protection for their children, are the foundation for minors to realize various rights, protect their children from harm, and prevent them from pursuing illegal and criminal paths. Therefore, regardless of the relationship between parents and whether they are divorced or not, resolving conflicts in a timely manner from the judicial system, appropriately isolating the relationship between parental emotional conflicts and child-rearing and education, minimizing the negative impact of parental emotional conflicts on children, and effectively implementing the most beneficial principles for minors in parental emotional conflicts.

10.4 Summary

The civil rights and interests of minors are closely linked to their personal lives. Strengthening the judicial protection of the civil rights and interests of minors is of great significance for safeguarding their rights. The concepts of maximizing children's interests, prioritizing the protection of minors, listening to children's opinions, and being child-friendly have been widely and deeply disseminated and recognized. The practical exploration of the public interest litigation system for the protection of minors, family education guidance, and guardianship and supervision system for supervising and supporting prosecution has greatly improved the judicial protection mechanism for the civil rights and interests of minors.

In the field of civil litigation, the legal provisions commonly used for the judicial protection of minors are mainly in the tort liability section of the Civil Code. Different remedies have been provided for the personal injury suffered by individuals without or with limited capacity for civil conduct in educational institutions, which provides good guidance for China's civil litigation procedures. In the process of handling cases, judges apply the relevant provisions of the Civil Code to strive for the maximization of the interests of minors.

Minors are the future of the country and the hope of the nation, so they should be protected with special and limited protection. At the same time, minors should also raise their self-awareness, remind parents, schools, and society to attach importance to legal education for minors and work together to create a clear and safe environment for minors, so that every child can grow up healthy under the sunshine of happiness and tranquility.

References

Chen, L. (2008). On the construction of special civil procedure for minors in China. *Juvenile Delinquency Issues Research, 1*, 49–53+48.

Liang, C. (2019). Research on the state guardianship system for minors from the perspective of public law. *Theory Monthly, 3*, 102–109.

Liu, H., & Huang, Z. (2025). The substantive allocation and procedural realization of civil liability for minors causing harm. *Journal of Soochow University (Law Edition), 3*, 76–87.

Xiang, Y., & Guo, Y. (2023). On the realization of the principle of the best interests of the minor in China's guardianship system. *Journal of Henan University (Social Science Edition), 5*, 54–58+154.

Xiao, S. (2019). The principle of the best interests of the child: Also on its enlightenment for China's juvenile law. *Study and Practice, 9*, 70–80.

Yu, L., & Zhang, C. (2010). The construction of an off-court dialogue mechanism between judges and age-appropriate parties in civil juvenile trials. *Academic Journal of Zhongzhou, 4*, 85–88.

Zhu, H. (2025). Liability for torts committed by minors. *Finance and Law Science, 1*, 71–88.

Chapter 11
From Substantive Rights to Procedural Guarantees: Protecting Children in China's Criminal Justice System

11.1 Introduction

In the legal system for the protection of children's rights and interests, the protection of children's rights and interests consists of substantive and procedural legal norms. Substantive laws specify the substantive rights of children, while procedural laws provide the rules, methods, and order for safeguarding children's substantive rights. The Criminal Procedure Law of the People's Republic of China plays an extremely important role in safeguarding the substantive rights of children to protection from abuse and the procedural aspects of criminal cases involving children (Jiang, 2021).

The Criminal Procedure Law of the People's Republic of China is a procedural law enacted by the State to regulate the conduct of criminal proceedings by the investigative, prosecutorial and judicial organs, and the participation of the parties and other litigants in the criminal proceedings, to ensure that the criminal law is correctly enforced, that human rights are respected and safeguarded while crimes are being punished, and that the unity of substantive and procedural justice is realized. In the process of safeguarding the rights and interests of children, the Public Security Bureau, the people's procuratorates and the people's courts, in keeping with the principle of maximizing the interests of the child, strictly guard the line of defense of safeguarding the rights of the child. The Public Security Bureau is responsible for investigating, detaining, arresting and pre-testing criminal cases; the people's procuratorates are primarily responsible for inspecting and authorizing arrests, as well as investigating and ultimately deciding whether or not to bring public prosecutions in cases that come directly to their attention; and the people's courts are responsible for adjudicating and passing judgment on criminal cases. The public security organs, the people's procuratorates and the people's courts all uphold the policy of educating, reforming and rescuing children who have committed crimes, and adhere to the principle of using education as the primary means of punishment, supplemented by criminal punishment. The three organs implement the

© The Author(s), under exclusive license to Springer Nature Singapore Pte Ltd. 2026
H. Li, P. Liang, *The Legal System for the Protection of Children's Rights in China*, Resilient and Friendly Living Environments,
https://doi.org/10.1007/978-981-95-9925-7_11

principle that criminal suspects and defendants have the right to a defense and to voluntarily plead guilty and accept punishment, thereby safeguarding the exercise by children of their independent procedural rights and allowing them to receive appropriate legal assistance in the course of criminal proceedings, while requiring investigators, procurators and judges undertaking criminal cases involving children to be familiar with the characteristics of children's physical and mental development. In order to further safeguard the rights and interests of children in criminal cases (Wang, 2013), *the Criminal Procedure Law of the People's Republic of China* provides for a special chapter on the litigation of criminal cases involving children.

This chapter will interpret the specific provisions of *the Criminal Procedure Law of the People's Republic of China* on special procedures for the prosecution of criminal cases involving children in the context of *the United Nations Convention on the Rights of the Child.* The main content includes the specific division of labor and cooperation between the public security organs as investigative organs, the people's procuratorates as prosecutorial organs, and the people's courts as adjudicative organs in safeguarding the rights and interests of children in criminal proceedings, thereby reflecting the principle of maximizing the interests of the child, and safeguarding the procedural rights and human dignity of children in the course of criminal proceedings.

11.2 Safeguards for the Protection of Children in Criminal Litigation

This section covers the protection of the rights and interests of children by the public security organs, the people's procuratorates, and the people's courts, and deals with the principles that should be upheld by the public security organs in the process of investigating children's criminal cases; the people's procuratorates, as the organs of public prosecution, review and approve the arrest and review and prosecution of children's suspected crimes, and, as the organs of legal supervision, supervise the correct operation of the law and safeguard the rights and interests of children; and the people's courts, as the organs of adjudication, safeguard the rights and interests of the participants in criminal proceedings in all aspects. The People's Courts, as adjudicating organs, are responsible for adjudicating children's criminal cases in accordance with the law, thereby safeguarding the rights and interests of litigants in all aspects of criminal proceedings.

11.2.1 Public Security Organs

The public security organs are an important part of the people's government and are administrative organs of the State; they are also tasked with the investigation of criminal cases, investigating criminal cases in accordance with the law and exercising the judicial power of the State, with both administrative and judicial attributes. The public security authorities, as the investigating authorities in criminal proceedings, should ensure the personal and individual rights of any criminal suspects during this period. Article 37 of the United Nations Convention on the Rights of the Child specifies the obligation of States parties: "No child shall be subjected to torture or to other cruel, inhuman or degrading treatment or punishment"; at the same time, children cannot be deprived of their liberty unlawfully or arbitrarily. Therefor the public security organs shall not be liable for any arrest, detention, or imprisonment of a child unless it is in accordance with the relevant provisions of the law. The arrest, detention, or imprisonment of children by the public security authorities should be in accordance with the relevant provisions of the law and should be used only as a measure of last resort and for the shortest possible period of time. In this regard, China has clearly stipulated that the public security organs may not, on their own initiative, decide to arrest criminal suspects, but rather that the people's procuratorates and the people's courts should decide to do so, and that any detention or imprisonment should be in accordance with the provisions of the law, failing which the public security organs should be held accountable. In addition, articles 278 and 279 of *the Criminal Procedure Law of the People's Republic of China* provide for the public security organs as follows:

Article 278
Where a minor criminal suspect or defendant has not appointed a defender, the people's court, people's procuratorate or public security organ shall notify the legal aid institution to assign a lawyer to provide for his or her defense.

This requires that child criminal suspects and defendants should be provided with appropriate legal assistance throughout the entire process of criminal proceedings, and that if they are subjectively unwilling or materially unable to appoint a defender, the public security organs, the people's procuratorates and the people's courts should notify legal aid agencies to assign lawyers to defend the rights and interests of the child. This is an implementation of the principle in *the Criminal Procedure Law of the People's Republic of China* that criminal suspects and defendants have the right to a defense, and also reflects the right of children who may be deprived of their liberty to receive legal assistance, as set forth in article 37 of *the United Nations Convention on the Rights of the Child.*

Article 279
When handling criminal cases involving minors, the public security organs, people's procuratorates, and people's courts may, depending on the circumstances, investigate the upbringing, causes of the crime, guardianship, and education of minor criminal suspects and defendants.

This article requires the public security organs to investigate, in the course of handling cases, the upbringing, reasons for committing the crime and the guardianship and education of child crime suspects and defendants, in order to understand the reasons for children's violation of the criminal law, and thus to take precautions for the prevention of children's crimes.

To sum up, the public security organs, as investigating organs for criminal cases, always implement the principle of maximizing the interests of the child in the investigation of criminal cases in which children may be suspected of committing crimes. In the course of the investigation, they safeguard the child's rights to personal integrity and physical integrity and ensure that they have the right to a defense in accordance with the law. In addition, the public security organs will investigate the reasons for the child's crime and related matters, thereby providing a factual basis for prosecution and adjudication by the people's procuratorates and the people's courts.

11.2.2 The People's Procuratorate

The People's Procuratorate plays a dual role in criminal cases involving children: as a prosecuting organ and as a legal supervisory organ. When the People's Procuratorate acts as a prosecuting authority, it undertakes the prosecutorial function of examining and approving the arrest of child criminal suspects and whether to prosecute child criminal suspects. When the people's procuratorates act as legal supervisory organs, they also supervise the filing and investigation activities of the public security organs, the trial activities of the people's courts, and the execution of criminal cases. The most important of these functions is the examination and approval of arrests and prosecution of suspected child offenders, with the procuratorates playing a crucial role in determining whether or not cases involving child offenders will proceed to trial in the people's courts. Thus, in handling cases involving criminal offenses committed by children, the people's procuratorates, in accordance with the law, follow the policy of "education, probation and salvation" and the principle of "education as the mainstay, punishment as a supplement", and strictly limit the criteria for reviewing and approving the arrests of children involved in criminal offenses, The principles of "fewer arrests, more cautious arrests" and the protection of children's privacy are all part of the defense of children's procedural rights, so as to safeguard the rights of children in criminal proceedings.

Firstly, the People's Procuratorates, in accordance with the law, uphold the policy of "education, probation and salvation" and the principle of "education as the mainstay and punishment as a supplement", and guarantee the procedural rights of children suspected of having committed a criminal offense in the course of reviewing their arrests and prosecutions. In fulfilling their duties, the people's procuratorates have always insisted on priority protection, special protection, and two-way protection, with the main purpose of helping to educate children and preventing them from reoffending. In this process, they work with other social forces to assist and educate children suspected of committing criminal offenses. When handling cases in which children are suspected of committing crimes, the people's procuratorates will designate procurators who have an understanding of the physical and mental characteristics of children to handle children's criminal cases; in the process of handling cases, if a child and an adult commit a joint crime, in general, in order to safeguard the child's right to privacy, the right to equal participation in litigation, and other rights, the child and the adult are handled in separate cases and prosecuted separately; if it is inappropriate to handle the child separately, special protection measures such as privacy protection and expedited handling should be taken for the child. Special protection measures, such as privacy protection and expedited processing, shall be taken for children. At the same time, after accepting a case, the people's procuratorate shall fulfill its obligation to inform accordingly, i.e., it shall find out from the child who is the suspect of the crime and his/her legal representative the circumstances under which he/she has appointed a defender, and inform him/her of his/her right to appoint a defender. If a defender has not been appointed, the people's procuratorate must notify the legal aid agency in writing, which will assign a lawyer to provide a defense for the child suspected of committing a criminal offense. If it is found that a public security organ has failed to notify a legal aid organization to assign a lawyer to provide a defense for the child, the people's procuratorate, as the legal supervisory organ, shall submit a written or verbal corrective opinion. In the course of discharging its duties, it may, depending on the circumstances, conduct an investigation into the upbringing, causes of crime, guardianship, and education of such children, and produce a social investigation report to be used as a reference for handling cases and education. When carrying out social investigations, people's procuratorates may commission relevant organizations and institutions to do so. However, in conducting social investigations, the privacy of the child shall be respected and protected, and information concerning the child's involvement in the case shall not be divulged to uninformed persons. In addition, if the public security organs have already made a corresponding social investigation report and referred it to the people's procuratorate, it shall be reviewed. If necessary, additional investigations may be conducted. The social investigation report produced by the people's procuratorate shall be transferred to the people's court with the case. In addition, in handling cases of crimes against minors, the people's procuratorates shall adopt methods appropriate to the physical and psychological characteristics of the minor victims, so as to fully protect the legitimate rights and interests of the minor victims.

The People's Procuratorates are fulfilling, in accordance with the law, the guideline on strict restrictions on the review and arrest of children involved in criminal offenses, and are safeguarding the procedural rights of children under review and arrest in accordance with the law. The strict limitation on the review and arrest of children involved in criminal offenses is consistent with the purpose of the United Nations Convention on the Rights of the Child, which requires that restrictions on the liberty of children be in strict conformity with the provisions of the law, as set forth in article 280 of *the Criminal Procedure Law of the People's Republic of China:*

Article 280

The application of arrest measures to juvenile criminal suspects and defendants shall be strictly limited. The people's procuratorates review and approve arrests and the people's courts deciding on arrests shall interrogate the minor criminal suspects and defendants and hear the opinions of defense counsel.

Minors and adults who are detained, arrested, and sentenced shall be detained, managed, and educated separately.

As the organs authorized to review arrests, the People's Procuratorates, because of the characteristics of children's development and China's relevant provisions on the criminalization of crimes committed by children, have adopted the principle of arresting children sparingly and cautiously. The procedure for examining whether or not a child needs to be arrested as a compulsory measure thus imposes strict requirements, namely, that the child must be questioned in order to find out clearly what crimes the child is involved in, i.e., the subjective malignancy of the child's suspected crimes, the nature of the acts, the circumstances, the existence of conditions for guardianship and social assistance, and the confession of guilt and acceptance of the penalty, and so forth, and to comprehensively assess the child's social dangerousness. At the same time, the child's defense counsel is heard on whether or not to arrest him or her, and if the conditions for not arresting him or her are met, a decision is made accordingly. If a child who has reached the age of 14 but is not yet 18 is suspected of a less serious crime and is not suspected of any other major crimes, and shows remorse for his or her crimes, and if the child's family, school, or community, residents' committee or villagers' committee in which he or she resides has the conditions for guardianship and assistance in teaching him or her, a decision may be made not to authorize an arrest or not to arrest him or her. If the child's crime is relatively minor, the child has effective custody conditions or social education measures, and there is no social danger or the social danger is relatively minor, the arrest of the minor criminal suspect shall not be approved. In addition, if the child has the first crime, negligent crime; crime preparation, suspension or attempt; over-defense, over-avoidance; surrender or meritorious performance; after the crime plead guilty to the crime or actively return the stolen goods, try to reduce and compensate for the losses, get the understanding of the victim; in the joint crime is not the main offender or the first member of the criminal group; belongs to the 14 years of age is less than 16 years of age of the child and so on one of the circumstances, even if the people's procuratorate may not authorize the arrest of a person who, even though the crime is relatively serious, has little subjective malice, shows remorse for his or her crime, and has the conditions for effective guardianship or social assistance, indicating that failure to arrest him or her will not create a social danger. When reviewing the arrest of a child, emphasis should be placed on whether he or she has reached the age of 14, 16, or 18, in accordance with the age of criminal responsibility, and if it is difficult to judge the actual age of the child, which ultimately affects the determination of the child's criminal responsibility, the arrest should not be authorized (Cheng, 2023).

When interrogating a child, the written opinion of the defender shall be attached to the file, and if the defender's opinion is that the child is not guilty, is guilty of a minor offense, or is mitigated or exempted from criminal responsibility, should not be detained, or that there is a violation of the law in the investigative activities, the prosecutor shall review this and set out the defender's opinion in the relevant working papers, and state whether or not the opinion is to be adopted. When a child, as a minor, is interrogated, the child's legal representative shall be notified of the child's presence, and the legal representative's procedural rights and obligations under the law shall be explained. While the legal representative present may exercise the child's criminal procedure rights on his or her behalf, he or she may do so in a manner that does not jeopardize the legitimate rights and interests of the child. Where it is not possible to notify, or where the legal representative is unable to attend, or where the legal representative is an accomplice, the people's procuratorate may also notify the presence of other adult relatives of the minor criminal suspect, the school, the unit or the representative of the villagers' committee, the residents' committee or the minors' protection organization of the place where the minor resides, and shall put the relevant information on record. Where a minor criminal suspect expressly refuses the presence of a suitable adult other than his or her legal representative, and there are valid reasons for doing so, the people's procuratorate may grant permission, but shall notify other suitable adults of his or her presence after consulting his or her opinion. Where a legal representative or other person present at the hearing considers that the procuratorate has violated the lawful rights and interests of the minor criminal suspect in the course of the interrogation, the people's procuratorate shall put the opinion on record. Reasonable comments shall be accepted and corrected. The transcript of the interrogation shall be read by or to the legal representative or other person present, who shall sign or stamp the transcript and affix his or her fingerprints. The questioning of minor victims and witnesses shall be the same as in the above-mentioned cases, and the questioning shall be conducted on a one-time basis, avoiding repeated questioning. When questioning a child suspect, his or her human dignity should be protected, i.e., the use of restraints is generally not permitted, and if there is a real danger to the person that they must be used, their use should be discontinued as soon as the real danger has been eliminated. Article 37 of *the United Nations Convention on the Rights of the Child* clearly states that "All children deprived of their liberty shall be treated with humanity and with respect for the inherent dignity of the human person and in a manner which takes into account the needs of persons of their age." In this regard, China's criminal procedure regulations stipulate that the interrogation of children who have not been deprived of their personal liberty should also respect their inherent human dignity, taking into account their age and psychological factors, and that, in the case of the interrogation of female juvenile criminal suspects, and in the light of the characteristics of female minors, the People's Procuratorates should assign female procurators to take part in the interrogation.

Furthermore, the People's Procuratorates strictly abide by the principle of "prosecute sparingly and prudently", and safeguard the rights of children in the process of possible prosecution in accordance with the law by applying the system of conditional non-prosecution in accordance with the law. When the prosecutorial authorities believe that a child who should be held criminally liable may not be immediately held criminally liable, they set a certain trial period. If, during the probationary period, the child concerned actively fulfills the relevant obligations and is able to show that he or she has shown remorse for his or her crimes, the prosecutorial authorities ultimately decide not to prosecute him or her in accordance with the law. The conditions for this are set out in Article 282 of *the Criminal Procedure Law of the People's Republic of China*:

> **Article 282**
> ***Where a minor is suspected of having committed a crime as set forth in chapters IV, V, and VI of the Criminal Law sub-chapters, and may be sentenced to less than one year's fixed-term imprisonment, and meets the conditions for prosecution, but shows remorse for the crime, the people's procuratorate may make a decision on conditional non-prosecution. Before making a decision on conditional non-prosecution, the people's procuratorate shall hear the views of the public security organs and the victim.***
>
> ***Where the public security organ requests a reconsideration of the decision on conditional non-prosecution, requests a review or the victim complains, the provisions of articles 179 and 180 of this Law shall apply.***
>
> ***Where a minor criminal suspect and his or her legal representative object to the decision of a people's procuratorate not to prosecute conditionally, the people's procuratorate shall make a decision to prosecute.***

From the above provisions, it can be concluded that conditional non-prosecution shall be applied under the following circumstances: the subject of application is a child who has reached the age of 12 but is not yet 18 years old; the crimes involved are limited to three categories, namely, crimes against personal rights, democratic rights, crimes against property, and crimes against the social order; the possible penalties involved are less than one year's fixed-term imprisonment; the procedural requirements for prosecution have been met; and the child's subjective view is that the child is remorseful of his or her crimes but that reconciliation with the injured party has not been required. There is no requirement to reach a settlement with the victimized party. Before making a decision on conditional non-prosecution, the people's procuratorate shall hear the views of the public security organs, the victim, the child, his or her legal representative, and his or her defender, and at the same time shall make a transcript of that decision and attach it to the file. After a decision on conditional non-prosecution has been made, the people's procuratorate shall promptly release the child from custody. If, in response to the decision not to prosecute with conditions, the child and his or her legal representative object to the decision not to prosecute with conditions, the people's procuratorate shall bring a public prosecution. If the child and his or her legal representative raise objections to the child's innocence, and the people's procuratorate examines and finds the reasons to be valid, it shall directly make a decision not to prosecute on the basis of the law, rather than attaching conditions for non-prosecution. If the child and his or her legal representative object only to the conditions attached and the period of probation, the people's procuratorate may, in accordance with the law, adopt a reasonable portion of the opinion and adjust the content, manner and time of the investigation; if the opinion is not conducive to the child's education, it shall not be adopted and the law shall be interpreted and reasoned. This is the implementation of the principle of maximizing the interests of the child in the Convention on the Rights of the Child. In addition, if the child and his or her legal representative withdraw their objection to the decision not to prosecute conditionally before the people's procuratorate makes its decision to prosecute, a letter of decision not to prosecute conditionally will be prepared and the decision announced to the child and his or her legal representative in person, informing them of the duration of the ordeal and of the regulations to be observed during the ordeal and of their legal liability for violating the regulations, and a record of the proceedings is prepared and attached to the file. If the public security organs or the victim requests a reconsideration, review, or appeal of the decision, it shall be examined by the department of the People's Procuratorate responsible for the prosecution of minors.

The test period for making a decision on conditional non-prosecution shall be 6 months or more than 1 year, calculated from the date on which the people's procuratorate makes a decision on conditional non-prosecution. The social obligations to be fulfilled by the child during the testing period are specified in Article 283 of *The Criminal Procedure Law of the People's Republic of China*:

Article 283

During the test period for conditional non-prosecution, the people's procuratorate shall supervise and investigate the minor criminal suspects who are subject to conditional non-prosecution. The guardian of a minor criminal suspect shall strengthen the discipline of the minor criminal suspect and cooperate with the people's procuratorate in the supervision and investigation work.

The test period for conditional non-prosecution is six months to less than one year, calculated from the date on which the people's procuratorate makes the decision to withhold conditional prosecution.

Minor criminal suspects who have been conditionally not prosecuted shall comply with the following provisions:

(1) Comply with laws and regulations and submit to supervision;
(2) Report their activities in accordance with the regulations of the inspection authority;
(3) To leave the city or county in which they reside or to move to another place, they shall report to the inspection organ for approval;
(4) Undergo correctional treatment and education as required by the inspection authority.

That means, during the probationary period, the people's procuratorate may, in conjunction with the child's guardian, his or her school, unit, the village committee or residents' committee of his or her place of residence, or a child protection organization, carry out regular visits to the child, educate him or her, or provide him or her with follow-up assistance and education. They also monitor the child's compliance with the above provisions during this period. In addition, the People's Procuratorate may require the child subject to conditional non-prosecution to introduce the completion of addiction treatment, psychological counseling, or other appropriate countermeasures to the community or public welfare team to provide public welfare labor, not to enter a specific place, to meet or correspond with specific persons, to engage in specific activities, to compensate for losses, apologize to the victim, etc., and to accept relevant education and other corrective treatment and education, and require the child to comply with other prohibitions to protect the safety of the victim and prevent recidivism. If the child complies with the corresponding obligations during the trial period, the People's Procuratorate will directly issue a decision not to prosecute upon expiration of the trial period; only if a new crime is committed or a serious violation of the regulations occurs during the trial period will the People's Procuratorate revoke the decision of conditional non-prosecution and prosecute the child concerned in accordance with the law. The specific provisions are reflected in Article 284 of The Criminal Procedure Law of the People's Republic of China:

Article 284
Where a minor criminal suspect who has been subject to conditional non-prosecution has committed one of the following circumstances during the trial period, the people's procuratorate shall revoke the decision on conditional non-prosecution and institute public prosecution:

(1) He commits a new crime or discovers that there are other crimes to be prosecuted before the decision on conditional non-prosecution is made;
(2) Violation of the provisions on public security management or the supervision and management provisions of the inspection authorities concerning conditional non-prosecution, where the circumstances are serious.
(3) Where a minor criminal suspect subject to conditional non-prosecution does not have any of the above circumstances during the test period and the test period expires, the people's procuratorate shall make a decision not to prosecute.

Upon expiration of the period of conditional examination of the child, without committing a new crime or a serious violation of the law, the prosecutor will make an opinion on the examination of the conditional non-prosecution in accordance with the law (Wang, 2019), and ultimately submit it to the Prosecutor General for a decision.

In the course of the People's Procuratorates' review of arrests and prosecutions, a system of leniency in pleading guilty and accepting punishment is implemented throughout the process for children. That is to say, if, during this period, the child voluntarily and truthfully confesses to his or her crime, does not dispute the facts of the alleged crime, or admits to the punishment, the punishment written statement of guilty plea and acceptance of punishment. For detailed provisions, see be lenient in accordance with the law, and the child will sign Article 174 of *the Criminal Procedure Law of the People's Republic of China*:

Article 174
Where a criminal suspect voluntarily pleads guilty to a crime and agrees to the sentencing recommendation and the application of the procedure, he or she shall sign a written statement of guilty plea and acceptance of punishment in the presence of a defender or duty lawyer.

Where a criminal suspect pleads guilty and accepts punishment, but the legal representative or defender of a minor criminal suspect disagrees with the minor's plea of guilt and acceptance of punishment, he or she is not required to sign a written statement of guilt and acceptance of punishment.

When a child pleads guilty and accepts punishment, the people's procuratorate is obliged to inform the child and his or her legal representative of his or her procedural rights, explain the legal consequences of the plea and accept punishment, and listen to and record the views of the child, his or her legal representative, his or her defender, and the victim and his or her litigation representative. The child's signing of a written statement of guilty plea and acceptance of punishment shall be done in the presence of the child's legal representative or defender; if the legal representative or defender disagrees with the child's guilty plea and acceptance of punishment, the child's decision not to sign the written statement shall not affect the possibility of being dealt with leniently. In addition, if a child's legal representative is unable to be present when the child signs a written plea of guilty or punishment, China has established a system of suitable adults, who may exercise the right to be present, the right to object, and the right to know on behalf of the child's legal representative. The people's procuratorate shall record the reasons why the child's legal representative was unable to be present, the reasons for listening to the views of a suitable adult, and the fact that the child's legal representative or defender disagreed with the child's plea of guilty and punishment, resulting in the child's failure to sign the plea of guilty and acceptance of penalty, and then transfer the material, together with the materials in the case file, to the people's court or attach the file to a file for sealing. The content of the plea bargain includes the child's truthful confession of the crime committed, agreement to the sentencing opinion and the application of the procedure, etc., and is finally signed by the child, his/her advocate and the duty lawyer, so as to provide appropriate procedural safeguards, thereby safeguarding the child's rights and interests in the proceedings.

In addition, when deciding to release a child from custody on bail pending trial, the people's procuratorate may not use both surety and bond guarantees, and may order the provision of one or two sureties instead of a bond guarantee, on the basis of the child's correctional assistance. If it is found that the child has shown remorse for his or her crime (Liu, 2023), and that not detaining him or her will not lead to social danger, a recommendation may be made to the authorities in charge of the case to release him or her or to change the coercive measures. This is also a reflection in The Criminal Procedure Law of the People's Republic of China of the safeguards for children's freedom contained in *the United Nations Convention on the Rights of the Child.*

Finally, the People's Procuratorates safeguard the privacy of children in accordance with the law. When handling criminal cases against children, the people's procuratorates, for the purpose of protecting the privacy of the child and allowing the child to grow up healthily, shall keep the information about the child involved in the case confidential, and shall not disclose or disseminate the child's name, residence, photographs, images or other personal information that may be deduced about the child. If a child is under 18 years of age at the time of committing a crime and is ultimately sentenced by a court to less than 5 years' imprisonment, the people's procuratorate will, in accordance with the law, seal his or her criminal record upon receipt of the people's court's effective judgement or ruling. If the effective judgment or ruling is issued by the people's court of second instance, the people's procuratorate at the same level of the people's court of second instance shall, at the same time, notify the people's procuratorate at the lower level of the sealing of the relevant criminal records in the same manner. The People's Procuratorate eventually binds up and encrypts children's criminal records, case files and other relevant information sealed in accordance with the law, and does not disclose them; it has also established a special database of children's criminal records, and implements a strict system of safekeeping, so that, except for the needs of the judicial organs for the purpose of handling cases, or for inquiries made by the relevant units in accordance with State regulations (Wang, 2025), it does not provide any unit or individual with the sealed criminal records, and does not provide proof that the child has a criminal record either. Proof that a child has a criminal record is not provided. Where the judicial authorities or relevant organizations need to inquire about criminal records, they must strictly comply with the relevant procedural requirements. Once a child's criminal record has been sealed, it may not be unsealed unless a new crime has been committed and a decision has been made to carry out an imprisonment sentence of more than 5 years after the new crime and the crime for which the record was sealed have been punished together. Alternatively, it can be unsealed if an omission has been discovered, leading to a decision to carry out an imprisonment sentence of more than 5 years after the punishment for the crime for which the record was sealed has been punished together. The fundamental reason is that children have unlimited possibilities for growth, and even if they have a criminal record, they should have the appropriate human dignity, be free from discrimination, and have the opportunity to rehabilitate themselves. In other words, human rights and legal safeguards should be fully respected, and the privacy of the child should be protected at all stages of the proceedings. In addition, if a people's procuratorate decides not to prosecute a child, it should also seal the relevant records, and not make them available to any organization or individual, except for inquiries made by the judicial authorities in accordance with legal procedures for the purpose of handling the case. If a child whose criminal record has been sealed applies for a certificate of no criminal record on his or her own behalf or on behalf of his or her legal representative, the people's procuratorate shall issue it, and if it is necessary to coordinate with the public security organs or people's courts in order to issue a certificate of no criminal record on his or her behalf, the people's procuratorate will assist in that endeavor in accordance with the law.

In summary, in handling cases involving children in criminal cases, the People's Procuratorates follow the principles of "fewer arrests and more prudent arrests" in the criminal proceedings of examining arrests and prosecuting cases involving children, in accordance with the physical and psychological characteristics of the children, and in interrogating, examining arrests, examining and prosecuting the children involved in the case, as well as sealing up the relevant information on the case that is ultimately developed, The principles of "fewer arrests, more cautious arrests" and "fewer prosecutions, more cautious prosecutions" are followed in criminal proceedings, and the principle of maximizing the interests of the child is always implemented. On the basis of the humanitarian principle and the principle of helping the child, the bond that the child may be involved in is replaced by a guarantor who can better help the child to correct his or her situation. Thus, in the course of the work of the prosecutorial authorities, the rights and interests of children involved in criminal proceedings are more comprehensively safeguarded.

11.2.3 The People's Court

The people's courts, as the adjudicative organs for cases, exercise their adjudicative power independently in accordance with the law and are not subject to interference by administrative organs, social organizations or individuals. When hearing criminal cases involving children, the safeguarding of the rights and interests of children is reflected in the entire process of hearing criminal cases, including the safeguarding of the rights and interests of children before, during, and after the hearing of criminal cases involving children.

First of all, the people's courts safeguard the rights and interests of children in the following two areas before hearing cases involving children in criminal matters:

On the one hand, the people's courts, as organs with the authority to make decisions on the arrest of accused persons, adopt the principle of "arresting fewer and arresting with care" in relation to the arrest of children who have been sentenced to imprisonment, i.e., strictly limiting the application of arrest measures to children, in accordance with the law and in strict accordance with the conditions for the arrest of children sentenced to imprisonment, and, in the event that a decision is finally made on the arrest of a child who has been sentenced to imprisonment, interrogating the child in question in accordance with the law and listening to the views of the child's counsel. In the event that an arrested child has not completed the 9 years of compulsory education, the people's courts and education administrative departments work together to formulate policies or take measures conducive to the education of the child concerned, so as to ensure that the child concerned receives compulsory education. In addition, if the compulsory measure of release on bail pending trial is applied to a child who has no fixed abode and is unable to provide a guarantor, the people's court, in order to safeguard the child's right to survival and development, designates a suitable adult as a guarantor in accordance with the provisions of the law, and, if necessary, arranges for the child to be placed on bail pending trial to be observed and protected by the community.

On the other hand, with regard to the choice of trial procedures, children's criminal cases are not subject to the speedy trial procedure, and the consent of the child and his/her legal representative should be obtained for the application of the summary procedure. That is to say, when the people's courts hear cases involving children in criminal matters, they fully safeguard the procedural rights and interests of children in criminal proceedings and do not resort to the speedy dictation procedure even if the conditions for its application are met. Detailed provisions can be found in Article 223 of *the Criminal Procedure Law of the People's Republic of China*:

Article 223
The speedy trial procedure shall not be applied in any of the following cases:
(2) If the defendant is a minor.

The people's courts safeguard the rights and interests of children in the trial of criminal cases involving children in the following four areas: the establishment of a system of suitable adults, the establishment of specialized institutions or persons responsible for conducting trials, the principle of in camera trials, and the safeguarding of other procedural rights of children in accordance with the law.

Establishment of the Suitable Adult System Since children, as minors, are unable to understand some of their own procedural rights and interests, the system of suitable adults is set up by notifying the child's legal representative or other suitable adults when the child is being questioned and tried in accordance with the law (Yin, 2021). Detailed provisions are found in Article 281 of *the Criminal Procedure Law of the People's Republic of China:*

Article 281
In criminal cases involving minors, the legal representative of the minor criminal suspect or defendant shall be notified of his or her presence during the interrogation and trial. If it is impossible to do so, or if the legal representative is unable to be present, or if the legal representative is an accomplice, other adult relatives of the minor criminal suspect or defendant, or representatives of the school, unit, grass-roots organization of the place of residence, or of the minors' protection organization may be notified of the presence of the minor criminal suspect or defendant, and the relevant information shall be put on record. The legal representative present may exercise the procedural rights of the minor criminal suspect or defendant on his or her behalf.

If a legal representative or other person present at the hearing believes that the case officer has violated the lawful rights and interests of the minor during the interrogation or trial, he or she may submit an opinion. The transcript of the interrogation and the court transcript shall be given to or read to the legal representative or other person present at the trial.

A female staff member shall be present during the interrogation of a female minor criminal suspect.

In the trial of a minor criminal case, after the minor defendant has made his final statement, his legal representative may make additional statements.

When questioning minor victims and witnesses, the provisions of paragraphs 1, 2 and 3 shall apply.

Respecting the rights of the child during the interrogation and trial of the child, and ensuring to the greatest extent possible the future survival and development of the child involved in the criminal proceedings, in accordance with the law, with the best interests of the child as the primary consideration. Thus, it can be concluded that during the trial process, not only will the child's own statement be taken into account, but the child's legal representative or other suitable adult, and the advocate's defense of the child's criminal involvement will also be heard, and, as stipulated in this article, after the child's final statement is made in court, his or her legal representative may make additional statements, which will ultimately be taken into account, in order to determine the child's guilt or innocence, and the seriousness of his or her guilt or misdemeanor. The gravity of the crime. When a child appears in court as a victim or a witness, provisions are made to safeguard the rights and interests of the child. This reflects the fact that the best interests of the child, as stipulated in the United Nations Convention on the Rights of the Child, are a primary consideration in criminal cases involving children. In addition, if a child's legal representative or a suitable adult is not present during the questioning or interrogation of the child, the corresponding witness testimony presented by the investigating or prosecutorial authorities must be corrected or reasonably explained, otherwise, it cannot be used as the basis for the conclusion of the case. In the trial of cases in which children have been sexually or violently victimized, measures such as simultaneous audio and video recording should be taken when questioning children to ensure that it is done once and to avoid secondary victimization of the child (Tong, 2019); if the victim or witness is a girl child, consideration should be given to the physical and psychological protection of the female child, and the questioning should be designated to be carried out by a female staff member.

Specialized institutions or persons shall be established to be responsible for the hearing of cases. In the course of the trial of a case, the judicial organ of the State shall identify specialized institutions or designate specialized personnel to be responsible for the trial of criminal cases involving minors. In this regard, there are specialized trial organizations for hearing juvenile cases, i.e., for cases where the defendant was under 18 years of age at the time of committing the alleged offence and under 20 years of age at the time the case was filed in the people's court. In addition, the judges who hear criminal cases involving minors should be specially trained, be more familiar with the physical and mental characteristics of children, and be adept at the ideological and educational work of children. People's assessors involved in the trial of criminal cases involving minors may be identified, on a priority basis, by random selection from a list of people's assessors who are familiar with the physical and psychological characteristics of children and who are concerned with the protection of minors. Where there are minor defendants in a joint criminal case or other criminal cases involving minors, the president of the people's court concerned shall decide, in the light of the actual situation, whether the case should be heard by a juvenile trial organization. In the case of minors or minor public security offenders who are charged in separate cases in the same people's court, the cases may be heard separately in order to safeguard the privacy of the children.

The principle of closed hearings. The rights and interests of children are fully safeguarded in the trial of cases involving children. Thus, the principle of in-camera hearings and the exception of public hearings are upheld in cases involving children. Detailed provisions can be found in Article 285 of *the Criminal Procedure Law of the People's Republic of China:*

Article 285
Cases in which the defendant is under 18 years of age at the time of trial shall be heard in camera. However, with the consent of the minor defendant and his or her legal representative, the school in which the minor defendant is enrolled and the organization for the protection of minors may send a representative to the trial.

Examination of whether a child has reached the appropriate legal age of responsibility at the time of committing the alleged crime or at the time of trial shall be based on a comprehensive judgment based on documents such as household registration certificates, birth certificates, or evidence such as school registration cards, census registrations, and testimonies of disinterested persons. If it is not possible to prove the age, the case shall be determined in favor of the child. Cases involving children in criminal matters are heard in camera, except with the consent of the child and his or her legal representative, who may be represented by the school in which the child is enrolled and by the organization for the protection of minors. The number and scope of representatives present is determined by law, and only by decision of the court may they participate in the education of the child in court. Unrelated persons other than those mentioned are not allowed to participate in the court proceedings, and those present are expressly informed that they may not disseminate information about the case. Even in cases that are heard in public in accordance with the law, in order to safeguard the privacy of the child in cases that may require the sealing of a criminal record, no one may be present.

Other procedural rights of children. When the people's court hears a case involving a child who has been sentenced to imprisonment, it is also required to fulfill the following obligations to safeguard the child's procedural rights. These include, when serving the child with a copy of the indictment from the people's procuratorate, stating the crime with which the child is charged and the relevant legal provisions in accordance with the law, and informing the child of the trial procedure and of his or her procedural rights and obligations. If, for whatever reason, a child does not appoint a defender throughout the hearing of the case, the people's court will notify the legal aid organization to assign a lawyer familiar with the physical and psychological characteristics of children to provide criminal defense for the child involved in the criminal case. If a minor victim and his or her legal representative do not appoint a legal representative because of financial difficulties or for other reasons, the people's court will assist him or her in applying for legal aid. Where the people's procuratorate transfers investigation reports on the character traits, family situation, social contacts, upbringing, reasons for committing a crime, performance before and after the commission of the crime, and guardianship and education of a minor defendant, or where the defender submits written materials reflecting the above circumstances of the minor defendant, the court accepts them and takes them into account in the process of deciding the case. Where necessary, the people's court may commission community correctional institutions, the Communist Youth League, social organizations, etc., to investigate the aforementioned circumstances of the minor defendant, or may do so on its own. Before the court session and when the court adjourns, depending on the circumstances, arrangements may be made for the minor defendant to meet with his or her legal representative or a suitable adult. The people's court shall set up a seat for the legal representative or suitable adult of a minor defendant on the side of the defense table near the spectator area. In the trial of a criminal case involving a minor who may be sentenced to less than 5 years' imprisonment or who has committed an offence by negligence, courtroom seating may be set up in a manner appropriate to the characteristics of the minor. In the course of court hearings, the adjudicator shall, in accordance with the minor defendant's degree of intellectual development and state of mind, use language expressions appropriate to minors. Where it is found that a minor defendant has been threatened, reprimanded, induced to confess or satirized, the presiding judge shall put a stop to it. Where both the prosecution and the defense propose that the minor defendant be sentenced to control or probation, they shall provide the court with written materials on the minor defendant's ability to obtain guardianship and education, as well as on the lack of significant adverse impact on the community in which he or she lives. The court shall review the investigation report on the situation of the minor defendant, as well as the written materials submitted by the defense concerning the situation of the minor defendant, and hear the opinions of the prosecution and defense. The above reports and materials may serve as references for handling cases and educating minors. The people's court may notify the person who made the investigation report to appear in court to explain the situation and to be questioned by the prosecution, the defense and the court. After a minor defendant has made his or her final statement, the court shall ask his or her legal representative whether he or she wishes to make an additional statement. In criminal cases involving minors, the pronouncement of judgment shall be made in public. In cases where criminal records should be sealed in accordance with the law, no one may be organized to observe the judgement when it is pronounced; if there are any observers, the people's court informs them, in accordance with the law, that they may not disseminate information about the case. In criminal cases involving minors in which sentences are pronounced at regular intervals, where the legal representative of the minor defendant cannot be notified, is unable to be present, or is an accomplice, the court may notify a suitable adult to appear in the courtroom, and after the sentence has been pronounced, serve a copy of the judgment on the adult relatives of the minor defendant. When a minor offender is sent to prison to serve his or her sentence or to community corrections, the people's court shall deliver to the enforcing authority an investigation report on the minor offender and materials concerning his or her performance in the trial of the case, together with the relevant legal documents.

Lastly, the people's courts, as adjudicating bodies, do a good job of following up and safeguarding children's criminal cases after they have been concluded, mainly in terms of the following protection of the right to privacy of children involved in criminal cases, and in terms of children's ideological and psychological education after they have been sentenced by the courts in accordance with the law: sealing of the children's relevant criminal records and reform and education.

(1) Sealing of criminal records relating to children. After a people's court has concluded a criminal case against a child in accordance with the law, it shall, in accordance with the relevant provisions of the law, safeguard the privacy of the child's crime and shall not disclose it, i.e., it shall seal the relevant criminal records of a child under the age of 18. Detailed provisions can be found in Article 286 of The Criminal Procedure Law of the People's Republic of China:

Article 286

If a person was under 18 years of age at the time of committing a crime and is sentenced to less than five years' fixed-term imprisonment, the relevant criminal record shall be sealed.

Where criminal records are sealed, they may not be made available to any unit or individual, except where the judicial authorities need to do so in order to handle the case or where the unit concerned conducts inquiries in accordance with State regulations. Units conducting inquiries in accordance with the law shall keep the circumstances of the sealed criminal records confidential.

With the exception of statutory circumstances, the people's courts are prohibited from disclosing to the public any information about a child's involvement in a criminal case, throughout the entire process of hearing the child's criminal case. This is a key aspect of safeguarding the future survival and development of children involved in criminal cases; for children, the completion of a sentence, or even if they are not ultimately sentenced, the disclosure of relevant information can have a significant impact on their lives, and may even jeopardize the child's rehabilitation. Therefore, criminal records of children should be sealed and should not be made available to any organization or individual without going through legal procedures. This includes the child's name, residence, photograph and any other information or data from which the child's identity may be inferred. The information in the case file that it inspects, extracts or copies, and which involves children, shall not be made public or disseminated. At the same time, if a criminal case involving a child is heard in court, in order to prevent secondary victimization and physical and psychological safety of minor victims and witnesses, they generally do not appear in court to testify; if they must appear in court, they are equipped with technical means to protect the privacy of minor victims and witnesses, as well as psychological interventions and other relevant protective measures, so as to ensure the child's physical and psychological well-being.

(2) Educational rehabilitation. After the conclusion of the court debate, the court may, in accordance with the physical and psychological characteristics of the child and the circumstances of the case, work with other organizations to educate the child as the accused and the child as the victim accordingly. In the case of a child who is the defendant, if the people's court ultimately decides that the child is guilty, the minor defendant shall be educated in the rule of law in accordance with the law after the verdict is pronounced. At the same time, the People's Law may, in the light of the specific circumstances of the child, have the child psychologically counseled by professional psychologists, and, in the light of the specific circumstances and with the consent of the child and his or her legal representative, the guilty child may be psychologically evaluated. The corresponding psychological counselling and assessment may be entrusted to specialized institutions and professionals. The resulting psychological evaluation report can be used as a reference for handling cases and educating minors in order to prevent children from committing crimes in advance. Based on the above educational situation, for the purpose of reforming and educating children who are determined to be guilty, where necessary, when educating a minor defendant, if the participation of an adult relative other than his or her legal representative, or of a teacher or counselor, etc. is conducive to the probation and salvation of the minor, the people's court will invite him or her to participate in the relevant activities, thereby promoting the rehabilitation and growth and development of the child as a convicted offender. In addition to the people's courts, the relevant government departments, people's groups and social organizations cooperate fully in educating and assisting children involved in criminal cases, thereby promoting the healthy development of children involved in criminal cases (Zi, 2018). In addition, since the people's courts, as the adjudicating bodies that decide whether a child is guilty or not guilty, and whether the crime is minor or serious, have a more detailed understanding of the process and causes of the child's involvement in a criminal case, in addition to adjudicating the case, they carry out in-depth research into the causes of crimes committed by children who are involved in a criminal case, while at the same time strengthening their cooperation with the relevant governmental departments, people's associations, social organizations and other groups, and conduct in-depth analyses of practical countermeasures for preventing children from committing crimes, thus promoting the development of the education and assistance

of minors. The development of people's juries for criminal cases, investigations into the situation, and placement and rehabilitation, so as to fully safeguard the legitimate rights and interests of children and actively participate in the comprehensive management of social security. At the same time, the physical and mental health of children as victims cannot be ignored, so in order to pay greater attention to the physical and mental health of children, the people's courts need to work with the relevant government departments, people's groups and social organizations to implement the necessary psychological interventions, economic assistance, legal aid, transfer to a new school and placement, and other protective measures for children who have been subjected to sexual assaults or who will be harmed by violence, as well as for their families.

In summary, the people's courts fully safeguard the procedural rights of children in cases involving children in criminal proceedings, in accordance with the law, and only the people's courts have the authority to determine whether a child's conduct constitutes a crime. At the same time, the inherent personal freedom and human dignity of children are protected in the proceedings, and children are interrogated and tried in the presence of a legal representative or a suitable adult, so that their right to a defense is guaranteed. After a final decision has been made as to the guilt or innocence of a child's actions, the child's criminal record will be sealed and the child will be provided with relevant educational assistance. This is a manifestation of China's commitment to the principle of the best interests of the child following its accession to the United Nations Convention on the Rights of the Child.

11.2.4 Special Provisions for the Protection of Children's Rights and Interests in the Entry into Force and Enforcement of Sentences

If, after the People's Court has ruled in accordance with the law, the People's Court decides that the child concerned is not guilty of the crime, the child shall be released from custody in the courtroom after the verdict has been pronounced. If the People's Court decides that the child's conduct constitutes a crime and imposes a corresponding penalty, the child shall be referred to a correctional facility for juvenile offenders for the enforcement of the corresponding criminal law. In the enforcement of penalties, the United Nations Convention on the Rights of the Child requires that children deprived of their liberty in States parties should be separated from adults in the execution of their sentences; China's detailed provisions on this are set out in article 284 of The Criminal Procedure Law of the People's Republic of China:

Article 284

Sentences for juvenile offenders shall be served in juvenile correctional facilities. The enforcement agency shall take the offender into custody in a

timely manner and notify the offender's family. At the end of the term of imprisonment or detention, the enforcement agency shall issue a certificate of release to the offender.

In the case of juvenile offenders, penalties should be enforced separately from those for adult offenders, with juvenile offenders having the corresponding penalties enforced in juvenile correctional facilities. In the execution of sentences for juvenile offenders, first of all, the people's procuratorates, as legal supervisory organs, have the right to supervise the implementation of the law in accordance with the law. The departments responsible for the prosecution of minors thus supervise, in accordance with the law, the activities of detention centers and correctional facilities for juvenile offenders in their supervision of minors, and cooperate in the education of minors; if, during this period, it is found that juvenile criminal suspects and defendants have not been detained and managed separately from adult criminal suspects and defendants, or that juvenile offenders are being detained to carry out their penalties in violation of the regulations, they shall, in accordance with the law, submit corrective opinions. If the department responsible for prosecuting minors finds that a community corrections organization has violated the relevant provisions on community corrections for minors, it should submit a corrective opinion on the matter in accordance with the law. Secondly, the people's courts, as judicial organs, in order to prevent children from committing crimes and to ensure that children are helped and educated, may establish contact with juvenile correctional facilities and other places where sentences are being served, in order to learn about the rehabilitation of juvenile offenders and to assist in the work of helping them to be properly educated and rehabilitated, and they may also pay return visits to juvenile offenders who are currently serving their sentences. When deemed necessary, they may urge the parents or other guardians of minor offenders who have been sentenced to imprisonment to visit them in a timely manner, thereby safeguarding a certain degree of parental guardianship over the child as he or she grows up, as well as close emotional ties between the two parties. In the case of juvenile offenders sentenced to control, probation, parole or provisional release, the people's courts may also assist community correctional institutions in formulating correctional measures. In addition, the people's courts may, in due course, visit juvenile offenders and their families who have been sentenced to control, probation, exemption from criminal penalties, ruled to be on parole, or decided to be sentenced to provisional imprisonment, etc., to find out how juvenile offenders are being managed and educated, so as to guide the families of juvenile offenders to assume the responsibility of correcting and educating them, and to create a favorable environment for juvenile offenders to reform and rehabilitate themselves. In the case of juvenile offenders who have been sentenced to control, suspended sentence, exemption from criminal punishment, parole, or a decision to be sentenced to temporary imprisonment, the people's court may, if they are eligible for schooling or employment, make a recommendation to the relevant authorities concerning their placement, accompanied by the necessary materials. If the people's court finds that the unit concerned has not fulfilled its duty to educate, manage, rescue, care for or protect minors, it shall make a judicial recommendation to that unit. Lastly, the people's courts shall, in conjunction with actual practice, carry out publicity and education on the rule of law for minors in accordance with the characteristics of criminal cases involving minors.

In summary, the enforcement authority for juvenile offenders is the juvenile correctional facility. In the course of enforcing the sentence, the people's procuratorate, as the legal supervisory organ, supervises the enforcement process in accordance with the law, The People's Court determines the appropriate measures based on the child's behavior during sentence enforcement to safeguard the child's rights and interests. In addition to the provisions of the criminal law, if the child's conduct does not constitute a crime, reference should be made to the provisions of other chapters of this book, such as *The Law of the People's Republic of China on Public Security Administration Penalties*, etc., and if community corrections are ultimately applied to a child's penal punishment, the relevant provisions of *The Law of the People's Republic of China on Community Corrections* are applied to the child's enforcement of his or her sentence.

11.3 Summary

As children are the future of national development, the United Nations Convention on the Rights of the Child clearly establishes the principle of the best interests of the child, requiring States parties to guarantee the right of the child to survival and development and to protect the child from abuse, and to deal with children in conflict with the criminal law in a manner that promotes the sense of dignity and worth of the other person, with an emphasis on the reintegration of children involved in criminal matters into society. In this regard, in China, the principle of the best interests of the child prevails in proceedings involving criminal offenses committed by children, and the policy of educating, reforming, and rescuing children who have committed crimes is being implemented (Yuan, 2020), with the principle of education as the mainstay of the proceedings, supplemented by criminal penalties, so as to maximize the interests of the child.

In the course of criminal proceedings in China, the public security organs, the people's procuratorates, and the people's courts each play their own role, dividing up their responsibilities while at the same time cooperating with each other, and safeguarding children's procedural rights in all aspects, from the investigation, examination of arrests and prosecutions, to the final adjudication and implementation of the final judgment in the case of a child involved in a criminal case. During this period, the People's Procuratorates have upheld the principle of "fewer arrests and more prudent arrests" and "fewer prosecutions and more prudent prosecutions" of children, which is a manifestation of the principle of maximizing the interests of children in the People's Procuratorates' performance of their duties in accordance with the law. At the same time, the People's Courts, in the entire process of adjudicating cases, have formulated and put into practice a corresponding system for the rights and interests of children before, during and after litigation. If a child suspected of having committed a crime has not reached the minimum age of criminal responsibility, the criminal procedure is not applied. At the same time, for children who have reached the age of criminality, the procedures for the application of justice are different from those for adults, so as to safeguard the substantive and procedural rights of the child, most notably the child's right to privacy, the right to a fair trial, and so on. It can be seen that, after the laws on children's rights have been well formulated and good substantive legal norms have been developed, there is still a need for sound procedural laws to guarantee the implementation of children's substantive rights in order to maximize the protection of children's rights.

In summary, The Criminal Procedure Law of the People's Republic of China is still exploring the protection of children's rights and interests, and it is believed that with the development of the times and the deepening of the concept of safeguarding children's rights and interests, The Criminal Procedure Law of the People's Republic of China will become increasingly complete in its protection of the rights and interests of children, so as to achieve the all-round safeguarding of the rights and interests of children in both substantive and procedural terms, and thus to promote the all-round and healthy development of children.

References

Cheng, L. (2023). Criminal procedure responses to the individual lowering of the age of criminal responsibility. *Local Legislation Journal, 6*, 113–129.

Jiang, N. (2021). The age of criminal responsibility for minors: A comprehensive interpretation of Article 17 of the criminal law. *Journal of Beijing Union University (Humanities and Social Sciences), 2*, 10–19.

Liu, R. (2023). Judicial application of the provisions on criminal responsibility of young minors. *Law Science, 7*, 59–76.

Tong, L. (2019). Difficulties and countermeasures in preventing and handling cases of sexual assault against minors. *Journal of Chinese Youth Social Science, 2*, 126–132.

Wang, M. (2019). The implementation and improvement of the conditional non-prosecution system for minors. *Gansu Social Sciences, 4*, 223–230.

Wang, Y. (2025). A stratified approach to the sealing of minor criminal records. *Legal Forum, 5*, 164–176.

Wang, Z. (2013). A brief history of the development of the juvenile criminal procedure legal system. *Juvenile Delinquency Issues Research, 5*, 82–87.

Yin, L. (2021). The presence of an appropriate adult during interrogation: A discussion centered on participation in interrogation. *Journal of National Prosecutors College, 2*, 135–150.

Yuan, N. (2020). Research on the jurisprudential justification and local construction of juvenile justice. *Henan Social Sciences, 10*, 84–91.

Zi, Z. (2018). The evolutionary logic and enlightenment of China's special criminal procedures for minors. *Jianghuai Tribune, 3*, 122–127.

Chapter 12
Operationalizing the Best Interests of the Child: Juvenile Protection in China's Community Correction System

12.1 Introduction

Children's rights deserve more attention, but while protecting their rights from infringement, the transformation of their re-socialization also deserves attention. Because some criminals' crimes involve children who can repent on their own initiative, non-custodial sentences are more favorable than fines, especially for children. Community correction is a non-custodial and socialized means of execution, which plays a positive role in punishing crimes and reforming criminals. Community correction plays an active role in promoting the repentance and re-socialization of those criminals whose crime circumstances are relatively the child and less harmful, especially for juvenile criminals. Because they are not fully developed physically and psychologically, they cannot take responsibility for their actions, and they are likely to rebel, abandon themselves, and even develop indifference and hatred towards the law. Therefore, the Community Correction Law of the People's Republic of China specifically provides for the community correction of children, so that their rights to education, privacy, and other rights are fully protected. This enables them to be educated and rehabilitated in a legal, reasonable and safe environment.

In order to promote and standardize the work of community correction, ensure the correct implementation of criminal sentences, criminal rulings, and temporary execution outside prison, improve the quality of education correction, enable community correction subjects to better integrate into society, and prevent and reduce illegal acts, China has enacted the Community Correction Law of the People's Republic of China in accordance with the provisions of the Constitution. This law specifically sets up a chapter for the work of juvenile community correction, and gives clear provisions on how to protect the rights and interests of children in community correction, which is an indispensable part of the establishment of a legal system for the protection of juvenile rights.

© The Author(s), under exclusive license to Springer Nature Singapore Pte Ltd. 2026

H. Li, P. Liang, *The Legal System for the Protection of Children's Rights in China*, Resilient and Friendly Living Environments,
https://doi.org/10.1007/978-981-95-9925-7_12

This chapter will be combined with legal provisions, from the general provisions on community correction to the special provisions on community correction for children, to interpret how *the Community Correction Law of the People's Republic of China* gives special protection to juvenile community correction objects, strengthens the protection of the rights and interests of juvenile community correction objects, and promotes their smooth return to society. How to respond to and implement *the United Nations Convention on the Rights of the Child* to maximize the survival and development of the child with the best interests of the child as the primary consideration.

12.2 The Basic Overview of Community Correction in China

12.2.1 The Development Process of Chinese Community Correction System

Since 2002, China has been actively promoting the localization of community correction. In early 2002, the Ministry of Justice established a community correction system research team to conduct extensive and in-depth research on the experience and practice of community correction at home and abroad. In August of the same year, the Research Report on the Reform and Improvement of China's Community Correction System was completed. This report provided a relatively comprehensive introduction to the work of community correction abroad and how to construct and improve the community correction system and put forward a preliminary idea. The introduction of the Opinions on carrying out the pilot work of community Correction has laid a solid foundation for the development of the next step.

After the introduction of the foreign community correction system, China began to carry out a community correction work pilot in some provinces and cities in 2003. The pilot work of community correction has been carried out in 47 streets and towns in Beijing, and preliminary exploration has been made on this basis. In 2003, the Ministry of Justice, together with the Ministry of High Law, High Procuratorate, and Ministry of Public Security, issued the Notice on Carrying out the Pilot Work of Community Correction, taking Beijing, Shanghai, Tianjin, Shandong, Jiangsu, Zhejiang and other six provinces and cities as pilots (Zhang, 2010). The implementation of this system marks the official launch of China's community correction system.

In 2004, China's Ministry of Justice issued the Interim Measures for Community Correction Work of Judicial Administrative Organs, which set out corresponding provisions on the organization and responsibilities of community correction work, the reception of criminals, corrective measures, and the termination of correction. It further promoted the institutionalization and legalization of the community correction pilot work, and further improved the quality of community correction work.

In 2005, the Supreme People's Court, the Supreme People's Procuratorate, the Ministry of Public Security, and the Ministry of Justice jointly issued the "Notice on Expanding the Scope of Community Correction Pilot", the pilot projects for community correction will be expanded from six provinces and cities to 18, and gradually develop in depth and breadth from east to middle and east to west. The promulgation of "Opinions on the Implementation of Community Correction Work in the Country" has expanded the community correction work of juveniles in our country. In general, in our country, community correction work started relatively late, but the development speed is very fast and has shown good momentum (Jiang et al., 2014).

The community correction in our country has been piloted from 2003 to 2009 and has achieved good legal and social effects. In the 2011 Criminal Law Amendment (VIII), community correction was included in the scope of legislation for the first time. The Eighth Amendment to the Criminal Law stipulates that "criminals sentenced to public surveillance or sentenced to probation or parole shall be given community correction in accordance with the law…" This provision also confirms from the level of Criminal Law that community correction is a kind of penalty execution mode coexisting with imprisonment. And "Criminal Law Amendment (VIII)" also includes juvenile offenders no longer into the subject category of recidivism, which also provides a legal basis for the application of probation to juvenile offenders who commit repeated crimes and their education and correction. In 2012, community correction was further implemented across the country.

In 2012, the Criminal Procedure Law of the People's Republic of China, based on China's long-term practical experience and achievements in the field of juvenile justice, made specific provisions for the trial procedures of juvenile criminal cases in Special procedures. The detailed provisions are made in the way of law, so as to provide a guideline of "education first, punishment as a supplement" for juvenile offenders to carry out community correction work. At the same time, the legalization of the legal aid system, the suitable adult presence system, and the conditional non-prosecution system is also an affirmation of the practical experience of juvenile justice and has played a good synergistic role in the implementation and implementation of the community correction system. The Criminal Procedure Law stipulates the social investigation procedure, which further standardizes the conviction and sentencing of children; The "sealing of Criminal Archives" and the "no need to declare previous convictions" provisions of the "Amendment (VIII) of the Criminal Law" organically combine entities and procedures, protect the legitimate rights of children, and allow them to better accept community correction and return to society as soon as possible.

On March 1, 2012, the Measures for the Implementation of Community Correction jointly formulated by the Supreme People's Court, the Supreme People's Procuratorate, the Ministry of Public Security, and the Ministry of Justice came into effect. The Measures for the Implementation of Community Correction are in accordance with the provisions of Amendment (8) to the Criminal Law and are combined with the work needs of the reform of the central judicial system. On the basis of summarizing and summarizing the pilot work of community correction in China, a normative document was introduced. The Measures for the Implementation of Community Correction aim to standardize and standardize the work of community correction in our country. It has perfected a series of effective correction methods such as pre-trial investigation and evaluation, correction group, classification management, individual education, and case correction. Key aspects of law enforcement, such as acceptance, supervision, punishment, and detention, will be unified and standardized. It is a set of procedure operation standards, which comprehensively standardizes the working system, system, and workflow of community correction. The "Measures for the Implementation of Community Correction" has made provisions on the principle of juvenile community correction and promoted its development in community correction. It indicates that the current community correction work in our country has gradually entered a new stage.

The Community Correction Law of the People's Republic of China was passed on December 28, 2019, and came into effect on July 1, 2020. At this point, the legalization process of community correction has really begun. The promulgation of the Community Correction Law of the People's Republic of China marks that community correction has gradually embarked on the road of legalization. The promulgation and implementation of *the Community Correction Law of the People's Republic of China* is not only a milestone in the history of community correction in China but also a milestone in the construction of the criminal enforcement system in the new era with Chinese characteristics. This is the first special community correction law in China, which will have an important impact on promoting the standardization, specialization, and rule of law of community correction work, and promoting the modernization of the national governance system and governance capacity.

12.2.2 The Value and Significance of Community Correction to the Protection of Children

In today's increasing juvenile delinquency, the education and protection of children have become a very prominent social phenomenon. For juvenile crime cases, not only should be different from adult crime cases in terms of conviction and sentencing but also should adopt special procedures different from ordinary criminal proceedings according to the characteristics of children themselves. Children are a special group of people, they are still in adolescence, psychologically immature, easy to impulsive, easy to get into groups, the negative impact on the outside world is greater, easy to become the subject of crime. Sending delinquent children to the community to correct their behavior and psychology can cultivate their sense of responsibility, promote their rehabilitation, and create a favorable environment for their future reintegration into society.

As a branch of the community correction system, the juvenile community correction system only targets children. According to the provisions of China's Criminal Law Amendment (XI), the system applies to juvenile offenders who are at least 12 but under the age of 18 and are sentenced to public surveillance, probation, parole, and temporary execution outside prison.

Compared with traditional imprisonment, community correction places children in the community, can prevent cross-infection, and children can establish correct moral values (Chen, 2014). Community correction attaches great importance to the educational function of penalty for children, reflecting the idea that "education is the first, punishment is the auxiliary". Community correction for juvenile offenders has positive significance in correcting children's bad behaviors, avoiding cross-infection within the prison, saving judicial costs, and preventing crimes.

The application of community correction to juvenile offenders, for the children themselves, helps to maintain a close relationship between children and their family of origin, ensures their growth and rehabilitation under the care of their parents and other relatives, promotes the coordinated development within the family, and avoids the learning of children' bad thoughts and criminal methods. With the acceptance of the community, let the juvenile correction objects get along with other children in the community and receive peer education, so that not only eliminate the psychological inferiority, but also complete the reform without any ideological burden, but also guards against promiscuity and effectively reduces the recidivism rate. It avoids the premature labeling of children as criminals and provides a new platform for children who have gone astray to reform, where they can accept correct and progressive ideological and moral reform, constantly abandon criminal thinking and illegal ideological means, accept the help of all sectors of society, promote the re-socialization of delinquent juveniles, prevent and reduce the re-delinquency and crime rate of children; For the whole society, this is a reflection of the modesty of criminal law and the humanization of punishment, which can better play the role of education and protection of juvenile criminals, help the whole society to strengthen the understanding of juvenile crimes, let all sectors of society join in the correction education of juvenile correction objects, and finally form a social value conducive to the harmonious development of public and individual interests. So as to promote the all-round development of individuals and society.

12.3 General Provisions of the Community Corrections Law

In China, community corrections place offenders within the community, where, under the assistance of judicially designated social organizations, non-governmental organizations, and community volunteers, their criminal mindset, deviant behaviors, and undesirable habits are corrected. This approach enables offenders to receive guidance and education within a normal living environment, thereby transforming their negative thoughts and behaviors and acquiring proper moral standards and behavioral norms. On this basis, community corrections provide the subjects with life, educational, and psychological guidance, facilitating their successful reintegration into society.

Given that leniency is the primary approach adopted for juvenile offenders in China, community corrections constitute one of the most suitable measures for this population. The *Community Corrections Law of the People's Republic of China* is the country's first specialized law on community corrections, providing detailed regulations regarding the principles, organizational structure, applicable subjects, and custodial management of community corrections. The rigor and comprehensiveness of China's legislative framework for community corrections reflect the government's significant attention to criminal correction work.

12.3.1 Working Principles

In our country, the work of community correction should be coordinated by many departments and play the role of all aspects. Community correction work should organically combine professional institutions with social forces. It is necessary to adopt the methods of classified management and individual correction and carry out targeted reform on the object of community correction so that they become a law-abiding citizen (Jiang, 2024). Although community correction needs to be implemented in accordance with relevant laws and regulations, it always adheres to the principle of "education first, punishment is auxiliary", and focuses on protecting the human rights of the objects of correction and protecting their various rights and interests from illegal infringement. At the same time, emphasis should be placed on educational assistance so that they can better participate in social practice. The provisions of *the Community Correction Law of the People's Republic of China* on the principles of community correction work are mainly presented in Articles 3 and 4:

> **Article 3**
> ***The work of community correction shall adhere to the combination of supervision and management with education and assistance, the combination of specialized organs and social forces, and the adoption of classified management and individual correction, so as to eliminate the factors that may cause the objects of community correction to re-offend and help them become law-abiding citizens.***
>
> **Article 4**
> ***The object of community correction shall receive community correction according to law and submit to supervision and administration. Community correction work shall be carried out in accordance with the law and human rights shall be respected and protected. The person's rights, property rights and other rights enjoyed by community correction recipients are inviolable, and they are not discriminated against in employment, schooling, and social security.***

12.3.2 Applicable Object

According to the Community Correction Law of the People's Republic of China, the community correction system applies to offenders who are sentenced to public surveillance, suspended sentences, parole, or temporary execution outside prison. Community correction system for children se A branch of the community correction system. Since its target is only children, according to the provisions of the Criminal Law of the People's Republic of China, it can be seen that the system is applicable in China to juvenile offenders who are between 12 and 18 years old and are sentenced to public surveillance, probation, parole, and temporary execution outside prison. Article 2 of *the Community Correction Law of the People's Republic of China* clearly stipulates the applicable objects of community correction:

Article 2
Offenders sentenced to public surveillance, suspended sentences, paroles, or temporary sentences outside prison shall be subject to community correction according to law. This Law shall apply to activities such as supervision and administration, education, and assistance to the objects of community correction.

12.3.3 Place of Execution

In order to better maintain the social relations of community correction objects, so that they can smoothly reintegrate into society, restore social relations, and prevent sudden changes in their daily life. In order to correct their illegal psychology and bad habits, to help them smoothly return to society. The community correction organs in our country determine the place of their execution according to the principle that is most conducive to their acceptance of correction and better integration into society. When choosing the correction place for the child community correction objects, the close relationship between them and the family of origin should be taken into account. It is necessary to ensure that they are corrected under the supervision and education of their parents and other relatives while trying to maintain the peer education of them and other children in the community to prevent their bad thoughts and behaviors from growing up. *The Community Correction Law of the People's Republic of China* mainly stipulates the place of implementation of community correction in Article 17:

Article 17
The community correction decision organ shall determine the place of implementation of community correction when imposing public surveillance, announcing probation, ruling on parole, and deciding on or approving temporary execution outside prison. The place of implementation of community correction is the residence of the object of community correction.

Where the object of community correction lives in more than one place, his regular residence may be determined as the place of execution.

Where the residence or habitual residence of the object of community correction cannot be determined or is not suitable for the implementation of community correction, the decision organ for community correction shall determine the place of implementation in accordance with the principles conducive to the object of community correction to accept correction and better integrate into society.

The decision organs for community correction referred to in this Law refer to the people's courts that, according to law, impose public surveillance, announce suspended sentences, order parole, and decide to temporarily serve sentences outside prison, and the prison administration organs and public security organs that lawfully approve temporary sentences outside prison.

12.3.4 Responsibilities of the Competent Authorities and Relevant Departments

In our country, community correction is the responsibility of the state judicial administration department. The judicial administrative organs of the local people's governments at or above the county level shall be responsible for community correction work under their respective jurisdictions. Public security, judicial, judicial, and other relevant departments shall, in accordance with their respective duties, carry out community correction work in accordance with the law (Zeng, 2025). Governments at all levels shall, in light of the actual situation, establish community correction committees. In the whole country, the public officials are the main body of community correction work, and the judicial staff is the main body of implementation of correction object work. The main force of community correction work is community correction law enforcement personnel, social workers, and social volunteers (Zhang, in press). The details can be found in Articles 8 and 9 of *the Community Correction Law of the People's Republic of China*:

Article 8
The judicial administration department under The State Council shall be responsible for the work of community correction throughout the country.

The judicial administrative departments of the local people's governments at or above the county level shall be in charge of community correction work within their respective administrative areas. The people's courts, people's procuratorates, public security organs, and other relevant departments shall, in accordance with their respective functions and duties, do a good job in community correction according to law.

The people's procuratorates shall exercise legal supervision over the work of community correction according to law. Local people's governments shall, when necessary, establish community correction committees, which shall be responsible for the overall planning, coordination, and guidance of community correction work within their respective administrative areas.

Article 9
The local people's governments at or above the county level shall, as needed, establish community correction institutions and be responsible for the specific implementation of community correction work. The establishment and cancellation of community correction institutions shall be subject to the opinions of the judicial administrative department of the local people's government at or above the county level and shall be subject to examination and approval according to the prescribed limits of authority and procedures.

The judicial office shall undertake the work related to community correction according to the entrustment of the community correction institution.

12.3.5 Specific Measures

In China, corrective measures and plans are customized. According to the condition of the community correction object, a correction team is designated for them and is responsible for implementing the relevant correction plan. The object of community correction should be educated in the aspects of the rule of law and morality, and their concept of the rule of law should be strengthened. Improve their moral character and sense of repentance, and combined with their personal characteristics, daily performance, etc., to their work and living conditions for comprehensive consideration, according to their aptitude. As for the target of juvenile community correction, it generally adopts concrete corrective measures such as public welfare labor, ideological education, legal education, and moral education.

Community correction institutions guide the objects of community correction to develop a good sense of social responsibility and prevent and reduce crimes by conducting public welfare labor and participating in social services. Through special education, psychological counseling, judicial guidance, and other ways to guide the community correction objects to establish a correct world outlook, outlook on life and values, and cultivate their good psychological quality (Yuan, 2019); Through the organization of social welfare activities, help community correction objects to develop good behavior habits and healthy mental state. See Article 24 and Article 36 of *the Community Correction Law of the People's Republic of China* for details:

Article 24

Community correction institutions shall, in accordance with the content of the judgment and the gender, age, psychological characteristics, health status, causes of crime, types of crime, circumstances of crime, repentance, and other circumstances of the object of community correction, formulate targeted correction programs to achieve classified management and individual correction. The correction program shall be adjusted according to the performance of the community correction object.

Article 36

Community correction institutions shall, as needed, educate the objects of community correction on the rule of law and morality, enhance their sense of the rule of law, and improve their moral quality and sense of repentance. The education of the objects of community correction shall be based on their individual characteristics, daily performance, and other actual conditions, giving full consideration to their work and life, and teaching them to different persons.

12.4 Protection of Children Under the Community Correction Law of the People's Republic of China

The Community Correction Law of the People's Republic of China is divided into general provisions, institutions, personnel and duties, decision and reception, supervision and management, education and assistance, dissolution and termination, special provisions for juvenile community correction, legal responsibilities, and nine chapters of supplementary provisions. Among them, the seventh chapter, as a special chapter for children, is worth our study and interpretation. Therefore, this section will be divided into two parts: the general provisions of community correction and the special provisions for children in community correction to interpret the embodiment of the law on the protection of children's rights and interests.

12.4.1 General Provisions of Community Correction for Children in China

The provisions on juvenile community correction are mainly concentrated in Chapter 7 of *the Community Correction Law of the People's Republic of China*. However, there are also some provisions related to children in other chapters. This section will introduce and interpret the provisions related to children in other sections.

First of all, the responsibilities of grass-roots organizations, related relatives, and units in community correction work are stipulated. For example, the guardian of the object of community correction shall perform the duty of guardianship according to law, create conditions for the object of community correction to receive education and reform, and supervise the performance of the duty of guardianship of the child object of community correction; The family members of the juvenile community correction object shall fulfill the obligation of bringing up and maintaining the juvenile community correction object according to law, and supervise the juvenile community correction object; The school shall strengthen its contact with the judicial and administrative organs at the county level of the place of residence, and assist in the education and management of the child community correction objects. These institutional arrangements can ensure that children can successfully complete community correction and return to school. To ensure that the personal information of the child's community correction objects is not infringed and leaked; It can ensure that children continue to receive compulsory education and employment. Guardians, family members, units, schools, etc. of community correction objects should give support to community correction work. Guardians, family members and schools of the child community correction objects have the obligation to assist community correction institutions in carrying out community correction work. Ensure that children can successfully complete community correction and return to school; To ensure that the personal information of juvenile community correction objects is not infringed and disclosed; To ensure that children receiving community correction continue to receive compulsory education and employment. In this regard, the provisions of *the Community Correction Law of the People's Republic of China* are mainly reflected in Article 12:

> **Article 12**
> ***Residents' committees and villagers' committees shall assist community correction institutions in doing a good job of community correction according to the law. The guardian, family member, unit, or school of the object of community correction shall assist the community correction institution to do a good job in community correction.***

The second is the provision of the formulation and adjustment of corrective programs. A targeted corrective plan should be developed. The correction plan shall meet the requirements of classified management and individual correction. In addition, correction programs should be adjusted according to the performance of community correction objects. Specifically, community correction objects re-commit crimes or commit serious violent sexual crimes such as intentional homicide, kidnapping, rape, etc. are revoked probation, and parole, and need to adjust correction programs. Correction programs should be adjusted according to their performance and other circumstances.

On the basis of comprehensive analysis and evaluation, a targeted treatment plan should be formulated. For juvenile community correction objects, according to their risks and needs, scientific development and adjustment of correction plans, to achieve classified management, teaching according to aptitude. In the community correction work, only by working out a targeted correction plan can we achieve the scientific correction purpose. Community correction staff should effectively implement the community correction plan, and make appropriate adjustments according to the actual situation to ensure its effectiveness. In the community correction work, only by working out a targeted correction plan can we achieve the scientific correction purpose. Therefore, in the community correction work, the community correction staff should effectively implement the community correction plan, and make appropriate adjustments according to the actual situation to ensure its effectiveness. Article 24 of *the Community Correction Law of the People's Republic of China* stipulates in detail the above contents:

Article 24

Community correction institutions shall, in accordance with the content of the judgment and the gender, age, psychological characteristics, health status, causes of crime, types of crime, circumstances of crime, repentance, and other circumstances of the object of community correction, formulate targeted correction programs to achieve classified management and individual correction. The correction program shall be adjusted according to the performance of the community correction object.

The community correction institution shall, according to the situation of the community correction object, determine the correction team for it and be responsible for implementing the corresponding correction plan (Utami, 2022). Determine that the correction team must:

Scientific identification of corrective groups. In accordance with the principles conducive to the implementation of educational reform and corrective measures for criminals, the members of the correction team shall be scientifically and reasonably determined according to the types of crimes, circumstances of crimes, expressions of confession and repentance, and the degree of influence in society. Before accepting the post-correction declaration procedure for the object of community correction, the community correction institution decides its members, and the correction team participates in a series of procedures such as the declaration of correction. The following aspects should be fully taken into account in the establishment of correction groups: the physical and social risks of community correction objects; Addressing the special needs of prisoners; Objective conditions, such as community correction personnel, social security, etc.; The composition of the correction team should be determined scientifically and reasonably according to the objective needs of community correction objects. Perform the duties of the corrective team. According to the legal status, characteristics, and advantages of the members of the correction group, the responsibilities of their work should be defined. To do "responsibility to the person", cannot complete the work responsibilities of the behavior to regulate, and carry out the corresponding punishment. Promote accountability among correction team members. The judicial staff in the correction team shall, as the leader of the correction team, be responsible for the education and management of the objects of community correction, and take the initiative to assume the main responsibilities. Members who cannot perform or incorrectly perform their duties and affect the supervision and correction work of community correction objects shall be replaced in a timely manner. The correction team insists on making measures according to the case and putting people first. The correction team should combine legal constraints, moral guidance, and kinship supervision, and take the initiative to implement appropriate correction plans under the guidance of community correction institutions and judicial offices so that the objects of community correction can better integrate into society. At the same time, the members of the correction team should also report the correction status of the community correction object to the community correction institution and the judicial office, strengthen contact, communication, and cooperation, and work together to do a good job in supervision, management, and education. The details can be found in Article 25 of *the Community Correction Law of the People's Republic of China*:

Article 25

A community correction institution shall, according to the situation of the object of community correction, determine a correction team for it and be responsible for implementing the corresponding correction plan.

According to needs, the correction team may be composed of personnel from the judicial office, the residents' committee or the villagers' committee, guardians and family members of the object of community correction, personnel from the unit or school they belong to, and social workers and volunteers. Where the object of community correction is female, there shall be female members in the correction team.

In addition, *the Community Correction Law of the People's Republic of China* also provides for the employment and schooling of community correction objects. According to *the Employment Promotion Law of the People's Republic of China* and the division of responsibilities of the government, the main units to promote employment are human resources and social security departments, as well as vocational colleges and vocational skills training institutions. Social organizations such as trade unions, the Communist Youth League, women's federations, and disabled persons' federations play an important role in promoting employment and protecting the labor rights and interests of employed citizens within the scope prescribed by law. In the process of socialist modernization, education is the most fundamental. Therefore, the work of community correction must guarantee the equal right of the object of community correction to receive education. The responsibility of community correction organizations is to coordinate with relevant departments and units. Community correction institutions should stand on the standpoint of legal service and coordination to ensure that community correction objects are not discriminated in the process of employment; ensure that relevant departments, in accordance with legal procedures, implement measures such as tax reduction and exemption, interest discount on loans, social insurance subsidies, and job subsidies. All departments and units shall perform their duties according to law. For the child community correction objects, such as school students and vocational high school students, it is more important to do a good job in education and employment to ensure their healthy growth and development. The provisions of *the Community Correction Law of the People's Republic of China* on helping community correction objects to find employment and study are mainly presented in Article 37:

Article 37
Community correction institutions may coordinate relevant departments and units to carry out vocational skills training and employment guidance for community correction objects with employment difficulties, and help school students in community correction objects complete their studies.

Finally, the relevant specific subjects of community correction (including their guardians and family members, as well as their units or schools) have a legal obligation to assist in education. For the objects of juvenile community correction, more attention should be paid to the help and education of their guardians and families. In their work, community correction institutions correctly evaluate the relationship with guardians and family members of community correction objects. At the beginning of the establishment of the relationship, it is necessary to explain the legal obligations to them, let them know the goals of community correction, reach agreement on the goals and cooperation methods, fully mobilize their enthusiasm, reach agreement to the greatest extent, and jointly educate the community correction objects. Properly handle the relationship between the work units and schools of the objects of education correction and the protection of their legitimate rights. Information about the sentencing of juvenile community correction objects and the implementation of community correction shall be limited to a small number of people closely related to them to prevent the spread of large areas. To avoid the adverse impact on the educational correction work of community correction objects.

The Community Correction Law of the People's Republic of China clearly stipulates the statutory obligation to assist relevant specific subjects in education in Article 39.

Article 39
The guardian, family member, unit or school of the object of community correction shall assist the community correction institution to do a good job in educating the object of community correction.

12.4.2 Special Provisions of Community Correction for Children in China

Chapter 7 of *the Community Correction Law of the People's Republic of China* is a special provision on community correction for children. It makes specific provisions on juvenile community correction in all aspects, and its content mainly includes the following four aspects

12.4.2.1 Differentiation Correction

Different from adult community correction, community correction institutions should take into account the age, psychological characteristics, growth needs, growth experience, crime causes, family guardianship, and education status of the child community correction objects when implementing community correction for children. Treatment with adult correction objects is different, so that children can truly reform during community correction, get the help of social education, and prevent cross-infection.

When community correction institutions organize relevant social education, they should still conduct juvenile community correction objects and adult correction objects separately. In order to better protect juvenile community correction subjects from re-education, integration into society, and discrimination, juvenile community correction subjects do not need to wear community correction-related clothing. When the community correction institution organizes the juvenile community correction objects to participate in social education, it should also separate them from the adult community correction objects to avoid the behavioral, psychological, environmental, and other inappropriate adaptations of the juvenile community correction objects. China's community correction will be the juvenile community correction object as the focus of attention in the community correction work, adhere to the "education first, punishment as a supplement" (Wong & Fung, 2023). Continue to attract the participation of social workers related to children, and set up correction teams to ensure that juvenile community correction objects are reformed and reintegrated into society to the maximum extent possible. To educate and rehabilitate children, so as to achieve the goal of community correction and promote their early reintegration into society. In this regard, Article 52 of *the Community Correction Law of the People's Republic of China* clearly stipulates:

Article 52
Community correction institutions shall take targeted corrective measures according to the age, psychological characteristics, developmental needs, growth experience, causes of crime, and conditions of family guardianship and education of the child community correction objects. Community correction institutions shall determine correction groups for juvenile

community correction objects, and shall absorb personnel familiar with the physical and mental characteristics of children to participate. Community correction of children shall be carried out separately from that of adults.

12.4.2.2 Family Guardianship Responsibility Is Strengthened

Guardians and family members of community correction objects, their units or schools should cooperate with community correction institutions to carry out community correction work. The guardian of the child community correction object should also bear the corresponding legal responsibilities. Where a guardian is negligent in performing his guardianship duties or refuses to perform his guardianship duties, he shall bear the corresponding legal consequences.

Children are the future and hope of the country. The judicial administrative organs have the duty to effectively supervise the juvenile community correction objects, and provide them with good education and guidance so that they can reform and become useful people in society. However, the child community correction object is often young, and lacks strong self-protection awareness, making them susceptible to criminal paths. Therefore, it is particularly important for guardians to effectively supervise children. The duties of the guardian of the child object of community correction are as follows: First, under the guidance of the community correction institution, the guardian of the child object of community correction shall cooperate with the community correction institution to do a good job in community correction and participate in the duties of the correction team; The second is to perform the duty of guardianship, undertake legal obligations such as upbringing and correction, ensure that juvenile community correction objects receive good education and development, reform, and reduce the education and social discrimination that juvenile community correction objects are subjected to because of criminal behavior. *The Community Correction Law of the People's Republic of China* clarifies the guardianship responsibility of the family in Article 53:

Article 53

The guardian of the object of the child community correction shall perform the duty of guardianship and undertake the obligations of rearing and correction. Where guardians fail to perform their duties of guardianship, community correction institutions shall urge and educate them to perform their duties of guardianship. If the guardian refuses to perform his guardianship duties, he shall notify the relevant department to deal with it according to law.

12.4.2.3 Identity Information Protection

Article 16 (1) of *the United Nations Convention on the Rights of the Child* provides that children shall not be subjected to arbitrary or unlawful interference with their privacy, family, home, or correspondence, nor to unlawful attacks on their honor and reputation.

The protection of the identity information of the child community correction objects is also a concrete manifestation of the protection of children's privacy. The staff of community correction institutions and other personnel participating in community correction work according to law shall keep confidential the identity information of children obtained in the course of performing their duties. Except for the need of judicial organs to handle cases or the relevant units in accordance with the provisions of the State, the file information of juvenile community correction objects shall not be provided to any unit or individual.

In order to better protect the security of children' personal information, necessary confidentiality measures must be taken and the obligation of confidentiality must be strictly enforced. Juvenile archives shall be managed and stored using special instruments and platforms. After the security work is done, it is managed and stored at different levels. Set a high level of access and transfer authority for children' file information to prevent confusion with other individuals' file information. The identity information of the child community correction objects can be better protected. In addition, Article 61 of *the Community Correction Law of the People's Republic of China* also makes corresponding provisions on the legal liability of relevant staff for leaking confidential information.

The protection of personal information of the object of community correction not only involves its personal files but also involves its social relations, personal privacy, and so on. Article 26 (2) of *the Community Correction Law of the People's Republic of China* stipulates that "community correction institutions shall protect the identity information and personal privacy of community correction objects during field visits." Therefore, in the field investigation of juvenile community correction objects, the participation of irrelevant personnel should be avoided, and the relevant signs of community correction should be hidden, so as to reduce the adverse impact on the daily life and education of juvenile community correction objects. Article 54 of *the Community Correction Law of the People's Republic of China* stipulates in detail the protection of the identity information of the child community correction objects:

Article 54
Staff members of community correction institutions and other persons participating in community correction work according to law shall keep confidential the identity information of children obtained in the course of performing their duties. Except for the need of judicial organs to handle cases or the relevant units in accordance with the provisions of the State, the file information of juvenile community correction objects shall not be provided to any unit or individual. Units that conduct inquiries according to law shall keep confidential the information obtained.

12.4.2.4 Education and Employment Support

The provisions of our legislation give full attention and respect to the characteristics and needs of children. Community correction institutions should strengthen legal, moral, patriotism, and other aspects of education. Through psychological counseling, psychological intervention, and other means, timely psychological correction. When implementing corrective measures for juvenile community correction objects, the study and work needs of juvenile community correction objects should be fully taken into account, and appropriate arrangements should be made for corrective activities. At the same time, it is necessary to continue to innovate the correction program, so that it meets the physical and psychological characteristics and development needs of children, and effectively ensures their schooling and employment.

In addition, the child community correction objects cannot be separated from the relationship between family and school in the process of receiving compulsory education, participating in work, employment, etc. Family education and school education play a very important role in ensuring the implementation of children' right to receive compulsory education. Community correction institutions should attach importance to the family education of parents and other guardians of the child community correction objects, help them correctly perform their guardianship responsibilities, and enable them to carry out legal upbringing and education of children. Community correction institutions and school departments should strengthen exchanges and establish a sound contact mechanism. Let juvenile community correction objects have access to compulsory education, and truly ensure that they receive systematic and comprehensive education at this important stage of education in their lives. In the implementation of employment, the advantages of social participation should be fully leveraged to create a favorable social atmosphere for the employment security of juvenile community correction subjects. Ensuring employment is a shared responsibility of society, which requires coordination and cooperation among relevant government departments as well as broad participation and assistance from the community. Community correction institutions shall actively coordinate with relevant departments and units, provide vocational training programs according to the specific needs of juvenile community correction objects and social development trends, and provide practical help for employment problems (Yuan et al., 2024). This part is also a response to Articles 28 and 29 of *the United Nations Convention on the Rights of the Child.*

The details can be found in Article 55 of the Community Correction Law of the People's Republic of China:

Article 55

For children who have not completed compulsory education, community correction institutions shall notify and cooperate with education departments to provide conditions for them to complete compulsory education. Guardians of the child community correction objects shall ensure that they enter school on time to receive and complete compulsory education in accordance with the law. If the object of community correction has reached the age of 16 and wishes to find employment, the community correction institution may coordinate with relevant departments and units to provide vocational skills training, employment guidance, and assistance.

The community correction of children shall also be assisted and participated in by relevant social organizations such as the Communist Youth League, women's federations, and juvenile protection organizations (Xie & Liao, 2024). In youth work, the Communist Youth League, women's federations, juvenile protection institutions, and other institutions play an irreplaceable role; In addition, the government will also provide legal support for social groups to participate in community correction work.

China is continuing to build and improve the social support system for juvenile community correction work. At the same time, communication and contact between community correction work and other departments have been strengthened, so that the Communist Youth League, women's federations, and juvenile protection organizations have played an active role in the work of juvenile community correction. The Community Correction Law of the People's Republic of China elaborates on the specific ways in which the Communist Youth League, women's Federations, and juvenile protection organizations can assist in accordance with the law. The function of each organization is divided, so that the work of juvenile community correction can be better integrated into society. The provisions of *the Community Correction Law of the People's Republic of China* on the participation of the Communist Youth League, women's Federations, juvenile protection organizations, and other relevant social organizations in juvenile community correction are mainly in Article 56:

Article 56

The Communist Youth League, women's federations and juvenile protection organizations shall assist community correction institutions in doing a good job of juvenile community correction according to law. The State encourages other social organizations related to children to participate in the work of juvenile community correction and provides policy support according to law.

The Community Correction Law of the People's Republic of China has made special provisions for juvenile community correction objects in terms of returning to school, further education, and employment. Juvenile community correction objects, like ordinary children, shall not be discriminated against by any unit or individual in terms of returning to school, further education, employment, etc. In cases of discrimination is committed, the departments of education, personnel, social security, and so on shall give corresponding treatment according to law.

The protection of the enrollment and employment rights of children in community correction in China is mainly based on the physical and psychological characteristics of children in community correction. An effective educational correction program is formulated to include legal knowledge, ideological and moral character, mental health, skills training, and other aspects to help children in community correction to go to school and employment. When the school refuses to accept the child's community correction object due to community correction, the community correction institution shall inform the education department and provide assistance. Refer to Article 57 of *the Community Correction Law of the People's Republic of China*:

Article 57
Children who are subject to community correction shall enjoy the same rights as other children in terms of returning to school, further education and employment according to law, and no unit or individual shall discriminate against them. Where there is discrimination, it shall be dealt with by the departments of education, human resources and social security according to law.

Finally, Article 58 of *the Community Correction Law of the People's Republic of China* stipulates that the relevant provisions of community correction for children shall not be terminated because the object of correction has reached the age of 18.

Article 58
If the object of juvenile community correction reaches the age of 18 during the period of community correction, it shall continue to be implemented in accordance with the relevant provisions of juvenile community correction.

12.5 Summary

The Community Correction Law of the People's Republic of China provides special protection for juvenile community correction objects, determines correction groups for juvenile community correction objects, and attracts personnel familiar with the physical and mental characteristics of children to participate (Niu & Fan, 2024). The law guarantees the completion of compulsory education for children in community correction and provides vocational skills training for them. Ensure that they enjoy the same rights as other children in terms of returning to school, further education and employment according to law. The legal rights and interests of children in the process of community correction are protected from all aspects and angles.

This chapter integrates all the laws related to the protection of children in *the Community Correction Law of the People's Republic of China* by enumerating and interpreting them. In this paper, *the Community Correction Law of the People's Republic of China* mainly protects the legitimate rights and interests of children in the process of community correction by distinguishing them from adults, protecting the identity information of the child community correction objects, supporting education and training of the child community correction objects, and strengthening family guardianship responsibilities. It is a response to the principle of maximizing the interests of the Child in *the United Nations Convention on the Rights of the Child.*

In the future, *the Community Correction Law of the People's Republic of China* will continue to improve the juvenile community correction system, formulate a phased and step-by-step community correction system for children, and realize the systematization and standardization of community correction for children (Peng & Yuan, 2024). Strengthen the training of community correction workers, and design corresponding correction plans for different juvenile community correction objects, so as to cultivate their psychological emotion and cognitive ability, so as to better reform and enter the society (Gong, 2021). Establish a scientific and effective evaluation mechanism for the whole process of community correction to ensure the effective operation of all aspects of community correction (Du, 2017).

References

Chen, L. (2014). Research on the community correction system for juvenile offenders in China. *Journal of Southeast University (Philosophy and Social Science), S1*, 158–162.

Du, Y. (2017). Legislative suggestions for juvenile community corrections. *China Youth Study, 6*, 107–112.

Gong, H. (2021). Practical problems and solutions in the community corrections of minors — Data analysis based on a survey of juvenile crimes in T City China. *Prison Journal, 3*.

Jiang, J. (2024). Rehabilitative control and penal responsivity: Implementing restraining orders in Chinese community corrections. *Asian Journal of Criminology, 2*, 183–202.

Jiang, S., Xiang, D., Chen, Q., Huang, C., Yang, S., Zhang, D., & Zhao, A. (2014). Community corrections in China: Development and challenges. *The Prison Journal, 1*, 75–96.

Niu, Z., & Fan, T. (2024). The institutional realization of juvenile community corrections in China: Multidimensional foundations and theoretical remodeling. *Community Corrections: Theory and Practice, 3*, 13–19.

Peng, W., & Yuan, X. (2024). The juvenile community correction system in China: Reflection and reconstruction. *Journal of Nanjing University of Aeronautics and Astronautics (Social Sciences), 1*, 71–81.

Utami, P. N. (2022). The role of community counselor in handling child clients in Class I Correctional Center of Medan. *Jurnal Penelitian Hukum De Jure, 2*, 271–284.

Wong, D. S., & Fung, C. S. (2023). Juvenile community corrections in China: The quest for a restorative approach. *Asian Journal of Criminology, 2*, 113–132.

Xie, Y., & Liao, S. (2024). Social support for juvenile community corrections: Value logic, current situation analysis, and path exploration. *Industrial & Science Tribune, 3*, 37–40.

Yuan, H., Song, L., & Dong, Y. (2024). Research on the practice and system of juvenile community corrections. *China Rule of Law, 7*, 69–77.

Yuan, X. (2019). Risk, risk assessment, and community corrections in China. *International Journal of Offender Therapy and Comparative Criminology, 14*, 2466–2482.

Zeng, R. (2025). Exploring the path of public security departments' participation in juvenile community corrections. *Society and Public Welfare, 11*, 116–118.

Zhang, J. (2010). A preliminary study on the juvenile community correction system. *Theory Monthly, 8*, 118–120.

Chapter 13
Complementary Legal Frameworks for Child Protection in China: Supplementary Laws and Regulatory Provisions

13.1 Introduction

The safety and development of the child are related to the harmony and stability of society. The establishment of a complete and comprehensive legal system is important for the protection and promotion of children's development. China has taken positive actions in many areas, such as establishing and improving a legal system to protect the child's rights and interests, and protecting the child's rights to survival, development, protection and participation. Moreover, China will continue to improve its legal system and policies in the future, and ensure that the child's rights and interests are fully protected.

In China, the rule of law is making continuous progress. China's legislation on child protection has been continuously developed and improved. There is a significant trend of active legislation concerning the protection of the child's rights and interests. Specifically speaking, three laws in China have completed major revisions to the age of criminal responsibility. They are *the Law of the People's Republic of China on the Protection of Children*, *the Law of the People's Republic of China on the Prevention of Juvenile Delinquency* and *the Criminal Law of the People's Republic of China*. Besides, there are many changes in China's law regarding the child. The Marriage and Family section of the Civil Code of the People's Republic of China has further improved the protection of the child. *The Law of the People's Republic of China on Maternal and Infant Health Care*, *the Law of the People's Republic of China on Public Security Administration and Penalties*, and *the Labor Law of the People's Republic of China* also have special provisions on the protection of children's legitimate rights and interests. At present, China has established a legal system for the protection of the child's rights and interests (Ye, 2022). In this legal system, the special law on child protection is the main body, and other laws, administrative regulations and other normative documents play a supplementary role.

© The Author(s), under exclusive license to Springer Nature Singapore Pte Ltd. 2026

H. Li, P. Liang, *The Legal System for the Protection of Children's Rights in China*, Resilient and Friendly Living Environments,
https://doi.org/10.1007/978-981-95-9925-7_13

These documents, from multiple angles and at multiple levels, provide legal protection for the healthy growth of the child.

The first 12 chapters of this book provide a detailed explanation of the main legal documents on the protection of children's rights and interests in China. In addition, China's provisions on the protection of children's rights and interests are also scattered in other legal documents, such as the Law of the People's Republic of China on Maternal and Child Health Care, the Teachers Law of the People's Republic of China, the Labor Law of the People's Republic of China, the Law on Public Security Administration and Punishment, and the Prison Law of the People's Republic of China, etc. This chapter will focus on the five laws related to the protection of children's legal rights and interests, and enumerates other official documents related to children in China in the form of a list.

This chapter aims to analyze the specific contents of other laws in China's legal system to protect children's legitimate rights and interests. At the same time, the author interprets the purpose and focus of the legislation on the protection of children groups in other laws and clarifies the complementary role of other laws in the whole legal system. Through the interpretation of this chapter, the book makes the legal system of protection of children's rights and interests in China more complete.

13.2 Other Laws Protecting the Rights and Interests of Children

Law is an important weapon to protect the legitimate rights and interests of the child. The first few chapters of this book analyze and summarize the design highlights and concepts of the legal system of protecting children's rights and interests in China. As a preliminary chapter, this chapter will be interpreted in accordance with the laws that may be involved in the different periods of a child's development. The growth of children goes through the process from birth to education, and then from labor to punishment after breaking the law. The author focuses on the provisions related to the protection of children's rights and interests in the five legal documents mentioned above. In this way, readers can have a deep understanding of the legislative tendency of China's legal norms to protect children's rights and interests.

13.2.1 Law of the People's Republic of China on Maternal and Child Health Care

The Law of the People's Republic of China on Maternal and Child Health Care regulates the social relations arising from activities to ensure the health of mothers and infants and improve the quality of the healthy population. This law is of great significance for safeguarding the health of the next generation, strengthening maternal and child health care, and safeguarding the rights and interests of women and children. The law was adopted at the 10th meeting of the Standing Committee of the Eighth National People's Congress on October 27, 1994, and went into effect on June 1, 1995. And then got amended twice, in 2009 and 2017. The Law of the People's Republic of China on Maternal and Child Health Care is divided into seven chapters, each chapter, in turn, is "general provisions", "pre-marital health care", "maternity health care", "technical appraisal", "administrative management", "legal responsibility" and "supplementary provisions". In different periods, this law has different requirements and measures for maternal and infant health care and protects the health of mothers and infants in an all-round process. The promulgation and implementation of the law have played an important role in protecting the legitimate rights and interests of women and infants.

Maternal and child health care in China sprouted at the end of the twentieth century and began to develop gradually in the twenty-first century. The Government has also begun to place maternal and child health at the core of its health work and to protect the reproductive health of women and children as the primary goal of its health work. Since the promulgation and implementation of the law, China has formulated a policy for maternal and child health work that "takes health care as the center, aims at safeguarding reproductive health, combines health care with clinical practice, focuses on the community and the grassroots and gives priority to prevention". Chinese laws have always adhered to the right direction of development and provided more comprehensive protection for women and children (Li et al., 2011).

Article 1 of the Law of the People's Republic of China on Maternal and Child Health Care specifies the legislative purpose:

> **Article 1**
> ***This Law is enacted in accordance with the Constitution in order to protect the health of mothers and infants and to improve the quality of the newborn population.***

The Chinese people's Government takes a positive attitude towards maternal and infant health care and provides necessary conditions and assistance for it. The development of maternal and child health care has been greatly encouraged and supported. In addition, the administrative department of health under The State Council shall be in charge of the national maternal and infant health care work, formulate the national development plan and implementation plan for maternal and infant health care work, and supervise it. The administrative departments of public health under local governments shall be responsible for the supervision and administration of maternal and infant health care within their respective administrative areas. Moreover, Local people's governments shall lead the work of maternal and infant health care and incorporate the work into their national economic and social development plans at the corresponding levels. For the management and implementation of maternal and child health care, Article 2–5 of *the Law of the People's Republic of China on Maternal and Child Health Care* provides guidance and legal basis:

Article 2

The State shall develop the cause of maternal and infant health care, and provide necessary conditions and material assistance to enable mothers and infants to obtain medical and health care services.

The state shall support maternal and infant health care undertakings in outlying and poverty-stricken areas.

Article 3

People's governments at various levels shall lead the work of maternal and infant health care.

Undertakings of maternal and infant health care shall be incorporated into the national economic and social development plan.

Article 4

The administrative department of health under The State Council shall be in charge of the work of maternal and infant health care throughout the country, put forward the guiding principles of classification and classification according to the conditions of different regions, and exercise supervision and administration over the work of maternal and infant health care throughout the country.

Other relevant departments under The State Council shall, within the scope of their respective functions and duties, cooperate with the administrative departments of public health to do a good job of maternal and infant health care.

Article 5

The State encourages and supports education and scientific research in the field of maternal and infant health care, disseminates advanced and practical technologies of maternal and infant health care, and popularizes scientific knowledge of maternal and infant health care.

In pre-marital health care, *the Law of the People's Republic of China on Maternal and Infant Health Care* regulates medical and health care. Medical and health institutions shall provide pre-marital health guidance, pre-marital health consultation, and pre-marital medical examination to citizens. The main function of these works is to enhance the theoretical understanding of both men and women on reproductive knowledge, reproductive health care, child genetic diseases, etc. It is of great significance for eugenics, improving the quality of the born population, and ensuring family happiness and social stability. The first step of "eugenics" is a marital check-up. Through the pre-marital examination can be found in time whether women suffer from diseases that seriously affect pregnancy or embryonic development, and lays a solid foundation for maternal health care work in advance.

In the course of pregnancy and perinatal care, medical and health institutions shall provide guidance on maternal and child health to women of childbearing age and pregnant women. This is essential for the health of pregnant women, mothers, and newborns. Pregnancy care is a comprehensive service activity. Through health monitoring, doctors can detect the abnormal situation of mother and child in time and give appropriate intervention. This can reduce birth defects or miscarriages and ensure the health of the fetus. At the same time, medical examination can also find out in time whether the fetus has genetic metabolic diseases, timely diagnosis, and treatment measures.

In newborn care, much needs to be done by the health care institutions. On the one hand, medical institutions should do a good job of health examination of newborns to ensure their health. On the other hand, the immunization of newborns should also be actively implemented. Specifically speaking, medical institutions need to do the following: Firstly, screening, diagnosis, treatment, and monitoring of neonatal congenital and hereditary metabolic diseases are carried out in accordance with relevant national regulations. Secondly, newborn visits should be carried out to prevent and treat common and frequently-occurring diseases in infants. Third, vaccines should be provided to young children according to a specified procedure and plan. Fourth, doctors should provide scientific and reasonable health care services for the growth, breastfeeding, and nursing of newborns. The implementation of this work can effectively improve the physical fitness of the child, reduce death and disability, and lay a solid foundation for their future growth and development. This legal provision is also in line with Article 24 of *the United Nations Convention on the Rights of the Child*. Article 24 recognizes the right of the child to the enjoyment of the highest attainable standard of health. Children have access to medical and rehabilitation facilities. At the same time, the State party should strive to ensure that no child is denied access to such health services.

For details, see Article 14 of the Law of the People's Republic of China on Maternal and Child Health Care:

Article 14
Medical and health institutions shall provide maternal and perinatal health services for women of childbearing age and pregnant women.

Maternal health services include the following: (1) Guidance on maternal and child health care: providing medical advice on the birth of healthy offspring and on the causes, treatment and prevention of serious hereditary diseases and endemic diseases such as iodine deficiency disorders; (2) Pregnant women and maternal health: provide pregnant and parturient women with health, nutrition, psychological and other consultation and guidance, as well as regular prenatal check-ups and other health care services; (3) Fetal health care: monitoring, counseling and medical guidance for fetal growth and development; (4) Newborn health care: Providing health care services for the growth and development, breastfeeding and nursing of newborns.

In the case of confirmed fetal malformations or serious defects, doctors have the obligation to inform and give medical advice on the termination of pregnancy. Such provisions can not only protect the maternal health but also protect the right to health of the fetus. See Article 18 of *the Law of the People's Republic of China on Maternal and Child Health Care*:

Article 18
Under any of the following circumstances after prenatal diagnosis, the doctor shall explain the situation to both husband and wife and give medical advice on the termination of pregnancy:

(1) the fetus suffers from a serious genetic disease;
(2) the fetus has serious defects;
(3) Continuation of pregnancy may endanger the life safety of the pregnant woman or seriously endanger the health of the pregnant woman due to serious illness.

In addition, the law also regulates healthcare institutions accordingly. Professional health care personnel are not only responsible for maternal physical examination, disease treatment, psychological counseling, and other work, but also for providing scientific guidance for maternal parenting, timely disease inspection, and vaccination of infants. In terms of newborn disease screening, the corresponding physical examination and related testing should be carried out on the newborn. It can be specifically seen in Article 24 of *the Maternal and Child Health Care Law of the People's Republic of China*:

Article 24
Healthcare institutions provide guidance to mothers on scientific child-rearing, proper nutrition, and breastfeeding.

Medical and health institutions shall give physical examination and vaccination to infants, and gradually provide medical and health services such as screening for diseases of newborns and prevention and treatment of frequently occurring and common diseases among infants.

In terms of the administrative management of maternal and child health care, China's laws put forward requirements for administrative organs and medical and health care institutions. Governments at all levels, as state organs in the management of public affairs, must give full play to their leading role. Only when all departments work together can we ensure the public welfare, equity, and accessibility of maternal and child health services. Since 1997, all localities have paid attention to strengthening the basic construction and connotation construction of medical and healthcare institutions. For the construction of obstetrics and pediatrics in grassroots hospitals, the policy is tilted in terms of human, material, and financial resources. This fully reflects the important role of medical and health institutions in maternal and child health care. It can be specifically seen in articles 28 and 31 of *the Maternal and Child Health Care Law of the People's Republic of China* (Li et al., 2004):

Article 28
People's governments at all levels shall take measures to strengthen the work of maternal and infant health care, raise the level of medical and health care services, actively prevent and treat the endemic and high-incidence diseases caused by environmental factors that seriously endanger the health of mothers and infants, and promote the development of maternal and infant health care.

Article 31
In accordance with the regulations of the administrative Department of Health under The State Council, medical and health institutions shall be responsible for the work of maternal and infant health care within the scope of their duties, establish norms for medical and health care work, raise the level of medical technology, take various measures to facilitate the masses, and do a good job in providing maternal and infant health care services.

In terms of the distribution of legal responsibilities, *the Law of the People's Republic of China on Maternal and Child Health Care* stipulates the legal responsibilities of the staff of medical and health care institutions. It is mainly determined by its status and role in maternal and child health care work. Workers engaged in maternal and child health care are the first to ensure the health of women and newborns. They are not only active advocates of health education, but also the undertakers of maternal and child health outpatient and primary medical services. Therefore, according to the relevant laws and regulations, personnel engaged in maternal and child health care should have the corresponding academic qualifications or professional qualifications, and obtain the maternal and child health care technical assessment certificate in accordance with the law. The law shall take strict measures to crack down on personnel engaged in maternal and child health care without the corresponding qualifications.

In this regard, Article 35–37 of *the Law of the People's Republic of China on Maternal and Child Health Care provide* in detail:

Article 35
Where a person who has not obtained the relevant certificate of conformity issued by the Government commits any of the following acts, the administrative department of public health under the local people's government at or above the county level shall stop it and may, according to the circumstances, give him a warning or impose a fine: (1) engaging in pre-marital medical examination, genetic disease diagnosis, prenatal diagnosis or medical technical appraisal; (2) performing an operation to terminate pregnancy; (3) providing relevant medical certificates as provided for in this Law.

The relevant medical certificate issued by subparagraph (3) above is invalid.

Article 36

Any person who, without obtaining the relevant qualification certificate issued by the State, performs an operation to terminate gestation or terminates gestation by any other means, resulting in death, disability, loss or basic loss of the ability to work, shall be investigated for criminal responsibility in accordance with the relevant provisions of the Criminal Law.

Article 37

Any person engaged in maternal and infant health care who, in violation of the provisions of this Law, issues relevant false medical certificates or conducts sex identification of the fetus shall be given administrative sanctions by the medical and health institution or the administrative department of public health according to the circumstances; If the circumstances are serious, the practicing qualification shall be revoked according to law.

Maternal and child health care is a work involving the whole process before pregnancy, pregnancy, and postpartum. It has the characteristics of obvious stages and strong professionalism. While providing high-quality maternal and child health care, it is also necessary to strengthen standardized management. Therefore, in order to better achieve the goal of protecting maternal and child health, China has established a complete management system. Through the enactment of the Law of the People's Republic of China on Maternal and Child Health Care, we can promote health care to improve the quality of services and reduce mortality of maternal and newborn mortality and disease morbidity. At the same time, extensive publicity of nursing knowledge, such as breastfeeding, scientific diet, and reasonable exercise, can ensure that people can provide protection for maternal and child health from multiple angles and levels, and implement the protection of children's rights and interests.

13.2.2 Teachers Law of the People's Republic of China

The general secretary has pointed out that, education is the foundation of the century-long plan; teachers are the foundation of education. Teachers are the foundation of the nation. The development of the country and the rejuvenation of the nation depend on talents, and the cultivation of talents and the improvement of quality depend on teachers. Teachers are the source of education. They shoulder the responsibility of making every child grow up healthily, and bear the responsibility of providing the best education for their people. Teachers are the promoters of social progress. They play an important role in children's education.

Teachers Law of the People's Republic of China was drafted in 1986. After 8 years of preparation and amendment, it was adopted at the fourth meeting of the Standing Committee of the Eighth National People's Congress on October 31, 1993, and came into force on January 1, 1994. Since then, the law has been amended in 2009, aiming to improve the social status of teachers and safeguard their legal rights. This law is of great significance for cultivating a high ideological and moral level and a high professional level of teachers. *Teachers Law of the People's Republic of China* is divided into nine chapters, each chapter is "General Provisions", "Rights and Obligations", "Qualifications and Appointments", "training and Training", "assessment", "treatment", "Reward", "Legal Responsibility" and "Supplementary Provisions". The enactment and implementation of the law have great practical significance for promoting the development of socialist education.

Teachers are important participants in children's education. With teachers as the target, the Teachers Law of the People's Republic of China elevates the state policy of respecting teachers and valuing education into law. It protects children's legitimate rights and interests from the perspective of youth education and provides a legal basis for children's right to education in China. At the same time, this law also clarifies the rights and obligations that teachers enjoy in the process of socialist modernization. This also coincides with the legislative idea of *the Compulsory Education Law of the People's Republic of China* (Li & Xue, 2021). Meanwhile, the law fully implements the provisions of Articles 28 and 29 of *the United Nations Convention on the Rights of the Child*. Every child has the right to a standard of living adequate for his or her physical, mental, spiritual, moral, and social development. The provision of the right to education can fully guarantee the full development of the child's personality, intelligence, and physical and mental capacity.

Teachers' rights refer to the rights and interests enjoyed by teachers in education and teaching according to law. The Teachers Law of the People's Republic of China stipulates that teachers enjoy many rights. Specifically, it includes the right to education and teaching, the right to scientific research, the right to manage students, the right to obtain remuneration, and the right to democratic management.

The right to manage students is one of teachers' rights related to children's rights. It means that teachers have the right to guide students' learning and development and to evaluate students' character and achievements. This is a kind of dominant right that teachers enjoy over students in teaching. To be specific, teachers have the right to provide targeted guidance to students according to their physical and psychological development and characteristics. They can give guidance to students in aspects such as specialty, employment, and further study. Secondly, in ideological and political quality, moral cultivation, academic work, and other aspects, teachers should give objective, fair, and appropriate evaluations. Finally, under the guidance of correct thinking and scientific methods, teachers should make students' personalities and abilities develop in an all-round way.

The specific content of the provisions on the rights of teachers in *the Teachers Law of the People's Republic of China* can be seen in Article 7, which relates to the rights of children in the third provision:

Article 7
Teachers shall enjoy the following rights: (1) Conducting educational and teaching activities, carrying out educational and teaching reforms and experiments; (2) Engaging in scientific research, and academic exchanges, participating in professional academic groups, and fully expressing opinions in academic activities; (3) To guide students' learning and development, and to assess students' conduct and academic performance; (4) Get wages and remuneration on time, enjoy the welfare treatment stipulated by the state and the paid leave of winter and summer holidays; (5) To put forward opinions and suggestions on school education, teaching, management and the work of the administrative departments of education, and to participate in the democratic management of schools through congresses of staff and staff or other forms; (6) Participate in advanced studies or other forms of training.

The law also lays down the duties of teachers. In order to fulfill the mission of teaching and educating, teachers need to undertake a series of tasks and assume corresponding responsibilities. The Teachers Law of the People's Republic of China stipulates in detail the obligation of teachers to ensure children's right to education. These obligations mainly include, but are not limited to, the obligation to abide by laws and morals, the obligation to abide by rules and regulations and to complete education and teaching, the obligation to cultivate students' correct outlook on life and values, the obligation to protect students' basic rights, and the obligation to regulate students' behavior.

First of all, the Teachers Law of the People's Republic of China stipulates the obligations of teachers in the cultivation of students' outlook on life and values. Teachers are required to educate students with a scientific outlook on life and world outlook. On the one hand, students should work hard to learn book knowledge while loving the motherland and socialism. On the other hand, it is necessary to allow students to set up lofty ideals while combining their own values with social services, and insist on hard work. Teachers should educate students to be good citizens who abide by the law, social morality, and civilized behavior habits. In this process, teachers should consciously strengthen students' patriotism, national unity, and legal education in order to promote the Chinese national spirit.

Secondly, the Teachers Law of the People's Republic of China stipulates the obligation of teachers to protect the basic rights of students, which means teachers should care about and love all students and respect the personality of students. This provision is the concrete embodiment of legal documents such as *the Constitution of the People's Republic of China*, *the Civil Code of the People's Republic of China*, and *the Protection of Minors of the People's Republic of China* in the field of education. Personal dignity is the most basic spiritual right of the right holder. The specific personality rights of the right holder reflect the requirements of personality dignity in different degrees. Students are also rights holders. Although they are in an educated position compared with teachers, they also enjoy personal dignity (Liu, 2009).

Finally, *the Teachers Law of the People's Republic of China* lays down the obligations of teachers in regulating students' behavior. The main content is that teachers should actively safeguard students' legal rights and promote their healthy development. On the one hand, the scope of teachers' suppression of wrongdoing is clear. In school work, teachers shall stop illegal acts that infringe upon students' rights. On the other hand, the scope for teachers to criticize and resist wrongdoing is in a general sense. Safeguarding children's legitimate rights and physical health is the common responsibility of the whole society, and teachers are naturally duty-bound. Therefore, teachers have the responsibility to criticize and resist illegal acts that endanger students' physical and mental health.

The specific content of the Teachers' obligations stipulated in *the Teachers' Law of the People's Republic of China* can be seen in Article 8. The third provision relates to the education of students' outlook on life and values, the fourth provision relates to the protection of students' basic rights, and the fifth provision relates to the regulation of students' behavior:

> **Article 8**
> ***Teachers shall perform the following obligations: (1) Abide by the Constitution, laws and professional ethics, and be a model for teachers; (2) To implement the educational policies, observe the rules and regulations, implement the teaching plan of the school, fulfill the appointment of teachers, and complete the tasks of education and teaching; (3) To educate students on the basic principles defined in the Constitution, patriotism, national unity, legal system, ideology, morality, culture, science and technology, and to organize and lead students to carry out beneficial social activities; (4) To care for and love all students, respect their personality, and promote their all-round development in moral, intellectual, physical and other aspects; (5) To stop acts harmful to students or other acts infringing on the legitimate rights and interests of students, criticize and resist phenomena harmful to the healthy growth of students; (6) Constantly improve ideological and political consciousness and the level of education and teaching.***

In addition to the rights and obligations of teachers, *the Teachers Law of the People's Republic of China* also clearly stipulates the welfare benefits enjoyed by teachers. This is an affirmation of the work of teachers to educate people and train the future successors of the country, and it is also an encouragement to the hard work of teachers. In addition, the Teachers Law of the People's Republic of China also encourages graduates to engage in education and teaching in ethnic minority areas and remote and poverty-stricken areas. This provision also reflects the protection of children's right to education in these remote areas. And this provision is also consistent with Article 33 of *the Compulsory Education Law of the People's Republic of China.*

For specific provisions, see Article 27 of the Teachers Law of the People's Republic of China:

Article 27
Local people's governments at various levels shall provide subsidies to teachers and graduates with secondary technical education or above who are engaged in education and teaching in areas inhabited by minority nationalities and outlying and poverty-stricken areas.

In terms of legal responsibility, the Teachers Law of the People's Republic of China stipulates the responsibility that teachers should bear for violating students' rights and interests, and investigate criminal responsibility for serious violations of students' rights and interests. Specifically, Article 37 provides:

Article 37
In any of the following circumstances, teachers shall be subject to administrative sanctions or dismissed by their schools, other institutions of education, or administrative departments of education: (1) Deliberately failing to complete the tasks of education and teaching and causing losses to the work of education and teaching; (2) Corporal punishment of students, which is not corrected after education; (3) Bad conduct, insult students, bad influence.

If a teacher has any of the circumstances listed in items (2) and (3) of the preceding paragraph and the circumstances are serious enough to constitute a crime, he or she shall be investigated for criminal responsibility according to law.

Teachers are the engineers of the human soul and play a vital role in the healthy development of children. Teachers can not only help students establish a correct outlook on life and values but also protect students' personal dignity and rights in education and teaching activities. Teachers not only have the right to manage students and ensure their independent personality development but also can criticize and resist illegal acts that infringe on students' health. *Teachers Law of the People's Republic of China* is the first law concerning teachers in the history of Chinese education, and its promulgation and implementation have important practical significance. On the one hand, the promulgation of the law is conducive to fundamentally improving the social status of teachers (Zhao & Hao, 2015), protecting their legitimate rights and interests, and laying the foundation for improving the quality of education for the child. On the other hand, the implementation of this law is also more conducive to strengthening the construction of teachers and creating a group of high-quality teachers. In short, China is committed to fully protecting students' right to education, promoting the development of socialist education, fully implementing the fundamental task of cultivating morality and educating people, and training socialist builders and successors who are well-developed morally, intellectually, and physically.

13.2.3 Labor Law of the People's Republic of China

Labor law was originally adapted by civil law. Since the rise of the Industrial Revolution in the nineteenth century, labor law has been increasingly incorporated into the legal system of various countries. In the course of the development of labor law, it has gradually separated from civil law and formed an independent legal department. *The Labor Law of the People's Republic of China* is a law established by the state to regulate the labor system. Its main purpose is to protect the legitimate rights and interests of workers, adjust labor relations, and maintain the order of the socialist market economy. The labor law is formulated and promulgated in accordance with the Constitution and is of great significance for promoting economic development and social progress (Guo, 2008). The Law was adopted at the Eighth session of the Standing Committee of the Eighth National People's Congress on July 5, 1994, and came into force on January 1, 1995. Since then, *the Labor Law of the People's Republic of China* has been amended for the first time in 2009 and for the second time in 2018. *The Labor Law of the People's Republic of China* currently in force is divided into 13 chapters. The chapters, in turn, include "General Provisions", "employment promotion", "labor contracts and collective contracts", "working hours, rest and Vacation", "Wages", "labor safety and Health", "special protection for Female employees and underage workers", "vocational training", "social insurance and welfare", "labor disputes", "supervision and inspection", "legal responsibilities" and "Supplementary Provisions". The fundamental starting point of the law is to take workers as the center, to protect the legitimate rights and interests of workers as the basis, reflecting the humanistic care for workers.

On the premise of ensuring the safety and health of the child, *the Labor Law of the People's Republic of China* allows the child to engage in work appropriate to their age and intelligence. However, the physical and mental development of children has not been completely fixed, and there is a gap with adults. Therefore, when arranging the labor of underage workers, we should pay attention to their physiological characteristics. For example, excessive physical labor, excessive tension, unsuitable tools, etc., will have a negative impact on the normal development of underage workers. The Labor Law of the People's Republic of China has made many special provisions to protect the legitimate rights and interests of juvenile workers. Such as the legal minimum age limit for employment, the requirements for the type of labor of juvenile workers, and the obligation for employers to arrange health examinations for juvenile workers.

The legal minimum age of employment is the age limit for natural persons to enter the labor field and form legal labor relations with employers, and it is also an important embodiment of the labor law's protection of the rights and interests of the child. In the provisions of the minimum age for employment (Zhou, 2013), the Labor Law of the People's Republic of China has made relevant provisions. A worker between the ages of 16 and 18 is a minor worker, and a child under the age of 16 cannot qualify as a worker. This provision is consistent with the rules on the identification of persons with full capacity for civil conduct in the Civil Code of the People's Republic of China. At the same time, it also meets the requirements of the International Labor Organization's Minimum Age for Employment Convention, 1973, which stipulates that "the minimum age for employment shall not be lower than the age of completion of compulsory education and in any case shall not be lower than 15 years of age". This restriction on the age of employment reasonably takes into account the physical development of children and the development of Chinese society and also protects the employment rights of children as much as possible.

The prohibition and restrictions on the employment of children in *the Labor Law of the People's Republic of China* can be specifically seen in Article 25 and Article 58, paragraph 2:

> **Article 25**
> ***An employing unit shall be prohibited from recruiting minors under the age of 16.***
>
> ***Units of art, sports, and special arts and crafts that recruit the child under the age of 16 must abide by the relevant regulations of the State and guarantee their right to receive compulsory education.***
>
> **Article 58 (2)**
> ***"Underage worker" refers to workers who have reached the age of 16 but not the age of 18.***

In addition, the meaning of "child labor" is not the same as that of underage workers referred to in the Labor Law of the People's Republic of China. The two concepts have obvious differences. First of all, in terms of age, child labor refers to children under the age of 16 who have labor relations with units or individuals and engage in income-generating labor or engage in individual labor (Wu, 2014). The term "underage workers" refers to the worker who has been employed by the employing unit and has reached the age of 16 but not 18. Secondly, in terms of legality, *the Labor Law of the People's Republic of China* prohibits employers from employing child labor. However, there are exceptions for art, sports, and special crafts units. And the recruitment of underage workers is permitted by law. Finally, from the point of view of liability, child workers are usually persons without or with limited capacity for civil conduct. They can't be legal workers. However, underage workers are regarded as persons with full capacity for civil conduct. They can sign labor contracts with employers as workers and get equal protection in law.

Women and the child are facing more challenges and obstacles in the job market because of the obvious differences between them and male workers in their physiological characteristics, educational level, and occupational status. Their equal employment rights are vulnerable to violation. Therefore, in order to guarantee the equal employment rights of such vulnerable groups, *the Labor Law of the People's Republic of China* provides special protection for female workers and underage workers. The law puts forward specific requirements for employers to arrange the underage workers to engage in prohibited labor and to carry out health checks on them. This is also consistent with the concept of protecting the social rights and interests of underage women in *the Law of the People's Republic of China on the Protection of Women's Rights and Interests*.

The Labor Law of the People's Republic of China strictly stipulates that the employer shall arrange the types of labor for underage workers. Employers are required not to arrange for the child to engage in a certain range of labor, mainly involving toxic, high temperature, low temperature, high intensity, and high risk, fieldwork, and other labor that may seriously endanger children's health. This legislative purpose is also consistent with Article 31 of *the United Nations Convention on the Rights of the Child*. It requires that "the child has the right to be protected from economic exploitation and from performing any work that is likely to interfere with or interfere with the child's education or be harmful to the child's health or physical, mental, spiritual, moral or social development". Article 64 of *the Labor Law of the People's Republic of China* provides as follows:

Article 64
No underage workers shall be arranged to engage in work underground in mines, work that is toxic or harmful, work with grade IV physical labor intensity as prescribed by the State, and other work that is prohibited.

In addition, other laws and regulations in China also provide for the treatment of underage workers who suffer from certain diseases or have certain physical defects (non-disabled types). It also requires employers not to arrange for them to engage in a certain range of labor and specifies the types of diseases and defects, and the types of labor. At the same time, employers should also pay attention to the protection of the health of underage workers. The law stipulates that employers should arrange regular health check-ups for underage workers to protect the legitimate rights and interests of children. Article 65 of *the Labor Law of the People's Republic of China* provides as follows:

Article 65
The employing unit shall conduct regular health examinations of juvenile workers.

On the assumption of legal liability, the Labor Law of the People's Republic of China makes corresponding provisions. For the illegal recruitment of children under the legal minimum age for employment by employers, and the illegal infringement of the legitimate rights and interests of underage workers, the law stipulates different administrative departments and different punishment measures for them. See Article 94–95 of *the Labor Law of the People's Republic of China*:

Article 94
Where an employing unit illegally recruits a child under the age of 16, the labor administrative department shall order it to make corrections and impose a fine. If the circumstances are serious, the business license shall be revoked by the market supervision and administration department.

Article 95
Where an employing unit violates the provisions of this Law on the protection of female and underage workers and infringes upon their lawful rights and interests, the labor administrative department shall order it to make corrections and impose a fine. If damage is caused to female workers or underage workers, they shall be liable for compensation.

The Labor Law of the People's Republic of China provides special labor protection for underage workers, which is based on the characteristics of underage workers and aims at protecting the special rights and interests of underage workers in the labor process. The law aims to ensure that they can grow up and work in a healthy, safe, and legal environment. Provisions on age restrictions, working hours and rest, work content and environment, education and training, and labor remuneration effectively protect the rights and interests of underage workers. The protection of underage workers is essentially the protection of the development of new productive forces. We should promote and enforce these regulations to ensure that underage workers can develop fully and become pillars of the country and society (Dai, 2012).

13.2.4 Law of the People's Republic of China on Administrative Penalties for Public Security

In the socialist rule of law system with Chinese characteristics, *the Law of the People's Republic of China on Administrative Penalties for Public Security* not only has the role of maintaining public order and ensuring public safety but also undertakes the task of protecting and educating the child and preventing them from breaking the law and committing crimes, just like criminal laws and norms. This Law was adopted at the 17th session of the Standing Committee of the Tenth National People's Congress of the People's Republic of China on August 28, 2005, and came into force on March 1, 2006, and was revised in 2012. *The law of the People's Republic of China on Administrative Penalties for Public Security* is divided into six chapters, each chapter, in turn, is "General Provisions", "Types and Application of Penalties", "Acts and Penalties for violating public security administration", "punishment procedures", "supervision of law enforcement" and "Supplementary provisions". The basic spirit of this law is the combination of empowerment and limitation of power, and the combination of combating violations and protecting human rights. It is necessary not only to fully empower the public security organs and their police to perform the necessary power for public security management, but also to help them better serve the social security order and public safety, but also to make stricter regulations on the exercise of police power to prevent the abuse of power; and it is necessary not only to punish those who violate the law but also to respect and protect human rights, paying special attention to preventing the improper use or even abuse of power from infringing upon the legitimate rights of citizens.

The Law of the People's Republic of China on Administrative Penalties for Public Security has adopted relatively lenient punishment measures for the acts of the child. In keeping with the legal spirit of protecting the legitimate rights of the child, this law stipulates the penalties for the administration of public security to the child. According to their age, intelligence, psychology, and growth characteristics, different education, rehabilitation, and deterrence measures are applied to help them self-correct, understand their mistakes, and avoid violating the law again. This concept ensures the individual difference and particularity of the child when they accept the punishment of the public security administration. At the same time, for the child who violates public security administration, the law emphasizes that parents or legal guardians are the subjects of children's education and guidance. Through their education, the child is guided to realize the negative consequences of their own behavior, which helps them to actively correct their mistakes.

In terms of the provisions of the age of responsibility, the provisions of the Law of the People's Republic of China on Administrative Penalties for Public Security are different from the norms of criminal law, which is mainly based on Article 30 of *the Law of the People's Republic of China on Administrative Penalties*. This article provides for different punishments for the child who have committed illegal acts according to their age. The child under the age of 14 who have committed illegal acts shall not be subject to administrative punishment but shall be ordered to be disciplined by their guardians. The child who has committed illegal acts between the ages of 14 and 18, they shall be given a lighter or mitigated administrative punishment. In view of the fact that violations of public security administration penalties are relatively minor violations and do not constitute crimes, the age of responsibility for public security administration penalties is only divided into three sections, namely under 14 years old, 14 years old to 18 years old and 18 years old and above. This is clearly different from the age range of 14–16 years as defined in *the Criminal Law of the People's Republic of China*. The specific provisions of *the Law of the People's Republic of China on Administrative Penalties for Public Security* can be seen in Articles 12 and 21:

> **Article 12**
> ***A person who has reached the age of 14 but not the age of 18 and violates the administration of public security, he shall be given a lighter or mitigated punishment; A person under the age of 14 who violates the administration of public security shall not be punished, but his guardian shall be ordered to impose strict discipline on him.***

> **Article 21**
> ***Where a person who commits an act violating the administration of public security has any of the following circumstances and should be subject to administrative detention in accordance with this Law, the punishment of administrative detention shall not be carried out: (1) Having reached the age of 14 but not the age of 16; (2) Having reached the age of 16 but not 18 and violating the administration of public security for the first time; (3) Over the age of 70; (4) Pregnant or breastfeeding her baby under one-year-old.***

The Law of the People's Republic of China on Administrative Penalties for Public Security has increased the severity of punishment for violations against the child who are the future of a country and a nation. However, in real life, the child often suffers from various forms of infringement, which is manifested in the infringement of their body, property, spirit, and so on. The law imposes harsher penalties for acts that harm the children's legal rights, such as beating, injury, and molestation, in the form of longer detention and larger fines. The specific content can be seen in the provisions of articles 40, 43, and 44 of *the Law of the People's Republic of China on Administrative Penalties for Public Security*:

Articles 40
Whoever commits any of the following acts shall be detained for not less than 10 days but not more than 15 days and shall, in addition, be fined not less than 500 yuan but not more than 1,000 yuan; If the circumstances are relatively minor, he shall be detained for not less than five days but not more than 10 days and shall, in addition, be fined not less than 200 yuan but not more than 500 yuan: (1) Organizing, coercing or inducing a person under the age of 16 or a disabled person to make a horrible or cruel performance;

Articles 43
A person who beats another person or intentionally injures another person's body shall be detained for not less than five days but not more than 10 days and shall also be fined not less than 200 yuan but not more than 500 yuan; If the circumstances are relatively minor, he shall be detained for not more than five days or fined not more than 500 yuan.

Under any of the following circumstances, he shall be detained for not less than 10 days but not more than 15 days and shall, in addition, be fined not less than 500 yuan but not more than 1,000 yuan: (1) beating or injuring another person in a gang; (2) beating or injuring a disabled person, a pregnant woman, a person under the age of 14 or a person over the age of 60; (3) beating or injuring others repeatedly or beating or injuring more than one person at a time.

Articles 44
Anyone who indecently assaults another person or intentionally exposes his or her body in a public place under aggravating circumstances shall be sentenced to detention of not less than five days and not more than ten days; Anyone who indecently assaults a person with intellectual disability, a mental patient, or a person under 14 years of age, or in other serious cases, shall be sentenced to detention for not less than 10 days and not more than 15 days.

In addition, *the Law of the People's Republic of China on the Prevention of Children Delinquency* stipulates that schools, relevant social organizations and their staff, and those who abet, coerce, or induce the child to commit undesirable acts or serious undesirable acts shall be punished by the public security organs in accordance with the law for public security administration when their acts meet the conditions for public security administration punishment. This provision closely links *the Law of the People's Republic of China on Administrative Penalties for Public Security* with the legal system of child protection and jointly contributes to the protection of children's rights and interests.

The Law of the People's Republic of China on Administrative Penalties for Public Security makes a special provision for the violation of the administration of public security by the child under the age of 16. One is that parents or guardians should be notified when investigating suspected offenders and dealing with illegal acts. Because the physical and mental development of the child under the age of 16 is not sound, and they do not have the ability to fully identify and control their own behavior. The child may make false statements or even refuse to make statements based on negative emotions, such as nervousness, anxiety or fear, in the absence of a parent or familiar adult relative during an investigation or questioning. This will make it more difficult for law enforcement officers to enforce the law. In addition, if parents or familiar adult relatives are present, it can also timely detect the possible violations of children's rights and interests such as intentional delay or fraud by law enforcement officers in the investigation process. So that to exercise the right of supervision at any time and protect the legitimate rights and interests of the child.

Consistent with the provisions of Article 270 of the Criminal Procedure Law of the People's Republic of China, the requirements for the questioning process are specified in Article 84, paragraph 3, of *the Law of the People's Republic of China on Administrative Penalties for Public Security*:

Article 84, Paragraph 3
When questioning a perpetrator of a violation of public security management who is under the age of sixteen, a parent or other guardian shall be notified of the presence of the perpetrator.

As minors, the child isn't mature enough compared with adults in terms of physical and mental development and cognitive level. As for some acts that harm their legitimate rights and interests, they are often unable to stop and defend their rights in a timely and effective manner. *The Law of the People's Republic of China on Administrative Penalties for Public Security* protects the child in a biased manner, and it is undoubtedly a powerful blow to the behavior that damages children's rights and interests. However, this is not to defend the rights and interests of the child only when they are infringed upon but to make people pay more attention to the disadvantaged groups and cherish the rights and interests of the child through the deterrent effect of the law, so as to provide more help and support to them. The protection of children's legitimate rights and interests also requires the cooperation of other relevant laws and the joint efforts of the whole society. Only in this way can we create a harmonious and safe social environment for the healthy growth of the child.

13.2.5 Prison Law of the People's Republic of China

Prison Law of the People's Republic of China is an integral part of the country's criminal law. It regulates certain social relations that take place in the execution of sentences in prisons and is formulated by the country and ensured by country coercion. The Prison Law of the People's Republic of China was amended and adopted at the 11th meeting of the Standing Committee of the Eighth National People's Congress on 29 December 1994, and came into force on 29 December 1994. It was amended once in 2012. From the perspective of content, the Prison Law of the People's Republic of China is divided into seven chapters. And each chapter, in turn, is "General Provisions", "Prison", "Execution of Penalties", "Prison Administration", "Education and Reform of Criminals", "Education and Reform of Juvenile Offenders", and "Supplementary Provisions". This law was enacted and implemented to protect the legal rights of detainees. It is of great significance to execute penalties correctly, punish and reform criminals, and prevent and reduce crimes.

The concept of prison law was developed along with the evolution of prison functions, and its history is as long as the length of punishment. In early China, the main forms of punishment were capital punishment and physical punishment executed in the form of exile, while criminal detention and imprisonment did not occupy a dominant position in the criminal punishment system. At that time, prisons were mainly guarded places for not convicted criminals and criminal defendants, and the proportion of convicted prisoners sentenced to detention was small. With the continuous development of society, a penal system with criminal detention and imprisonment as the main body has gradually come into being. The main function of the prison has gradually evolved to carry out the punishment of criminals sentenced to criminal detention and imprisonment. In accordance with this, prison law becomes the law for executing punishments on criminals.

In terms of detention and management of detainees, the Prison Law of the People's Republic of China adopts the mode of separate detention and management. At the same time, it gives special attention to children among detainees. On the one hand, separate detention mainly solves the problem of the detention system, that is, separate detention according to gender, age, type of punishment, and level of sentence implementation. And it is divided according to the nature of the crime, creating conditions for classified correction and classified education, and avoiding cross-infection. On the other hand, separate management mainly deals with the problems of the management system. It is mainly to systematize the original decentralized management mode and give appropriate treatment according to the reform effect of prisoners and the length of their sentences. Moreover, according to the characteristics of various types of criminals, the law gives proper control to give full play to the functions of management such as restraint, correction, training, guidance, punishment, and incentive. This provision is similar to the differentiated correction method stipulated in Article 52, paragraph 3, of *the Community Correction Law of the People's Republic of China*. They are both special provisions for juvenile offenders to provide a relatively healthy education and reform environment.

It is an effective way to protect the rights and interests of juvenile criminals and an important principle in the management of juvenile criminals to detain juvenile criminals strictly separately from adult criminals. This provision can effectively prevent juvenile criminals from being adversely affected by adult criminals, and prevent them from being bullied by adult criminals. And it is of great significance to protect the personal safety of juvenile offenders and purify the environment for their incarceration. At the same time, the practice also facilitates the implementation of special treatment of juvenile offenders. According to the characteristics of the physiological development of juvenile offenders, the law requires targeted legal knowledge education and corresponding cultural education for juvenile offenders. The implementation of separate detention and management can better carry out the education and correction of juvenile offenders, promote their reintegration into society, and lay a solid foundation for better punishment and reform of juvenile offenders.

The specific provisions can be seen in Article 39 of *the Prison Law of the People's Republic of China*:

> **Article 39**
> ***Prisons shall separate the custody and administration of adult male and female prisoners and juvenile prisoners. In the reform of juvenile and female prisoners, consideration shall be given to their physical and psychological characteristics.***
>
> ***Prisons detain prisoners separately and administer them in different ways according to their types of crime, types of punishment, length of sentence, and performance in reform.***

In addition to the provisions on the division of custody and supervision, the *Prison Law of the People's Republic of China* also provides a special chapter on the education and reform of juvenile offenders. This law stipulates that the place of execution of punishment for juvenile offenders is a juvenile correctional institution. As a type of prison, the juvenile correctional institution is the national penalty execution organ, that undertakes a special social mission. It is not only a place where juvenile offenders are punished, but also a special place of education and reform. In terms of the management of juvenile offenders, the department also attaches great importance to the protection of their legal rights and strives to create a reform environment conducive to the physical and mental health of juvenile offenders and their positive progress, so that they can form correct values and outlook on life. Legal norms also clearly stipulate that in daily management, prison staff can use the term "student" for minor offenders. This provision is specifically reflected in Article 74 of the *Prison Law of the People's Republic of China*:

> **Article 74**
> ***Juvenile offenders shall be executed in juvenile correctional institutions.***

As for the principle of education and reform of juvenile offenders, *the Law on the Protection of Children of the People's Republic of China* clearly states that "the principle of education, rehabilitation, and rehabilitation shall be carried out, and the principle of education first and punishment as a supplement shall be adhered to". It is also included in *the Prison Law of the People's Republic of China*. These laws and regulations put forward the basic requirements of "education first and punishment as a supplement" for the education and reform of juvenile offenders. In view of different cases and juvenile crimes, different treatment is implemented according to the nature, circumstances, and social harm of juvenile crimes. The law strives to educate and save the majority, and severely cracking down on a small number of especially serious criminal acts. The specific provisions can be found in Article 75:

Article 75
Education and reform should be the main focus in the execution of criminal punishment for minor offenders. The labor of juvenile offenders shall conform to the characteristics of minors and shall mainly focus on learning culture and productive skills.

Prisons shall cooperate with the country, society, schools, and other institutions of education to provide necessary conditions for juvenile offenders to receive compulsory education.

In general, a juvenile correctional institution is a place for the education, rehabilitation, and rehabilitation of young people over the age of 14 and under the age of 18. For juvenile offenders who meet the above age conditions, they need to enter juvenile correctional institutions to serve their sentences. If the sentenced juvenile has reached the age of 18 during the time of serving his sentence and cannot meet the conditions of the juvenile correctional institution, does he need to be transferred to a prison for adult offenders to serve the remainder of his sentence? In this regard, the Prison Law of the People's Republic of China clearly stipulates that those with remaining sentences of not more than 2 years may continue to serve their sentences in juvenile correctional institutions. This provision takes into account the physical and mental development of children during the sensitive period of transition to adulthood and the fact that their transfer to a post-adult prison environment may result in the failure of previous educational rehabilitation. This fully reflects the humanity of the law and protects the healthy growth of minors in another way, safeguarding their legitimate rights and interests. Such provisions take into account the physical and mental development of minors in the sensitive period of turning into adults, which fully reflects the human nature of the law. In addition, if juvenile offenders are transferred to adult prisons, their previous educational reform may be weakened by the influence of the environment. This could lead to the failure of previous educational reforms. Article 76 of *the Prison Law of the People's Republic of China* provides as follows:

Article 76
When a minor offender reaches the age of 18, if the remaining term of his sentence does not exceed two years, he may still stay in a juvenile correctional institution to serve the remaining term of his sentence.

The relevant provisions, such as separate custody, management, setting up special juvenile correctional institutions, and focusing on the principle of education and reform, are the special provisions of the Prison Law of the People's Republic of China for juvenile offenders in the process of executing punishment. This is consistent with the relevant provisions of *the Criminal Procedure Law of the People's*

Republic of China and *the Community Correction Law of the People's Republic of China*. The general provisions for juvenile offenders in prison, such as the execution of punishment, prison administration, education, and reform, are the same as those for adult offenders. This can be seen in particular in article 77 of *Prison Law of the People's Republic of China*:

> **Article 77**
> ***Where the administration, education, and reform of juvenile offenders are not provided for in this Chapter, the relevant provisions of this Law shall apply.***

Due to incomplete physical and mental development, lenient management measures for juvenile offenders are more easily accepted by society and the public. Therefore, many leniency measures were initially tried in the management of juvenile offenders, and after successful experience, they were gradually introduced in adult prisons.

The promulgation and implementation of *the Prisons Law of the People's Republic of China* is an important milestone in the history of China's socialist legal system. It indicates that the prison administration of our country has entered a new stage of construction. As part of social governance, *the Prison Law of the People's Republic of China* also fully takes into account the physical and mental development of juvenile offenders in terms of safeguarding and regulating the legitimate rights and interests of juvenile offenders. The law upholds uphold the concept of tolerance but never connivance, on the one hand, it provides special care in the system design for errant children to help them correct their ideas and learn from their mistakes. On the other hand, *the Prison Law of the People's Republic of China* also pays attention to the connection and coordination with other laws and regulations, constantly optimizes the system design, and requires prison administrative organs to rely on state power organs and state judicial organs. Conscientiously perform the functions of supervision and inspection, and investigate, verify, and handle the complaints and reports of juvenile criminals. At the same time, on the basis of laws, regulations, and rules, conscientiously perform the functions of supervision and inspection, and investigate, verify, and handle the complaints and reports of juvenile criminals. Thus, the laws and regulations of prison management can be further improved, the legitimate rights of juvenile offenders can be effectively safeguarded, and prison management work can be promoted to the legal and standardized track.

13.3 Summary

This chapter takes the age development of children as the guide and interprets several legal norms involved in the growing process of children in detail. First of all, the fetus is the starting point of the natural person's life formation, growth, and development, and the protection of the fetus reflects the level of a country's rule of law. As a law to protect the health of mothers, fetuses, and newborns, *the Law of the People's Republic of China on Maternal and Child Health* has strengthened the work of maternal and child health from the root and has ensured the health of the next generation. Growing up from an infant to an adolescent is a process of qualitative change, which requires school education. In this process, teachers play a crucial role. *The Teachers Law of the People's Republic of China* clarifies in legal form the important position and role of teachers in promoting the healthy growth of students and maintaining normal teaching order and protecting the legitimate rights and interests of children. To leave school and enter society, labor is essential. In order to fully protect children's right to equal employment, *the Labor Law of the People's Republic of China* gives preferential protection to vulnerable groups such as underage workers, which shows that lawmakers attach importance to children's labor rights and interests.

In the process of children's growth, factors including family situation, living environment, social influence, and other factors will lead children astray. The educational reform of juvenile offenders affects the stability and development of the country. In order to protect the legitimate rights and interests of juvenile offenders, *the Law of the People's Republic of China on Public Security Administration and Punishment* and *the Prison Law of the People's Republic of China* clearly define the particularity and difference of the child. These two laws strengthen crime prevention and legal awareness education for children through education and guidance give mild treatment in punishment methods, and effectively protect the legitimate interests of juvenile offenders.

We must make it clear that the protection of children's rights and interests requires not only the support of the law but also the joint efforts of the whole society. Families, schools, and all levels of society should provide a better growth environment and more comprehensive protection measures for children's development. Only in this way can we ensure the healthy growth of children and contribute to the harmony and stability of society.

In the context of the rule of law, China's law on the protection of children's rights is a legal system with *the Constitution of the People's Republic of China* as its core, and *the United Nations Convention on the Rights of the Child* as its programmatic guidance. *The Law of the People's Republic of China on the Protection of Children* and *the Law of the People's Republic of China on the Prevention of Juvenile Delinquency* serve as specialized laws within this system, with other laws as supplements. A child protection legal system with Chinese characteristics covering civil, administrative, and criminal matters has been initially established, providing strong legal support for the protection of children's legitimate rights and interests (Zheng & Shu, 2024). Moreover, there are other policy documents for multi-level and multi-angle supplements, together to form a complete set of child protection systems. In addition to the ten or so laws mentioned in this chapter of this book, other legal documents are listed below, and the detailed interpretation will not be repeated.

References

Dai, M. (2012). Theoretical and empirical analysis of labor adult system. *Chinese and Foreign Jurisprudence, 3*, 503–520.

Guo, Z. (2008). Contract theory of labor relations and its practice. *Social Science Research, 4*, 29–33.

Li, C., Li, C., Li, X., Gao, G., Wang, D., & Yan, G. (2011). Management and development of county-level maternal and child health centers. China Maternal and Child Health Care, 20, 3045–3047.

Li, J., & Xue, E. (2021). Compulsory education policy in China: A perspective of legal analysis. In *Compulsory education policy in China: Concept and practice* (pp. 1–14). Springer Singapore.

Li, J., Liu, L., & Hu, C. (2004). Survey on the implementation of the maternal and child health law in Rizhao City. *China Maternal and Child Health Care, 12*, 78.

Liu, J. (2009). A brief discussion on the moral basis and legal guarantees for the realization of human dignity in China. *Morality and Civilization, 4*, 108–111.

Wu, H. (2014). Research on children's rights protection and children's welfare legislation. *China Youth Research, 1*, 36–40.

Ye, X. (2022). The concept and institutional system of legislation on the protection of minors. *Chinese and Foreign Law, 3*, 724–743.

Zhao, S., & Hao, S. (2015). Analysis of China's education development under the threshold of law. *Education Academic Monthly, 6*, 15–20.

Zheng, G., & Shu, J. (2024). In the name of protection—A critical analysis of China's legal framework of children's personal information protection in the digital era. *Computer Law & Security Review, 53*, 105979.

Zhou, B. (2013). Protection of minors' rights and interests: What labor law can and cannot do. *Journal of China Youth Politics Institute, 3*, 29–33.

Chapter 14
Conclusion

In modern society, ensuring the physical and mental health of the child is the proper meaning and goal of the law; at the same time, the law is an important weapon for safeguarding the rights and interests of the child, and only through the continuous improvement of the legal system for the protection of the child can the capacity and level of protection of the child's rights and interests be continuously enhanced. In the past, China has been committed to improving laws related to the child, practicing the concept that "the highest law is to make the people happy". The efforts made by the Chinese government in safeguarding the rights and interests of the child are not only reflected in the improvement of the domestic legal system but also in the active implementation of the United Nations Convention on the Rights of the Child, which highlights the globalized nature of China's safeguarding of the child's rights and interests. As stated in the preface, the purpose of this book is to take the Convention on the Rights of the Child as the basis and combine it with China's legal norms for safeguarding the rights and interests of the child, to show the world China's legal system for safeguarding the rights and interests of the child and the achievements of China's child protection endeavors, and to provide the world with a Chinese solution for the legal construction of safeguarding the rights and interests of the child. By studying and analyzing China's practice of the Convention on the Rights of the Child and its legal system for safeguarding the rights and interests of the child, this book will help readers better understand China's achievements in safeguarding the rights and interests of the child, and will also help readers better understand China's efforts to safeguard the rights and interests of the child from an international perspective.

Convention on the Rights of the Child

One of the key words of this book is the United Nations Convention on the Rights of the Child, which is recognized as the most comprehensive and extensive international convention regulating the child's rights in the world. Based on the principles

© The Author(s), under exclusive license to Springer Nature Singapore Pte Ltd. 2026

H. Li, P. Liang, *The Legal System for the Protection of Children's Rights in China*, Resilient and Friendly Living Environments,
https://doi.org/10.1007/978-981-95-9925-7_14

of non-discrimination, the best interests of the child, respect for the rights and dignity of the child, and respect for the child's views, it specifies four basic rights of the child, such as the right to survival, the right to protection, the right to development, the right to participation, etc., which should be enjoyed by the child according to law. This book focuses on analyzing the contents of the Convention that are related to China's legal system for the protection of the child's rights and interests, as it has a far-reaching impact on China's legal system for the protection of the child's rights and interests. Since its accession to the Convention, the Chinese government has attached great importance to the active protection of the child's rights and has earnestly implemented the Convention. On the premise of fully understanding and assimilating the legislative purposes and principles of the Convention, China has successively issued legal norms and policy documents on the protection of the child's rights and interests, setting high standards and requirements for the cause of protecting the child's rights in China, and fully demonstrating China's determination to promote and protect the rights of the child and to set up a better legal system for child protection. At the same time, the establishment of the principle of "what is most beneficial to minors" is the inheritance and development of the concept of "child-centeredness" of the Convention on the Rights of the Child, and is also a manifestation of the development philosophy of the Communist Party of China, which has always been "people-oriented" in the context of the child's rights protection. It is also the implementation of the Communist Party of China's "people-centered" development philosophy in the area of child protection.

China's Legal System for the Protection of the Child's Rights and Interests
Another key word in the book is the legal system for the protection of the child in China, at present, the socialist legal system with Chinese characteristics has been put in place, the legal system for the protection of the child's rights and interests covering civil, administrative and criminal areas has begun to take shape, responding to the current social problems in the protection of the child's rights and interests, for the protection of the child's legitimate rights and interests provides a strong legal support. In building a legal system for the protection of the child's rights and interests, China follows from the four rights of the child included in the United Nations Convention on the Rights of the Child, Strive to fully protect the rights and interests of the child, so as to build a protective barrier for the healthy growth of the child, with the Constitution of the People's Republic of China as the entry point and the protection of the human rights of the child as the core, emphasizing the principles of equality for the child, respect for the child's rights and freedoms, protection of the child's education and protection of the child from infringement, for other laws and regulations have made clear the correct direction of the protection of the child's rights and interests, and played a programmatic guiding role, and formed a legal system of the protection of the child's rights and interests based on the Constitution and the protection of their rights and interests and supplemented by other laws. According to the needs of social development and the legislative work in the new era, from the principle of the best interests of the child, China has enacted the Law on the Protection of Minors of the People's Republic of China, and the law makes a

top-level design for the construction of the legal system for the protection of the child's rights and interests in China from the legal level, the Law of the People's Republic of China on Prevention of Juvenile Delinquency, the Anti-domestic Violence Law of the People's Republic of China, the Family Education Promotion Law of the People's Republic of China, the Compulsory Education Law of the People's Republic of China, the Law on the Protection of Women's Rights and Interests, the Civil Code of the Peoples Republic of China, the Criminal Law of the People's Republic of China, the Civil Procedure Law of the People's Republic of China, the Criminal Procedure Law of the People's Republic of China, the Community Correction Law of the Peoples Republic of China and a series of laws and regulations is an important part of the rights and interests of the child safeguard the legal system, the combination of these laws and regulations has jointly supported China's legal system for the protection of the child's rights and interests, all aspects of the protection of the child's rights and interests should be included in the scope of legal protection from various fields, perspectives and levels, such as health, safety, education, family environment and legal protection. At the same time, the protection of the child's rights and interests is related to the development and destiny of all mankind and involves the most fundamental interests of human beings beyond the nation, country, and skin color. Under the global background of care for the child, China has a firm determination and attitude, in the legislative process, China pays attention to integrating with the international community, and attaches importance to echoing the contents of the United Nations Convention on the Rights of the Child, and implements the concept of international child protection into Chinese legislation, make Chinese the child's rights and interests protection legal system with both China's national conditions and international concept.

The value of this book lies in the fact that while exploring China's legal system for the protection of the child's rights and interests, it also emphasizes the content of China's legal system for the protection of the child's rights and interests that borders on the United Nations Convention on the Rights of the Child in the context of global care for the child, demonstrating the globalized nature of the protection of the child's rights and interests, which is an important step in our efforts to present China's legal system for the protection of the child's rights and interests to the world. China's legal system for the protection of the child's rights and interests has been established and is quite effective, providing solid legal protection for the healthy growth of Chinese the child, and has been widely recognized domestically and internationally. It must be clear that the child's rights and interests will be more reliably safeguarded only if the challenges facing the current legal system for protecting the child are squarely faced and actively addressed, and if scientific and reasonable measures are taken to improve China's relevant laws and regulations. In the future, China's child's legislation will continue to be based on China's national conditions, draw on advanced international experience, and continue to pay attention to the latest concepts and trends in the international community regarding the protection of the child's rights and interests and make unremitting efforts to build a more comprehensive and rigorous legal system for the protection of the child's rights and interests. China will always actively contribute Chinese wisdom and solutions to the protection of the child's rights and interests, and hopes to join hands with other countries in building a community of human destiny, jointly promoting the development of the global cause of protecting the child's rights and interests, and realizing the great solidarity and victory of the people of the world!

Attached List: Relevant Legal Documents on the Protection of Children's Rights and Interests in China

Law

"Sports Law of the People's Republic of China"
"Law of the People's Republic of China on Basic Medical Care and Health Promotion"
"Drug Administration Law of the People's Republic of China"
"Vaccine Administration Law of the People's Republic of China"
"Law of the People's Republic of China on Safeguarding Public Cultural Services"
"Law of the People's Republic of China on the Prevention and Control of"
"Administrative Punishment Law of the People's Republic of China"
"Patriotism Education Law of the People's Republic of China"

Administrative Regulations

"Provisions of the People's Republic of China on the Protection of Minors in Schools"
"Regulations of the People's Republic of China on the Internet Protection of Minors"
"Regulations of the People's Republic of China on Labor Security Supervision"
"Measures for Registration of Adopted Children by Chinese Citizens"
"Measures for the Implementation of the Maternal and Child Health Care Law of the People's Republic of China"
"Regulations on the Implementation of the Law of the People's Republic of China on the Promotion of Private Education"
"Regulations on the Prevention and Rehabilitation of Persons with Disabilities"
"Disability Education Ordinance"
"Provisions of the People's Republic of China on the Prohibition of Child Labor"
"Measures for Registration of Children Adopted by Foreigners in the People's Republic of China"
"Measures for the Implementation of the Law of the People's Republic of China on the Prevention and Control of Infectious Diseases"

Judicial Interpretation

"Interpretation of the Supreme People's Court and the Supreme People's Procuratorate on Several Issues concerning the Application of Law in Handling Criminal Cases of Rape and Molestation of Minors"
"Interpretation of the Supreme People's Court on the Application of the Criminal Procedure Law of the People's Republic of China"
"Interpretation of the Supreme People's Court on the Application of the Civil Code of the People's Republic of China on Marriage and Family (1)"
"Provisions of the Supreme People's Court on Safeguarding the Legitimate Rights and Interests of the Parties in the Review of Death Penalty and Execution Procedures"
"Reply of the Supreme People's Procuratorate on Whether Compulsory Measures of Criminal Detention for Minors under the Age of 16 Suspected of Theft are Illegal"
"Interpretation of the Supreme People's Court on Several Issues Concerning the Specific Application of Law in the Trial of Juvenile Criminal Cases"
"Interpretation of the Supreme People's Court on Several Issues Concerning the Specific Application of the Law in the Trial of Criminal Cases Involving Abduction and Trafficking of Women and Children"

Other Laws, Regulations, and Policy Documents (Excerpts)

"Outline for the Development of Chinese Children"
"Opinions of the State Council on Establishing a Rehabilitation Assistance System for Disabled Children"
"Opinions of the State Council on Strengthening the Care and Protection of Left-behind Children in Rural Areas"
"Opinions of the State Council on Strengthening the Protection of Children in Difficulties"
"Circular of the State Council on Resolutely Combating the Criminal Activities of Trafficking in Women and Children"
"Guiding Opinions on Strengthening Mental Health Care Services for Children in Difficulties"
"Notice of the National Health and Health Commission on Printing and Distributing the Action Promotion Plan for Healthy Children (2021–2025)"
"Opinions on Further Promoting the Optimization, Quality Improvement, Innovation, Transformation and High-quality Development of Child Welfare Institutions"
"Guiding Opinions on Promoting the Construction of Child-friendly Cities"
"Notice on Further Improving the Work Related to the Protection of Factual Unaccompanied Children"

"Notice of the National Health and Health Commission on Setting up the National Children's Regional Medical Center"
"Notice on Doing a Good Job in Rescue and Protection of Children with Lack of Guardianship Due to the Impact of Pneumonia Epidemic in COVID-19"
"Provisions on the Protection of Children's Personal Information Network"
"Measures for the Administration of Child Welfare Institutions"

Index

© The Editor(s) (if applicable) and The Author(s), under exclusive license to Springer Nature Singapore Pte Ltd. 2026
H. Li, P. Liang, *The Legal System for the Protection of Children's Rights in China*, Resilient and Friendly Living Environments,
https://doi.org/10.1007/978-981-95-9925-7

GPSR Compliance
The European Union's (EU) General Product Safety Regulation (GPSR) is a set of rules that requires consumer products to be safe and our obligations to ensure this.

If you have any concerns about our products, you can contact us on

ProductSafety@springernature.com

In case Publisher is established outside the EU, the EU authorized representative is:

Springer Nature Customer Service Center GmbH
Europaplatz 3
69115 Heidelberg, Germany

www.ingramcontent.com/pod-product-compliance
Ingram Content Group UK Ltd.
Pitfield, Milton Keynes, MK11 3LW, UK
UKHW021615260926
475829UK00010B/66
* 9 7 8 9 8 1 9 5 9 9 2 4 0 *